PASSAGES

Linda Trubridge

A MOTHER MEDIA NZ book

First published in New Zealand in 2018 by MOTHER MEDIA NZ

For more information about our titles go to www.mothermedia.nz

A catalogue record of this book is available from the National Library of New Zealand

ISBN 978-0-473-43707-7

Cover photograph by David Trubridge.

Cover design by Reuben Maybury.

Passage: Passing transit; transition from one state to another; liberty, right to pass through; voyage crossing from port to port; right of conveyance as passenger by sea; bird of ~, see Bird. 2. Passing of a measure into law. 3. Way by which person or thing passes; corridor etc. giving communication between different rooms in house. 4. (pl) What passes between two persons mutually, interchange of confidences, etc. 5. ~ (of or at arms) fight (freq. Fig.). Part of speech or literary work taken for quotation etc.
Oxford Illustrated Dictionary, Oxford University Press 1962

PASSAGES

A family's voyage towards spiritual discovery

This exciting account of a nomadic life follows a voyage that began some thirty years ago when the Trubridge family left everything to sail halfway around the world with their two small children. Linda invites us on board to experience those challenging ocean crossings, personal storms, and ecstatic landfalls.

The story's strength lies in its weaving of past and present together, to reveal how that adventurous lifestyle was a catalyst for the extraordinary futures of all those on board.

"The waves of the ocean have formed these passages. I hope they speak to those who love the land and sea; that they awaken a desire to step into the unknown, to discover the spiritual dimension within us all."

"All these words are for David, Sam, and Billy;
without them there would be no story and no happy ending."

CONTENTS

INTRODUCTION

"Where do we come from? What are we? Where are we going?"

Paul Gauguin

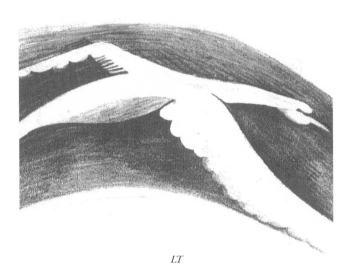

LT

I write with the encouraging words of friends and family ringing in my ears, inspiring me to set off again on the journey that brought us to this place and time. Although it is raining, the sun shines through the mist and there is no beginning, no end to the magic of the elements dancing together. I have always found it easier to make sculptures in my kitchen, to meditate in the living room and so, I begin, placing one word after the other, gleaning memories and facts from journals and drawings. Just as an event may be seen through countless eyes, told with many voices, the truth has numerous interpretations. Although I am not proud of everything I relate, this is how it was. *Passages* reflects on those years when our family stood alone with only self-belief to guide the way. Come with us now, experience that sometimes harmonious, often tumultuous time of living on the ocean.

David and I had created a fulfilling lifestyle with a predictable future, but no sooner was our family complete with two lovely children than a spontaneous idea spun us onto a new course. There was no turning back as we discarded everything to buy a yacht and escape a culture that had lost its reason. Hornpipe would carry us on the most profound passage of our lives, safeguard us through those times when we practiced our beliefs and lived our philosophy.

Before venturing into the unknown, David and I prepared ourselves as best we could, believing that we should live our truth so that we might return something of value to the world. The challenge of voyaging at the whim of the elements was overwhelming, the burden of nurturing my family sometimes quenched my joy, and I often wondered whether I was brave enough for the life we chose. But those ocean passages shaped our children: William the freediver; Sam the performance artist. They are the foundation for my art that speaks of the human predicament; David's design that supports an earth in crisis.

FOUNDATION STONES

"I will build a temple to the sun and moon and trees
In the middle a spreading oak tree and around it an eternal ring of stone.
The sun will spread patterns of stony shadow
the tree will rustle its changing leaves
I'll worship the dying embers of sun and the new threads of moon
And I'll bury my ashes deep in the earthy oaken roots.
I'll create a spirit and it will live forever."

David Trubridge, 1975

The dry stone wall at Aros   LT

When I visited Aros on that windy spring day I expected to find my friend Rachel, and as I gazed beyond the lonely house to the purple fell I wondered why she had chosen to live there. Golden as summer sunshine, Rachel had shone amongst the students on our sculpture

5

course. At weekends, we had ridden bikes to gather bluebells, stopping for a ploughman's lunch at a country pub. Somehow we had remained in touch. On knocking, I waited, and when the heavy door was thrown open it was her boyfriend, David, who emerged from the cavernous interior as a wild beast from a lair. His woollen clothing hung like pelts and he glowed with a golden haze of wood dust from the sculpture he had been carving. I was enthralled. David's appearance seemed to evoke the mythological stories that had always entranced me, and when he said Rachel had gone, my soul reached out to share his inconsolable sorrow. He would say of that first time we met: *"Your eyes scared the shit out of me."* But I remember David's tormented energy, how he talked of expressing his heart and soul through the raw wood culled from a growing tree, of transforming its substance, himself, the world. And I had believed his every word.

Following that encounter Rachel persuaded me to write to David, and on returning to London I sent him a letter, some comforting words to explain her change of heart. Having lost interest in tepid relationships I had found my fulfilment elsewhere. Each evening and weekend I navigated the vacuous Underground, going against the press of commuters to join a dedicated gathering of yogis. My spine vibrated to my teacher's resonant chant, shook with laughter at repeated jokes as I adhered to his commanding, *"Be Here Now."* While many spiritual leaders solicit adulation and surrender, Alan maintained that yoga should be accessible to all. Wise beyond our knowing, he was surrounded by a following of swamis, sris and pundits who encouraged us to question and seek our own truth.

I was often exhausted when I arrived for a Friday meditation, yet I left with energy to paint into the early hours. Saturday yoga was followed with rambling walks that entwined London's history with Indian philosophy, and our summer yoga retreat concluded with a meditation where it seemed I balanced on the brink of a void. A siren song enticed me towards a commitment but I wavered and an opportunity passed. In despair, I gazed through the window at clouds passing without pause, and without hesitation my heart opened to the unknown. In that moment, I felt a glorious transcendence towards the light, *"My eyes flowed with tears and my heart burst in glory. A realm of new sights and sounds overwhelmed me with intense colours and fragrance."* Everything had changed. As autumn, winter, and spring flowed ever on, my spirit absorbed each moment of bliss knowing that those days of wonder would also pass.

England's summer of 1976 was a phenomenon. London basked in a heat wave that went on and on. And so it would be with my new life and love. Making my escape I drove north with a friend who had a home on the Welsh border. The road coiled in a shining river of light and as we passed Birmingham's giant cooling towers the fiery sky opened my eyes and heart. I sought out Rachel, who was living her romantic dream in a tumbling Welsh cottage high above the clouds. The harmonious surroundings soothed my soul and when I woke amongst the sun-drenched mountains my exhausting sense of purpose had thawed. Simple actions were an homage to nature's magic. I bathed in a waterfall, felt a tingling release as, throwing my arms wide, I joyfully ran into the future. *"Why don't you visit David in Northumberland,"* suggested Rachel. And following an irresistible instinct I set out on an adventure, perhaps knowing, but not yet aware, of my secret hope.

That journey from North Wales carried me on, through towns and villages until, as the evening shadows lengthened, I caught the last bus from Haltwhistle to Coanwood. From there I walked a narrow lane that climbs uphill between the dry-stone walls that fringe the fells. I was an incongruous figure in my embroidered peasant pinafore. A copious rucksack and boots indicated a nomadic disposition; the fading light adding mystery to intense eyes and wild hair. As I walked my mind raced ahead. Opening receptive hands, I repeated the mantra, *"Be still, oh mind; when walking, walk."* And on drawing nearer the solitary house my mind bubbled with uncertainty. Was I stretching the bonds of friendship, would these ancient stones reward me with a welcome? Was I brave enough to accept the consequences? I told myself, *"What have you got to lose? Be brave, walk on, think no thoughts. Brave, be, walk, feel!"* All this and then, as the sun's last rays caressed the fell, a golden form condensed from the horizon. The colossus crystallised into a man, David ran into the unknown seeing only a silhouette, raven black against the road. Our passages met. Elated by buoyant breezes two paths became one, and with that first embrace it was known, yet hidden; that this would be for all time.

The Aros community welcomed travellers with an open door. A French family had arrived and the table was laden with homemade cheese, breads, and quiches from their farm. After eating, as the summer evening mellowed, David carried his duvet onto the fell and I curled beside him in my sleeping bag. We shared our hopes and dreams, watching the silent stars, fading into sleep. David woke first and on watching my hands deeply etched with crevices from sculpting he realised, *"These are the hands that will hold me through all of my life."* Some forty years would pass before he shared this thought that had inhabited a precious place in his memory.

On that rare sunny day we walked over the moorland heather and lichen-crusted rocks of the fell. Dropping down to where a stream sprung from the undergrowth we followed its tumbling passage through mossy gullies and pebbled pools sheltered with saplings. Stopping beside a grassy bank we moved closer to where the sun cast patterned lights upon a leafy carpet. David reached out to hold me, saying, *"I've been wanting to do this ever since you arrived."* And without question, we shed our ugly clothes and lay beneath the sky, as though we had known each other forever. I had waited an eternity for that moment. All of nature's bounty was in that embrace. Our spirits unfolded to the comforting earth as, swept along on a wave of becoming, we floated a while, serenaded by tinkling water, warmed with the sun, caressed by a breath in the trees. This was a celebration of everything that we were and all that would follow. Walking on, we silently acknowledged the fragile seed of change that was growing deep in our hearts, a secret that belonged to us alone.

The following afternoon we took a last walk through luscious meadows to where the Lambley Viaduct arced the River Tyne. As the hour drew close to when I must leave I hurried to keep up with David's giant strides. When I hesitated beside a gully that a flood had gouged through the marshes David called, *"Go on, you can do it. JUMP!"* Destiny hung in balance. Jumping, I fell short and, twisting my ankle, unable to walk, I had the perfect excuse for staying. When David's friends left for a holiday we found ourselves alone with a chance to explore a future together. Summer's pungent fragrance of wood smoke and flowers conspired to make that weekend the rest of my life. On sunny days we abandoned the moors for the shady valley, where we swam in river pools, our white bodies slipping through sepia ripples. If my sore ankle hurt, David lifted me in his strong arms. Returning home with baskets of fruit, we boiled vats of jams and chutneys for the larder, listened in the mellow dusk as the ethereal voices of Monteverdi's *Vespers* echoed around the stone walls, soaring as larks to the heavens. Those days resonated with an ecstasy of birdsong, while by night the wailing curlews and booming snipe soothed us with their sorrowful poetry. Time drifted as we floated on a sea of tussock grass, and when I returned to London it was to say farewell.

Although I had dedicated myself to yoga's spiritual truths, I had always known that if my heart called I would follow. Just as the sage Krishnamacharya had been commanded by his Guru to shun asceticism and academia for a family life, I too made a choice. Alan understood and my friends wished me well. But I was

"I balanced on the brink of a void" LT

a few days late in giving notice and my employer demanded I remain until Christmas, saying, *"If you break your contract I will ensure you never get another teaching job."* David had not forgotten Rachel's change of heart - he needed a commitment. So I discarded my profession and caught the train to Newcastle. We drove home with a balmy wind caressing our skin. David emptied a drawer for my clothes and my fears dissolved. But once, needing an affirmation of support, I asked, *"What would have happened if I hadn't come along?"* And when David said, *"If not you, it would have been someone else,"* the truth in his comment shattered my self-worth. Although I knew that David was still recovering from the depth of his feelings for Rachel, I needed an assurance that I was *The One*. Meanwhile, our relationship would reveal more surprises and a *happy ever after* that would take time to evolve.

I had blindly stumbled into David's home and life. Three years previous he had financed the purchase and renovations of Mount Pleasant with an inheritance from his grandmother and compensation for a leg broken in a car accident. During a year on crutches David managed an overland trip across Europe where, visiting Rudolf Steiner's *Goethe Annum*, he was overwhelmed by the philosopher's allegorical sculpture, hewn from raw wood. Inspired by an urgent desire to build a home where he could work as an artist, David spent his final university year searching for an affordable building, coming across a ruin standing at a thousand feet on the edge of the Northumberland fells looking north towards the undulating backbone of Hadrian's Wall, and west to the purple hulk of Cold Fell. Others with similar aspirations had settled in the area, and scattered habitations, with names like Howley Winter, indicated a savage environment that had driven away the original tenants. The Northern Fells, with their all-embracing earth and sky, could be energising or oppressive. One stood alone, fighting the elements with the determination of a wild beast and the words of The Who's *Baba O'Riley* would become David's anthem, *"Out here in the fields, I fight for my meals, I put my back into my living, I don't need to fight, to prove I'm right, I don't need to be forgiven."*

From hunting the mammoth to motor mechanics, men find companionship in shared projects. And so it was, as David and his friends extended the tribal affiliation of their student years, living rough, toiling through the twilight days of 1973's harsh winter, suffering snowfalls that lasted into April. After reclaiming the ruined Mount Pleasant from the birds that had sheltered in the dwelling, they named it Aros, the Celtic term for home. The house, with its basic furniture and threadbare carpet, retained a practical authenticity. Clothes were hand washed, food cooled on a stone slab, meals and hot water heated on the Aga cooker. Rebuilding the interior and windows had taught David woodworking skills, and after buying a lathe he started turning wooden bowls to earn a living, his whirling drowning the sounds of the thundering generator. As a boy, David had made model boats from matchsticks collected from the gutters on Bournemouth's promenade, a hobby that led to him creating authentic wooden models of sailing ships, including the Golden Hind. Although academically able, David was most fulfilled in the art department, however an art career was *just not done*, so he chose to further his interest in sailing, studying naval architecture at Newcastle University, an enthusiasm that waned when his course focused on designing oil tankers. But years later David would apply those engineering and drafting skills in creating furniture, houses, lights, and sculpture, eventually going full circle: designing boats and windsurfer sails.

The sparse northern light barely penetrated Aros' deep apertures, yet it was infused with a gentle radiance and during winter's cruel storms the house became a vessel, adrift on an ocean of snow. Its crew huddled around the fire, playing card games in the cavernous dark while the ghosts of previous inhabitants watched from the shadows. Friendships blossomed into relationships and an unspoken ownership settled on those who remained to brave the elements. Pip, Tim, and toddler Joe emanated the morality of a Millais family, the pathos of Picasso's Blue Period. Pip chose to embrace the monotony of working class drudgery I had striven to escape, her flowered frock and duffle coat displaying her empathy with the common people. Tim had abandoned his middle-class education for a soul-destroying job restoring antique furniture; returning from work grey and bitter, his unfulfilled intellect poisoning him as surely as the chemicals he used to strip the ugly furniture. Yet although Tim and Pip appeared wane and worn they exuded a confidence I lacked.

Pete, with his loose grin and wispy hair, lived amongst us as a hermit, garnishing his existence with wry observations, and legend had it, a rock strung at head height over his bed. Maybe his geology degree lent some meaning to this, but being clumsy, Pete encountered the rock on a daily basis. When questioned, he answered, "*Because I have to learn to live with it!*" as though life's truths could be discovered through pointless hardship. This might have explained why Pete tolerated working for the neighbouring farmer who, manifesting some incomprehensible grudge against David, murderously accelerated his Land Rover to race past the house. Pete found comfort huddled around a fag, randomly flicking ash towards the coal scuttle, punctuating our silences with abandoned laughter.

Soon after my arrival David and Tim bought and began renovating the nearby barn of Dyke Head. At last, after centuries, the ruin's skeletal timbers enclosed the sky. I joined the team, gathering stacks of slates from a derelict railway cottage, thinking nothing of participating in a physical toil that blackened my face with soot. I had grown up wearing my brother's cast offs; had identified myself as a person preferring adventures to posing *pretty as a princess.* Unaware of gender choices, I played the page and prince, free to rough and tumble until Tommy Fisher threw me in a ditch of stinging nettles for refusing to show him my knickers. At school I sought solace in outdoor pursuits. Camping, climbing, and canoeing often coincided with my period and when I inevitably capsized I would suffer that horrid, sodden mess; sooner die than reveal the shameful truth. Somehow I overcame the curse, but how often has crippling embarrassment thwarted women's activities and aspirations? My relationship with nature led me to teach art and drama at Brathay Hall Outdoor Education retreat in the Lake District while David sought his freedom in the Outer Hebrides; eking out the petrol, turning off the motor and headlights of Bumble, his battered van, to coast silently, recklessly downhill.

The words of Tom Paxton's song, *"I'm a mighty restless man in a mighty restless land and I'm bound for the mountains and the sea,"* speaks for David both then and now. And at last I was happy. After teaching adolescents, it was a novelty to carry steaming mugs of tea and cakes to the workers, and when our friend Marilyn visited she turned to David and said, *"Well! You landed on your feet!"* And he had, for I would have willingly spent my life baking cakes for him and his friends. Making a stand for equality was my last concern; all I wanted was to please David.

Despite living in the wild we longed for ever more remote places so, in late summer, we took the ferry to Mull and while David joined his friend Douglas on the prawn boat I walked over a headland to bathe in the crystalline sea. Travelling on to Barra we pitched our tent on a cliff and hardly noticed the sun's absence when rainy days kept us inside, while Bran, David's border collie, slept beneath the fly sheet. Absorbing the land and each other we walked on through meadows of flowers, lit a fire in the drizzling rain to cook a kipper and staunch our hunger. Dawn saw us huddled in the bilge of a fishing boat, crossing over to the purple headland of South Uist. There we traversed the wild moorland, striding through heather high as our waists, bathing in streams, glad of the rabbit Bran caught for our stew; slept in the hollowed rings of stone, ruins of the Black Houses, all that remained of those who had abandoned the bleak Hebrides for the colonies of Australia and New Zealand. From a bluff, we saw a yacht in the bay and, waving, we fantasised about the owners taking us for a sail. There was no response but as we walked on our minds spun with the imagined freedoms of travelling on a boat.

On our return, David resumed his part-time job working in the woods of the local estate; developing a knowledge and love of trees alongside a fellow forester. Old Alan became family and during lunch times soup, bread, and cheese he regaled us with stories of his childhood in Newcastle and of marching with the Jarrow Coalminers who, barefoot and starving, walked to London to protest their plight. Bran enjoyed those days and I often joined them, seeking out a witch's cottage, gathering bitter sloe berries or meadowsweet to make jugs of sparkling wine. Sometimes David returned with arms full of flowers or branches of beech leaves to soak in our bath and it seemed those sweet pleasures would last forever. We aspired towards an independent lifestyle, embraced the purity of toil.

David and I dug a stony field to plant potatoes; Pip established a wattle compound where chickens scratched the bare earth, and on the edge of the fell the skeletal frame of a wind generator awaited the day when we would transform the relentless wind into electricity. When Dykehead was sound, Tim started making traditional kitchen cabinets while David created spinning wheels and furniture, sharing their machines, ideas, and philosophies with an intimate ease and what David described as, *"The empowerment of knowing that I could make anything I wanted with these tools in this workshop."* Despite Dykehead's twenty-inch walls, the driving rain forced a way through and it was a wonder the wood burning stove never ignited the dust that hovered in the air. The guys never wore masks or ear muffs, giving no thought to their ears and lungs as they suffered the building's inadequate ventilation; considered their backs as they sloshed through mud carrying the finished furniture up the field, sometimes borrowing a tractor and trailer used to haul manure; wiping splatter of the newly oiled wood.

I accompanied David on timber buying excursions and on passing an irresistible place he would inevitably say, *"Why don't we stop here?"* And walking hand in hand into the dappled light of a remote forest, or following a stream as it tumbled over sparkling pebbles we drew closer, gathering a raw energy from the earth. I was so intent on echoing David that I failed to see how we complemented each other; that his bronze beard framed a golden sun, while my face glowed with silvery moonlight. And where his eyes were set wide as a lion mine were intense as an eagle. Since discarding his fringed suede jacket and the purple velvet hipsters he had rent asunder when starting his motorbike, David had taken to wearing homespun jumpers and patched jeans that blended with the landscape. I had gleaned my garments from various ethnic sources and with my flapping skirts, woollen ponchos, and wooden clogs, I seemed to step out of *Wuthering Heights*. However, I was still a new arrival with an uncertain relationship.

I suppose it all began when my mother asked my father for a dance at the City of Bath's Pump Room ball. He was dashing in his naval uniform, and she so beautiful with her abundant auburn hair. Doreen had cheekily chosen her partner for life and exchanged Starr, her maiden name, for Mrs King with that *Ladies Excuse Me* dance. I was just four when we moved to the chilly brick house and unruly garden in the Midlands. My parents immediately set to improving their circumstances and the audacity of Mum's jaunty, tweed clad figure brandishing a tasselled umbrella was not wasted on the villagers who called her *The Queen of Cosby*. There was a warmth in their local greeting, *"Ow are yer me duck,"* however Mum said she was nobody's duck. And she held true to the Somerset endearment, *my lamb*, her dialect and differences making me feel special. At Christmases, when my parents lyrically danced to Calypso music they evoked the mysterious island of my birth, and while my brother felt no connection with a life that had passed us by, faded photographs of Bermuda fed my passion to return.

Bermuda was light years from that paltry post war Britain. Homes were bereft of carpets and long before recycling the daily news was reborn as toilet paper. Gathering around the coal fire we simultaneously scorched and chilled as we played games and listened to the radio, but Mum enfolded us in a love as warm as the downy hollow of a bird's nest, filled our minds with her stories of hedgehogs and rabbits. Dad cycled to work and spent his spare moments gardening, renovating, making our furniture and toys. As soon as he passed his driving test we set off to visit my grandparents in Bath; the car snaking along the bendy lanes, Mum administering boiled sweets. I succumbed to travel sickness soon after the cat had noisily vomited into its cardboard box but I can still picture that first jubilant view of the city; the toppled buildings pocked with bomb cavities, sinister edifices blackened with soot. And after driving up impossibly steep empty streets we came to my grandparents' house and they took us across the road to the sweetshop.

I dared to hope that my dreams could come to something when on a fresh spring morning I waited for my interview at Loughborough College of Art and Design, feeling confident in the polka dot mini dress Mum had bought in defiance of my father's suggestion of a grey suit. I presented my folio that expressed a love for the mesmerising act of drawing, the intense observation that rendered a copper kettle with a reflection so real one could almost reach out to seize the wooden handle. The panel accepted me on the provision that I achieve the necessary O levels and I never considered what I would do if I failed. Once at art college I never looked back. Barely seventeen and ill equipped for independence I awaited my student allowance; hungry and homeless I learned that freedom requires financial security; that there were those less fortunate than I. My flatmate Angie's limbs were swollen with rheumatoid arthritis and she depended on me to carry her easel and paints. Although the psychedelic discos obscured Angie's twisted body all her dates were one-night stands. Yet it was Angie who taught me to embrace life and when she died the woods were full of bluebells; the colour of her eyes and spirit.

One of my first art college projects was to illustrate William Golding's novel, *Pincher Martin*, in a contemporary style. That account of a drowning man's hallucinations was a strange story to set a teenager but despite my ignorance of

"She's leaving home"

modern literature and art I read the book and began scribbling like a child, hoping that abstraction would spontaneously occur. The illustrated series I produced was rich with symbolic images that inspire me to this day. A fertility goddess, formed of colossal stones, towers over an island surrounded by a perpetual sea of emotion. Birds soar amongst billowing clouds, while a figure, floating suspended in a glass jar with a narrow neck is an eerie premonition of my son William ambiguously flying or sinking into the cavernous Blue Hole of the Caribbean. I continued making visual references to waves and water, swirling paints and inks until my head spun and, unaware of the element's connection to sexual instincts, I resolved to continue my art education somewhere near the sea.

Choosing Exeter College of Art, I met Rachel, and together we rejected illusionary painting for the reality of sculptural form. While some students wasted those years in an alcoholic stupor, to be deservedly culled, I never comprehended why Rachel was rejected without reason or qualification. She would thrive as an art therapist and our friendship eventually led me to David. Before then I would travel to Greece, Jerusalem, Africa, the Caribbean, South America. Following my long-distance boyfriend's posting as a Voluntary Service Overseas teacher in Zambia, I also applied, but the interviewer's *"Could you drive a tractor?"* revealed my limitations. When they asked, *"Are you a practical or romantic person?"* I saw that my frilly blouse and long velvet skirt had given me away. How could an adventurous artist, a romantic traveller, an enigma, serve humanity? The answer to my conundrum appeared in the form of an advertisement in *The Times Educational Supplement*. I was miraculously accepted for the job, and at twenty-one I left England for the life I had always dreamed of.

Not far away, the man who would become my husband had also developed a desire to travel; his affinity with the ocean. Following the war, David's father Geoffrey studied at Oxford and on being appointed language master at Gordonstoun School the family moved to Scotland where Josslyn home-schooled her sons until, at the tender age of eight, David was sent away to Blairmore School. There he joined a pack of lost boys who endured outdoor exercise in all weathers, followed by an icy shower and porridge. While David blamed his mother for the betrayal, his father was equally involved in choosing what they believed was a superior education. As the classmates grew from children to adolescents they brutalised each other and discussed their bodily functions with blunt naivety. Where boarding school had set out to make a man out of David he would emphatically denounce the institution that deprived him of a family and incarcerated him in an emotionless environment.

In his free time, David wandered the mountains, gathering strength from the magnificent solitude, developing an empathy with wild places that would nourish him throughout his life. One June day, when David was nine years old, he was called to the headmaster's study. The brief altercation was concluded with a handshake and after that momentary diversion of being told that his father had died from a brain abscess he was marched back to class, to the *"Bad luck, Trubridge,"* consolations of his school-mates. It was as simple as that. But it wasn't, when the most important person in David's life had been spirited away, leaving him with a bottomless pit of questions; no opportunity to acknowledge his father's passing. Photographs of Geoffrey show a profile sharpened by post war conventions, and a lean, athletic build that David inherited along with the height that protected him from bullies and contributed to him becoming a powerful rower and runner. Few memories remain of the father, teacher, and Scoutmaster who inspired countless Gordonstoun boys; the heroic Officer who had won the respect of his company of Nepalese Gurkhas. More than half a century would pass before David read a student's funeral tribute that described Geoffrey to a son and grandsons who had inherited his qualities, *"No one could have been more alive, more youthful. No man and no boy here could beat him for fitness. I once said to him after he had completed the assault course, 'How do you manage to keep fit enough to do that so fast?' and he said with a sort of modest surprise, as though he himself could not quite understand it, 'You know I never find anything difficult about it.' It is part of the irony of things that he should have been the one to go. I remember him racing along the rope as though the air were his element. I remember him in his canoe as though he belonged to the water."* David has said that Laurie Anderson's words, *"When my father died it was like a whole library had burned down,"* best describes his loss and I recall how at a tender age the shocking thought, *"What if Mummy or Daddy died,"* was too traumatic to contemplate.

Following the tragedy, Josslyn left Gordonstoun's cloistered courtyards, bought a bungalow in Bembridge on the Isle of Wight and worked as House Matron of a nearby school, hiding the family's grief from the world and themselves. Privileged with a youth of travel and an education, Josslyn was a reserved, private person. Remaining single, she devoted herself to providing her sons with an education, the future she valued. David continued travelling to Blairmore, catching an overnight train from Kings Cross until he was old enough for Tonbridge School. Josslyn came to depend upon David to fill Geoffrey's shoes and, where most teenagers would have rebelled, he fulfilled his responsibilities. Their home atrophied into a museum of fading memories. Gifts, shaped by clumsy schoolboy hands, squatted upon the mantelpiece, defending a territory of broken dreams. And while David recoils from sentimentality and has an affinity with change, a residue of those values endure for, when something becomes old or damaged, it will be mended and patched, its life extended. Our frugal childhoods heralded an era of profligate plenty when shopping would become a leisure activity, diminishing quality and integrity until all that remain are labels and broken promises. And as our society consumes more and more it becomes vital that we turn the tide and restore that which is broken.

TIES THAT BIND

"In learning to look, feel, and hear, as for a first time,
Movement becomes adoration,
Our voices become true and we live as warriors of peace."
Linda Trubridge

David and I followed our instincts and five months later we married. Discovering a chapel beside a gushing stream that ran down from Wolf Hills, I imagined a bridal procession dancing and singing along their way to that mossy building with its forgotten tombstones. But that ceremony of white mists and wild flowers remained a dream. Our relationship was too new and fragile to shine a spotlight on, so we kept our pact secret; however we needed a witness, so David asked old Alan if he would join us on a trip to Hexham. There was a twinkle in Alan's eye when he replied, *"Whay aye lad, I'll see yah tamaraaw."*

On *The Day*, David wore jeans topped with his father's tweed jacket. My hooded velvet coat hid an embroidered wedding dress from Palestine, the treasured gown making me feel special. But I had one concern, and as Bumble gathered momentum I purposefully asked David if he had everything he needed. His, *"Why, what's wrong?"* indicated a concern that I was criticising his clothes. It wasn't a good start. *"Everything,"* I persisted, drawing a blank look. We were almost at Alan's house so I cut to the chase, *"Well, what about the ring?"* A stunned silence was followed with, *"What ring?"* My timid hints about the formalities of a ceremony that obsessed girls from their earliest years had gone unnoticed. David didn't know anything about rings and weddings. He was here and wasn't that enough? As we raced towards Old Alan's house I wondered how to own up. With no time for subtleties I drew from my pocket: a wedding ring! *"So, what was all the fuss about, when you had that all the time!"* laughed David. Ever practical, I had bought the ring in Carlisle, asking the jeweller, *"If I don't need it, can I bring it back?"* David was highly amused by this diversion to the mysterious commitment he was making. All was well and when we stopped outside Alan's house he hugged me tight.

After Alan had eaten a breakfast of pie and mushy peas we were ready for the ceremony that was conducted in an ancient council hall, overlooking Hexham Abbey. Then we drove home to find that no one was surprised by our secret. Pip continued sweeping the floor, Pete turned up the volume on his Bob Dylan record. Was their disinterest a first indication that the strands of our communal lifestyle had worn thin? Or a justifiable disappointment

The Wedding Dress   LT

at our hidden tryst? When my parents visited, they expressed relief that we had married, *"With no fuss!"* And when I reflected upon their wartime wedding, I understood. They had looked splendid, my father in his naval uniform, mum in a rakish trilby and the simple dress she had turned inside out and sewn to look like new. And when I look at their wedding photo with everyone wearing silly hats to create a sense of occasion, I cannot help but smile.

Although I had maintained my independence since leaving home at sixteen, David suggested I break free from my parents. There were few opportunities to be close, and when my husband appeared to find his friends more stimulating than my company, I never realised he had replaced his cloistered childhood with a communal lifestyle. Afraid of revealing my inadequacies I became hidden and inhibited. Once, in those early days, I alluded to David as a spreading oak, myself the ivy that wound around its trunk. I was pleased with my description's implied balance of yin and yang, but when he responded that 'ivy inevitably strangles the tree' I wished I could swallow my stupid words. And all I could do was to secretly vow to prove my worth.

After meeting Josslyn for the first time, mother and son had walked across the field to Dykehead, she carrying a copious black handbag that held everything one might need; an emergency screwdriver, rain hat, clean handkerchief. I had wondered if I was the subject of their conversation; wished that I could speak for myself. At Christmas, we journeyed south to David's home in the Isle of Wight and as we drove the island's winding lanes, feeling our way through the heavy clouds that rolled over the downs, it appeared as if we travelled back in time. Our days were spent visiting significant milestones of David's youth. There was the dockyard where he had been sacked from his first job; the seafood van above Brading, where he had sold cockles, jellied eels, and whelks; the wall he had climbed to watch Hendrix, The Who and Bob Dylan perform. And in a cloistered garden beside a secluded beach hut David and I abandoned ourselves to the open air and a passion that was never lacking.

The Trubridges fell into family traditions, and following a Christmas day swim it seemed unsociable to refuse the turkey, so I ate meat for the first time since embracing a *satvic* life. After repeating the celebrations in Cosby, we drove the slushy road north to Scotch Corner. There we turned left for Barnard Castle and the climb up Teasdale and over the Pennines. On reaching that higher altitude the veiled track lost definition and we debated whether it was foolish to continue; that if we slid off the road, we could be lost in the frozen wasteland. A tide of relief surged through me as Bumble rattled down the cobbled streets of Alston and over the bridge into the Tyne valley. We followed the river as it flowed through white pastures, past quiet pools where we had bathed in summer, and at Coanwood we abandoned the valley for a winding track that lay hidden beneath a snowy petticoat. The light faded as Bumble skirted the shrouded fell and came to rest beside the stony house and skeletal trees. The journey's obstacles had seemed more than physical and although a party was underway we crept away. A little baby was cradled in a cot in our room and while her parents celebrated we lay cocooned in each other's arms, sleeping through the last hours of that momentous year. Meanwhile Gemma Jones, who had been born on the sixteenth of September, slept, unaware that her presence would herald the arrival of Sam exactly nine months later.

Those years coincided with the British craft revival, a time when creating functional items from wool, leather, clay, and wood melded into a self-sufficient lifestyle. David and I had shared a passion for the artist Brancusi whose sculptures transformed spirit into matter, sowing the seeds of contemporary design. While I identified with Gauguin and William Blake's earthy mysticism, David admired the ethereal landscapes of Turner. Natural forms were acceptable, however my strangely sensual sculptures and study of yogic philosophy appeared self-indulgent in those rugged surroundings. My companions had never known me in other circumstances and with no child to establish my self-worth I felt inconsequential, a feeling that was reinforced by the arrival of a crumpled paper parcel that David opened to reveal a treasure beyond compare: a jumper that his mother had spun from a raw fleece on the first spinning wheel he had made. In moving to Northumberland I had sacrificed a career that spanned five years of tertiary study followed by four in the classroom. Teaching had stretched me to my limit but neither David nor his friends had any concept of what I had endured, the commitment I had made when I abandoned all that. Setting up a loom I tried weaving and began teaching yoga in the Slaggyford village hall. Despite my students insisting they needed a halfway break for a cup of tea and a fag they somehow made it through. But I had much to learn. When a plump farmer's wife spread her legs to sink into the splits, a competitive grandma twisted into a lotus position, and as I untangled the situation I prayed her psychotic son would not shoot me. It was only the happy news of my pregnancy that interrupted those yoga classes.

The previous September, David and I had been lying under a tree gazing up into the spreading branches when the russet dart of a red squirrel flashed like an elfin arrow. That day we met a man called Sam and somehow the synchronicity of his happy-go-lucky name and the fleeting messenger generated our spontaneous response, "*Sam's a good name for a baby.*" David's hankering for an adventure, to explore the Russia of the writers and poets he venerated, was abandoned. We chose Sam, and as the dream became reality the happenings within my body distracted me from other changes. Although my pregnancy was a mutual choice, David appeared repulsed by my fecundity. While Pip was also pregnant I sensed I had invaded her territory and could not understand why we were so close yet light years apart. Then, one sunny, unsuspecting afternoon, Tim erupted into a savage volley of accusations, and despite having no idea what I had done, his eloquent soliloquy convinced me that I alone was accountable. Shocked into silence I curled in a foetal position in the bath, where despite the frigid water I found some release. I was pregnant and alone; the friends I venerated had stolen my carefree love. And as those miserable days unfolded, shame turned to despair. Singing songs to the glowing light of my unborn child I somehow resisted darker inclinations.

Stunned into mute acquiescence I was unaware that David's closest friend Jonathan had encountered similar problems; that after helping build Aros he and his girlfriend had avoided the confrontations by leaving. David would have given anything rather than destroy happy memories. His father had died, Rachel and Jonathan had left; home and possessions have no value when compared with a life, first love, and friendship. He instinctively sought solace in creativity, crafting a rocking chair and cradle to feature in his first exhibition, *Wood Rhythms*, at a gallery on Hadrian's Wall.

While I longed to be cherished I was silenced by my lack of confidence. Where David and his friends shared the entitlement of a private education, mine had left me socially inept. My school's greatest insult was to be called *dead common*, however it had become fashionable to emulate those once despised colloquial accents. Everyone wanted, *"To live like common people,"* but Jarvis Cocker's lyrics describe a working class who still lack a voice and the confidence to use it. I venerated Tim and Pip so I never questioned the generosity that prompted David to relinquish our established house. Pete, who had silently observed the proceedings, moved out to renovate an old barn and we started work on transforming Mount Pleasant's adjoining ruin into a dwelling, our faltering relationship into a family.

My growing child, and the task of pointing the cottage's stonework, gave me some comfort, and in late May we set off on a camping trip to northwestern Scotland. There we ran naked along a remote beach and slept beneath the stars, beside the sea. While David climbed a mountain I wandered into a valley where wild horses gathered; drew their sensual forms and flanks, their tossing manes and tails. We visited David's brother who was living on remote Handa Island, counting shags for the Royal Society for the Protection of Birds. Three years younger than David, Mike was a voluntary exile controlling the tourists with the authority of a man who had found his natural element. Spending an evening with a couple on a cruising yacht, they suggested we sail with them to the Hebridean island of St Kilda, their enthusiasm dissolving on realising I was pregnant. I had experienced sailing the previous year when, borrowing a small yacht, David and I spent hours tacking the choppy seas off Iona. As he cranked the ropes tighter my anxiety grew greater, when the mast heeled lower my pulse quickened. And on asking David, *"Will the boat come back up when it tips?"* he flippantly replied, *"Well, maybe it won't."* When we turned for the shore I hid my relief. But despite the outing undermining my affinity with the sea, a desire had surfaced that would lead us to renounce everything without a glimmer of remorse.

Another trip took me south to London; a fecund form gracing Alan's yoga class, my friend Naomi and I sleeping amongst the roses in her fragrant garden. Despite being a generation older, with a husband a further twenty years removed, she supported my new love and the imminent birth. Comforted and compelled to make a new start I returned to work all hours, helping David complete our frugal cottage. On finishing the spiral staircase, he claimed a freedom motorbike trip across the border while I moved our few possessions into that first home, arranging a crude table and chairs in the living area, a mattress on the bare boards above. On David's return we made a vital trip into Hexham, to exchange Bumble for a reliable van. That evening as he read to me I laughed until I ached, attributing my painful pangs to a leaden mackerel that was jostling for space in my crowded abdomen. It seemed that those months from fertility to harvest, our first days alone, had passed in a moment. And as we shared the blissful awakening of our relationship, the gift of my blossoming body, I wished the evening would last forever.

When David fell asleep I continued my yogic breathing, observing a recurring sensation. Time passed in a hazy stupor and as the contractions increased to surging spasms I reached to waken David, and with a sudden *ping!* a warm flood flowed from me. Sam seemed determined to follow and as I scrambled for my clothes that brittle vulnerable feeling became overwhelming. *"We must go, quickly!"* I gasped as David lurched awake. When constructing the spiral staircase, we hadn't considered my bulky belly or its passenger's determination to escape. At last we stepped out into that auspicious night, beneath the sparkling stars that held a special truth for this child who was to be born. I held tight as Sam made another bid for freedom, then climbing into the new van I was ready. David turned the key to no response, and although he tried and tried, cursed, and swore, the vehicle had died. I desperately waited while David burgled Tim and Pip's car and as we sped towards Haltwhistle, condensed into a ball, legs crossed, teeth gritted to contain that frenzy within. The spasms escalated as we pounded the hospital door. The baby seemed sure to arrive as I hobbled along the passage. As I climbed onto the delivery bed the surging sensation reached a crescendo. But at last I could give myself up, and when old nurse Murphy said push, I pushed. And there he was! SAM! While my body opened with the contractions my heart opened to creation. The birth of love. And as the silence was filled with that first cry I exclaimed, *"It's a baby!"*

I reached out to hold Sam and then David and I clung together trembling and laughing with the magic of it all, gazing at each other, three of us forever ONE. Soon after he left, Sam was bundled away by the midwife and I was transported to another room. Overwhelmed by the fast, natural birth, I was unprepared for that beginning of everything I would hold most dear. During those hours of powerful yogic breathing my mind had been swept into a cosmic creation. The secret friend that had curled in my body was gone and I was alone, imprisoned in a white room. There I lay, afraid of my mysterious body, the chasm that had given of its secret. I waited in wonder for someone to break the spell of the night. At last the day dawned, and when a nurse came to ask, *"What would you like for breakfast?"* I implored, *"Please, can I see my baby?"* They brought Sam to me, packaged as efficiently as a fish dinner and when I hesitantly released him from the swaddling wraps tiny arms shot out; expressive hands explored the air. I watched Sam through the long day, observing how his limbs surprised him, how his eyes darted here and there, entranced by the light. And at last someone showed me how to feed him.

Sam's welcome was somewhat hesitant because both our parents had been crushed by the death of their first child. I remained in the hospital,

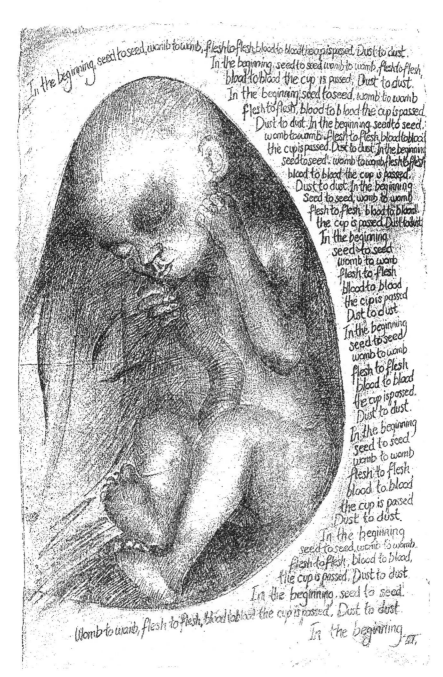

In the beginning, seed to seed, womb to womb, flesh to flesh, blood to blood the cup is passed. Dust to dust. In the beginning, seed to seed, womb to womb, flesh to flesh, blood to blood the cup is passed. Dust to dust. In the beginning, seed to seed, womb to womb, flesh to flesh, blood to blood the cup is passed. Dust to dust. In the beginning, seed to seed, womb to womb, flesh to flesh, blood to blood the cup is passed. Dust to dust. In the beginning, seed to seed, womb to womb, flesh to flesh, blood to blood the cup is passed. Dust to dust. In the beginning, seed to seed, womb to womb, flesh to flesh, blood to blood the cup is passed. Dust to dust. In the beginning, seed to seed, womb to womb, flesh to flesh, blood to blood the cup is passed. Dust to dust. In the beginning, seed to seed, womb to womb, flesh to flesh, blood to blood the cup is passed. Dust to dust. In the beginning, seed to seed, womb to womb, flesh to flesh, blood to blood the cup is passed. Dust to dust. In the beginning, seed to seed, womb to womb, flesh to flesh, blood to blood the cup is passed. Dust to dust. In the beginning.

Journal LT

watching mothers and babies arrive and leave while David built our bed, using worn timbers from a stable. Each evening he slumped asleep in the hospital chair. When the bed was complete I was released. Carrying my baby into the sunshine and driving out of the valley we passed trees, orange with their autumnal blush. At last our cottage came into view. Here was all I had dreamed of. As I pushed the door open my senses overflowed with fragrant colours. The simple room was a palace, jewelled with a sunbeam tapestry of flowers gathered from the fields and forest. Small woven mats graced bare boards that had been swept to a silvered shine; the living flames of a log fire crackled in the hearth. My lover had created a home that would hold us forever secure, and as I drunk deep from that cup of humanity I wondered if it was I who had been born.

Although the cottage was unfinished and sparse, it was ours. Sam and I were intertwined in an irresistible cycle of love, giving and receiving, sustaining and depending on each other; a blossoming flower, opening secret petals. The dark shadows had passed, but over those first weeks I often woke from a nightmare to find myself desperately searching the bed for the elfin child, fearful he had flown away. I would find Sam, safely sleeping, at anchor in his stout cradle. This, David's first furniture design, was a synthesis of woods: Dykehead's earthy oak beams, grown in the forests of Merry England, combined with teak panels, recycled from ships that had sailed the world's oceans. On featuring the piece in an exhibition, a response, *"Your cradle makes me want to have a baby,"* voiced what many felt on meeting Sam who, with his big brown eyes and curly hair, was magical in more than his mother's eyes.

Shortly after our homecoming, David planned a final fling before selling his Velocet Venom motorbike, claiming this excursion would celebrate our transition to parenthood. Before becoming a mother I had been fearless. I remember free climbing Cornwall's Bosigran sea cliffs, leaping from boulder to boulder with no other thought than keeping up with my friend. That on hearing he had fallen to his death, I realised how an extreme life may end. Motherhood had stolen that reckless spirit and separation from Sam went against all my instincts. Longing only to be with my baby, unsure of where my relationship was taking me, I agreed. I should have known better. As I handed Sam to Pip, my primitive impulses screamed a warning and when David dragged the heavy bike onto the road I wanted to turn and run. Buckling on the clumsy helmet I climbed onto the bike, hugging closer as we sped away, cutting through a sharp wind. Turning onto the open road David increased throttle. Gathering momentum, we undulated over the swelling waves of land. I pressed into my lover's braced body as, elevated above the moorland, silhouetted against the sky, we hurtled into oblivion. The force of our passage tore the helmet from my head, released my thrashing hair. Speed distorted my scream and feeling a tighter embrace, hearing my shout as an ecstatic *"Faster, faster,"* David accelerated and we shot, as a missile, along the road that follows Hadrian's Wall. Legions of centurion ghosts stepped aside as we echoed through space and eternity. Lost in the volition of metal and madness my senses rippled with a fearful thrill. Whooping and howling we flew on, into infinity. And after a time that had lasted forever, when I was finally beyond hope, we looped back into the winding lanes that led home. Quivering with relief I held Sam in my arms and breathed again. David was elated and satisfied. Doing the ton had initiated his child into the world. But for me it was different. I had realised that my life was no longer mine to lose; it was precious for my child's sake. The fearless mouse had become a mother tiger and only the passing of time would quench her fire.

While those days with my new baby were bliss, memories linger of fingers swollen with chilblains and a line of nappies, frozen as flags, on an arctic expedition. Sam was my constant companion, a being closer than my spirit. I performed for him as I did the housework and he returned my exuberance with laughter. It filled me with delight to sing his name and the magic of sharing our love made every moment a pleasure. Our cottage lacked electric lights, hot water, a stove and as autumn became winter the scant daylight demanded I complete all the tasks before the four o'clock twilight dwindled to darkness. Then a flickering pool of candlelight served as I nursed my baby through those bitter nights, huddled beside the embers of our bedroom fire.

David and I maintained some freedoms, sneaking out to watch Werner Herzog's *The Enigma of Kaspar Hauser* with my precious bundle hidden beneath my shawl. While Sam's inquisitive nature filled my soul with joy I was often torn between my husband and baby who both wanted my complete attention. David refused to submit to the cycle of domesticity that orbits a child, and when Sam woke at mealtimes he would say, *"Leave him, he needs to learn to wait."* I never managed to suppress that overwhelming need to comfort Sam and David would turn to me laughing, saying, *"You and your little baby,"* ever surprised at the turn of events. Braving the fells I walked to the bus in an icy wind with Sam snuggled beneath my poncho. As I clambered aboard, the driver glanced at my round body and sympathetically enquired, *"When's your bairn due hinny?"* After a further hike we were welcomed into a room full of mothers and babes and suddenly Sam was gurgling and laughing. It was then I realised that his need to interact was as vital as food and shelter, and years later, on seeing Sam surrounded by his circle of theatrical performers, I remembered my little boy, that early observation.

Ours was a rugged existence but independence nourished our souls, work strengthened our bodies, and the fluctuating seasons fulfilled a need for diversity. There was always bread dough or earth beneath my nails. Chopping wood, cooking and hand washing clothes took most of the day and any spare time was spent building the house we named Redthorn Cottage after a hawthorn tree that grew beside the door. The two dwellings huddled together as if united against the storms of life, yet

"Sam was magical in more than his mother's eyes" LT

28

the only connection Pip and I had was through our children. When she took Joe to the playgroup I looked after her baby, and although there was less than three weeks between Tessa and Sam, they were total opposites. I grew fond of the tempestuous little girl who needed constant attention, while Sam grew into a determined toddler, with a fresh awareness that consumed the days and brought nights of fitful dreams. I often climbed into his bed to reassure him and once, when he suddenly cried, *"There's a monster in the bed,"* I ricocheted into a foetal position, fearful that I was the monster that inhabited my child.

Countless generations had weathered the windswept moors before we came along yet the locals were generous enough to affectionately describe us as, *"Those hippies that live on the fell."* The black Galloway cattle that trampled the rough pastures around Dykehead belonged to Stan who also grew tatties. Drinking tea with him and his wife, Gladys, in their suffocating kitchen, I plumbed the depths of what to say and inadvertently suggested ways of livening up his bland potatoes. Stan's horrified, *"Why ya diven't want to do thart to yer tatties?"* taught me a lesson. My man and I had evolved into responsible parents, fallen into age old roles, but my inability to drive restricted my independence and undermined the core of my being. Having left home at sixteen, driving had passed me by. David took me through the basics but Bumble's complex gears required strength and advanced skills. In recurring nightmares, I hurtled downhill out of control. Reality could be just as traumatic. One memorable afternoon saw me perched upon cushions holding my own on a busy road, with Bran on alert behind my driving seat, his head switching from side to side; watching out for rabbits as the countryside flashed past. All was going well; and then Bran leapt into my lap. The situation became dire as David's explosion of expletives ejected the cringing dog onto the floor between my feet and the pedals. In sheer terror, I powered into oblivion, my feet kicking at Bran and the brakes. The experience compounded my anxiety and a first driving test reached a crescendo when the van door flew open on a bend. The next saw me squeezing my pregnant body behind the wheel for another attempt with an inevitable result. While these blunders were not responsible for my fear of technology, that sense of inadequacy would remain.

With David's first dining table and chairs commission came an opportunity to establish himself as a designer craftsman. On attracting more, he developed a structured, organic style that balanced traditional and contemporary design. The repetitive processes refined David's skills and aesthetic. Avoiding tropical woods that appeared garish in the mellow English light he chose native timbers to reflect the lands delicate hues. His forestry work taught him to respect trees as living entities, to understand their growth and the nature of timber. Sometimes David and Alan felled a tree to process themselves, slicing the trunk into planks to dry and shape into furniture. For this they used the estate's enormous saw that had been set up in a damp hut; one of a cluster that had housed German and Italian prisoners of war. As the whirling blade whipped the wind into a frenzy, David feared for his limbs. The trepidation kept him focused. Accidents are more likely in random moments of distraction. One summer day David arrived home early, his face a sickly white. "*What can you do about this?*" he said, removing his scarf to reveal a savage gash. While working alone clearing undergrowth, David had stopped for a pee, resting the hooked sickle on his shoulder. But as he fumbled for his zip the freshly sharpened blade fell, slashing David's neck a fraction from his jugular. My head spun with the gravity of what might have been; red blood pooling on the grass, our bereft family, a man cut down in his prime.

After extending the stone walls of our cottage David and I started work on the interior. The novelty of building had worn thin, time was limited and while I mixed buckets of plaster in the freezing shell of our new kitchen, Sam had to be contained in a playpen. Was there ever a time when families were free of challenges? We were shaping a home to last a lifetime, and when an enormous roof timber had to be wedged I stood, solid as a Caryatid on a Parthenon column, supporting the beam while David set it in situ. Jobs came far worse, like the weekend when David, Tim, and Pete dug a septic tank for our waste water. Endless rain had soaked the battlefield of trenches and the glutinous clay defiantly clung to our gang's boots and shovels. We despaired of finishing, but the day came when David struck the conclusive nail. It was then he noticed the fifty-pound note, payment for a worker, was missing from his pocket! Where else could it be, but entombed beneath our feet. We could not bear to rip the floor apart, or afford the lost money. There was nothing to do but laugh at the foolish mistake, easily made under stress.

On sunny afternoons, I set off with Sam on my back, sometimes seeking David in the woodlands or crossing the Tyne to where Rachel lived in an old farmhouse called Low Burnfoot. She and Peter had returned after two years researching a mountain community in Northern India, had visited on a pretext of asking, *"Does Low Burnfoot harbour any ghosts?"* David and Peter felt an immediate rapport, developed a friendship untainted by shadows, and I remain eternally grateful to Rachel for bringing us together. The love that David and Rachel had known need not be compared with ours, it was simply different. Before meeting David, I had remained true to a boyfriend who had undermined my self-esteem. When I was affectionate he accused me of being a nymphomaniac, taunting me with tales of other women, the nun he led astray, promiscuous girls who were such fun. Victim to my need to be loved I had tried and failed to be them all; had longed to be told just once that I was special. Thirty years later he contacted me to say how admirable and beautiful I had been, and I could only laugh. At last I am fulfilled, but if not for Rachel those years would have been lonely. While I respected her creativity, she admired my independence and visiting Low Burnfoot was made more special because of our shared past. In summer we filled bowls with raspberries or sat sewing in shards of sunshine with our children crawling about our feet. Sometimes we trundled at a toddler's pace, catching fragments of conversation while Sam and Albert discovered every insect that crossed our path and, having built our homes, friendship, and future, it seemed those blissful days would last forever.

THE IDEA

"He who binds to himself a joy
Does the winged life destroy;
But he who kisses the joy as it flies
Lives in eternity's sunrise."
Auguries of Innocence and Eternity, William Blake.

On completing Redthorn Cottage I painted the wall with a tropical beach scene and prepared a Caribbean feast for our friends who, arriving with blackened faces, brandishing placards stating *"Keep Coanwood white,"* displayed a derogatory sense of humour that would not wash in today's world. And as we danced to a reggae beat the contrast with our monotone surroundings betrayed a secret desire for a more stimulating life. My grandfather's death proclaimed Billy's conception and as my pregnancy advanced David and I ventured south to London. When walking on Hampstead Heath I recognised the familiar stature of my yoga teacher, Alan, and after reflecting on which of us had invoked that crossing of paths he laid a hand on David's shoulder and said, *"Look after Linda, she's a treasure."* Alan's presence could not be doubted; he influenced my belief that nurturing a child could be as spiritually profound as the way of a hermit, and David never forgot the encounter that released me from the turmoil that had crushed my spirit.

Moving on we visited David's mother and the island's boat yards, going on board a yacht that was a miniature home containing everything required for an adventure. An idea was forming in David's mind fuelled by Britain's political climate. When the Thatcher government told its people to stockpile food and tape their windows in the event of a nuclear war I felt like a sitting duck. I cried for days, despairing for our unborn child. Meanwhile David believed that if we owned a boat we could escape across the Atlantic. This metamorphosed into us buying a Bobcat catamaran and naming her Tormentil, after the delicate yellow flower that grows on the fell. David planned sailing her north shortly after the baby's birth, and with the passing days he became increasingly restless as he dreamed of her waiting in the Isle of Wight. In my ninth month we ventured out to a fancy-dress party, and while I exposed my pregnant belly in Turkish pants, veils and beads, David wore my yoga tights and a forked tail beneath cricketing whites, dramatically abandoning the baggies to don red horns and reveal, a *devil in disguise.*

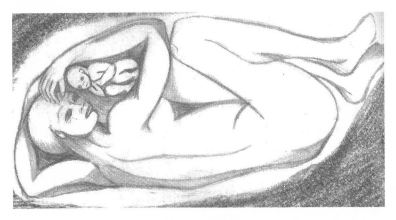

Mother and child LT

I had resolved to have this second baby at home, to avoid the panic we experienced when Sam was born on that moonlit autumn night. Our baby happily floated in the amniotic fluid of my inner ocean until, on a buoyant sunny day, while stretching to peg out the washing, those waters broke. I assumed that this was IT, that the birth would follow. There was no telephone at home so little Sam, Bran, and I hobbled down to the lonely lane to stand there, scanning the cattle that grazed the fields between us and Dykehead, where David was at work. Although traffic rarely passed our cottage I felt no panic. We waited a while, and then with a rattling rumble, a coal lorry rolled over the hill and screeched to a halt. Out jumped a man dark with the dust of ancient forests, "*Haweay, wots ooup wah yee ma hinnie pet,*" the Geordie bellowed against the idling motor and although my fecund form and wet dress said everything I completed the story, "*I'm going to have a baby, and my husband is in that barn.*" And with an, "*Al' rheet hinnie pet,*" he was away, running over the field, disappearing into the workshop. David and Tim were startled when a tattered apparition with wild eyes in a soot black face appeared like a demon from hell with a rousing, "*Haweaay lads thee watters haea braken; haweay!*" Such was the story of the heroic coal man who heralded William's birth.

After waiting a day and night with sleepy birdsong and humming insects providing a soothing soundscape, nothing had happened and the midwife conceded that for safety's sake I must go into hospital. "*But first, we could try raspberry leaf tea.*" David knew a hedgerow where fresh leaves were unfurling, flowers opening to reward summer seekers with ruby berries. Returning with fists full of foliage he compressed the bitter leaves into two mugs and added boiling water. Without hesitation, I ate and drank it all; enough raspberry tea to birth a battalion. I was aimlessly doing the dishes when my body awoke to a primitive power as for two excruciating hours great claws gripped my belly. As the seismic contractions accelerated to an agonising intensity that strong back squeezed through my pelvis and at five minutes past three on May the twenty-fourth, 1980, William surfaced and took his first breath. Holding him close I saw him awaken to his glorious life; Sam and David welcomed him into our family. Then we bathed and weighed the wriggling baby, balancing two bags of wholemeal flour and a tub of margarine on the scales. Years later Sam would describe their first meeting, "*I expected you to arrive with a suitcase and umbrella like big bear at the train station. I find it hard to think that at some point we were actually strangers. For the only time in our lives we must have looked at each other like aliens.*"

Although William had arrived on a summer breeze to the sound of new lambs, I have heard that an intense, fast birth may be traumatic for both mother and child. Our genesis continues to impact upon our lives. As a new being completes their passage into the world they encounter an overload of stimulus. Is that first howl one of a being outcast from the mother? Or a joyful cry of independence? The sound of one who has harmonised with the spirit? It has been said the atmospheric pressures of diving deep emulates the birth experience. As William dives in his mother the ocean he experiences a breathless world, surrenders to sensations that may be subliminally reminiscent of that first passage towards the light. Is it possible that my sons' rapid births enable Sam to embrace his creativity, embolden William to dive deep? For despite the hazards of freediving he returns repeatedly to that ultimate union with the ocean he describes as paradise.

Ten days after the birth David left for the Isle of Wight, to prepare and sail Tormentil around Land's End and up Britain's west coast to Maryport in Cumbria. While David's mother enjoyed his company, I struggled through long days and nights when Sam stayed awake to ensure he missed none of the attention being given to the newcomer. Billy's needs left me impatient with Sam, riddled with guilt at neglecting my first born. One desperate day I loaded my children in the pram and pushed it the two miles to the phone box. After telling David my concerns he said that Sam would soon get over it, adding his mother's advice: that women were often emotional after giving birth. Having reverted to his singular state David persevered with his plan, but following six hours trying to round Portland Bill he conceded the catamaran would not sail to windward. He and his crew spent a futile week waiting for the westerlies to abate before returning, only to set off again, determined we would use the boat that summer. Billy was six weeks old when David victoriously arrived in Maryport, after encountering savage lightning and the mysterious St Elmer's Fire. His mother acknowledging her heroic son's voyage with an adaptation of Rudyard Kipling's *If*, concluding *"Yours is the Earth and everything that's in it, And - which is more - you'll be a man, my son!"*

I loved both my children with all my being but during those early days I was isolated and overwhelmed. Though David's absence had taught me to stand alone, I often wondered if Sam would ever forget how the new baby had stolen my heart. My first baby's intense birth and our tranquil years together had created a foundation of love that transcended all else. Sam had become an exuberant child, our home a lively, noisy place that was incompatible with Billy's need for quietness and affection. As I dashed around in a whirlwind of perpetual motion, the children watched from the sidelines. There was a still centre in the storm. Although I began the nights alongside David, I moved to a spare bed with Billy and we fell asleep enfolded in a sublime embrace. Was it the uncertainty of my presence that made him drink until he was utterly satiated, an emergence of that obsession William would give to every project he pursued? From the start he aspired to keep up with Sam, bracing all the muscles of his little body, attempting to stand long before it was possible. Our isolated lifestyle would be abundant with contemplative times when our children's souls were filled with the wonders of the universe. A flickering fire in a dark room, the silence of snow or a star falling from the sky would awaken deeper sensitivities, and while Sam would continue to entrance me with revealing insights, Billy remains forever mysterious, instinctively part of my being.

"Billy could never get enough of that loving comfort that flowed between us" LT

Despite the distance from Maryport harbour, we regularly made the trip to the boat, loading the van with nappies, food, and outboard engine. I had naively embraced the new venture, even boiling spaghetti in sea water, rendering it inedible and fortunately avoiding contamination from Seascale's nuclear reactor. Tormentil was little more than a floating caravan with inadequacies that surfaced at inconvenient times. It was a white-knuckle event for David's mother when, approaching the harbour entrance, the outboard spun off the stern, plunging steaming and bubbling into the sea. Jokes about using it as an anchor were not well received; Josslyn had judged and failed us. On mistiming the harbour's four-hour tidal window for entering and exiting, Tormentil floundered in thigh deep mud, and while Sam took advantage of the jaunty angle of the cockpit to slide and lark around, the local lads made cheeky comments, *"Have yous lot jest sieled uver from Ireland."* One fine day on a windless sea David spontaneously plunged into the water to initiate a man overboard practice, giving directions to drop the mainsail to cradle and winch him on board. As he shivered uncontrollably we adopted a simpler rescue procedure, however despite the watery sunshine, sailing gave us access to wild places; the luxury of a home on the sea. One weekend we voyaged over the Solway Firth to Scotland's Kirkcudbright Bay and when Tormentil dried out on the falling tide we walked ashore and over the hill for a picnic on the sands of Brighouse Bay.

Through those growing years we stuck with what we did best. I looked after the home and David earned our living. Returning from Dykehead he would lower his head of golden curls, asking *"What wood is this?"* and I would attempt to detect the fragrant body of a tree felled in a forest planted centuries before our birth, pretend that I recognised the bitter smell of ash, a fruity aroma of oak. David was involved with every part of the process, from nurturing the forest plantations to sourcing, selecting, and having a sawmill cut a tree for a particular design. After slowly drying the timber in a kiln the planks were ready to be formed into furniture. David's sensitivity to the wood's structure and pattern combined with his feeling for innovative design rapidly led to national recognition. While never compromising his craftsmanship, my husband worked efficiently to ensure that his pieces were affordable. Group and individual exhibitions led to prestigious commissions such as a treasure box for the Victoria and Albert Museum in London; the promise of a lifelong career.

As David's reputation and business blossomed he gave up his forestry job. Bran was moping around the house needing more walks than I could manage, and when friends offered to take him into their home and hearts we were relieved. A long overdue day came for an indulgent shopping trip to buy a cosy mat for the hearth. Rachel and I trailed our children around Newcastle, completing a list of errands before our return. On cresting the hill above Redthorn Cottage we saw my table, chairs, and cooking pots strewn outside. What had happened to my home? That morning, before setting off for Dykehead, David had opened our Aga cooker to draw the flame and had forgotten to shut it. After he left the wind whipped the fire into a blazing conflagration. Fortunately Tim, returning for a fag break, smelt the fire, and ran into the flaming kitchen, bravely seizing the gas bottle that fuelled our emergency stove. His action prevented an explosion that could have destroyed the entire habitation. On hearing Tim's shouts David raced up the field and together they fought the blaze and when the panic was over the Haltwhistle fire truck arrived. In those days we never so much as locked a door when going on holiday. Our home had felt inviolable and although most of the damage was melted furnishings, a soot blackened interior that was restorable, it was demoralising just when we thought we were finished.

A year after Billy's birth we set sail for a holiday around the Isle of Man. I stood my first watch, following a compass course, and dawn revealed the hills, bays, and 'foreign' port of Douglas. There we went alongside the dock, scaling its high wall to be greeted by the local fishermen who, impressed with our venture, donated a pile of fresh shellfish, casting wicked, wrinkled winks towards David saying, "*Arrh she'll be good for the binge ternight lad, arrh.*" They surveyed our nautical love shack for signs of action, however any amorous intent was atrophied by their curious glances and Billy who screamed whenever I moved out of range. Our return to Maryport proved salutary when we met a rising gale that was blowing into the Solway estuary. The prevailing westerly was extremely hazardous for a boat that could not sail to windward, an outboard motor that lacked power. Anchoring off Workington with a plan of waiting for dawn and the incoming tide that would allow passage over the Maryport bar, we rapidly saw that our anchor was dragging. David calculated and I helplessly stood watch as the tossing waves and howling wind pitched us towards Maryport. Inside Tormentil our trusting little ones slept in their warm nest and I avoided imagining the consequences if the tide was not high enough to scrape into the harbour. I dressed the children in their life jackets and when crossing the bar was unavoidable David started the outboard. Trusting to its throbbing beat, I aligned Tormentil to the harbour wall and steered for the centre of the turbulent water. Any hesitation and we would be fouled or blown into the treacherous estuary. Rising on the bar wave Tormentil surged through the entrance and spun into the harbour. It was a born-again experience. Dizzy with redemption, awash with relief, anxiety switched to elation and we wandered into town to eat a cafe breakfast; the best Maryport could offer. We served our children's needs with gratitude, knew that we had cheated disaster and acknowledged this in each glance, touch, and word. A thought passed between us, that if we wanted to pursue our adventures afloat we must take heed of Tormentil's inadequacies and make a further commitment.

Far from curtailing our activities, the sailing epic had fuelled David's fire, but the incessant building had sapped his energy and he craved new horizons. Northumberland's persistent wind tormented him and there was no peace on stormy nights when rain blasted our house and found devious ways of penetrating its walls. Maybe the pointing was leaking, perhaps the flashing was at fault? The tortuous drip, drip, drip drove David insane with its tittle tattle tale of jobs to be done. He talked more about the sea, recalling how, on rounding Land's End, he had longed to just keep on going, out across the Atlantic. The permanence of weathered stones and growing forests had been replaced with a yearning for the fluid freedom of sailing, and when a London exhibition coincided with the Earl's Court Boat Show, David went along, returning with the seed of an idea that would change our lives.

I should have known how potent an idea is once it catches fire. Although I had spent my childhood as far from the sea as is possible in Britain, my aspirations lay far beyond the sleepy village of Cosby. My romantic imagination had seized on Bermuda, the island of my birth, and my determination to return changed my life just as growing up on the island of Malta inspired my father to write, *"This period of my life was to impress me more than anything else in deciding my future."* Thinking that reading would quench David's thirst for adventure, I sought out the sailing books in our mobile library, finding *Daughters of the Wind,* an account of New Zealand explorer Doctor David Lewis' circumnavigation with his wife and two small girls and *Children of Cape Horn,* that Rosie Swales had written while sailing the world. These tales of alternative family lifestyles posed the salient question, *"If they could do it, why not us?"* And in that instant, the idea broke free to fly. We could continue on our predictable path, or sell everything and sail into the blue; passively await a nuclear holocaust, or take control of our future. There was a world out there waiting to be explored and no other response than, *"Why not!"* In a heartbeat, a tectonic shift had occurred and, once spoken, the decision could not be revoked. Although my sense of being an outsider was no reason for leaving, a need to prove myself may have precipitated a longing for adventures, sunshine and the zingy essence of ozone and salt. After giving our all in building a home to last a lifetime, we were ready to sacrifice everything; to sell up, buy a yacht, pack and GO. The plan was cast in stone and though we had not considered whether ours would be a circumnavigation or one-way trip it seemed like a salvation. David could hardly wait to share it with his mother.

Josslyn's summer and Christmas holidays with us were the highlights of her year and after dinner we sat before a celebratory pile of profiteroles as David told the exciting news. Her response was immediate and volatile, *"How could you be so irresponsible? Why would you deny your sons their English upbringing?"* David was stunned, his mother had encouraged him to buy Tormentil and he had imagined her taking an enthusiastic interest in this, his latest venture. The exotic dessert lay in ruins and my immediate response was to abandon our plan. We had forgotten how much David's mother needed us, that she had lost so much that was precious. Josslyn's first baby had died at birth and she had been over forty when David was born. Following her husband's death her world had pivoted around her sons, and Sam and Billy were the sunshine in the evening of her life. This latest escapade must have seemed a ridiculous jaunt to one of a generation that had sacrificed everything for the security we were squandering. Her pleadings were met with David's persuasions and as the evening progressed both stubbornly stood their ground. While my support of the scheme classified me as a traitor I felt her anguish. Tears tainted expectation of Josslyn's blessing and when she voiced her final objection, *"You don't have the right temperament,"* David could not have been given a greater incentive. Nothing could have antagonised him more than his mother's lack of faith. Maybe he imagined that his father would have been more encouraging, for although he never lived long enough to question David, in the eyes of his son he would always be a hero.

Secretly shocked by David's uncompromising attitude I was aware that a similar issue had tainted my parents' relationship. The tropical lifestyle of Bermuda had granted them a freedom unknown to their generation, and when my dad was offered employment at the Regent Oil Company in Trinidad, they enthusiastically wrote to my mother's parents. My grandfather's warning that they would disown their only daughter if her husband took the job could not be ignored, for my father was eternally indebted to them for supporting his wife at a time when the Navy had denied him leave to comfort her following the death of their first child. Giving away the life they craved, my family sailed for England. All that remained of Bermuda were fading photographs of my happy parents on coral beaches and a lack of fulfilment that manifested in my mother's breakdown, my father's unresolved bitterness.

My parents had never understood our homespun values but they related to our desire for a place in the sun; the life they had wished for themselves. Others questioned our exposing the children to danger, and I was acutely aware we must do everything to ensure their safety and happiness. The harrowing tale of a family who had spent months in a life-raft after their wooden yacht hit a whale influenced our choice of a steel hull that might more likely survive an encounter with a shipping container, reef, or whale. David and I scanned magazines in search of a suitable yacht, but few travellers chose to return to Britain. We briefly considered building, but we had suffered enough drudgery and self-sacrifice. After extending our search overseas we found a yacht in the British Virgin Islands. Molly Bloom, a forty-foot cutter, with separate fore and aft cabins, sounded ideal, and following a glowing report from her broker we met the owner who had returned to England with her three toddlers. Despite an ominous shadow of shattered dreams, Molly Bloom perfectly suited our needs and we were ready to buy. When a potential sale of our house fell through it gave David an opportunity to check out *our yacht*, and he left for the tropics wearing the donkey jacket, jumper, and jeans that he could not imagine surviving without.

David returned from a week of snorkelling, sailing, and reggae, convinced we were leaving England for paradise. But Molly Bloom was another story. Her bold red hull, hastily painted for a quick sale, had blistered into a jungle of trailing weed, electrical wires exploding from her rusty engine's ravaged guts, and where bunks and a galley should have been there was nothing but vacuous space. The decrepit state of the yacht mirrored the broker's moral fibre; having made a corrupt deal to support a friend, he appeared oblivious to the damage his dishonest report might have caused. Molly Bloom was a poisoned chalice and David hardly dared imagine the scene, had we arrived in Tortola after exchanging our home and thriving business for her corroded hulk. With no place to stay or funds to rebuild, our venture would have been doomed. Nonetheless David had made friends and found work. His stories of coral beaches and turquoise seas lent reality to our dream, however we desperately needed to sell Redthorn Cottage before winter revealed the extreme nature of our stunning surroundings. But how would we attract a sale?

In Britain, the idea of sailing around the world with small children was rare enough to be newsworthy, so we offered our story to Newcastle's *Evening Chronicle*, generating a front page spread with a photograph of our family under the title *Into the Unknown*, concluding with the vital message that the scheme was dependent upon selling our *"beautiful home"*. Some thirty years later we met an old man who remembered our story, because, *"People in England didn't do that sort of thing."* The article attracted two separate buyers and a bidding hike that fortuitously increased our funds. Then an advertisement in the autumn *Yachting Monthly* attracted our attention and David immediately set off to view the forty-five-foot steel cutter that was sitting in southern Spain. Although our budget would be stretched to afford her, Hornpipe was perfect. Fitted with everything we needed for blue water cruising, she was a manageable size while spacious enough for our family. Hearing that her owners had separated when their voyage from Australia concluded with the husband breaking both legs jumping into soft mud, gave cause to wonder about the ominous demise of relationships afloat. However, we were the lucky ones. The delay and increased finances from the sale of Redthorn Cottage made Hornpipe affordable, and despite missing an autumn departure, our charts of prevailing weather patterns indicated that early spring was an option; that once the northern hemisphere's storms had passed we could expect the trade winds to blow us across the Atlantic leaving several months for cruising before the Caribbean's hurricane season.

As we prepared to venture beyond the reach of doctors and hospitals we adopted a strategy of prevention rather than cure. On long forgotten school days my girlfriends and I had gazed into the clouds, sharing our aspirations. While it was assumed we would leave at fifteen and get married, with babies soon after, the more instinctive pattern of accidental pregnancies marred many lives. My irreplaceable children were a choice, but they were all that we could adequately nurture so David decided to have a vasectomy. I am eternally grateful that he liberated me from a lifetime of invasive contraptions for despite the pill liberating our generation, all contraceptives come with a sting in the tail. There were no downers in this decision, no lack of libido, then or now. My impacted wisdom teeth were next and our children came under fire for numerous injections. Billy felt things deeply and howled louder with each jab. It was his helplessness that hurt most, and while Sam appeared completely detached, watching the needle enter his arm, many years later he would explain that although he felt the pain his concern about what was being done to him made him pay attention.

Determined that our kids should experience a regular childhood I began teaching four-year-old Sam to read so that any learning issues could be resolved without panic. I have heard that a mother's unconditional love is a vital factor in nurturing a child's self-confidence and believe David's homeschooling protected him from the later adversities of boarding school. While Josslyn's gentle guidance nourished his ability to learn, at my rough and tumble school I dreamed the days away and had turned eight before my mother taught me to read. Entranced by the mysterious symbols, the secrets they revealed, I stood in my pyjamas, reading by the hall light when I should have been asleep. After bestowing that precious gift, Mum went on to train, to teach at a progressive primary school. Her advice provided a foundation for teaching my kids and I attribute their love of learning to her simple, effective techniques. Our daily school time gave Sam and I opportunities to bond in ways that had been limited since Billy's birth. We were partners on a quest to retrieve our happy-go-lucky relationship. And as Sam began drawing in his scrapbook I never imagined this was the first of many journals that would overflow with a cornucopia of sketches, cartoons, and collages of people and places he would experience.

When friends who had travelled Scotland in a gypsy caravan suggested crewing for us our venture seemed more real, given the possibility of company. We talked of how their two small boys would be playmates for Sam and Billy, but fortunately their interest waned before we discovered that a boat at sea has barely enough emotional space for one family. On meeting Gerry at an art exhibition in Newcastle, we talked about mucking about in boats and immediately knew he would be the perfect companion on our voyage. Gerry's unruly mop of hair and healthy disposition from surfing in a British climate balanced the attributes of a young nurse who had answered our advertisement for crew. Catherine's practical disposition were key credentials, but she and Gerry were yet to meet and share a cabin. While keeping, options open for a circumnavigation we anticipated having to earn our living along the way and when David's Aunt Julia proposed we build her a house on a plot of land near Mullumbimby we applied for an Australian residency. The plan was primarily a security investment which, along with the toxic rift between Julia and Josslyn, could be resolved later.

On selling Redthorn Cottage to a young couple we pared our possessions to essentials that would fit in our trusty van for the trip to southern Spain. We held an auction to raise funds and when my shaker rocking chair, the first item of furniture David had made, sold for twenty-five pounds I was grateful for every penny. After sacrificing my eclectic record collection of yogic chants, Mariachi bands, and Jamaican classic *The Mystic Revelation of Rastafari* David parted with the Bob Dylan soundtrack to his life that even he could sing along to. Then we gave away our remaining belongings and abandoned our home for a rented cottage in Featherstone. There we braved the worst winter ever. While the walls of our bedrooms were coated with ice, our kitchen shrouded in a forest of drying nappies, visions of the future gave warmth and comfort. Sam viewed the pending trip as an adventure story featuring the characters of Molly Bloom, Gerry, Hornpipe, and Catherine and having grown used to his entertaining ways we assumed that this was a healthy dimension of his imagination, until Pip cautioned me about his insecurity. Such concerns were lost in the escalating events that left no time for more than a belief that all our problems would be resolved on arriving at our new home.

After the Christmas celebrations we waved a last sorrowful goodbye to my parents and David's mother, whose parting, *"I knew that no matter what I said you would do it anyway,"* epitomised the helplessness of being a mother. Then we counted down the jobs, with David completing a last commission of twelve altar chairs for Edinburgh's Saint Mary's Cathedral, while in spare moments I sanded them and sewed bright patterned cushions to transform Hornpipe's interior. After giving away a host of soft toys, I realised I had broken Sam's bond of affection with his favourite teddy. It was too big for Hornpipe, but there was another reason. The bear, a gift from my mother, had been a first indication of her mental trauma, that Christmas a decade ago.

Following my homecoming from Jamaica my parents, grandparents, and I had shared the Christmas festivities with my brother and his wife in Coventry. There had been no indication anything was amiss when, after eating far too much, the conversation settled on my single status. Then we melted portholes in the Anglia's icy windscreen and drove home beneath the gloomy sodium lights that cast urine stains upon the defiled snow. I barely breathed as, isolated in that tunnel of night, I sat squeezed amid the generations of a family that was about to explode. Dropping off my grandparents we continued home. I was half asleep when my mother burst into my room screaming *"I've killed Daddy!"* I found him shuddering in bed. *"It's all right Lindy,"* he said. But it wasn't. There was no murder, but the shock could not have been greater. This was a travesty of the mind. And while we reasoned, Mum deconstructed her life into a litany of incriminations, reliving past traumas that were more real than the present. We tried to console her as she cowered from the blasts of fighter planes blitzing the City of Bath, soothed her as she experienced the death of my baby sister, listened to her recall how her black dog Lucky had been poisoned by a neighbour.

Back then I believed whatever I was told. My only experience of mental disturbances was my Art College friend Julie waking me one morning to say that Jesus had entered our room to claim his bride, and knowing nothing of schizophrenia, I wondered why he had chosen her. As Mum denounced the charade of her life, my Dad and I tried to soothe her turmoil. But we could not dispel the demons. Eventually we entrusted her to the care of others, and by the time the doctor arrived Mum had lost touch with reality, insisting we join hands with our old teddy bears and the new one she had given me for Christmas. I spent the last days of that memorable year supporting my Dad, visiting Mum in the mental hospital where lost souls wandered, their white faces wiped of a past and future, gowns flapping open to reveal shameless bodies. I was informed Mum had suffered an extreme mental breakdown, that she had been given electric shock treatment and sedatives. It was claimed menopause and the strain of looking after my grandparents was the cause. But I felt it was something more. An extension was being built onto the house, and as my grandparents' move became imminent it seemed Mum had suddenly realised how their close proximity would kill my father's spirit. It was too late to abandon that plan and I returned to London, coming home every weekend. Dad was dependent upon me for emotional support and when he asked my opinion I had no choice but to say, *"Mum seems better."* However she had changed and I had lost the mother I loved.

I subsequently hated the oversized bear for its connections with that terrible Christmas, but back then nothing was discarded, so Big Ted had been passed to Sam, whose lingering memory pictures him abandoned on the woodpile behind Redthorn Cottage. How small my heart felt when compared to that huge guilt. I gave Sam my long loved Sooty bear, who had entered my life when I was four years old; going everywhere with me in those days when he was *The Bear*. And although Sooty's growl had worn thin and straw had burst from his threadbare fur, he was off on the journey of his life.

BREAKING FREE

"The thunder is rolling, growling like a bear.
Down to the depths it shatters;
Roaring, bellowing like a bull pierced by the matador's sword in its heart.
Rumbling, tumbling, rolling, crashing to the gaping cliffs in glee.
The storm is breaking as day comes with dawn.
The nightmare is past and the sea is calm."

Linda King, 1962

When the local newspaper boasted that it was warmer at the South Pole we knew it was time to leave. But as our final day dawned, ominous clouds loomed over the fells and we feared a fresh snowfall could isolate us in a crystalline limbo that would take days to clear. Once Rachel had collected our boys to play with Albert and Jesse, I set to packing while David spent his day lying on the frozen floor of Stan's shed, struggling to fix the mechanics of our tired van. It was then he discovered the universal joint on the propeller shaft was terminally worn. A breakdown would sabotage our journey, but nothing could be done so he avoided mentioning it.

In an era of smaller vehicles, our van was no more spacious than a car. As we loaded it with books, charts, toys, and David's old tuck box packed with chisels and planes that would earn our living in some far-flung land, the van sunk on its axles. When Rachel arrived with our sleepy children we climbed aboard with me sitting beside David, baby Billy on my knee and my legs wedged amongst the essential nappies, and food. Sam lay in the back, cocooned in a pile of bedding. Waving goodbyes, we turned away from homely lights and friendly faces, and as the frozen sky contemplated scuppering our voyage, we drove away. Insurance was prohibitively expensive and with no emergency funds every action was vital; however we were embarking on a glorious adventure, and as the old van gathered momentum our doubts slid away.

The road out of Coanwood lay muffled beneath a blanket of snow and through our frosted windscreen we caught farewell glimpses of the fell shrouded in a silvery mist. On joining the motorway at Carlisle we followed a singular track through banks of sullied slush with the occasional beaming light of a lorry illuminating our cramped interior before it thundered past with a tectonic roar. Drifting snowflakes blurred our vision and the engines rhythm lulled us with a soothing spell. Dreams were more real than this. What glorious pageants were evolving in the minds of our sleeping children; what inspirations would be born of that wasteland of swirling snow. Sam stored the essence of those experiences in the catacombs of his mind. He would remember stony houses, tunnels the wind scoured in the drifts; a snow plough scooping cavernous gouges in the whiteness, and sometime in the distant future he would translate those insights into a spectacular performance that explored the deeper nature of waking and sleeping.

As our wheels climbed the slopes of Shap pass, which divides the Pennines and Lake District, we dared to hope. Voyaging through time and space we coaxed our humming engine, and when it seemed the incline would never end we swept over the cresting wave of Shap. The incantation relented to a comforting purr, our pace quickened, the snow relented and moorland gave way to a gentler landscape. When the smoking towers of Birmingham were subsumed in our wake, I remembered that first journey I had made to Mount Pleasant. Sharing the driving I tightened my grip upon the wheel to speed along the familiar roads of Devon, which told tales of my previous life, of emotions that tugged the strings of my helpless heart. As Dracula, we swept through the land, to board that ship before phantom dawn could break the spell, and onward we raced, to Plymouth Hoe, where ancient times ago Sir Walter Raleigh had bowled upon the greensward. Some thirty years previous I had completed my first ocean passage, from Bermuda, to arrive in Britain, a babe in my mother's arms. On sighting those misty hills, had I anticipated leaving this harbour on my return to the sunshine?

On pulling into the carpark, tiredness melted to jubilant relief. We hardly believed that we had made it so far. As that murky February the seventeenth dawned, we boarded the ferry for Northern Spain. Our worries dissolved. If our old van would go no further we could push it off the ship and hire a vehicle to continue south. When the shores of old England faded, we felt no regret. Our Union Jack hung slack. David's schooldays had sabotaged his patriotism; my parents' disappointments had tainted my loyalty. And as we steamed towards the horizon I believed the stars would guide us, the wind carry us on that passage towards our spirit.

LT

We had broken the mould of what we expected to be.
Now as nomads we must wander the sea.

Once Britain had disappeared, we explored the empty ferry and found vacant cabins below, but before we could settle in, a steward ushered us back to our deck class accommodation. There we claimed a garish playroom, sharing the cushions with a mother and her daughter who played with Sam. After a day and night, a glorious sunrise welcomed us to Santander and magically our van revved into action. Driving through the orange groves, we inhaled freedom in every breath. Billy wriggled on my lap, Sam played in the back and as the miles coasted past it seemed nothing could stop us. As we cruised along the motorway a truck gestured for us to pass. We hesitated to cross the no overtaking line, but there was no danger and I waved to the friendly driver. Shortly after a police car raced past with sirens blazing, indicating us to Stop! On pulling over we were met with a tirade of accusations and a sixty pound fine. It was a set up; the truck driver had propositioned us before reporting our offence. Handing over the cash we drove on under a cloud of gloom. Our funds would barely stretch to provisioning for the voyage and there would be no more until we found work in the Caribbean, an ocean away. The betrayal and unpredictable expense had shattered our euphoria, as with only our silent thoughts for company I optimistically considered worse scenarios while David's anger calcified into predictions of further disaster.

At dusk we briefly stopped to eat, paying an exorbitant price for a dish of greasy meat. Then the children burrowed amongst our belongings to sleep away the miles of that velvet night. When the road deteriorated into a mountain track we became anxious and by the light of a sinister moon we made a brief stop. It was then David discovered petrol puddling beneath the exhaust pipe. He scrambled in the gravel to survey the carnage and with a sinking feeling saw the overloaded van had stretched the springs and rubbed a hole in the fuel tank. We requisitioned a nappy to bind the pipe, Billy's potty to gather the precious drops of petrol. Then as David drove on I sat bolt upright, uptight, scanning the rubble, tensing my internal organs as if I felt the jagged rocks clawing our vulnerable underbelly. Could we outrun the leaking fuel to reach Marbella before our vehicle collapsed? In the early morning we passed Madrid and as the sun rose, Sam and Billy woke to play amongst our muddled belongings. When they became restless we revived ourselves with a fizzy drink at a roadside bar and as we climbed the last mountain range before Marbella we risked a stop beside a lake. An exhausted elation flooded our veins; from there it was all downhill and surely we would make it.

Although the old van had surpassed our expectations, on reaching Marbella her gears froze. We hovered at intersections willing the cars to continue before we lost momentum, knowing that if we stopped there would be no starting. In a dizzy delirium we found ourselves on the motorway heading for Puerto Banus. It was then we witnessed the last drama of a stranger; the accident slowing the traffic to a crawl, the shock numbing our jubilation. Then, on rounding a corner we caught a first glimpse of the glittering ocean and Puerto Banus framed against the Sierra Blanca mountains. As the grand coastal highway dwindled to a single street with an adobe façade, we beheld a forest of masts bobbing within the walls of an opulent marina, and at half past three on the nineteenth of February we switched off the engine, confident that if necessary we could push our wheels those last metres. We had not ceased since docking at Santander and after the constant rhythm of driving it seemed that our hearts had stopped beating. Hornpipe was within reach, but a uniformed guard mockingly barred our way and when David said, *"We have a yacht here,"* he shook his head and laughed. On showing our ownership papers we were allowed to enter the marina where Hornpipe waited and as exhaustion evaporated into tears of gratitude we embraced the dream that had sustained us for months.

Beach boys LT

Hornpipe appeared as a mirage, her crisp white hull reflecting the rippling water on which she floated like a swan. Even my inexperienced eye recognised her fluid lines, the simplicity of her single fifty-five-foot mast. Climbing over the rails into the deep cockpit that would be our safe-haven in high seas, David unlocked the steel doors that could have done good service on a submarine. And stepping into Hornpipe's saloon I found that her previous owners had left us a Pandora's box of wet weather gear, housewares, tools, and diving equipment. Superman sheets featured high on Sam's list, however it was the dials and knobs on the electrical switchboard that impressed him most. Then realising that lunchtime was long gone, we bought bread and tomatoes and ate, sitting on the aft seat in the Mediterranean sunshine. Trundling the kids past the marina we found a small beach and running into the sea found it was warmer than an English summer. I calculated we could afford a drink at the tapas bar and as our children played around our feet we celebrated a joy as fresh as the first kiss of a love affair.

Puerto Banus was suffering a radical reconstruction from a scenic fishing village into the new kid on the block of the Costa del Sol, and we kept asking ourselves *"What are we doing here?"* It was only later we realised what an incongruous sight we had made when we arrived, exhausted from four days of travel. We had encountered some villains on our trip but our decrepit van had earned the name *Hero.* Tourists posed beside the rusty hulk and then our Danish neighbours paid us fifty pounds and set to restoring Hero. Those first days were spent recovering and carrying the remnants of a previous existence into our nautical home. Hornpipe was rich with sensations as unreal as those of another planet. A sharp definition of steel and salt replaced the pungent aroma of earth and smoke, that kinetic throng of swaying masts and clanging halyards created a soundscape that would become forever familiar. On drifting into sleep we heard the crackling of tiny shrimps echo through Hornpipe's hull and wondered what other creatures lived in the depths. As our senses tried to keep up I constantly repeated, *"This is your home, this is where you live."* But it was all a dream.

David's most vital task was to practice and perfect his celestial navigation. Although our voyages on Tormentil had required only coastal navigation, previous yacht deliveries had given him some understanding of the theory. When hitching a ride on a boat leaving Cowes bound for Marseilles the skipper had passed the Needles before saying, *"Oh, by the way, can you navigate?"* After studying the charts David had guided them safely across the Bay of Biscay as far as Gibraltar using radio direction beacons, but our trip from Gibraltar to the Canary Islands would be his first opportunity to practice celestial navigation. David would have no backup, or second chance in finding the small group of islands. The procedure of shooting the sun would require a steady hand, patience, and balance to counter the rolling, lurching, rising, and falling ocean swell. So every day he walked out along the seawall to where he had an unobstructed view of the sun and horizon. While he was practising, a seasoned seaman offered help, which David gratefully accepted and over the weeks they regularly met to refine the skills that would lead us to our destination. After taking a precise reading of the sun's angle David would return to Hornpipe's chart table, where he consulted our books of sight reduction tables and the nautical almanac's astrological tables. On completing his calculations of the latitude and longitude David triumphantly announced our position. The answer remained the same, but with repetition the process became intuitive.

Our family had woken from hibernation to the luxury of sunshine and freedoms rarely found in Britain. While I practised yoga on the beach the children played, leaving traces in the sand the tide would wash away, a pattern we would repeat on a string of beaches stretching to the other side of the world. I tried rowing our aluminium dinghy in the sheltered waters of the harbour, but being accustomed to the forward paddling of a kayak the wooden oars clashed each other or slipped beneath the surface sending the tubby dinghy spinning, only holding a linear course when an unblemished hull lay within its trajectory. The pleasure yachts were rarely used so these collisions went unnoticed. It seemed an illogical way of moving through water and I wondered how, when, or if I would ever row in a chosen direction, but the dinghy would be

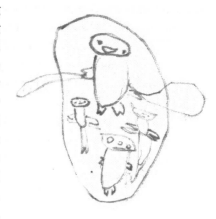

Rowing ashore ST

our only connection to the shore so I must master the skill. Memories of my driving failures goaded me on and at last the oars relented and the satisfaction of propelling my family through the water fuelled my confidence.

There were numerous jobs to accomplish, the first one primarily cosmetic with David replacing Hornpipe's stainless steering wheel with his newly made wooden one. We erected netting around the railings to safeguard the children, who would never be allowed on deck at sea unless accompanied by an adult, and while Sam was sensible enough to follow instructions Billy couldn't yet climb out of the cockpit. After considering fixing the freezer we opted for security over cold beer, to save our engine and fuel for propelling the boat. While filling Hornpipe's stainless-steel tanks we estimated how much water we would need for the Atlantic crossing. Then the foolish mistake of turning the hose to full pressure revealed a bodged job. Under force the water overflowed into a corroded tank and on noticing it dripping into the bilges we realised the previous owners had disguised a leak by blocking it off. That fortunate revelation about our reduced water capacity saving us from the catastrophe of running dry in mid Atlantic.

After fixing the tank we continued our preparations, wondering what we might find next. Hornpipe's marine toilet, or *head*, was another source of concern. Flushing on board requires opening a sea cock that effectively creates a sinkable sized hole in the hull. We would meet yachties who avoided this risk by using the self-explanatory *bucket and chuck it*. However that method had its episodic nightmares, when a slip on the way to the firing line or a freak wave *returned goods to sender*. Stories of exploding toilet pipes circulate through the yachting fraternity with the victims gleaning a modicum of satisfaction from telling their tales. So it was with trepidation that David heroically overhauled our beastie. Hornpipe had two *heads*, with the more effective Lavac situated as an *ensuite* inside our cabin. While this design applied a vacuum principle, the antique head opposite the galley munched its solids with a slurping glarp, glurk, glarp, glurk. Everyone breathed a sigh of relief when the occupant escaped the confined space in time to view a toxic cloud eject into the ocean. From underwater Hornpipe may have looked like a giant pooping fish, however the sound of frenzied pumping ensured no one ventured overboard.

Gas was not deemed a safe fuel at sea, but replacing our stainless-steel cooker with a paraffin stove would have been inconvenient. Being heavier than air, gas could sink and accumulate in the bilges, exploding if ignited. Opting to remain vigilant we bought a sun shower and jettisoned a gas water heater that consumed unsustainable amounts of fresh water. Then, while David ripped up Hornpipe's shit brown linoleum I replaced her curtains and cushions with the cheery ones I had made. On hanging pictures saved from our previous life, the boat became a home filled with colours and light. All that remained was for our crew to arrive. Gerry and Catherine met for the first time at Marbella airport, knowing they would spend days and nights flung together in a confined space. Gathering in the cockpit for a bottle of *rough as guts* red wine the mood shifted to party time. Our merry band was setting off on an adventure, and this time I was on an equal footing with David, or so I thought.

CAST OUT INTO THE DEEP

"Outward bound upon a journey without ending
Outward bound, uncharted waters beneath our bow.
Far behind, the green familiar shore is fading into time
And time has left us now.
So farewell, adieu, so long, vaya con Dios
May they find what they are looking for
Remember when the wine was better than ever again
We could not ask, we would not ask for more."

Tom Paxton

In times to come starting Hornpipe's engine and untying her mooring ropes would become routine, but everything was new on that momentous eighth of March when we embarked on what was potentially a voyage around the world. After creeping past the breakwater where David had practised his navigation we hoisted the sails, but despite ever-hopeful upward glances there was no sign of wind. Selling up to go sailing had required a giant leap of faith and anticipating this maiden voyage had sweetened the monotonous preparations, but we had yet to feel Hornpipe lift her wings to the breeze and as we picnicked on the deck we longed for our bird of passage to fly.

Eventually admitting defeat we dropped canvas and cranked up the engine. And as its vibrating pulse escalated to a seismic beat, hatches juddered and small items danced on the table. David regretted every moment not sailing and as we pushed our path through the Mediterranean his complaints reached a crescendo. While this was only the beginning of our relationship with the mechanical beast that inhabited the engine room, Obelix was doing his boisterous best to shatter the romance. The relentless pounding reminded us of our eroding budget, that a profligate use of his services would risk his being worn out on some day of reckoning. The day faded to night as we bedded the children down to sleep in Hornpipe's belly, and long before Gibraltar's lights appeared Obelix's thundering pistons had pummelled our brains into submission. As we wove our way into the dockyard the spreader lights cast eerie shadows that created many margins for error. This, combined with an unfamiliar boat and wharf, led to an inevitable conclusion. Somewhere between fore and aft, port and starboard, we rammed a power unit. And despite Hornpipe bouncing off, David's pride was damaged by that first landfall.

Hornpipe family   LT

Amongst the yachts preparing to cross the Atlantic there was one with a wind vane sporting an image of a Victorian matron with an umbrella. Mary Poppins surpassed our misgivings about Hornpipe's name and while Buchanan, her rugged skipper, regaled David and Gerry with stories of crossings, we took stock of his knowledge. Then we set to gathering provisions to last until we reached the British Virgin Islands. Gerry scoured the town for mechanical parts and obscure foods returning with a bargain crate of bull's blood red wine, and four huge salamis, but best not dwell on what form those offal and grease truncheons had taken in a previous incarnation. The spirits of their rightful owners would haunt our intestines, and long after we bequeathed the remains to the ocean they would be remembered for introducing the word *biff* into our vocabulary.

While our isolated lifestyle had taught us to fix problems and entertain ourselves at sea, we would be beyond the care of doctors and hospitals, so staying healthy by eating well was a top priority. In Northumberland

I had mostly cooked vegetarian food. The children were used to eating whatever was put before them and would come to endure Gerry's head banging curries with bravado. Although we intended supplementing our diet with vitamin pills and hoped to catch fresh fish, we needed a dependable source of protein. This led to us purchasing seventy-two cans of corned beef, that with culinary genius could be transformed into curries, tacos, pies, moussaka etc. After coding the tins with indelible ink, we stripped their labels to avoid blocking the bilge pump if they became wet. Then, as Catherine mapped where the items were stored I stashed the redundant freezer with honey, marmite, coffee, milkshake, chocolate; the cupboards with rows of dried fruit, pulses, nuts, condiments, and spices. When every nook and cranny was full we raised the saucepans, dishes, and cups on a bed of packets and tins. After requisitioning the forward shower for tubs of margarine, dried milk, sacks of flour, and oats I hung string baskets bulging with vegetables and fruit against the galley wall. We would eat the perishable tomatoes and lettuce first, the oranges, cabbages, and carrots later.

Hornpipe carried an extensive health kit augmented with bandages, medications, and secret phials of morphine Catherine had nicked from the hospital and these we hid for that dire emergency we prayed would never occur. She dedicated herself to making baggy wrinkle, uncoiling the worn ropes before knotting their strands into soft brushes that sheathed the metal shrouds - upholding a nautical tradition that prevents the sails chaffing against the rig. Meanwhile David was often found with his head down, bottom up, overhauling Obelix, causing me to recall his proposition that I become Hornpipe's engineer to complement his knowledge of sailing. How I wished I could save David the frustrations of his most hated job. After all, my dad had spent his war in the engine room of a British Navy Ship. I visualised myself, emerging triumphantly oily from fixing the motor, and in my feminist heart I longed to prove myself, but my fear of machinery presented an insurmountable problem.

Despite working equally hard looking after the kids I felt guilty for my limited participation in those *real* jobs. Before leaving Gibraltar, I decided to immerse Sam and Billy in an experience that would sustain them on the empty ocean. Riding the cable car to the top of the rock we gazed over the hazy city and vast ocean that evaporated into a horizon we would go beyond. Then, turning our backs on that sunny afternoon, we entered the passages of an underground cathedral, wandering those dark depths, awed and alone with the columns of stalagmites and ethereal stalactites. Was there ever a more profound farewell than that pagan rite of passage? In the depths of the cavern I voiced a primitive prayer to mother earth and any god that was listening. Saturated with silence we stumbled into the sunshine and, after feeding the Barbary macaques, set off for the port. Billy fell asleep in his buggy, Sam stood on the foot rest as we traversed those narrow passages and baroque terraces, our journey metamorphosing from caverns to the tankers, squatting grey and grim upon the ocean. And on reaching the wooden pier, lapping water, and Hornpipe, the children bubbled over with stories of monkeys, caves, and ice cream, all to be written of in Sam's journal.

Unsurprisingly, in Greek Mythology the straits of Gibraltar had marked the limits of the known world, for they are notoriously swept by a ferocious wind that hurtles down from the mountains, tearing sails and shattering masts. This, along with prevalent westerlies and adverse currents, renders it near impossible to sail out of the Mediterranean. Throughout our time at the Rock a low-pressure system over Morocco combined with a high over Spain had delivered a favourable easterly wind. There came a day when, despite hoping for more preparation time, it became foolish to squander the force eight that would blow us out through the straits. So, after hastily setting up a safety cable on Hornpipe's deck, at thirteen hundred hours on the thirteenth of March we set sail. Friday was a taboo, the thirteenth doubly disrespectful of God and the Devil, yet despite an armada of superstitious seamen warning us we tempted fate by starting our venture on that day of days. Maybe David remembered the compelling words, *"Launch out into the deep,"* chiselled on his father's tombstone in the Gordonstoun cemetery; the biblical passage from Luke 5:4 commanding him to head for the open seas. Our Captain held to his decision and Gibraltar's Pillars of Hercules, that with its twin on the edge of the African continent, mark a gateway to the Mediterranean, allowed us to pass. And as the monolithic wedge of rock receded the Atlantic Ocean opened before us, and it seemed that we were fulfilling a prophecy.

The erratic wind set us to goose-winging Hornpipe's mainsail to starboard, genoa to port, emulating a great bird with wings outstretched. But when the breeze dropped we rolled in the heaving swell, our sails slating and crashing, and it was only after many changes that our yacht settled to, dipping through the ocean's crests and gullies on a close reach. David expected our voyage to the Canary Islands would take approximately a week, but as the Iberian Peninsula faded Gerry joked, *"Maybe that was the last time we will ever see land."* And where we had fearfully gritted our teeth there was suddenly laughter. Gerry's wry comment hit the nail on the head and we assumed the gravity of his remark was yet another manifestation of his dark humour. However Catherine would confess they had discussed their odds of surviving the voyage and many years later we would learn that Gerry suffered from an anxiety syndrome that tainted every situation with dread.

As the horizon dissolved into blackness an ominous swirling beset our collective stomachs. Despite trying to go with the waves I was overwhelmed with a dizzy nausea. This was only the first day of our voyage around the world and already I was sick. If I had been a passenger I could have acquiesced to the fluid motion, but *taking to my bunk* was not an option with the children to look after, watches to keep, meals to prepare. I had enjoyed the rolling gait of the ship that carried me from Jamaica to England, had weathered Tormentil's gait as she bobbed like a duck upon the abrupt waves of the Solway Firth. Surely my nautical heritage and that first Atlantic crossing as a babe in my mother's arms counted for something. But none of us had experienced an ocean swell from the deck of a small yacht; the rapid downwind pace that afforded the mast no stability to prevent the rolling that, combined with our angle across the waves, created a stomach churning corkscrewing motion.

Having prepared for every circumstance it was deeply disturbing to discover I had escaped society only to be locked into the inadequacies of my body. Seasickness surprised us all but we were soon passing the bucket as amicably as a tray of drinks. After throwing up there was a euphoric intermission while our minds and bodies reclaimed a momentary equilibrium. Grasping that brief opportunity, I desperately cleaned, cooked, and served the children's needs but the black void inevitably saw me crawling into the cockpit, my brain awash, stomach spiralling into oblivion, rallying for another attack. Nausea was accompanied by a debilitating lethargy and mindless miasma that rendered simple calculations impossible. And, at a time when it was vital I protect my children, my feet had been swept from under me; my adventurous spirit crushed. Free of nausea, David believed my problem sprung from a lack of faith in his capabilities. As I cowered in a corner he was at one with the ocean. Empowered by an intense sense of purpose he jubilantly laughed at dangers as though they never existed. Here was everything David had ever dreamed of and he wanted to share his excitement with me.

Following the Moroccan coast we mirrored an overland trip that David and friends had made in the early seventies. On arriving at the country's border, they had been obliged to cut their long hair, their curls blowing over the sea, the waves washing them back to the sandy shore. Driving south through Fez and Marrakech they spotted a picture of a camel, with a sign that read, *"Fifty-Two Days to Timbuktu."* One evening David and Jonathan had decided to explore the rocky slopes of a gorge. Descending in failing light they were unprepared for the crumbling ridges, and routes that often ended on the edge of cliffs. As darkness fell their friends tried to guide them down with the van's headlamps and by the time they found a way they were desperately cold, thirsty, and hungry. And now, off that same shore, David and family were involved in another adventure.

Our course followed a busy shipping lane and by night the lights of ships kept us on alert. When a steamer passed close by, David switched on Hornpipe's spreader lights to indicate we were a sailing vessel that must be deferred to. She surged through the energetic sea, a buoyant swell rolling underneath, lifting her high, showing us who was in charge. A rattling clang of tins, jars, pots, and pans; the soundtrack of chaos resonated from below, asserting a claim on our bamboozled brains. And as I steered, looked after the children, cooked, and coped, a singular thought, *"I wish I could go home,"* clawed at my mind; to be answered by a rational, *"Going back is impossible. We are all at sea!"* Our family had become flotsam and jetsam, at the mercy of the wind and waves. The coast was lost to windward, a thousand feet of water lay beneath us, and our escalating downwind pace prevented any return to the comfortable house and business we had built and sold.

I come from a family of seafarers, an association with the sea that includes grandfather, great grandfathers, maybe more. As a boy, my father's one aspiration had been to enlist in the Navy. Exactly forty years before, his ship had encountered a fierce gale in the very waters we sailed. When his ship's engine foundered, the convoy sailed on leaving a solitary corvette to guard them and their cargo of ammunitions. My father wrote, *"Dawn found us wallowing in heavy seas with part of our deck cargo consisting of forty, five gallon drums of aviator fuel that had broken adrift."* Although the crew managed to secure the volatile cargo, on reaching Cape Town their vessel was assigned to escort the convoys that were supplying the beleaguered island of Malta. Dad described the six days and nights of Operation Vigorous, *"I spent my twentieth birthday during this period and I don't think I've ever felt so frightened in my life, before or since. The continual strain of living with noise was shattering. My own action station was in B boiler room with an officer standing at the top of the exit ladder complete with loaded revolver as a deterrent to panic as the noise and vibration of our guns firing and bombs exploding near and distant multiplied in that sounding box below the water."* My father came to hate the life he had venerated, writing, *"Joining the Royal Navy was the greatest mistake of my life. Many thieves and murderers have less of a prison sentence with more privileges and comfort than I did during my honourable contract of service to the country and my signature at the age of fifteen, (eighteen months before the start of WWII) when the coming of age was twenty-one, was sufficient to bind me to an unbreakable bond until I was nearly thirty-one."*

On that first day at sea, David released the bronze sextant from its wooden box, hooked his lanyard on the safety line and climbed onto the roof of the aft cabin. Then, bracing himself to Hornpipe's twisting roll, he seized the moment, catching the sun's glowing orb in the mirrored discs, calling out his reading of the angles which we recorded along with the precise time each sight had been taken. Following the nine thirty and noon fixes, David calculated and indicated our position as a cross on the chart, initiating a routine of taking sights and plotting our course that would dominate every ocean passage we made. Navigating would have been a fun diversion if we had not been consumed by sailing procedures, domestic chores, and child care. After, we gathered over the chart table to view our position and speculate on the efficiency of Hornpipe's sails. Over subsequent days that singular cross initiated a faltering line that inscribed our passage towards the Canary Islands; a line that would become our assurance of a future.

On leaving the security of land we had given ourselves up to David's expertise, accepting his decisions and knowledge of processes that only slightly differed from nautical methods that had been used for hundreds of years. Satellite navigation lacks that connection with the elements and cosmos. Though computer charts connect to a GPS system, making plotting locations and distances instantaneous, those using it depend on technology and often have no understanding of what to do if the system fails. We understood our place in the universe, our connection to the sun, moon, stars, and planets. Our traditional approach was demanding, but if we encountered a problem while navigating and propelling our yacht across the ocean, we could adapt.

Watch keeping was set as a three hour rota, with the person going off remaining on call for sail changes. Log entries record the repetitive flap, slap, thwap of flogging sails and how often we lost steerage way as Hornpipe skewed out of control. By our third day we were battered and bruised from the pitching, thrusting gait. Night fell with Hornpipe pounding through huge seas, racing on a rapidly increasing thirty-five knot wind. When unpredictable squalls prompted Gerry and David to hurriedly don their harnesses and scramble on deck they found the mast pumping. Springing to action they dropped the flogging mainsail. Amidst the drama, a tanker passed close by and dolphins streaked beneath Hornpipe's bow, slashing the inky waves with phosphorescence. Fresh soakings and the euphoria of an averted catastrophe had invigorated our boys and they thanked their lucky stars Hornpipe had not been dismasted. Meanwhile the children and I were shut in the aft cabin with the steel door latched against the waves that smashed into the cockpit. Intoxicated with seasickness, I lay strewn on a pile of abandoned sails, a captive audience to Sam and Billy as they rolled and tumbled in the anarchic muddle. When their antics culminated in nausea they briefly joined me, and on reviving returned to leaping around, until finally they sunk into a jumbled, submissive sleep.

During the night the storm abated and my dawn watch was calm. Although my energy was spent I blearily prompted Sam to sound out the words of his *Janet and John* books as, mystified by the squiggly letters, he thrived on my participation. Billy's small sentences were revealing a window into his world and he kept up a noisy chatter as he drove toy cars into a lump of playdough, while Sam busily drew in his journal demonstrating that he was doing important work. Resigned to Hornpipe's persistent bucking and skewing we somehow kept up with the day's demands until an indecisive wind at dusk prompted repeated sail changes, and when a miscreant wave swung the cooker's contents onto the floor we had no choice but to scoop up and eat the remains of our supper.

The deep, safe cockpit had become the nucleus of all activities. Its airy connection with the ocean making it easier to tolerate the motion but on those odd occasions, when the self-steering worked, we ate, tightly wedged around the saloon table. While believing the ritual supported good eating habits, mealtimes were more fun than formality. Hornpipe thundered along like the runaway train from the children's *All Aboard* tape and when the helms-person shouted, *"Big wave!"* we braced ourselves; but there were never enough hands to hold onto bowls, food, and children. Dishes launched themselves onto the floor and plates slid to and fro, as dinners changed owners. I longed for it to stop, we all did, but the ocean was in control, rolling and twisting with a momentum that continued through day and night. Yet I never slept as deeply as those precious hours when I rocked in my cradle, safe in Hornpipe's belly. Later, when asked whether we came to a standstill to rest for the night, I explained that the ocean never sleeps, how even a calm sea could smash with an inconceivable violence, that Hornpipe's sails and keel held her in an equilibrium that was infinitely preferable to being tossed around under a bare mast.

Our extended family had bonded into one, as if we had always lived together. Sam thrived on the attention of four adults while Billy found a security in Hornpipe's miniature scale. Gerry and Catherine had blossomed into their role as surrogate parents, and with them calling me Linda, the children abandoned calling me mummy. Daddy suffered the same fate and sailor Sam and bosun Billy considered themselves crew of the jolly Hornpipe. We helped them join in the safer activities but they mostly amused themselves with toys and books. The saloon floor was ever awash with Lego and, lacking television, videos, and opportunities to play outside, they needed stories and diversions. This was how Bouncer entered their lives. Born of a long line of country spiders, Bouncer had wandered into the tuck box where, on making a home amongst David's hand tools, he became an unwitting stowaway. Sam and Billy spotted him hanging around the galley, constructing a new web; and in the absence of a dog or a cat Bouncer became their pet spider. Our children's travels bore a resemblance to those of Bouncer. They also trusted to familiar comforts and a secure bed or web to fall into after exploring uncertain territory. The story of Bouncer's voyages will unfold, and whether it was the same spider we glimpsed scuttling behind a cupboard is irrelevant, for it was certainly one of his lineage.

We had expected Hornpipe's automatic helming device would take over the tedious task of steering, but what should have been a labour saving blessing sorely tried our patience. Although the brand name Aries would imply lightness and flight, David described the contraption as, *"A worthless piece of junk!"* The mechanism of ropes, brackets, and blocks was connected to the steering wheel through a cat's cradle of pulleys and cords that divided the cockpit with an obstacle course to outwit the bleary-eyed sailor. Salient ropes threaded their way to the stern, from where they manifested their worth through a cryptic assemblage of corroding zinc and aluminium pipes, rigged to a vane that tilted with the wind pressure, thus activating a twisting action in a paddle that projected from Hornpipe's stern. As the rushing water, pushed the paddle onto its side, ropes and pulleys responded by moving Hornpipe's wheel or tiller, to theoretically steer a consistent course.

Somewhere in that communication between oar, rudder, wind vane, and wheel, a message was being lost; and despite our boys spending long hours fiddling with and discussing its intricacies, the Aries was absent without leave. The inanimate machine played a larger than life role in on-board dramas and thus far it had proved more useful as a climbing frame for getting on and off the stern of the boat. Where the robotic watch keeper should have given us respite from the arduous task of steering, we had spent endless hours trying to control its deviances. The Aries was the bogey man of our boat and the ship's log reverberated with vitriol. David believed that if given the right tweak or tightening of ropes, the Aries would magically fall into line. In a well-rehearsed scene, I steered as the boys tried another strategy. *"Give it a click,"* David shouted from the stern to Gerry in the cockpit as they obsessed over details of the wind vane's tilt and response. They rehearsed tactics to outwit the cunning contraption, believing that if they solved its riddle we would be released from the monotony of steering. But the Aries persistently behaved like a stubborn ram and appeared determined to spoil our trip. I wondered whether the diabolical machine had been the demise of Hornpipe's previous owners, and would have volunteered to steer all watches if I could have never heard the name Aries uttered ever again.

Amidst the nautical regimes and domestic routine, we could not underestimate our crew. Catherine balanced Gerry's zany pathos with a certainty that all would be well, and when he joked about catastrophes she just gave her enigmatic smile. Catherine remained mysterious as a sphinx and all that Gerry would glean from the vaults of her personality was that her father was *loaded*, with a collection of antique cars and a big house in Berkshire. We waited for a riddle to unlock Catherine's secrets and wondered why she had chosen to sail with us. She must have known how many night watches she would stand without a gin and tonic, the toddler bottoms to wipe, the risks that must be endured. Catherine would prove herself as efficient as is possible without batteries, however her presence, along with Hornpipe's life raft and a grab bag of fishing gear, lemons, and medications, enhanced our peace of mind. After asking about the mysterious box strapped to the deck, Sam incorporated, *"Going in the life raft,"* into his fantasy games, a reminder that despite our thoroughness, the unpredictable ocean could outwit us all. And though I optimistically believed I could become accustomed to a life at sea, a realisation that our vulnerable children were unlikely to survive a sinking or capsize remained an insurmountable anxiety.

When my fourth night watch rewarded me with calm conditions that the Aries could manage I began a patchwork quilt that might boost our cruising funds. Where gazing at the tiny stitches had previously proved

all do - there must be the there must be exceptional land, but I feel we
all do - there must be exceptional people who are more at home
out here battling with these elements and I'm sure its mostly a
matter of finding confidence and understanding of all these huge
creatures of waves and sky and ones place between the two

Need a thicker pencil
and less howly wind

All I write sounds tired, uninspired and its hard to write
as a concerned mother and wife or just a frightened kid
its not what I wish to express or feel but maybe I can somehow
sort these out and feel more able to care without just being had

too much for my fragile stomach I was now able to sit sewing in the saloon. The simple task saturated me with contentment. Remaining tuned to Hornpipe surging through the waves, her sails fluttering in the breeze, I periodically dashed to the cockpit to scan the black ocean and check the course. That constant back and forth, the detailed stitches, and self-reflection had interrupted my equilibrium. Turning from the swaying Tilley lamp, I darted outside to be struck by a blinding beam of light, a ship towering over our yacht. My mouth dried; a silent scream died as a paralysing wave of terror swept over me. A shout froze in my throat, my knees folded and I crawled upon the cockpit floor, clawing for the switch that would activate the spreader lights to render Hornpipe visible. And as the spotlights illuminated our mainsail I cried, *"David come quick! A ship, a ship!"*

Had the ship seen us? I dared not look into the path of imminent disaster. Moments passed as futile prayers and expectations of that terrible collision regurgitated through my mind. Then David was in the cockpit, rubbing bleary eyes, gazing around and following the direction of my pointing arm. In his presence, under our reassuring lights, I was brave enough to look beyond, to see with an overwhelming and sudden realisation that where I had visualised an imminent disaster, the moon sailed amongst the clouds, shining glorious rays upon our deck. On my fleeting, flitting into the cockpit, dense clouds had obscured her light. My intense focus, the transition from dark to light, had bamboozled my vision and when the moon emerged from behind an inky cloud her beaming light appeared as that of a ship at such proximity a collision seemed imminent. It had all been a lunar trickery of my mind, and now it was just the moon ploughing her course through the velvet waves of night. David laughed, hugged me, and laughed again. *"Can I go back to bed?"* he asked, *"Or are we going to get hit by another moon?"* And after a trickle of shame my tide of relief bubbled into effervescent laughter. Everything was different out there on the ocean, and the moon could be a ship, if you happened to see it that way.

By the sixth day our minds had tuned into a rhythm of flapping sails and straining rigging that was only broken by the syncopated blasting of Obelix charging the batteries. Sleepless nights of sail changes had taken their toll. Our limbs were wracked with Hornpipe's persistent corkscrewing as she tunnelled through the heaving swell with a sweeping, swinging momentum. Despite our bracing against the bulkheads, Neptune delighted in making every job a challenge, preparing the simplest meal a gravity defying performance. The task of opening a cupboard to extract a tin required the ingenuity of a choreographer, the balance of a gymnast. If the galley wretch could sustain the focus of a Zen master, we might eat that night. One thing led to another and if that humble cook stumbled on a step or lurched through a doorway, a corner would deliver a punch to bruised ribs, cruel cuts to elbows and shins. Chaos was inevitable and when that long sweated-over stew sloshed on the floor the spill amounted to hungry bellies and a cleaning task of immense proportion.

During the night, the wind persistently backed the foresail and when it became too gusty for the Aries, Catherine capitulated to hand steering. Yet by the time David relieved me from my watch it had dropped, causing his comment, *"Linda propelling us by waggling the rudder."* I had dreaded waking David from his heavy stupor, how he growled and groaned in reluctant incomprehension, followed by a quizzical analysis of Hornpipe's progress that left me feeling accountable for any discrepancies. After his graveyard watch, Gerry reported, *"Lots of fun, two ships, one shooting star, one aeroplane, and the moon rose. Total interest time, ten minutes in three hours."* And later when two turtles swam past they seemed to define a change in the seascape.

As our garland of crosses inched closer to the Canary Islands we began imagining mountain ranges in every bank of cloud. Following David's noon sight he estimated we were too far east to pass between Tenerife and Gran Canaria, so he set an alternative course to approach a side of the island that was lit with beacons. Unspoken anxieties lingered in every comment, exacerbated by David's warning that while we longed for land we must be prepared to sail away and seek safety at sea if the conditions were unsafe. Every glance revealed a longing for land and we found ourselves listening for a change of tempo that might pre-empt a victorious announcement. While we thinly disguised our obsession by fidgeting with trivial jobs, David made directional sail changes, repeatedly checking the course, mentally preparing himself for that first landfall. And all the while the metallic sea undulated towards the hard horizon, mocking our desire for land – land, at any cost. The hours stretched to an interminable length with David picking up conflicting radio direction beacons in the direction he believed the land lay. Yet another dusk darkened to night. Then, at nine twenty, David identified the 'La Isleta' light on Gran Canaria, shouting a *"land ho,"* that rung as music to our ears. And that night we kept watch and went to our bucking bunks knowing we would soon sleep in stillness and safety.

As dawn illuminated the pinnacles of Gran Canaria, a gusty north easterly sprung up, becoming fickle and furious as we drew near the mountains that tower over Porta Aringa. When the wind abruptly ceased off Porta Maspalomas we cranked up Obelix and by noon of the twentieth of March, Hornpipe was tied stern to against the high walled dock of Puerto Rico's inner harbour. Bouncer gave a sigh, spun himself a hammock, and settled to an uninterrupted sleep. By the time he awoke his web would be swaying again. But after seven days our brains had finally accepted the ocean, and on clambering ashore the land set to that rolling, rumbling, twisting, and a tumbling we had so recently endured. Nausea dizzied our brains and just when Billy had thought to have mastered the skill of walking he found himself a novice again, his logical mind posing the question, *"Why is the land moving?"* He was not alone and we laughed as we wove along the wharf, taking those first steps together. Following a luxurious sleep, we cleared the mess of our voyage and prepared for the one ahead. While Sam formed a friendship with a boy on a neighbouring boat, I set to (with a 'bucket and scrub it' technique) on an enormous pile of washing. The guys worked on the Aries, which we were using as a ladder to scale that imposing stone wharf built for fishing boats and high tides, with no consideration for mothers with toddlers. One time I climbed ashore and set up Billy's collapsible pushchair, but before I could sit him in it a gust of wind had spun the buggy along the dock into the harbour. Along with a plastic potty this was our only child gadget; but since it had sunk beyond reach we had to do without.

The port appeared uncannily similar to Puerto Banus. After the totality of sailing, the beach presented a separate reality, with fully grown palm trees arriving by boat, just like us. Catherine and I walked there with Sam and Billy, carrying buckets and spades, only to find the shore crammed with bare breasted girls. A pungent aroma of coconut oil hung on the breeze and occasionally a languid duo would administer lashings of tanning oil to gleaming bodies, rearrange a hint of clothing before sauntering beside the frothing waves, playfully scooping glistening beads of water over their buttocks and breasts. These performances were directed at groups of males who scanned the fleshy panorama like meerkats on a

TV commercial. While the girls' futile attempt at cooling their bodies barely disguised an intention of raising the meerkats' temperature, we were equally incongruous. Our British skin had barely seen the light of day, and our voluminous bikinis looked stuffy amongst that hotbed of thongs and flosses. Catherine and I set to on some serious tanning while Sam and Billy played their innocence games. They were oblivious to the pulsating hormones, glad of the freedom and the treat of an ice cream as we wandered home. The following day we sent Gerry along, who on his return commented that it wasn't just the racks of ripe flesh on display, but the hedonistic preening and posturing that was so intimidating.

At last, when Hornpipe was ready to go, we hired a vehicle and set off to explore the island. David had replaced his jeans with shorts, Gerry was making a fashion statement with a white boiler suit, and my red jumpsuit contrasted with Catherine's sensible skirt. The beach buggy had seemed a fun way to travel, until the road deteriorated into a gravel track which became increasingly precipitous as we wound uphill. Stopping to wonder at the sparse foliage that clung to the friable red scoria, we found small mosses patterning the algae studded rocks, cacti prickling with menacing spines and luminous flowers. After craning our necks to where the convoluted pinnacles of a natural Sagrada Familia seared the dazzling sky, we took a last look out over the silky patina of burnished waves, before turning inland to buzz over the snaking mountain road. At a solitary tavern high on the central plateau we ordered icy fizzy drinks, the sparkling air and sharp lemon exciting our palates. Craving action we headed down the east coast to the fabled sand dunes that had blown over from the Sahara. Staggering into a miniature desert we clambered up and slid down slopes with the abandon of those who had been imprisoned. At last, with every orifice impregnated with sand, when our ocean passage had been exorcised, we completed the day in an off season 'all you can eat' restaurant, which proved the perfect solution to our budget and hunger. After filling our plates to overflowing and going back for more, we left, driving the beach buggy through the night with the sleeping children curled in our laps.

Before leaving, David and I hitched a ride for a quiet walk in the countryside. Our perception of each plant and rock was heightened in knowing that those moments must sustain us through weeks of empty ocean; that reaching out to the earth was a refreshing drink before entering a desert, a last longing glance when departing from a beloved. When the day came, Gerry uncoiled the rope and jumped down onto Hornpipe's deck, severing that last tenuous connection with land. Then we motored until we could sail close hauled. However, after three hours we had made little progress and the adverse winds and falling barometer confirmed it wasn't worth persevering. Turning, we sailed back to arrive at dusk. Picking up the mooring had been an exacting task the first time around, and as David reversed our stern toward the dock, we awaited the final act: Gerry's star performance. As Hornpipe's transom neared the harbour wall David shouted, *"Jump."* Gerry gathered himself for a leap of faith, hesitated and…tiredness and the dwindling light played their part as, to Sam and Billy's enormous satisfaction, Gerry hit the water with a resounding splash. The spectacular plunge shattered our silent disappointment and Gerry, willing as ever to enjoy a joke, surfaced, spluttering and laughing, to scramble up the harbour wall and tie our stern rope to a bollard. And it was then we saw his white boiler suit had been washed clean of the orange sand of the Sahara, in readiness for the translucent waters of the Caribbean.

ALL AT SEA

"The dew is on the lotus! Rise Great Sun!
And lift my leaf and mix me with the wave.
'Om mani padme hum' the sunrise comes
The dewdrop slips into the shining sea."
Edwin Arnold

True to absurd fate it was April Fool's Day when we again motored out of the harbour, waving to Sam's friend Florian farewelling us from the breakwater. There were many backward glances as we mechanically hoisted Hornpipe's sails, trying to convince ourselves this would be our last sight of land for three to four weeks. In seafaring tradition, a ship's log records the action of *sailing towards*, rather than proclaiming the certainty of arriving at a predesignated spot. Those simple words reveal the characteristic humility of those who voyage the seas, establish that nature has the upper hand. And with three thousand miles between us and Antigua, where and when would we next see land? A storm could hit at any time, but fatigue presented the greatest threat to our safety. Though tiredness is nothing new to parents of young children, the broken nights and exertion of sailing is relentless when added to seasickness. It was vital we maintain our energy so I divided our bunk with lee cloths - and with a sail bag holding me womb tight I slept soundly, rocking in my canvas cradle on the ocean.

After motoring to charge our batteries we sailed close hauled while David tinkered with the Aries, believing it would free us from the drudgery of helming, concluding with the words, *"But it's supposed to work."* There was no alternative but to stand three-hour watches, staring at the compass, trying to keep the wandering arrow on track, and despite an afternoon breeze fluttering the sails, by dusk they were flogging. As the arid mountains faded into haze, an unspoken, *"Here we go again!"* passed through our minds, and when sloppy waves and a dancing horizon destroyed our appetite for Gerry's spaghetti bolognaise he commented, *"The only cure for seasickness is to stand under a tree."*

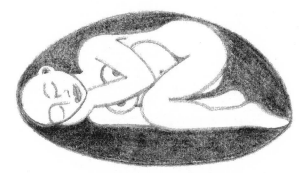

Asleep on the waves LT

I woke to the thunder of Obelix blasting through the ocean in search of the elusive trade winds. Hornpipe slowly came alive as each person clambered into the cockpit to comment on our progress. Sam had risen at five thirty followed by Billy with yet another dry nappy; however, having lain in bed looking at books he was miserably seasick, clinging to me as I struggled with the cooking. A lack of sleep and our yacht's loose roll afflicted everyone with a mindless lethargy. The navigational fix proved unrewarding when there was just so far to go. We all longed for a miraculous arrival in Antigua, and following lunch an uncharacteristic hush descended on the boat.

At sea nothing remained the same for long and when a fresh breeze sprung up it seemed we had at last found the trade winds that would carry us across the Atlantic on that faster, if less direct, route that sailing vessels have always used. Hornpipe was soon surging through the waves and we were grabbing for hand holds and bracing to avoid being thrown against the walls and deck. The simplest tasks became impossible; cupboards spilled their contents, food slopped from bowls, but the exhausting momentum was exhilarating and as a pod of porpoises emulated Hornpipe's rolling gait we squealed in response to their squeaks. A tanker passed close by and when David called on the radio he was so surprised at making a connection he forgot to request they inform Lloyds of London. Another came into view, but the transmission was lost in indecipherable crackles. It seemed we were truly on our own and as the clouds fluctuated from cirrus to mackerel David predicted a warm front with light winds, which was frustrating, given our chart indicated force eight trades.

That night David's efforts with the Aries proved worthwhile and we were released from helming, making only the occasional adjustment as Hornpipe hurried along under a starry sky, her bow wave whispering a sensuous tune. Our third day of sailing was all we had dreamed of. Taking advantage of the sunshine we rigged the deck hose and while the engine recharged the batteries took turns washing with refreshing sea water. But as we were pumping water into the cockpit to swill out the debris that had accumulated beneath the mat, David saw the engine's cooling water was boiling. Throwing Obelix's switch he was just in time to avoid wrecking the engine and investigations revealed that a plumbing fault allowed debris from the outlet to clog the inlet pipes. Confidence in Hornpipe's working mechanisms plummeted and when the noon fix revealed our previous one hundred and twenty-five mile run had amounted to just a hundred, everyone was deflated. And yet the day had been peaceful and serene and, after a Gerry curry and a banana toad in the hole I had absorbed enough contentment to write, *"Today was the first day that I enjoyed being on the sea."*

Following the distractions our night watches allowed us to dwell on deeper truths. Though no words could describe the ocean, it seemed we traversed the cosmos upon a substance without feature or form; that the indigo ink of existence echoed from those depths. As Hornpipe cut her path through the rolling swells of cobalt and azure the ocean erased all evidence of her passing. Our secrets were swallowed into eternal silence. Years later, on a trip to Japan, David and I found ourselves in an art exhibition looking at a collection of black and white photographs by Hiroshi Sugimoto. As we gazed at those almost imperceptible images we discovered the slightest definition of a horizon; and suddenly we were there again, upon the ethereal sea, under an infinite sky. Tears ran down our faces; memories returned to that spiritual space and we turned to each other with the same words on our lips.

On the morning of our fourth day Hornpipe was romping along, pitching and tossing, jarring our bruised bodies. Although glad to be making progress I longed for it to stop, even if just for a moment. Catherine and Gerry had not slept, however they valiantly cooked lunch and helped Sam with his reading. Amidst the devastating noise and chaos David was trying to make vital navigation decisions and this, his first experience of being constantly around our children, made him view my role in a new light. Though he could not anticipate the future, Sam was able to measure the changes, to find sailing a miserable substitute for the life we had left behind. Kicking against the discomforts he took out his frustration on Billy, creating problems only I could solve. Later we helped Sam make a cut-out spider, avoiding altercations as Billy joined the fun of printing potato cut Easter chickens. Then we threw all the cushions into an avalanche in the back-cabin, and as the children leaped and bombarded each other with pillows Hornpipe resounded with shrieks of happy laughter. It reminded me of Saturday mornings when my brother and I transformed our blankets and pillows into castles, of winter days at Redthorn Cottage when I had upended the settee to create a fantasy landscape where Sam and Tessa danced to the music of *Tangerine Dream*.

Sometimes it seemed we lived a timeless existence, destined to travel forever on that infinite glassy ocean. Egyptian mythology tells how the sun god Ra dies into the fiery sunset, to sail a barque through the serpentine body of night and be reborn in the sunrise. The sea's kinetic fluidity had us in its spell but what intrigued us most was the 'green flash' that was said to occur as the last sun rays disappear beyond the horizon. While we eagerly anticipated every sunset, we speculated on that momentary effect, whether we had been fooled into believing a fictitious story. The green flash had become the holy grail of our trip, but each evening the horizon dissolved in grey cloud. The other phenomenon was that, despite all Gerry's efforts, we had not caught any fish. Were the oceans depleted or were we bad fishermen? Meanwhile the twin cords of the fishing line and Walker log stretched ever hopefully from Hornpipe's stern and it would be sometime before we learned that the rotating paddles of the device that recorded the watery miles of our passage had been scaring the fish.

Dolphins appeared, kindred spirits darting through the waves, their bodies sparkling with phosphorescence, while above and around Hornpipe's mast, Leaches' Storm Petrels fluttered, causing us to wonder whether they were travelling with us or following a petrel migration path. Flying fish propelled themselves over the ocean, swooping like the swallows that flew around our Northumberland home. We watched them echo the ocean's rise and fall, their rainbow wings skimming over the swell, bouncing off the crest of a wave to disappear in a flash of blue. Sometimes at night Gerry and Catherine heard a whirl of tiny wings on the deck above their cabin, and in the morning discovered the stiff scaly bodies of those that had stranded, dull with death, a reminder of our intrusion on the ocean. We also found small squids, and surmised they must have shot out of the water in fright. Gerry used them as bait, hoping they would smell and look more authentic than our lures. Decades later he solved the mystery of how they propelled themselves through and out of the water, sending us diagrams and the comment, "*It's been keeping me awake for thirty years.*"

As Hornpipe sailed west on the latitude of the Cape Verde Islands, an advancing line of crosses over our chart was the only indication we were not inscribing a circle. Although the voyage had only just begun, most conversations anticipated our arrival. The fluctuating wind demanded constant sail manoeuvres with gibing and poling out the genoa a demanding procedure that involved all of us. While Catherine and I stood by to helm and manage the sheets, David and Gerry fastened their harnesses and climbed onto the pitching deck. After dropping the jib our boys jousted the pole, reset and hoisted the sail. But of course it was never that simple, especially when wind fluctuations and subsequent bouts of pole combat competed with every evening meal.

The children were programmed for survival. They needed an adult to guide their play and instinctively knew I was wired to protect them. Although the domestic chores were synchronised with our three-hour watches, navigation and fixing things stole David's time. We were stretched to our limit as, despite the exhaustion of period pains, I again took his place on the cooking rota. That day he was trying to mend the wind instruments that were giving misleading information – the batteries that mysteriously lost charge, forcing us to run the engine. Before rousing Obelix he had to loosen the stern gland which ran through a stuffing box of greasy hemp rings that prevented water leaking along the shaft. On switching off he wrapped a strap around the propeller shaft to stop its spinning, but sometimes it broke loose, resounding a mesmeric ommmm through the boat. While Sam recalls the polyphonic vibration soothing his sleep, David registered yet another summons to the torture chamber of the engine room, with a potential lost finger or worse adding stress. None of us understood enough to help, so he carried the burden alone, hesitating to ask Catherine and Gerry to do more. After all, this was not their boat or children.

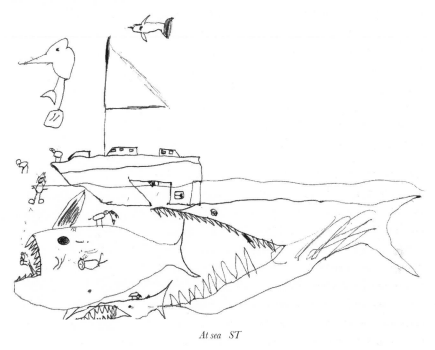

At sea ST

The morning of our sixth day saw Hornpipe headed downwind with her sails full, the sheets creaking as they flexed around the winches. Then the wind dropped and once again we were going nowhere with all hope of a consistent day's cruising crushed in the slam and bam of flogging sails. After three hours motoring we realised we were missing an obvious way to enjoy a calm sunny day. Hornpipe's engine had subsided into stillness yet we drifted on over the incandescent sea. The momentum of her roll brought a cacophony of sound, a heaving slosh as she wallowed in the swell, a clang of halyards, the galley pots and pans dancing to a new beat. Throwing out a rope we were considering our next move when David spontaneously leapt overboard, to surface an alarming distance astern. Swimming after the boat was obviously challenging, but as soon as our Captain had seized the rope Gerry jumped off the rail before climbing out and up the mast to dive from the spreaders. Catherine and I watched from the deck and then, taking turns we descended the Aries and clinging to the safety rope's umbilical cord, slipped into the radiant blue. Separating from our mother ship felt as unnerving as stepping into outer space. It was like standing on a cliff surrounded by sky, when that desire to leap into the void beckons one to fly. My mind recoiled from the knowledge that I swam in three thousand fathoms of ocean and dreadful premonitions washed through my being, of falling through that liquid depth, down, down into an abyss of crushing darkness.

The silky water was so refreshing and I knew Sam wanted to swim, wished he could experience that release from the confined boat. But it would have been difficult getting him back on board, and when Catherine noticed the purple pink sail of a Portuguese man o' war jellyfish we scrambled up the Aries. The ensign was fluttering so we hoisted the drifter to release an expanse of blue spinnaker fabric that was perfect for the gentle breeze. The afternoon was suffused with a peaceful contentment that set me to baking chocolate biscuits, and following teatime we began throwing cooling buckets of water over each other which became a game with Sam darting behind the compass, his slippery elf body outwitting us all. No one cared if we were going anywhere and as Gerry tried fishing, Catherine sewed flags we could use to communicate to passing ships. After bathing Billy in a bucket, I lathered my hair with sea-soap to rinse away the accumulated salt with the abundant ocean, conserving fresh water, just as my mother had wrapped ice cubes in a towel to refresh herself during Bermuda's summers.

It seemed we had negotiated a truce with the elements and after a tactical sailing adjustment of downwind tacks our problem with the Aries dissolved, with the comfortable motion more than compensating for the marginal difference in distance travelled. Sam would say he thought David and Gerry played with the self-steering in the same way he and Billy occupied themselves with Lego. That morning he had made a contraption, "*A machine for killing people when they get too old and won't die.*" He showed us the place where they go in to be shot by arrows, how the mechanism was transported on wheels. What could I say or do – where was the sweet, innocent child I had nurtured? Sam and Billy with their perfectly formed bodies and hair bleached golden from the sun appeared so angelic and it was disturbing when their games exposed cruel attempts at comprehending the world. When a Greek freighter altered its course to call on the radio, "*Hullo sailing boat on my port bow this is Greek ship Elaine, do you receive me, over."* A crucial aerial cable was too short and Catherine's attempts at finishing her signal flags were too late. The lost opportunity was disappointing when we knew our anxious parents would be reassured by a message, that a record of our location could prove vital if things went terribly wrong.

As Hornpipe's momentum became less violent the children and I ventured beyond our confined circle of cockpit and cabins. Clipping their harnesses to the safety line I clambered onto the deck, sheltering Billy and Sam as they crawled past the salt encrusted windows of the saloon, making faces at those within. I hustled them forward to huddle behind the upturned dinghy and lie in the mainsail's swinging pool of shade, gazing up the mast, feeling the pendulum motion. Gaining confidence, I guided them to Hornpipe's bucking bow, where we clung to the railing watching her slice a path through the ocean, laughing as the waves struck the hull, shooting columns of spray skyward, showering us with jewels of light. On further occasions I carried a picnic, or a book to read a story, sitting on the wooden seat at Hornpipe's stern, our perch swooping and dipping with the waves that roared beneath us, sweeping away forever. Those extreme escapes were our equivalent of playing in the garden when, despite wearing harnesses, I felt my children were as exposed as if I had taken them for a walk along a motorway.

During the evening David practiced sighting the stars that momentarily appeared in the brief twilight while the horizon was still visible. Later, when the bright moon presented further opportunities he took more, saving his calculations for morning. Having adjusted the ship's clock our day correlated with the children's natural orientation to the light. The heat and humidity rendered us lethargic and nauseous so it was a relief when the mainsail's shadow swung over the cockpit, as Hornpipe's increased speed created a refreshing breeze. If we had located the kids' volume switch it would have been heaven. They had energy to burn so David took them up top for a splashy water fight, with him hauling buckets of seawater which they scooped in plastic cups to throw at each other. While Billy was too small to enjoy rough and tumble, Sam loved the game and afterwards I sat with my arm around him, sounding out the words of his stories, taking turns at reading together. The gentle learning process was working and he had started taking books to bed where he laboriously read by himself.

Over lunchtimes we discussed our noon fix, following dinner with a review of the day's progress. That evening's meal began with a fresh hors d'oeuvre of tuna from the flesh of our first fish. The children had watched the killing and gutting, asking questions about life and death, expressing immense satisfaction with each gory detail, *"Ooooh look there's lots of blood."* The tasty starter was followed by Catherine's cheese loaf which Gerry described as *"livelier than the tuna."* When a pitching wave threw it out of the oven for the second time we gave up and ate it, for we could not afford to waste food or the time spent in preparation. As we sat in the evening's gathering dusk Sam asked about *"The cold place."* When I explained, *"We're not going back, this is our home now,"* a horrified expression washed over his face and he said *"Aren't we going to see land again, just sail along for ever and ever?"* Sam's response served a reminder that our children had never chosen to be there. It was an indication they had no comprehension of anything beyond the daily discomforts, that they had no idea when or if the persistent tossing and turning would end. Their days playing with the same toys in that tiny space on or below the saloon table must have seemed interminable. By contrast, my childhood was spent running wild in a garden with fields beyond, a brook to fall into, trees to climb. I had danced with cows and watched foxes burrow in the copper earth, enjoyed a freedom denied to Sam and Billy.

Our confidence was boosted by calculations that, during our first week at sea, Hornpipe had averaged a hundred and twenty miles a day. With the Aries' co-operation we were keeping up with the chores while periodically checking the helm; living those days in the present, leaving no mark upon the ocean. A flotilla of fluffy trade wind clouds traversed the sky, the occasional black cloud threatened a squall. The barometer remained steady with each day passing just like the last. The ocean's pulsing heartbeat echoed through our sleeping and waking and we had become one with the waves that caressed Hornpipe's hull, massaging her with fluid flowing fingers. We were returning to the source, following the sun and stars, moving to familiar steps, with a rhythm and tune we would never forget. It was a dance that was lyrically balanced, in harmony with the elements, a sailor's dance, a Hornpipe.

By the end of David's watch the wind had risen and, before kissing me awake, he deliberated whether to reef the main. The previous day he had tethered the boom to the gunwale with a kicking strap halfway along its length. Although it had proved an efficient means of flattening the mainsail it required a huge effort to dismantle and adjust our rig, so he decided to leave it until later. As if to prove a point the wind dropped to a steady four or five knots before he fell asleep. During my watch I had prepared hot cross buns for a Good Friday breakfast, leaving them rising for Catherine to bake. And as I woke to that rich aroma wafting from the galley ambiguously mingling with the salty breeze I anticipated them spicing up an uneventful morning, celebrating a barbaric Christian ritual on the ocean a thousand miles from land. It was luxury enough for David and I to awaken together, sheer bliss to know that life was going on without us. Freed of responsibilities we lingered in bed soothed by the rolling waves, serenaded by a gentle breeze. The familiar sounds of Sam and Billy scrabbling in their Lego box, Catherine getting their breakfast, sounded far away and it was so good to drift in and out of sleep together.

Our minds were tuned to that all-pervading music of moving things; a change of tempo could alert a nagging unease, a whispering wind in the rigging could reassure or ring a warning bell. Within the bowels of the engine room the propeller shaft broke free of its strap, gathered momentum, roaring to a crescendo, to be joined by the sound of throbbing canvas and straining rigging, reverberating with a persistence that should not have been ignored. Although we sensed an increased momentum, this was our turn to catch up on lost hours. We were fooling ourselves. The wind was building, shifting, compromising our yacht's rig, and with each rolling wave she drew closer to a tipping point. But, just a few more breaths of stillness and peace; one blissful moment more.

And then it happened! Hornpipe summited a wave and skewed into its trough, carving a curving course. As fresh wind hit the back of her mainsail a wrenching crack blasted above our heads. Catherine yelled as David leaped from the bunk, girding his loins to disguise a waning erection. Fearing the worst I kicked the wardrobe in a turmoil of despair. Daring to look I saw the boom, folded and broken, draped over the steering column amidst a tangle of ropes. Meanwhile, the backed foresail was holding Hornpipe hove to, and she was straining in the swell, with her sheets trailing in the sea. Great green globs of water bashed the hull raining spray upon the deck. The children watched from the saloon door and Sam said, "*That's not how to sail a boat.*" And shamed by his observation I doubted we could ever amend the catastrophe.

Gerry came blinking into the light and we set to clearing the mess. With the boom broken it appeared our mainsail was useless, and we were only a third of the way into a three-thousand-mile crossing. Going back was impossible but how could we go on? We ate breakfast, the hot cross buns congealing in our mouths as we avoided incriminating comments that might add to Catherine's sense of responsibility. She should have told us the wind had freshened, that helming was difficult with Hornpipe riding closer to the wind than her rig could manage. However, David knew he should have taken the precaution of releasing the kicking strap and reefing the mainsail; should have acted on his instincts instead of lying in bed. And I had distracted Catherine with my domestic indulgence, preparing for Easter as though we had no other care in the world. I remembered Sam's comment about sailing on forever. That there are no second chances at sea. And when all seemed lost I wrote, *"There must be exceptional people, who enjoy battling the elements, but I need land; we all do. And although I write as a concerned mother and wife I feel like a frightened child."*

.

REDEMPTION

"Won't you help to sing, These songs of freedom?
'Cause all I ever have, Redemption songs."
Bob Marley

Ocean passage   LT

The disaster had taught me that I could not relax my vigilance. While my first thought had been that sailing on to Antigua would be impossible, as we talked through the options it seemed our situation wasn't so bad. While we could sail under a bare mast using our polled-out genoa to pull us the two thousand miles to Antigua, David proposed we try to repair the boom that had snapped at the point where he had set the kicking strap. As regrets dissolved into a plan the atmosphere became charged with positive energy. Years of renovations had taught David to innovate with limited resources and he and Gerry wasted no time adapting the mahogany timbers that supported the dinghy into a plug that could be slid inside the fractured boom. After gluing four lengths with plywood sandwiched between each piece they bound the rough plug with rope and set it aside to bond overnight.

Lacking the shady mainsail the cockpit was a heat trap and by afternoon we were scorched. Hornpipe's languorous downwind roll had been replaced with a ruthless, thrusting lurch that jarred our bodies. Powered by the genoa, her course cut across the waves on a heading due west, directly towards and on the same latitude as Antigua. While grateful to have averted the catastrophe we found ourselves thinking, "*Why on earth have we subjected ourselves to this?*" The children appeared oblivious to the discomfort, until the Lego skidded over the linoleum followed by their protesting screams. Sam had used his colourful mechanics set to construct a sextant which he operated from the safety of the cockpit, giving the order, "*I'm going to do some sextanting, you take the time.*" Followed by intermittent shouts of, "*Now!*" concluding with his abrupt announcements of degrees and minutes. And before bed he diligently returned "*To take a sight of the moon.*"

That night David slept in the lower bunk where he had more leg length and could see the wind instruments. On waking he found that, despite the absence of her mainsail, Hornpipe had managed a day's run of a hundred and forty-three miles since the disaster. Fortunately the boom's metal structure had not torn or twisted, and while Gerry extracted the pop rivets David crawled to the far side of the engine room to retrieve the Skilsaw. Then cranking up the generator he cut the plug into a hexagonal cross section which he spoke-shaved into a rounded beam. It was incongruously reassuring to hear the screech of machine tools; to see wood shavings floating away, over the ocean. As the men worked I prepared supper, suppressing pangs of seasickness with forays into the cockpit to gaze at the horizon and breathe deeply.

While we were relishing a triumph over adversity the children were imitating our behaviour. Billy was trying out new words and that evening it was "*bug-ger,*" to Sam's self-righteous, "*You shouldn't say that word.*" Striving to preserve normality I had baked a traditional Simnel cake, a reminder of Easter on Tormentil a year and a world away, and after helping the children make chocolate nests we sat fluffy chickens inside. During my watch, I hid eggs around the boat and the day dawned to Sam's shout,

"The Easter Chicken has been!" And while eggs and books were discovered and consumed David and Gerry continued, sliding the plug into the tube of the boom before winching it into position, bolting the kicking strap through the wooden core and replacing the mainsail track. Then they rigged the sail and cautiously hoisted it high. There was no bend or movement. Our men had achieved their complex repair thousands of miles from land, and were convinced that a professional workshop couldn't have done better. Meanwhile the wind had strengthened, Hornpipe was broaching, and having found that sailing was more enjoyable at a steadier pace we dropped the mainsail, happy to take longer on our passage if necessary.

That night David wrote, *"Still wondering with amazement what we are doing out here in the middle of the Atlantic."* Since leaving England there had been no time to ponder on changes and events, but on reaching halfway it all made sense. After leaving Gibraltar on that omnipotent Friday the thirteenth, fate had chosen April Fool's Day for our departure from the Canary Islands. Hornpipe's boom had broken on Good Friday and her mainsail rose again on Easter Sunday, which had fallen upon a full moon. Were these auspicious dates coincidental or is every day invested with a meaning that is only revealed when we join the dots? While we tried to disregard malevolent signs, it is easy to understand why seafarers and those whose destiny is dependent upon nature's whim become superstitious.

Repairing the boom had left no reserves for David's other responsibilities and when the Aries failed he had no choice but to steer his watch. Woken by his curses there was nothing for it but to take the helm and allow him to sleep. Sometime later I wrote in my journal, *"When listening to music, I understand the waves, move with them and express myself and it makes me realise how many entrancing moments remain undiscovered in this babble of living. I know that my concern for Sam and Billy are the reason I have been slow at getting to know the sea. The best time was my early watch as the children woke to the excitement of Easter morning. Sam came for a glowing cuddle and when Billy popped out we shared the magic of the hidden eggs, followed by thrills, wondrous surprises, and greed. My seasickness has developed into debilitating indigestion. Even after eleven days at sea I still feel grotty. David's vulnerability and tiredness cause me concern. We all depend on him, so it is frightening when he is out of control and I wonder whether it is wise to do this again, know that I deserve criticism for not participating in navigating and mechanics. These times of disorder and despondency threaten to engulf us, yet we have not been tested by the weather. How would we cope in really difficult conditions or without such an understanding crew?"* Writing had provided comfort and after visualising a walk over the fells I had a good cry and readied myself for another day.

Easter Monday was a quiet day of recovery from our exertions, with amongst the entries in the log the startling revelation, *"Gerry wiped Billy's bum,"* an indication our heroic crew had become close as family. After pouring buckets of cool ocean over our salty bodies we cautiously hoisted the triple reefed mainsail, and as the wind veered we tried gybing and goose winging the genoa, balancing the rig in hopes of avoiding the numerous sail changes that interrupted our nights. The following day David turned over the folded chart to plot our position on the other side. And when he marked that humble X in the middle of the Atlantic Ocean we saw we had come as far from land as we would ever be. Most exciting was the outline of Antigua at the far side of the chart and following that noon fix Gerry began stepping out the dividers to calculate the days ahead. Torn between the emotional ups and downs I both longed for our destination and believed I should live in the moment. The mental and physical effects of seasickness had undermined my self-esteem and while looking after the children and supporting David was my top priority I never gave myself credit for being the only one who could comfort Billy, or with the patience to encourage Sam with his schoolwork. His reading was taking him into a world where Billy could not yet go, and this gave him a confidence that overflowed into other activities. The most important factor in teaching was to avoid negative responses, and Sam's enthusiastic, *"I love maths"* dispelled my doubts. Despite the limitations of his chaotic classroom my son was happy and achieving; the least I could do was to remain patient and consistent.

A flock of storm petrels and two tropic birds with long white tails fluttered around Hornpipe as if mocking her pedestrian pace over the miles they flew so swiftly. On finding a few flying fish and tiny squid that had stranded during the night David expertly fried them for supper. Then we adults found ourselves sitting around the table in the dwindling dusk sharing our first relaxed evening. But serving the whims of the wind and sea was constant and that night was no exception. Once we were in bed the wind shifted and everyone had to be roused to gibe the genoa back alongside the mainsail, and when it increased we were woken again.

Dropping the mainsail and reefing it in the dark was an arduous task, involving scrambling up the mast to free the sliding cleats that jammed in the track, so when the wind dropped half an hour later David decided to wait and shake out the reefs at dawn. As Hornpipe laboriously sloshed and slewed through the heavy sea she frequently lost momentum, her sails bellying and voiding with a resounding crack. Rolling over a wave she momentarily swung off course and it was then the wind caught the back of the mainsail, sending the boom crashing. Despite the repair sustaining the blow, David continued fretting over the flogging sails. When the slamming and banging became too torturous we dropped the main and poled out the genoa, with the drifter balanced on the opposite side held with a stout cactus stem our Danish friends had given us.

The cockpit was ablaze with reflected light and with nowhere else to go we sat through a sweltering afternoon fantasising about ice cream. By contrast the night was chilly and we donned wet weather gear to steer through the rain, our teeth chattering as gusts and sixty-degree wind switches rendered the Aries untenable. The dismal dawn revealed a grey cloudscape with a murky sea. *"The children woke late with Billy saying all that could be said about the view, 'sky, sea' followed by a kiss, the first of hundreds that day. Sam emerged, complaining that it should have been his turn to sleep beside me, while despite the kids eruptions our crew slept on with David lying like a fallen giant in the humid aft cabin. Then it was my turn to hover in the heat, slightly above sleep. We had added another hour to our day and with everyone tired after the night's sail changes we soon retreated to our patches of shadow. Sam and I set to school work and when the novelty wore off I invented some creative projects with David helping make a pop up witch and ghost, jokey things that Sam loves. During the afternoon, the children painted the papier mache sea we had made, with Sam giving orders of no consequence, as to where Billy was to paint. Their ocean became mostly blue as Sam obliterated Billy's green. A lot of paint was daubed onto their little brown bodies and this inspired Catherine to decorate Sam - fun until it came to washing it off to his indignant howls."*

Impatient with the light wind David listlessly dragged himself through the morning and slept most of the afternoon. Then he set up an engineer's vice on the stern seat and, selecting a small piece of wood from his store in the engine room, he started cutting the rough shape of a pair of earrings. In carving the delicate interlocking pieces he gained control over his predicament. David's creative diversion had restored his spirit, however my attempts at helming while eating dinner had proved frustrating, with the fickle wind intruding on every mouthful. During my solitary watch I recalled other long nights, sitting in my rocking chair, nursing Sam beside our bedroom fire and while I was nourished by reflecting on the past, David gathered his strength from observing the ocean, "*I watched the white flecked water rustling past lacking substance, ethereal, floating mesmerically, twisting and weaving on and on endlessly timelessly for ever and ever.*"

Although Billy had adapted to boat life, Sam's needs were more complex. Leaving Northumberland had deprived him of friends and as Billy began talking, playing with Lego, drawing pictures, and participating, he eclipsed his older brother. Sam responded by being increasingly precocious, claiming attention in any way possible. David, in his role of provider, had never realised how the children totally consumed my time and he wrote, "*It's unfortunate that we have hit this trip on this particular moment in their development. It makes the days hectic and unrelenting. Poor Linda bears the brunt of it.*" Although David still maintained that children should fit into a pattern of adult life, he had become more aware. However the kids would grow to adults before we balanced our expectations. Since Billy's birth usurped Sam's position I had become torn between my boys and that night their rivalry sparked a bedtime dispute. Previously they had fallen asleep in their own bunks but when David began moving Billy beside me to vacate the convenient lower bunk, Sam protested that it was his turn to sleep in the big bed. We agreed on condition that he be fast asleep, and on managing a convincing impersonation, we moved him; but that night Billy had a traumatic nightmare that left him fragile throughout the following day, making me wonder where it had taken him.

Since starting his carving project David had become more content, and when we passed close to a tanker plying the New York to Cape Town shipping route he said he felt almost indignant anyone else should be out there on our ocean. Hornpipe was holding a steady downwind course, her bow wave rushing along the hull, rolling over to drift away in our wake. Combating lethargy, we scooped buckets of water to splash over our hot bodies, with Sam standing still, quietly enjoying the sensation while Billy, who was even wary of the baby bath, needed encouraging. The following day was a scorcher with an unpredictably light wind. We dropped our sails for a swim but were still making some headway ten minutes later when, combating shark anxieties, we drifted with one hand on the rope; a stray foot brushing against the Walker Log line causing heart flutters. Then we hoisted the sails to continue on our way with David completing his navigational calculations, Sam his schoolwork. The sky was clear but for a few clouds and as the sun dipped towards the horizon the immense space intensified. David and Gerry scrambled onto the cabin roof to catch the last rays, hopeful of seeing the green flash. We all froze in anticipation of a miraculous enlightenment and as the bloated sun sunk into the sea, a last blip of orange blooded to red. And there it was! A flash of green, briefly winking, an electric glow. It was gone in a moment but it was real. We had experienced the green flash!

On my watch I wrote, *"I don't feel passionate about when we arrive. I am at ease, enjoying this soothing pace."* Then, following another morning beneath the relentless sun, we gathered around the chart table for the daily revelation, the latest in that line of crosses boldly marching from the Canary Islands towards the Caribbean. And when Catherine and I said, *"We'll get there when we do, there's nothing we can do about it!"* our acceptance drove the men mad. Day and night, male and female, sun and moon, we were all programmed for survival. David and Gerry registered the wind and speed fluctuations deep in their psyche. They were obsessed with setting the sails and adjusting the Aries to increase Hornpipe's efficiency. By contrast, whether it was sailing, cooking, child care, or just keeping the peace, Catherine quietly served the situation. Meanwhile Sam's objective was to outwit Billy, who in turn clung to me, orbited me, trusted in me alone. Everyone depended on Hornpipe while, oblivious to us all, she danced with the wind and waves.

The days had settled into a rhythm with Catherine mending a tear in our number two genoa, pushing the stubborn needle through the heavy sailcloth while I beat the cream for profiteroles, making a special pudding to follow a corned beef moussaka, listening with pride as Sam slowly read his latest book. His reading and writing countered Billy's evolving vocabulary, rewarded him the stimulation that would resolve his behaviour and release an infinite realm of possibilities. And Sam loved repeating the staccato syllables, correlating letters with sounds, recognising and creating the words and sentences, *"Look Kathy. See me run. I can run. See Mark run."*

Meanwhile our night watches had become cathartic confessionals and rapturous ramblings, *"The sounds of creaking ropes and a feathery fluttering of sails is accompanied by a metallic clang from the rigging. A roar from the resonant depths. The omm of wind and sea overwhelming everything. By night there is an absence of those other activities we inflict upon our miniature world of hopes and dreams. This afternoon two tropic birds flew overhead, their wheeling and diving linking sky and sea, inviting us to observe our scene from another perspective; to look down from on high or to see ourselves from a fish's point of view. I have always imagined myself into other places or times, woven together the vibration of those that share our space on earth. Out here we can forget we come from an overflowing world. And I am reminded we are at the mercy of the ocean, that it will transform time into the present and leave no evidence of our passing. And as I write the sky curdles, clouds stretch milky claws towards the moon and I realise I could have sailed into several ships while expounding my philosophy."*

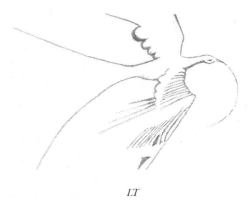

LT

On those magical nights with Hornpipe rolling downwind it was as though we could sail for ever, knowing no wants or needs. The children had taken their incessant chattering to dreamland and sounds that were jagged by day became softly sensual in that velvety darkness. David no longer read but sat listening to the waves, gazing at the stars, content with the here and now. Finding a cool place upon the deck he started writing, *"I lie here watching the brittle blue sea slipping past, lulled by the bow wave. I think of the noise and purposeful bustle of land that clashes with the timeless serenity of nature. And it came to me again, my expressed reason for sailing: the intimate closeness with nature it allows you. Free from the false and illusory dominance over nature that modern life on land creates."* A pervading sense of oneness with our surroundings overflowed from those nights into my day. *"I watch the sun rise into a turquoise sky blotted with smoking clouds. The vast sky mirrors the circling sea, the dream world of my imagination. 'La Lady Luna' slides into a billowing cloud monster that swallows her slender crescent in a gulp. The sun thrusts through the clouds and a tropic bird, our spirit guide, flutters around, sharing the loveliness. I have no desire to be anywhere but here; below the silent sky, above the singing sea, with Hornpipe holding us safe as babes in the cradle of her belly. Soon Billy and Sam will wriggle into another day of chaos, but for now their perfect limbs lie abandoned in sleep. Sam whispers remembered dreams, stretches, and is suddenly awake, playing with a toy. I plan the day's diversions, hunt the thimble, hide and seek or maybe a picnic upon the deck."* And those were my plans for what could have been my last happy day.

Though we had all become experts in creating space and privacy, our projects had elevated us beyond the daily routines. While David finished carving his first earring, I practiced yoga before sewing a quilt. Catherine pulled out the tatting she had brought for quiet times, and after press-ups Gerry studied the navigation charts. Later the children scooped water from the baby bath, pouring it over David as he sat in a puddle enjoying the cooling trickle and teasing tickle of tiny fingers. It was the perfect game until Gerry joined in. During the evening Billy was hammering the nails of a miniature woodworking kit when he stopped and indicated he had lost something. Opening his mouth, pointing within, he said two words, *"Pin! Gone!"* followed by a confused silence. This could mean only one thing! The blood drained from my face as I realised Billy had put the nail into his mouth and swallowed it. Catherine decided we must get him to sick it up, so we tried everything, a glass of liver salts, fingers in the throat, all to Billy's protesting screams, *"Noo, nooo, nooooo!"* Nothing worked; the nail had gone! When Billy recovered, we asked again, but words were limited and he could only respond with an indecisive *"Mmnnn,"* his mouth quivering, big eyes pleading. Had he actually swallowed anything? We were so afraid for Billy and tried to think of something we could do, but all attempts to make him regurgitate the nail proved futile. We had no contact with the outside world; hospitals and doctors were four sailing days away. And as Billy sobbed and implored, *"Toys! Bed!"* we ceased the cruel torture.

David and I hugged Billy's little body and tried to imagine his terror as those he had depended on turned against him. We had broken a trust, betrayed our gentle affectionate child, and there was nothing for it but to give him Smarties and ruefully put him to bed. I faced the long anxious night, terrified of what it would bring. Sometime during that night of watching my baby sleeping, helplessly serene, I expressed my anxiety, *"I don't know how to write of little Billy and the nail that he may or may not have swallowed. I dare not think of the possibilities as over and over again I acknowledge the depth of my love for him in a prayer. Our children are more precious than life. That deepest love is held by the flimsiest thread, and as this terrible freedom threatens to steal my child I wait, an empty husk, humbly waiting.*" It was only when day dawned to the familiar chaos that I felt strong enough to question Catherine. She told me that if a sharp object had lodged in Billy's gut, this would manifest as a slowly increasing lethargy that could linger for days before the situation became critical. Catherine's revelation was reassuring. Even that worst outcome wasn't as sinister as what I had imagined in my darkest hours. And Billy was not subdued; he had popped up, bright as ever, seemingly no worse for his ordeal. Although we examined the contents of his potty the nail was never found, but the incident had thrown me off balance and that dark night of dread would remain, a reminder of my child's mortality.

Despite clocking a hundred miles on the previous day David became tormented by the sails' listless flapping and fretting. Having forgotten the joy of Hornpipe surging through the waves with the wind filling her sails he vented his frustration and boredom on trying to make contact with the outside world. Billy's scare had alerted us to that vital need to communicate and on finding ourselves in a shipping lane David switched on the radio. Following his futile attempt Gerry started rotating the dial; we were becoming irritated with the buzzing static when a voice from the outside world echoed through the boat. Captivated by the West Indian announcer we gathered around, and as the twanging notes of a bass guitar throbbed out a tune we absorbed every note and nuance. It was not reggae, but a ballad, sung with raw words. Our collective silence was followed with a, "*What was that?*" Bob Marley's unforgettable *Redemption Song* had initiated us into the Caribbean culture. We were so close, and it felt like we were coming home.

I remembered when, a decade before, I had arrived in Jamaica to take up my first teaching position. How my doubts were quenched in that first rum punch under whispering palm trees, with a Calypso band singing an inevitable, "*Oh island in de sun.*" That on my first day at the Catholic boarding school a seemingly sweet girl named Hyacinth had slapped me; how my surprise dissolved on realising she had merely swotted a mosquito. Within my cloistered artroom I enacted a profane creativity, encouraging my students' self-expression, oblivious to the nuns who used guilt as a teaching tool, the wrath of God for failing a test, eternal damnation for cheating. Jamaica was in its prime, Bob Marley was king, and when I walked into Brown's Town I moved to a syncopated beat blasted from the rum bars that framed the dusty street. Even the abusive shout, "*Pig ooman, gyah byak hyam!*" could not quench my joy.

Shortly after term commenced the Mother Superior tearfully announced that a higher power had decreed that within the year the school would close. With my contract broken I set to exploring Jamaica's coral beaches and crystal waves. I saw Rastafarians emanate from the orange earth and discovered children with round bellies and hungry eyes existing a stone's throw from my house. Flying to Mexico City for Christmas celebrations, I saw the New Year at a mariachi bar, and watched a folkloric performance at the Grand Opera House, never imagining some thirty-three years later my husband would lecture there and receive a standing ovation from a crowd of thousands. I rode a night bus to a mountain lake where fishermen drifted in canoes, their butterfly nets floating on the still water. A shepherd followed me along a lonely track to a village that had been submerged by a volcanic eruption, and when Manuel begged me to marry him I was confused because back then I knew nothing of poverty or border restrictions.

When my money ran out, cheap rooms with dodgy plumbing revealed Mexico's underbelly, and by the time the school year finished I was sleeping with a machete under my bed, but whether I could have used it was another matter. Grasping a last opportunity to travel I set off for Bogota and the Peruvian city of Cusco, high in the Andes. There I photographed fluffy alpacas laden with sacks of *coca*, and drank milk infused with the leaves to ease altitude sickness. I bought colourful *ponchos* to brighten my winters and learned that before the Conquistadors pillaged their gold the Incas had playfully adorned the trees and crops with golden apples and stalks of wheat. Taking a train that followed the snaking Urubamba River I wandered amongst the abandoned stones of Machu Picchu, and reaching out to touch the mountains vowed to return and walk those pathways in the sky. Flying on to Iquitos in the upper Amazon I exchanged a bag of salt with the Yagua people, beads for a bag of salt which was all they required to maintain their independence. Satiated with adventures I embarked from Jamaica on my second Atlantic passage and woke on that last day at sea to a view of England's familiar shores.

One afternoon Gerry, David, and I drifted into a discussion about religious beliefs that went further than most. Catherine had quietly slipped away and it was, typically, just the three of us. In fact, it was her turn in the galley, where she cooked a spectacular corned beef, egg, and potato flan followed by homemade brandy snaps. We could have created a recipe book entitled *Seventy-Seven Ways with Corned Beef* to match the number of tins we had stowed for our trip. But who would have wished to emulate such a gastronomic fiasco. Following Catherine's feast we brewed a rare pot of ground coffee that was somewhat annulled by adding an hour to our day; then after another spectacular sunset we argued whether we had seen the green flash. Despite Billy seeming fine I felt a haunting apprehension as I tucked him into bed, but as David read an earthy tale of a giant turnip, by the light of the Tilly lamp, it rounded off that homely day at sea with a feeling of security.

Wednesday the twenty first of April marked our third week since leaving Gran Canaria, a departure that seemed long ago, as though it had belonged to other people. While the benign weather had favoured the children and I, the lack of wind had tormented David, and I wondered how he would fare sailing through the Pacific. He could not understand why Buchanan had warned us to expect a consistent force eight during our crossing, as after another morning of calm we gave up sailing and prepared for a swim. This time Sam joined us, remaining symbiotically attached to Hornpipe, and although he rapidly became tired of being dunked by the splashy waves, he had swum in the Atlantic Ocean. Once Sam had climbed up the Aries to join Catherine, I dived underwater to see Hornpipe suspended like a great whale, her keel heavily swaying. Diving was being and seeing as a fish and it was a revelation to swim down and fly up through the shimmering water to where my family watched from the gunwales. When I tried going deeper it was all too much and David said he heard me squeal as I shot to the surface, up the Aries, to the security of home. After motoring a further two hours we swam again and this time Sam stayed with Billy on Hornpipe, playing at shooting Gerry who fell from the cabin with a blood curdling "*Arghh*," as Sam fired his toy gun. Since finding the cowboy gun in a muddy puddle in Puerto Banus, shooting had become Sam's favourite game and Gerry enjoyed it just as much, eagerly climbing the transom to be shot, again and again, forming a friendship that bridged the generation gap to remain true decades later.

On climbing back onto Hornpipe we found a tattered land bird perched on her rigging. I sang to Sam of how the other birds had mocked our outcast and how it had flown away for an adventure. Leaving the wayfarer to recover we continued sailing with the drifter catching just enough wind. When the noon fix revealed we were a mere hundred and eighty-six miles from our destination David consulted the navigation books and identified radio beacons on both Antigua and Guadeloupe. Taking the hand-held Radio Direction Finder to the stern he twiddled the dial, and there they were – a certain proof of land. While he was euphoric we had long placed our absolute trust in David. Soon after we become distracted by an ominous hiss from a locker beneath the cockpit seat where the gas bottle was stored, in a hot spot between the engine and beaming sun. The terrifying prospect of an explosion propelled us onto our hands and knees sniffing around, fearing gas had seeped into the bilges. Although all that was discernible was an oily, salty aroma we opted to take turns pumping the phantom gas and when David deemed it safe he nervously lit a match to heat, or blow up, the remains of our previous meal. Following that redemption we fell into our bunks to dream of uninterrupted slumbers; to once again drag our reluctant bodies from the sticky sheets, to raise and lower sails through another night of variable wind.

With the sun's first rays two golden heads peeped around the curtain we had rigged over our door in hopes a darkened interior might extend their sleep. Then, in David's words, *"Another day began, of breakfasts to get, potties to empty, squabbles to resolve, screams to endure."* On his dawn patrol David had noticed the bird pecking at a few crumbs. Alas it wasn't enough, for somewhat later we found the little creature dead on the deck. Sam stroked the feathery body and committed it to the deep. Sadly, our little friend would never again dip his beak into a hibiscus flower to taste the honey centre, or accompany us to land and a hero's welcome.

While sorrow passed quickly amidst the morning's tantrums, unknown to us a less comfortable voyage was ending on the nearby island of Guadeloupe. Lone yachtsman, Steven Callahan, had set sail from the Canary Islands two weeks before our departure from Britain. His yacht, Napoleon Solo, had been headed towards Antigua on the course we would later follow, however, just six days out from Tenerife she was hit and holed by a mysterious object. While Steven had barely time to clamber into his life raft he survived the ordeal, collecting rainwater, and developing a symbiotic relationship with a pod of dorado that provided him with company and food. Alone in his six-person life raft Steven pondered its inadequacy to sustain even his one life, and despite spotting seven ships none saw his emergency signals. Constructing a sextant from pencils Steven predicted his arrival in Guadeloupe following seventy-six days adrift. Only a few days and miles of empty ocean separated us as we gained ground on Steven's slower passage, however it would be some thirty years before his story came to our attention.

A festive atmosphere illuminated that morning, as Hornpipe's billowing drifter steadily pulled us toward our destination, until, on dropping the sail for a cooling swim, we discovered that despite David having recently replaced the hank at the top of the halyard the friction of the sail swaying back and forth had virtually worn it through. After fixing another imminent disaster we were roasted beneath the noonday sun, and then we realised that there was an alternative. Dragging the heavy canvas awning from the sail-locker we draped it over the boom and tied it to the stanchions, transforming Hornpipe into a river boat steaming through the jungle. And as we luxuriated beneath its shade with framed views of the ocean we imagined frosted drinks clinking with ice and slices of lemon, relishing a breeze that was more refreshing than any cocktail.

Amidst the distractions of our imminent landfall Sam found diverse ways of provoking his little brother. After days of stretching our imaginations to engage him, only a beach would satisfy Sam's need for space. Following another brief swim the dying wind presented an Obelix opportunity and as we thundered along a tanker came close. We could see figures on the deck but despite longing to hear fresh voices there was no response to our radio call. As the ship merged with the sunset it gave three blasting hoots which was all very exciting. On hoisting the drifter for a peaceful evening, David's star sight set us seventy miles from land. When the lights of Antigua and Guadeloupe appeared on a compass heading of two hundred and ninety-five degrees, the precise direction David had plotted from his fix, he said that the satisfaction of perfectly aligning us to our destination after sailing three thousand miles was the biggest moment of his life.

Like most Caribbean islands, Antigua's north-east coast was poorly lit with a shore riddled with reefs that presented as more treacherous when sailing downwind, towards an obstacle that could not be seen or heard. Consequently, David set our course between Antigua and neighbouring Guadeloupe so if a squall hit we could run through the channel. And when the strengthening wind roused us for yet another sail change, we were reassured by our Captain's caution. During David's watch Antigua's loom became brighter and his rough bearing indicated we were just thirty miles away. *"Floating into land on the fading trade wind, the mast curving and dipping over the twinkling starry dome, the airy drifter swaying and dancing before us like a supple gymnast swinging between the parallel bars of the rigging. The sails are no longer black against the shimmering starlight, a dazzling light from ascendant Venus and then a laden orange glow begins to fight against the blackness. The swaying stern becomes a silhouette as it rises against the sunrise. Amidst the loom of Antigua, glistening clusters of homely lights appear. What will be revealed by the inquisitive new rays of the sun? What lies there for us? New sights, new experiences, new people. A new beginning of the next stage in a new dawn."*

Sunrise LT

Our passage would soon be over and that sense of being one with the ocean would never again touch us in quite the same way. On my last watch I opened my heart in gratitude to the sea and sky that had brought us safely to land, *"The waters murmur omm. That first and last sound reverberates through the ocean's throbbing belly. Myriads of stars pattern the robe of night. Garlands of phosphorescence mimic their sparkle, expire in a flash, leaving transient impressions on this ocean that leads us to our destiny. We have dared to live on this flowing flux, reached out to the mighty power that lies beyond, above, and below."* We remembered the generous seafarer who had assisted David with his navigation, an ocean ago. His wisdom that had helped guide us to our destination. He had tapped his forehead and said, *"Something will remain, up here."* And it had, but it was a something beyond words, a seed of experience that would grow to transform our lives forever.

WHAT SHALL WE DO WITH THE DRUNKEN SAILOR

"And the background's fading out of focus
Yes, the picture's changing every moment
And your destination you don't know it. Avalon."
Brian Ferry.

Flooding with elation we slid into English Harbour. After twenty-three days our voyage was over and our anchor had barely touched down when Gerry and David leapt overboard with a "Whoop!" Catherine and I hastily pulled on the children's water wings and, holding hands, plopped into the sea, all weariness dissolving in the soothing water. Following our splash David went ashore for customs clearance to learn that in our absence Britain had reclaimed her far flung colonial power over the Falkland Islands; that Thatcher's warships had crossed our path heading south. When David said he was glad we were out of it, the official's, *"Don't be so sure, you could be called up!"* abruptly reminded him that our fortunes were still linked to Britain's political machinations!

After David had phoned his mother she conveyed news of our arrival to my parents, this being all we could afford back then. On his return we swam ashore, towing Sam and Billy in the dinghy, and as they played we lay beneath shady palms, absorbing the colours and aroma, the sound and feel of land. Following more than three weeks of empty ocean everything appeared unreal, as though Antigua had merely floated into our circle of sea and sky. But we quickly came to our senses when a round of drinks at a beach bar cost a shocking twenty dollars, making us concede this must be the celebratory drink. On hearing the elegant racing yachts crowding into the harbour were arriving for the world renowned Antigua sailing week, that many had crossed the Atlantic for the event, we wondered at our ignorance. Wandering further we stumbled on a free rum punch party. We were in the Caribbean, with white sand between our toes, turquoise waves lapping our feet, a balmy breeze soothing our senses. Was this heaven, or what?

The curtains had opened on a theatre of ultimate freedom and all the while the forest of masts was amassing, yachts rafting in bunches of three or four to party and prepare for racing. Their decks bristled with crew, bronzed bodies posed and waved. We were equally toned and tanned from the perpetual tension of countering Hornpipe's twisting motion. Catherine's English complexion had become a bronzed rose, Gerry and I a burnt umber while David's hide had pixelated into a montage of all our skin tones. Mirrors reflected glimpses of the wild creatures we had become. David's beard suggested an old sea salt, or a friendly lion, my snaking black mane a frenzied medusa. But appearances were our last concern. It was carnival time and as our icy cocktails were replenished the responsibilities of weeks, months, and years evaporated. *"Whah warry baht a ting!"* Sobriety faded with the sunlight, and it was the children who guided us along the beach to the dinghy. *"No Daddy, don't be silly, stop falling in the water!"* Somehow we made it back to Hornpipe. It had been a long day but now we could sleep a whole night through.

Following that glorious arrival we spent a gentle day squandering our energy on a cleaning session before lying on the beach, drinking coconut water, talking about the trip. Watch keeping, seasickness, anxiety, and exhaustion were forgotten, and going to bed early in clean sheets was the greatest treat. Having learned to sleep through anything, the all-night parties never woke us. After watching a parade of gleaming superyachts their spinnakers flying high depart for a three-day race, we filled our water tanks to discover we had used a mere seventy or eighty gallons. Gerry and Catherine set off for an evening walk while David and I shared a first family time since leaving Spain. Then we escaped the crowd, sailing close-hauled to nearby Mamora Bay, relishing that first sensation of Hornpipe tightly dipping to windward, powering through a strong wind and tide. After anchoring with her keel skimming the sand our gang dropped the children and I on the beach and set off for the reef. As we rolled in the blissful waves I remembered that first swim in Jamaica when, hot from the classroom, we drove downhill, dropping a thousand feet through poinciana groves; how all weariness washed away as we wallowed in the buoyant waters of Runaway Bay. Now I was sharing that purest of joys with my children who, but for the orange water wings sprouting from their little arms, were naked, free to run and jump as they pleased. I sat motionless beneath the whispering palms with Hornpipe hovering close by, the black dot of the dinghy in the distance. And as I watched my children's tanned bodies glowing in the sunshine and sparkling sea, all cares dissolved. Secure in my circle of stillness Sam and Billy burrowed in the warm sand, splashed in the shallows. All was well with my world, why go any further.

Sam swimming with water wings   LT

Eventually we heard the Seagull outboard buzzing happily through the waves and the adults returned with stories of snorkelling with coloured fish in a translucent sea. We collected stores of green coconuts and, cracking a heavy nut, drank the pure water, scooped the soothing flesh with spoons shaped from the husk. Then we returned to English Harbour where Sam learned to snorkel, forgetting rivalries as he drifted face down in the shallows. The adults watched windsurfing races, wove little palm leaf birds and rode a bus to Antigua's capital, St John, gazing at jungly foliage and brightly painted shacks. On his return David fixed our VHF Radio with a longer cable and we were soon eavesdropping on the yachting chitter chatter, becoming engrossed in their soap opera of relationships, banter, and bullshit. One evening we walked over to Falmouth Harbour's floating bar and found ourselves drinking with two rugged *Pirates* whose tattooed faces whetted our curiosity about what they were doing amongst that crowd of drifters. We staggered home carrying the kids and when Catherine valiantly offered to put them to bed David, Gerry, and I rowed ashore to dance in a daze to the throbbing boom of a reggae band.

Through the week we watched the blue waters of the crowded harbour transform to a milky murk and wondered what we were doing there. The celebrations extended to the beach, and as Billy and Sam dug sandcastles, a wet t-shirt contest got into full swing. Once again, it wasn't the bare flesh that troubled us but the obscenity of women displaying themselves for a sleazy peepshow. After voting Catherine and I winners of the *brownest boobs in Antigua,* our men invested their competitive spirit in a last-minute entry for the rafting race. Despite the water container raft disintegrating, team Hornpipe had participated in the Antigua Sailing Regatta. Soon after, Gerry bought a snazzy red and yellow surfboard and David borrowed a windsurfer to try what looked so easy as, undaunted by the difficulties, he decided it was worth another go.

Having speculated on the seaworthiness of a yacht romantically named Camelot that resembled Captain Pugwash's ship, I saw there were children on board. In Sam's interest I befriended the family and one evening I babysat Oliver and his little brother, arriving to find Alison settling her boys to sleep in the galley while John adjusted his Admiral Horatio Nelson attire for a fancy-dress ball at Nelson's Dockyard. Their departure left me alone for the first time in years; lounging in the grand cabin, where plush velvet settees and bed had been set for the final act. More surprises awaited in the bathroom where a swarm of cockroaches scurried like kinetic wallpaper. I was woken by a distraught Admiral who implored, *"Where is Alison, she should be home!"* And on dissolving in tears Horatio confessed that due to him playing around his Lady Hamilton had gone off in a huff. While he scoured the anchorage, I stood watch and at dawn I left their domestic crisis to run its course.

Before leaving England, David had obtained a ten-year American visa from their embassy in Glasgow, but despite queuing all day at the Antigua office the bureaucrat refused my visa until I showed him my husband's passport. Eventually I was presented with a two-month visa and a surly, *"Maam, when we know you we may extend it to a year. If you don't like it go back to Glasgow, get your visa there!"* Arriving home, I found the Hornpipers set for an evening departure with Catherine speculating about a plainclothes policeman she had met on the beach. And then the mysterious *Pirates* rolled up in their ramshackle wooden boat to whet our curiosity and share their fish. Late that night we sailed for Nevis, the next island en route to the British Virgin Islands. Gerry and Catherine stood watch and at dawn we anchored in the open bay beside the capital, Charlestown. While our crew slept, David and I cleared customs, and on scouring the shops for essentials we found filthy shelves and exorbitant prices. Recalling Camelot and fearing that cardboard boxes would be riddled with roaches we resolved to make do. On buying a drink in a run-down bar a brute of a man, a British Navy Officer from warship HMS Exeter, accosted us and assuming we had something in common, bragged of his intention to "Bash the *wops.*" And after telling him what we thought of Thatcher's War he vented his wrath on the locals who could not afford to shun his patronage.

On our return we found Hornpipe rolling heavily, so we headed north to Majors Bay, St Kitts, where we replenished our supply of coconuts while the children confidently wandered away to play. On awaking to grey skies that obscured the mountains of Nevis and St Kitts, we saw that they resembled the Hebridean Islands off Scotland. Dreams of finding the perfect beach motivated an early start and after sailing to the capital, Basse Terre, we obtained customs clearance and fresh food for a remote experience. Then, after an exhilarating reach around Horseshoe Point, we beat back into Majors Bay where David and Gerry set off through burnt scrub to climb the mountain that towered over the island; black clouds and driving rain reminding them of home, a stinking salt pond, and a monkey appearing incongruously out of kilter.

The following day we motored around to Sandbank Bay and cautiously anchored in a narrow channel with coral beds and breaking waves to the seaward side. Then we went our separate ways, Gerry paddling over to surf the bar while I rowed ashore with Catherine, Sam, and Billy to practice yoga on the white sand. David had remained on Hornpipe preparing for snorkelling, when the hum of a launch pervaded the silence. After circling Gerry and observing our beach group, the police and customs officer came alongside to inform David we had broken a law, that our clearance only applied to Basse Terre. They had travelled many miles to reprimand us but an unspoken *"Why didn't you tell us,"* could not be voiced. After they left, we hauled in our anchors and, retracing our steps, motor-sailed through the long day. Once again David trailed to the customs office, to be chastised by their report, stating, *"The naked females and children were flaunting themselves on the beach."* Eventually, our passports were stamped, and once again we sailed for Majors Bay. Following a rainy night we sailed at dawn and by breakfast we were anchored in paradise.

Those days of swimming, snorkelling, and play seemed to never end. Gerry spent most of them surfing and we all had a swoosh on the smaller waves. With Hornpipe anchored close to the coral that fringed the shore it was easy to hone our diving skills, to practise equalising the pressure in our ears. Diving deeper every time we wove through coral arches, among fronds of elk horn forests alive with colourful fish. Those encrusted passages soon became as familiar as taking a leisurely walk in a garden blooming with flowers, blessed with birds. Drifting in that wonderland took me back to my first time snorkelling, at Negril in Jamaica where, after clambering over calcified crags I glimpsed a crystalline pool. Pulling on my new mask I pushed off and found myself floating on liquid air with cliffs and caverns looming beneath. It was all too much, gasping with disbelief I erupted to the surface! And again, I launched into imperceptible space, to fly high above rocky gullies, my senses assailed with expectations that at any moment I would fall. Yet I transcended gravity and physicality, was set free to dance in the brittle sunlight. That first dive flight revealed sights beyond ordinary perception. Vestiges of the child, who had found a world of possibility in the deeper end of the municipal swimming pool, hovered overhead, while safely hidden within, the child who was yet to be, who would dive deeper than anyone, smiled, and returned to his sleep of becoming.

Sandbank Bay was a perfect playground, the place where Billy became happy in water. Sam too gained competence in his *goggeling*, gripping David's hand as he splashed along the surface with his bottom in the air, diving down to return in a flurry of bubbles, gabbling about the fish he had seen. Many years later Sam would use this fluency with water to launch himself into a form of creative expression that changed his life.

When Sam told us he intended staging Shakespeare's *The Tempest* in a swimming pool, his scheme sounded ambitious for a first-time director. However, our son's determination won through. Sam directed and staged the production at Auckland's Tepid Baths and when the student actors' skin wrinkled from weeks of rehearsing in chlorinated water, no one minded; they were having too much fun. The performance glowed with youthful vitality, water nymphs transported the audiences to sensual depths, and the antics of clowns and villains were augmented with fluid lighting that portrayed the stormy ocean, a sea of blood, and Prospero's magic.

Sam's *The Tempest* ran for ten packed nights to radiant reviews. William played a tortured Prince Alonso entering underwater, surfacing to speak his lines without pause for breath. With eyes dramatically blackened, brow furled, William was a vision of aquatic nobility and I hardly recognised the boy who had left home a month before. He had done time lifting rocks as makeshift weights to prepare for baring his chest. And it was all worthwhile. William attracted a following of high school girls and his brother said, *"I heard their jaws drop, heard them whisper, 'Alonso, Alonso,' in the foyer."* Sam was on fire and when I asked, *"How did you convince the actors you could direct a play?"* he replied, *"They knew about acting but they had never acted in water. I know everything about water; I've been performing in it all my life."* Sam had spent his childhood directing dramatic fantasies on an interactive stage of beaches and oceans and his creative confidence had blossomed out of the environment he knew and loved.

The days drifted past. David climbed the hill to photograph Hornpipe at anchor with coral twenty metres to starboard, breakers twenty metres to port, confident that the compass coordinates he had taken would provide a way out if the wind got up in the night. His lofty perch revealed a view over the sand dunes to a salt pond still muddy from a storm surge that had swept over our benign beach. Far below, Gerry surfed a wave, Catherine lay in the shade, and I practiced yoga while watching the children run in and out of the water. I also ventured up the burnt hillside to render a smudgy sketch of the curving bay that swept towards the distant hills, and on my return David and I played beach volleyball, marking out a sand court as we had on holidays in Ireland and Scotland. Freed of responsibilities I enjoyed the presence of my children while they played on the beach from morning till night, their brown bodies protected by the moist tropic air. Sam and Billy wore the bare essentials: sand shoes, water wings, a sun-hat. Sun block had proved a sand magnet but an Elastoplast over the nose remained intact, and when Billy grew tired of digging and delving he flopped into a sleepy slumber. Although we enforced the vital rules that would save our sons' lives, we avoided nagging about trivialities that might dilute the salient danger of falling overboard. Sam understood that he never went on deck without permission, and as Billy became more agile we stretched a net over the cockpit so he could not stray at night. Living on a boat required constant vigilance, but where possible I avoided intruding on our children's discoveries, saving interventions for life or death situations.

Beach Billy LT

Gerry and David spent hours diving to provide a feast of lobsters, and just before our departure they discovered the perfect habitat and shot three in half an hour. Sandbank Bay had been a beautiful place to reflect on the transition from our former lives. Our relationship with Gerry and Catherine had blossomed and we were completely comfortable in each others' presence, but with many islands yet to explore it was time to sail that well-trodden route back to Basse Terre. On the fourteenth of May we anchored in the deep-water dock and caught a taxi through lush sugar plantations up Brimstone Hill. The old fort revealed immense views over to Nevis, Statia, and Saba, along with cannons that delighted Sam, who sat on top making explosive sounds, shooting everything including our taxi. Meanwhile Billy, who had no clue of what was happening, copied him. Returning, we goose winged towards the tiny island of Saba and were soon motoring beneath rocky crags with coloured houses perching on high. And it was then we fouled our propeller in a lobster net. As Gerry dived to free the tangled ropes we anxiously gauged Hornpipe's distance from the jagged shore. It was too deep for anchoring and there was no wind for sailing so it was a great relief when Gerry freed the propeller. After securing Hornpipe and rowing ashore we set off up a narrow gully that wound between precipitous cliffs to a plateau high above the sea, and ordering a drink in the only bar in the village called Bottom, we wondered what we might find at the settlement of Top.

The following day we took a taxi tour, holding our breath as Vincent spun along the twisting road, all the while pointing out fruits, vegetables, and dwellings poised on precipitous cliffs. After collecting tree gooseberries for jam, we stopped at a hotel where Sam almost fell in the swimming pool. Then Billy, who appeared to have lost his fear of water and everything else, calmly stepped on the surface, as if doing a Jesus impression. David would swear I hit the surface before Billy. My first thought was for my child, and it did not matter that I was soaked in the process.

With torrential rain the road became a foaming cascade. While we spent the morning grouped around a tap doing the laundry, David confronted yet another frustrating mechanical problem. Eventually he stormed up the muddy road towards Bottom and there I found him at the snack bar talking with some lonely locals whose desperation reminded him of the Coanwood farmers, and as we walked back to a cacophony of cicadas it seemed the walls of the gully closed in on us. It was with relief we turned our backs on Saba's tumbling cliffs and crashing seas, sailing close-hauled for St Barts on a wind that died as we tacked into Gustavia. After clearing customs and filling our water tanks we explored the sophisticated French town, enjoying its tasteful opulence. After talking to an architect about the possibilities of producing furniture on the island, we considered a change of plan, with David hitching out to look at a potential workshop. Gerry began an oil painting while I walked with the children to a beach on the other side of town. As I sketched Sam's wide-eyed gaze two young locals scrutinised my every movement and when I finished they indicated I should draw them. While they scanned the horizon with frozen expressions I drew and drew, appreciating the opportunity to observe their ebony skin that reflected the light, absorbed the shade, suited my chiaroscuro style. Although unaware of how they would influence my artistic expression, I had begun a practice of drawing strangers I encountered on my travels, and it was only after they left I realised our interaction had been entirely without words.

David walked home through the pungent darkness, disturbing basking lizards on the warm road, arriving intoxicated by the wonders he had seen, the potential of staying in this romantic place. Houses were being constructed and it appeared likely he might find skilled joinery work. He carried his album of photographs everywhere as he enquired about purchasing woodworking machinery and printing leaflets to advertise his furniture. Sailing had opened David's mind and given him time to conceive of designing a house where the furniture integrated into the building, however his concept depended on finding an enlightened client.

After shopping for Billy's birthday, we walked out to Le Presidente to view another workshop, and on finding a neglected building we wended our way home through the intoxicating darkness emboldened by rum punch. Next day we motored over to Goat Island, which true to its name demonstrated the devastation a herd of goats could wreak on a natural habitat, where in contrast to the verdant green of other islands the red earth was devoid of all vegetation. Across the bay beneath an orange cliff floated the wreck of a rusting coaster with a familiar rough wooden yacht tied alongside. Gerry, who recognised our *Pirates'* boat was intrigued by the enigmatic scene and he immediately began a painting. Meanwhile Catherine and I were concocting our own pirate story, drawing up a treasure map with clues, and then, *"Surprise! Surprise! Look what we found."* The map was produced and we trundled off, around the island in the blazing sun, prompting Sam and Billy to solve the clues. At last the treasure, a bag of chocolate coins saved from Christmas, was found under a rock. Sam was good enough to go along with the theatrics and the melting coins were sucked, resulting in two piratical chocolate grins that could only be washed away by walking the plank. So we wedged an oar blade over the dinghy, which Sam clambered onto and jumped off with abandon. Billy, as with many games, had no means of understanding what was happening. Wearing nothing but his water wings and red plimsolls, Billy stepped onto the plank, and while I steadied his trembling body he cautiously edged forward like a little bird. As his balance wavered he put his hands over his head and fell. After the dunking, it was home to supper, bed, and dreams of treasure.

Laying the trail had given David the opportunity to walk over the island and climb its volcanic plug. From that highest point he commanded a view back to the islands of St Barts, Saba, Statia, St Kitts, Nevis, and Antigua; forward to St Martin and Anguilla, our next ports of call. On visiting each island we respectfully flew a courtesy flag. We did not have a Dutch ensign for St Martin so as we sailed, Catherine and I hastily patched one from pieces, colouring details with felt pens. Then on entering Philipsburg harbour we saw a police launch rafted up to our *Pirates'* yacht. Gerry's curiosity got the better of him and he rowed over, taking his wet oil painting of their yacht alongside the wreck at Goat Island. When they snubbed his gift and avoided any association with him Gerry was bemused, but later, rumours of drug smugglers made him wonder whether he had unwittingly recorded a crime, suspect that our *Pirates* were the real deal. Following hours hanging around the dirty customs offices, David wandered home, past shops displaying cameras, stereos, and brash rubbish; wasted resources that symbolised our dependence on machinery which inevitably broke. We hastily departed to celebrate Billy's birthday with a beach barbecue. I had created feathered headdresses, fringed trousers, and waistcoats from my old clothes, and as we danced around our campfire, and sang songs, I harboured a hope that our children might sympathise with indigenous cultures; that bows and arrows would replace guns and cowboys. It seemed unbelievable that Billy had been born just two years before, that the baby, who had breathed his first breath in a windswept cottage high on the fells of Northumberland, was now a little brown boy who had sailed an ocean.

Returning to fill the gas bottle I took the children to a hotel pool and drew them swimming, Billy's sleek elfin cap contrasting with Sam's tousled curls. At last we sailed away, racing around the point before beating into Marigot Bay with the fading light. Then, with the help of Bob Marley and a bottle of Jamaican rum, we spontaneously erupted in a bop on the deck. After yet another day of fixing broken gadgets, David and I went ashore for a drink to bump into two drunken American girls who challenged us to race their yacht, Encore Sloopy. The following morning they stole away early and when we arrived first in Anguilla's Rendezvous Bay they evaded defeat by sailing on, leaving us to enjoy our breakfast while a violent storm with thirty-five knot gusts spun and swung Hornpipe from side to side. The sea fizzed with rain but when the misty veil lifted, it revealed the island of Anguillita sparkling in the sun. Then we tacked through smooth seas up to Road Bay with its little village of Sandy Ground. Going ashore we met a band of English architects who were playing darts and bottle walking at the Barrel Stays Bar. The game involved inching forward, supported on beer bottles, to place one as far as possible, beating a retreat without collapsing in the sand. And after David had been crowned *champion bottle walker* we departed in triumph, wondering how it was he won all the games.

Waking tired from the previous evening's excesses we continued our habit of sailing on before breakfast, tacking around to Crocus Bay. While Catherine and Gerry walked up to the shops at The Valley, I cleaned the boat and began an urgent sewing job, constructing a new bikini from three embroidered serviettes. Being economy sized, there was fabric to spare in my creation with its strategically placed pink flowers. David had rowed the kids ashore where they watched the locals' exuberance as they experimented with our diving gear, discovering their familiar playground anew. Following a late lunch and siesta, we sailed north to Cliff Bay. We set a second anchor on a little beach just a step from Hornpipe's stern, and when I went ashore to practise yoga with Billy it seemed I could almost reach out to touch the limestone cliffs. We were woken before dawn by local fishermen who requested we evacuate the bay while they cast a net across the narrow entrance. Meanwhile the village women and children had gathered on the cliff to signal any underwater activity and when a shoal appeared they shouted at the rowers. Sadly, the hungry, toothless old men were too slow for the fish and we watched them row home, hunched over the oars they had bodged from poles and planks.

After re-anchoring in the cove David and I drifted on the ethereal currents of that cathedral cavern while Gerry turned up the volume of our tape deck, awakening those cloistered sepulchres to the celestial sound of Monteverdi and Bach. When Gerry switched to Roxy Music we returned the favour, passing a blissful morning. Sometime later, Sam, Billy, and I swam the few metres to the beach where they played, sometimes joining me as I practiced yoga, sinking into the rich orange sand, sluicing it off in the warm sea. Yoga had sustained me since my art college days when a flatmate suggested it would dissipate my frenetic energy and give everyone some peace. I had continued on beaches, compromised by sun, sand, insects, and onlookers; balanced on a rolling deck awash with Lego, at the beck and call of my children, all the time trying to let go of a desire to immerse myself completely. But on that special day my children's presence transformed yoga into a joyful celebration I will remember forever.

In the late afternoon we motored over to Scrub Island, battling a stiff wind and negotiating the tricky reef to anchor close to the beach. By morning our dinghy had almost sunk, and while our crew circumnavigated the island, David set to bodging the leak and replacing its rubber gunwale. Then, from nowhere, a young couple appeared on a beach buggy and after inviting us for a drink at their luxurious hotel they asked endless questions about our cruising life. While we were equally curious about how they could afford to own an isolated island, we would never have traded places. Our home allowed us spontaneity, freedom, and priceless luxuries. Ocean breezes cooled our nights as we drifted upon a swimming pool and playground surrounded by an abundant supply of fresh fish.

That night we sailed back to Cliff Bay and set our anchors by the light of the moon, and when the fishermen returned Gerry and Catherine were awake and ready to up anchor. Thankfully the old folks filled their nets, and after buying five bar jacks we motored over to Crocus Bay for Anguillita's around the island sailing race. Gerry ran into the Encore Sloopy gang and joined them, drinking cold beer from their seemingly endless supply. We wandered over to where a row of brightly painted yachts was lined up, their sails billowing in the wind. Shore men strained on the ropes that held the delicate boats, which with the starter gun were released to speed away. They rapidly disappeared around Flatcap Point with us spontaneously giving chase, along with Encore Sloopy. But with no time to prepare Hornpipe for sailing close hauled, it was chaos on board, and as she heeled items fell from cupboards, toilets slopped over, and waves sloshed through portholes. Though I longed to share the fun I was desperately trying to keep up, my frenzied efforts at sustaining a domestic equilibrium equalling David's frustration with Hornpipe's maintenance.

By the time we arrived back in Crocus Bay it was teeming with drunk people. Music blared from a sound system and an ancient man was setting up a flimsy rope, his twisted fingers struggling to tie the knots and exert tension on the line. Eventually he managed to string it between two trees, just metres from the ground. Then, without decorum, he contorted into a faded carnival costume, pulled on a pair of ragged plimsolls, and hoisted himself into the foliage. His bird face appeared amidst the branches, as with chest convulsing, he struggled to erect a decrepit umbrella. Revellers and barking dogs ridiculed his every move as he attempted a first wobbly step onto the rope. A scrawny ankle stretched into space, stick arms clawed the branches, and knowing it would be beyond him to walk a line drawn on the ground I turned from the sad sight. It seemed our cruel world had eclipsed his stunt, had forever changed this small community.

And I was reminded of my village childhood, of those visiting circuses with their tired performers and abused animals.

When an enraged black woman separated me from the crowd I became swept up in my own drama. The piercing eyes of her children had me cornered, her flailing arms stabbed an accusation, *"Whiyat wooman! Yoh dissgustin! Whah yoh go shoh yohsel naked? Whah yoh no wear panties?"* My brain fast tracked to my new bikini. Were all three serviettes in place? Then it dawned on me. The high cut briefs must give the impression I was stark naked beneath my loose top! *"Woah! Wait a minute lady."* I demonstrated, *"Look! I am wearing panties. They're the latest style!"* In the tropics, day follows night, without wasting time dawdling through twilight. Her transformation was as immediate, and the sight of Sam and Billy tugging at my hands clinched the deal. I was a mother! Her fury melted in sweetness, *"Shoh me thah stayle. I gon mek one panty lak dat fo mahsell. Sary I caus yoh grief Sisstah!"* We hugged, exchanged names, and then my new friend and her armada of children disappeared in the throng.

Other boats had anchored off the beach and we were swapping origins and destinations with their owners when a slight, balding man stepped forward, introducing himself with a handshake, *"Roger's the name; Rogue,"* as he gestured towards a buttercup yellow yacht. Despite his shorts and t-shirt Roger looked like a bank manager, and when he concluded with a, *"We'll meet again,"* it seemed certain we would. As the evening deteriorated we slipped away and much later the girls from Encore Sloopy dropped by. They were deeply into God, yet we had never seen them sober or anyone so drunk. While they failed to convert Gerry, his foredeck seduction was scuppered and he spent the following day lying under a tree supervising the children, nursing a headache.

The hurricane season officially began on the first of June so we sailed away but on passing Anguilla's Dog Island we caught sight of Rogue's yellow hull with Roger waving us aboard. There, on revealing a huge flagon of rum, he repeatedly plied us with burning shots while gallantly cautioning us about its potency. Roger regaled us with classical music and tales of entertaining an operatic trio who had sung as they sailed the Pacific, and as the evening lost focus his questioning turned to relationships. On learning that Catherine and Gerry were not a couple Roger barely disguised his enthusiasm. While we too were curious about our crew's romantic disposition Gerry would admit that something intimate had occurred on the ocean crossing, that circumstances had not conspired for more.

The following morning we sailed for Tortola, hoping that the weather would allow us to stop at Sombrero Island. Our sails efficiently pulled us along and we were soon anchored beside the solitary slab, beneath its towering lighthouse. Nearby, a ladder ascended to where a smiling West Indian invited us ashore for a tour and table tennis tournament. But first we briefly dived overboard to found that the clear water distorted the size of the fish, that those hovering at depth were enormous, but so friendly that shooting them seemed barbaric. Then, rowing over to the rock we scrambled up the ladder to where the four lighthouse keepers waited to show us around, bantering all the while. This, the great shining light they manned, there the frugal shed they inhabited, and that was all. The hundred metres of smooth rock lay just fifteen feet above the undulating waves. On that benign day Sombrero's briny puddles were crusted with salt, its terrain splattered with bird poop and feathers, but the complete absence of plant life indicated that it was often awash. The lighthouse cast a horological shadow over all, delighted in pointing a profane finger to the heavens as it broke that unwritten rule in Sombrero's horizontals of sea and sky.

The keepers were obviously lonely in their ocean prison so after playing rounds of table tennis we invited them for a drink and spent the following day enjoying their company. Having estimated that our passage to the British Virgin Islands would take more than a day we hauled our anchor at midnight of the fifth of June and sailed from Sombrero under the mainsail and number two genoa. As the night progressed, we were beset by the self-steering dysfunctions that had dogged our Atlantic crossing and despite our pleas, the Aries was absent without leave. At dawn David discovered a course discrepancy, so we gybed the foresail to a goose-wing rig that carried us to Virgin Gorda and on to Tortola. There we anchored amongst a cluster of cruising yachts as for a first time I sighted the islands I had heard so much about. During the year of my birth my father's ship, H. M. S. Snipe, had conveyed the Governor of the Leeward Islands around his dominion of Antigua, Barbuda, Anguilla, Montserrat, St Kitts, and Nevis, which my father had described as, *"All unspoilt with perfect white coral beaches fringed with coconut palms and crystal clear waters into which local children dived for the coins we threw."* While his duties as engineer allowed no opportunities to enjoy the beaches, as Snipe passed through the British Virgin Islands they anchored off Dead Man's Chest, where he wrote of the sailors' antics, *"Traditionally we landed a party of sixteen men and a bottle of rum with orders for them to sing that well known song as they drank it. 'Fifteen men on a dead man's chest, Yo-ho-ho and a bottle of rum. Drink and the devil had done for the rest, Yo-ho-ho and a bottle of rum'."*

Since Hornpipe's arrival in Antigua we had celebrated a newfound freedom. But our relationship with our crew had changed since the routine watches of the Atlantic. Gerry's wit and wonder had complemented Catherine's steady certainty and their contribution had ensured the success of our voyage; however the end of that ocean passage had marked the beginning of a new chapter in our lives. Although throwing spaghetti at the wall to test it was *al dente* had been funny in those circumstances, it became vandalism when I was the one who cleaned up. As David slipped into the same group dynamic that had thwarted our time in Northumberland, I felt betrayed. Our family needed physical and emotional space, to reclaim Hornpipe as our home. Shortly after our arrival Roger the Rogue resurfaced to whisk Catherine away for a cruise along the chain of Caribbean islands. They were an incongruous couple with Roger harbouring hopes of a relationship, Catherine setting her sights on younger men with *nice legs*. And while Gerry stayed on to sail around Tortola before flying home for the English summer, that was not the last time we would spend together.

LIVING JAH LIFE

> *"Oh, island in the sun*
> *Willed to me by my father's hand*
> *All my days I will sing in praise*
> *Of your forest, waters, your shining sand.'*
>
> Harry Belafonte

The British Virgin Island of Tortola stretches like a lizard with the American Virgin Islands and Puerto Rico its head, snaking towards the tail of Virgin Gorda to the east. At its belly lies the harbour of Tortola's Road Town, where we anchored amongst the cruising yachts, and rowed ashore to meet a neglected character from our past. That sight of Molly Bloom's trailing fronds of green weed, her decks and red hull bleeding rust, reminded me of how close we had come to pinning our future on her. Fortunately, when things fall apart they often make space for a better solution. And having heard he might find work with an eccentric cosmetic surgeon David set off to meet Robin Tattersall at his legendary Purple Palace. The surgeon eagerly scanned David's portfolio before employing him to replace the French doors to his clinic that clung to the cliff overlooking Road Town's colonial buildings. And after shifting his chest of hand tools and a radial arm saw into Tattersall's tiny shed, David made a start on the menial task that had been set to test his ability and attitude.

On that first weekend, we sailed along the string of islands that flank the wide channel that stretches from Tortola to Virgin Gorda; past Norman, Peter, Deadman's Chest, Salt, Cooper, Ginger Islands, and finally the

112

tumbled terrain of Fallen Jerusalem. As we drew closer to the enormous granite boulders of Virgin Gorda, The Baths appeared as precariously balanced as if it were yesterday they had erupted from the earth. Anchoring amidst the charter yachts we set off for the giant's playground. Scrambling through crevices and canyons we wove our way amongst the boulders that had been smoothed by the fluxing tides of seventy million years. We swam through pools of shimmering silver fish and on scaling a cliff emerged in brilliant sunshine to find we had climbed to the top of the colossal pile. From that lofty peak we looked down at a muddled mass of rocks and rampant foliage, up at elegant palms that bowed to the tropical breeze. Delving through the layers of the labyrinth we found a grotto where a single beam of sunlight pierced a secret pool of sparkling water. There we came upon Sam, crouched motionless in the shadows, a sinister figure, a scene set for a performance or ritual. He had found a toy gun and a place where a drama could unfold. What was Sam thinking of? Had he been touched by a premonition of primal Caliban, or was he just an innocent child at play, measuring the distance between reality and fantasy. The image sparked our debate about guns as toys, which always returned to their purpose of killing. Our belief in nonviolence belied the presence of Hornpipe's pump action shotgun and rifle that her previous owners had purchased as defence against the notorious Red Sea pirates. When considering the event of an aggressive attack we felt that producing a gun could inflame a volatile situation; that unless we were prepared to kill we were more likely to become the victims of our weapons. I visualised alternative ways of dealing with such encounters and eventually we threw the guns into the ocean, glad to be shot of them.

During our family's early years together the land had entered our being. David and I had built foundations of earth and stone that provided us with purpose and direction. But as we became swept up in the carnival culture of the Caribbean our relationship woke to the sunshine of a new day. Although the Bermuda triangle has a reputation for mysterious disappearances I had been born of that enigma. Caribbean voices had soothed my dreams but before I had a chance to dip my toddler toes in the Atlantic Ocean it had been time to leave. Jamaica had deepened my connection with the West Indies and, a decade later, our return gave me a glorious sense of coming home.

As the fluid sea dissolved the permanence of our past we entered a realm of sensual pleasure. Dragging our mattress onto Hornpipe's deck we lay beneath the vast cosmos, as we had on our first night together. There we slept to the soothing sound of waves, the wind's caressing touch. We relished our privacy, remembering an early morning before our crew departed, when our affectionate position prompted Billy's proclamation, *"Look Sam, Linda and David are doing exercises!"* How we ceased all activity while I prayed that Gerry and Catherine still slept. We had become lean and bronzed by the sun and although we wore swim gear when anchored off Road Town, clothes made no sense in hot watery surroundings. A bare body scared tourists and solitude was preferable so, when a charter yacht anchored unnecessarily close, we casually continued, au natural. We sometimes dived with Billy watching from the dinghy. On one occasion I held Sam's hand while David swam in front, and when our eyes picked out a shadowy shape hidden amongst the boulders Sam squealed into his snorkel, and David quietly said, *"It's all right, it's a nurse shark."* This was the largest sea creature we had encountered, however the languid plant eater was completely harmless and as we watched we saw a smaller one hidden beneath. On returning to Billy, patiently waiting in the rocking dinghy, Sam couldn't contain himself, shouting, *"I saw a shark! I saw a shark!"* to Billy's nonchalant, *"I saw a whale."*

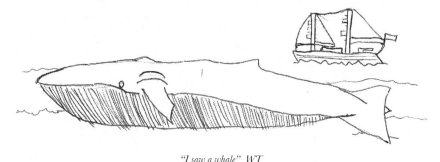

"I saw a whale" WT

On hearing the kindergarten needed a teacher, I sought out Prue to learn that she was also a seawife, but that her husband Peter had sailed their yacht, White Squall, from New Zealand while she and her small daughters flew the distance. Following a casual interview, I began teaching, with Billy trailing me through the mornings. Sam's admittance to Saint George's primary school was subject to a reading test. He cowered behind me as we entered the dragon's lair of the principal, Mrs Clough, who, thrusting a book in Sam's hands, eagerly anticipated his failure. And as he read with ease a ripple of confusion crackled her reptilian features. Sam became her school's youngest pupil, wearing his green gingham shirts with pride despite my lop-sided hand sewing. On his first day, Sam met Oliver from Camelot, and I discovered a girl I had taught in Exeter was the parent of one of my kindergarten kids. Sam's motherly West Indian teacher eased her pupils through Saint George's antiquated regimes while amidst the rows of wayward children at battered wooden desks Sam thrived, imbibing confidence as he drew, read, and drifted in dreams. At last he could make friends and play in the branches of a vast banyan tree, falling to the red earth, ripe fruits with unbreakable limbs and only the dragon Mrs Clough to darken their nights.

Sam's brief name has always said everything about him; however, William would accumulate a host of nicknames. While the most enduring was Billy, others were derived from his favourite t-shirt, featuring an elephant wearing football boots, a *'booty shirt'* that generated *Booky* and *Wook*. As Billy's vocabulary increased, my boys' rivalries were replaced with a friendship as complete as two parts of a whole. This compatibility evolved through their student years and when William joined Sam at Auckland University they shared a flat and a passion for creating theatre. William was elected president of *Stage Two Productions*, and the *Antipasto Theatre Company*, that Sam and friends founded in 1998. And they performed *A Midsummer Night's Dream*, with Sam the leader of the Mechanicals and William, a virile Lysander, once again seizing the opportunity to whip off his shirt and charm his audience.

Although a year younger than the kindergarten kids, Billy joined every activity. While Prue encouraged the little ones to interact with each other I contributed creative projects and taught the older ones to read. Despite considering the reading exam abhorrent, it was standard Caribbean practice, so I sat with my arm around each child in turn, sounding the letters to form those first magical words. Later in the morning we all gathered in a circle for singing and action rhymes. Though many children were beaten at home they responded to positive behaviour and no one hit or bit at the kindergarten. The raised two roomed building was set in a playground with swings, a Wendy house, and decrepit boat which the kids crowded into for fantastical voyages. One day an excited child ran to tell us, *"We're racing some little lobsters that we found under the house."* And Prue used the broom to dispense with the scorpions in the same way she dealt with tarantulas. Around this time, I grew concerned about Billy. Why did he paint his pictures black? Was he simply transforming the white paper in the most absolute way, or recreating the darkness before birth, premonitions of the depths? While Billy screamed loudest, to claim my attention from the forty others, his friend Alex delighted in provoking this explosive response; whereupon he threw his arms around his friend, and as if by magic the noise stopped. Gentle Billy fell for it every time and Alex's demonstrative affection became a beguiling behaviourism in a symbiotic relationship punctuated with noisy altercations.

Every weekend we sailed to a new island and despite wincing when David cranked Hornpipe's sheets to the max I embraced the challenges. The deep cockpit limited my visibility so I sat on top the aft cabin, moving the wheel with my toes or stood, legs spread wide, a foot on each seat. Days were spent diving, with Billy joining us in exploring the ocean's coral gardens and the ways of fishes. After buying a *Waterproof Guide to Corals and Fish*, the book became the children's bible with them scanning the pages to memorise the names and characters of every fish. There was always boat maintenance to keep up with and at such times we dropped the kids on the beach where they played within sight and sound, exploring the flotsam and jetsam of shells, coconut husks, their cars, and animals. Sam could swim and Billy was unsinkable in his securely fastened life vest - a golden purchase from a jumble sale that transformed our lives. While they thrived on independence and benign neglect, David and I frequently glanced towards those small silhouettes. Even from a distance we could interpret their body language and when the fun ran out we heard them chant, "*We - Want - To - Come - Back - On - The - B - o - a - t,*" as they waited with their bag of toys, hot, tired, and all played out.

A child finds enough stimulation in daily life to spark endless games. My earliest memory is of travelling by train, pushing a toy between the seats to gather the fluff of human passage. Hazy impressions remain of solitary days when, with my brother at school, I lay on the warm paving watching a microscopic line of ants. But I was terrified of the enormous spiders that, as autumn turned to winter, found their way into the house. A spider could sprint from beneath my bed with a reckless speed that filled me with dread. And how many daydreams were tainted with fears of that fleeting scuttle and spindly shadow? Sam and Billy had no phobias, they relished the sight of an insect going about its business and on catching a glimpse of Hornpipe's spider they would cry *"Look there's Bouncer!"* in a way that made him feel special. Before they could catch him, Bouncer had raced away, but he loved the children's stories and wished someone would write about him. Most of all he enjoyed the music that boomed around the boat, making his legs twitch, his heart brave enough for somersaults. He tried to find where the magic sound came from and decided it was another feature of Hornpipe, that his yacht was a new age tuck box, a spaceship in disguise.

Although Sam had settled into school I hesitated when it came to their sports day. We avoided contests and I doubted if he had a clue of what a race was, however my observations of other parents told me their offspring were groomed to win. As the schoolkids lined up, their parents urged them forward, and with the starting gun, Sam shot off, imitating the others, until a distracting thought entered his head. When he came in last I cheered and we ran on, laughing together. Such races were not going to help anyone succeed, they would more likely generate a sense of failure. Meanwhile Sam's healthy lack of rivalry protected him from the shame of losing and would lead him to achieve in his own unique way. My school reports had repeatedly mentioned daydreaming and despite inhabiting his own world my son was academically top of his class. Sam's alert eyes and mind observed everything and he would retain that individuality along with his dark curls. On leaving home for Elam School of Fine Arts, Sam proved he could be loved for himself as he shook off teenage inhibitions and became known as *Wild Thing* for his extravagant dancing. And I recall my shock, when the chat at a Tortola coffee morning switched from promoting England's defunct monarchy to racial purity and gender issues. That on being asked what I would like my son to become when he grew up, I could not resist being provocative: *"A ballet dancer,"* I said, predicting Sam's career in creating, directing, and reviewing contemporary performances.

The island's consistent breezes and warm water would be ideal for windsurfing so with our first spare cash we bought a board and rig, practising with one of us on rescue duty in the dinghy. We were soon flying over the sea or sailing with the children lying on the board. Even falling off was fun, except when I hit a cluster of spiny sea urchins. As I staggered to my feet, bottom bristled with spines, Billy began screaming about a small cut; I was his mother and he needed all of me. After buying another, faster windsurfer we swooped over the sparkling waves, David practising his gybes while I performed back-bending head dips. He reflected on his youth, canoeing the coast of the Isle of Wight, developing an affinity with the sea. *"A pattern had been formed in my impressionable young mind and soul. Now with all the responsibilities and struggles of an adult this was the key to a spiritual release, a freedom, a closeness to nature. My body is wholly in tune with the elements, the wind, and the waves. With nature."* And whether on windsurfer or yacht, David's instinctive response is to head towards the horizon and there, where the sea meets sky, he finds himself.

The plastic surgeon fortuitously had a new house and partner to impress. When he asked David to consider making him some furniture it was just what we had in mind. Our official story was that I was earning our living while my husband renovated the boat. However, David was working illegally and from his tiny workshop he could have dropped a stone on the roof of the immigration office below. My application for a work permit involved regular visits to that office when, tired from the morning's teaching, I queued for interviews, fearful of crumbling under pressure, worried that Sam or Billy could betray us with an innocent comment. Following the ordeal, we walked up the hill to the sanctuary of the Purple Palace's weathered stone walls that had repelled pirates in bygone days, and there amid the gothic statues and mossy fountains was a swimming pool we could use if we were quiet. I practised yoga, the children played, and after a picnic I sat Billy in the collapsible buggy with Sam standing on the footrest. Then, slinging my bag on my back, I started the long walk home. I wished we could take the bus, but with boat maintenance gobbling our funds we could not afford that luxury. Marine insurance was prohibitively expensive and we had no savings or back up for emergencies. Hot and weary I walked the mile along the curved crescent of the harbour pushing the sagging pushchair into the blazing sun.

After swimming, Sam and Billy occasionally remained behind, watching children's television with Diana's little boy, Matthew. Subsequently the cartoon characters, He Man, Skeletor, and Battlecat, entered innocent minds that had been shielded from commercialism. Childhood impressions remain forever and Sam recalls sneaking a red lollipop from Matthew's jar of sweets, and how David abstractly talked about it as they walked home through the fragrant twilight. Years later Sam wrote his confession, *"I felt bad and sorry and scared of David. He asked if I was lying and I said no I wasn't. Then we saw the moon. Maybe I used it to move the attention away from me, or maybe David pointed it out himself. Either way, both of us were happy to focus on something else. It was a thin crescent of gold in the deep blue and lavender sky. But what captivated me the most was that upon its dark edge we could see a faint outline, tracing its full shape. To my four-year-old mind it was a surprise, and a wonder. I had thought that I understood the moon, but this new mystery opened up all kinds of new possibilities. We gazed at this moon, David and I, as we walked home, and he made some progress in explaining it to me. Something about it being round, and catching the light in different ways."* In Sam's memory, the stolen lollipop, his first lie, and the hidden side of the moon had all rounded into one.

Sometimes I looked after a child whose mother taught at Sam's school. Her family had exchanged the troubles in Northern Ireland for Caribbean sunshine, but when her husband stepped backward into a bucket of water while using a power tool, his life ended along with their dreams. The children were sad, their mother exhausted, and there was no escaping the gutted home that looked out on an empty swimming pool, full of broken promises. Another friend carried the weight of an alcoholic husband whose addiction had rendered him blind, her schizophrenia spelling disaster for a daughter who believed she was a princess. The bars were full of tragic characters who wandered, drink in hand, through their lives. With rum priced at two dollars a bottle, drinking often became both hobby and habit; relationships frequently subsided into divorce. By contrast, when David became friends with Robin's West Indian mechanic he heard that his family had never been beyond Tortola, so he invited them for a sailing trip and picnic at a nearby island. But we soon realised that they were as uneasy around us as they were fearful of the water and learned that their evangelical church dictated how they spend their weekends.

On completing the door frames David moved the tuck box and bandsaw into the living area of the house which would serve as a workshop, using Robin's old car for transport to the building that looked out towards Brandywine Bay. David's designs had to accommodate limited machinery and the three quarter inch ready dressed Fijian hardwood that he laminated if extra thickness was required. But he was excited at the opportunity to develop new works which he presented in perspective drawings. Although Robin's taste was classical, after some discussion David's appealing designs won the day. Use of a car gave us a new freedom and we often drove the twisting road over to Tortola's northern coast with the children chanting,

"Up the mountain, up the mountain," gathering momentum for their ultimate, *"Up the mountain to the TOP!"* On summiting we briefly snaked along the island's spine before descending to the mantra, *"Down the mountain, down the mountain, down the mountain,"* until the jungle gave way to the garland of coloured shacks that adorned the beach of Cane Garden Bay. Then the release of tumbling in the waves, before filling our bellies with chips and cocktails from a beach bar, sharing space with Rastas and slender girls wearing scraps of clothing. Then relishing the ease of transport we drove home with the pulsing reggae and kids chatter subsiding into sleep.

One afternoon we visited Robin and Diana who were staying in an exotic house on a high ridge. An open Indonesian style roof allowed cool breezes to blow through rooms that featured the raw landscape. A waterfall gushed over a colossal granite boulder before flowing through the building and into a clifftop swimming pool with a water-slide. The shoot culminated in a terrifying moment as the victim was propelled into the sky, seemingly destined to end that ride of a lifetime in one fell swoop, then at that moment of enlightenment, one hit the surface of yet another pool. Sam and Billy repeated the sensation again and again; setting a precedent for their university years when they would jump from waterfalls or hurtle down sand dunes, riding a wooden plank. After measuring the height of the dune and timing their trajectory, William calculated they had reached up to seventy kilometres per hour. But his sums were flawed when he dived from a Las Vegas hotel balcony into a shallow swimming pool – an antic that marked the end of William's adolescence with a broken nose that caused him severe sinus problems during his early years of freediving.

The sensual humidity of the Caribbean complemented our intensity and we cast off our inhibitions as easily as one sheds unnecessary clothes on a sunny day. Tortola's nirvana was light years from Northumberland's homespun ways, and when David wrote an article for the Hexham Courant I imagined how our new life must appear to those farmer-folk whose days were spent dagging and dragging sheep from dykes and ditches. We had no regrets, *every little thing was gonna be alright*, and although we spent that hurricane season ready to seek sanctuary in the mangroves, the summer passed without event, unlike the previous year when boats had taken cover thirteen times. The only storm was on my birthday when, for a treat, we had sailed over for a meal at the Peter Island hotel. When the staff insisted the children sleep in the lounge we danced on, my orange dress fluttering like a hibiscus in the wind that rustled the palms. The rain lashed down but the kids were snug inside, watching their first movie, *Singing in the Rain,* with an uncontained excitement. And when the hotel invited us all for a hurricane dinner, the occasion was not wasted on Sam and Billy who gregariously ate through course after course until they were fit to burst.

Christmas, our only opportunity to overhaul Hornpipe, unfortunately coincided with David's mother's visit. Her news from home was of my Granny Starr who had died just weeks before, and as I reflected on this wisp of a woman who had been born in 1900 I realised my parents were finally alone. Sid Starr, like other survivors of trench warfare, had been unable to share his experiences and his wife Ida, had a lonely life. On my departure for Jamaica her question, *"Do they have the same moon and stars as us?"* had indicated the Caribbean was as incomprehensible to her as life on Mars and, sadly, our generation's ease of communication arrived too late to liberate her isolation. Having survived two world wars in a century of dramatic change, Ida despised anything old, and within her frugal means she replaced wood with plastic, nylon in preference to wool. I recalled how, as a small child left in her care, she had rubbed my body slick with the cod liver oil that it was intended I swallow. Later, on my mother's insistence, I visited my grandparents as they watched sport on the grey box; cheering gangs of men chasing a ball, boxers punching within a roped square. If they had shared their stories I would have been drawn into conversation, but war was deemed cruel, family history too personal, so I answered their questions and ate their chocolates, pocketing the silver coins they pressed into my palm. But I had pondered Granny's revelation that her family had prevented her wandering the Cheddar hills. Had she been an independent spirit, a young girl like me? I had never given enough thought to Granny when she was alive and now that she was gone there were many unanswered questions.

While Hornpipe languished in the Virgin Gorda haul out yard precariously propped on wooden chocks, we lived on board, surrounded by an ocean of grass. Without the luxury of water, it was excruciatingly hot and inconvenient. Gran sat knitting on the beach, watching over Sam and Billy, while David and I worked, perched atop oil drums, holding the heavy grinders overhead. As we cut through the toxic layers of paint, abrasive grit scoured our skin while the screeching disc assailed our ears and severed our connection with the real. We kept going, fearful that high humidity or rain would result in a bad job; that somewhere far from land we could suffer the consequences. When the exposed metal revealed extensive craters and bubbles oozing a chemical discharge, we learned the steel acne was electrolysis, that stray electric currents had cannibalised Hornpipe's hull. After agonising on how to slow the corrosion we decided to bolt four zinc anodes to her keel in hopes the softer sacrificial metal would provide a solution. Finally, we painted the raw steel with thick layers of epoxy, and as the powerful fumes blurred our focus we raced to keep up with the setting times accelerated by the sweltering temperature. Then we coated the underwater area with anti-foul to deter barnacles and weed, and at last the rolling crane lifted and lowered Hornpipe into the Caribbean Sea.

Proud of our gleaming yacht, relieved the job was over, we set sail with Gran watching from the aft seat. Under her gaze we always goofed up and on the familiar passage from Necker Island to Virgin Gorda we misjudged and briefly went up on the coral. Despite this being a first, Gran added our cock up to her list. Her inability to relate to our lifestyle made me wish my parents could have the pleasure of visiting their grandsons in a setting that would remind them of Bermuda. I was dreaming. My mother's claustrophobia prohibited her from flying. She had never learned to swim, but my dad had spent his childhood in Malta and a sepia photograph of my grandfather, clad in swim trunks, portrayed his family's love of the sun and sea. In turn my father had introduced his daughter to swimming at the municipal pool. My favourite moments were spent diving under, into fluid tranquillity, and on returning to the bathers splashing on the surface, those three metres intoxicated me with a sense of achievement that was sustained by my mother's green ginger wine. While I had ventured beyond I never imagined some twenty years later my children would transcend the ocean of bliss they had known before entering my world.

Sam and Billy's bunk at Hornpipe's peak was separated from the galley with a curtain we had salvaged from Redthorn Cottage. Billy had chosen the port side, Sam starboard, sleeping with a family of toy animals at their feet, bathed in a breeze from a canvas scoop that directed air through the interior. Drawers beneath the bunks contained their few clothes, and shelves overhead held much read books. After my kindergarten day I was all used up so David read bedtime stories from *Tintin, Asterix, Swallows and Amazons, The Lord of the Rings,* and many more. They sat with their backs against the slatted door of the anchor locker where fathoms of chain lay in clanking coils. Sounds precipitate images, and this was how *The Man with the Long Nose* came to be. The children believed they heard him rattling in the creepy locker, sensed him stealing through the galley, elongating to skulk inside the mast. On still nights they heard his groan and when the wind blew, *The Man with the Long Nose* leaped through the rigging, clanging as he flew. Who knows why he had chosen to haunt us but I recall the silent scream of a child who, paralysed for fear of the witch in the wardrobe, spent her nights in fear that even a thought might betray her presence.

David and I were drinking *piña coladas* at a beach bar when he asked me to visualise a bed for Diana and Robin. My childhood fantasies of sleeping in a four-poster condensed into the scribble I drew on a paper serviette. That dream would one day come true, meanwhile I was content with an extension to the width of our bunk, a tiny fan that created just enough breeze. Knowing that his patrons' romantic bed would demand all his experience and strength, David seized on the concept of curving pillars sweeping up to a central circle. When he began laminating the Fijian yucca into four great posts it was inconceivable that the chunky wooden assemblage, bristling with clamps and oozing glue, could ever become an item of furniture. But David loved a challenge and knew exactly what he was doing. He had begun his self-taught apprenticeship turning bowls on a lathe, progressing to replicating hundreds of spindles and spokes for spinning wheels, starting to make furniture when the process became boring. After constructing the bed posts David turned them on a lathe at a local workshop, shaping sinuous curves and rounding the bases into elegant spheres. Only David could have devised and produced the masterpiece of contemporary furniture that he wrote of in his journal, *"The act of creation must be an instinctive one and an accumulation of experiences and spiritual wisdom."*

The following April, Robin and Diana set off for Antigua's Race Week leaving us to look after Matthew and their house with its ocean vista, pillars, and vaulted roof that resembled a Greek villa. While the living area remained David's workshop, there were plans for furnishing it with a dark yucca to complement the kitchen's benches, cupboards, and drawers he had finished with a honey coloured Fijian kauri. The glorious bed filled a room that opened to a central courtyard, swimming pool, and jacuzzi. But where did Matthew sleep? There was no evidence of his existence. Then Diana led me past the pools down a steep flight of steps to where Matthew slept in a converted bathroom. On telling me that if Matthew woke in the night he knew where to find her I was too shocked to respond. I resolved to talk to Diana later and in the meantime I filled the tiny room with mattresses, instructing the kids that if any of them woke in the night they must all shout loudly and wait for me to come.

Diana had told us that after years in the tropics Robin was immune to the mosquitoes that multiplied in the water tanks. Sure enough, before dawn on our first day, we heard their whining drone and felt savage stabs as, despite cowering beneath the sheets, they inserted their proboscises through the weave, into our flesh. We abandoned ourselves to the debauchery of flopping in the jacuzzi before breakfast and amidst the fun of propelling Billy across the pool he suddenly swam by himself. Matthew thrived on family life with two brothers and Prue and I staged a kindergarten summer camp in nearby Brandy Wine Bay, cooking, tie dying, and clay modelling with the kids while their mothers lazed by the pool.

On our return to Hornpipe we moved to a seemingly safe mooring in the mangroves until one morning when we saw a boat drifting towards us with black smoke billowing from its deck. While I hastily shifted the gas bottle, David leapt into the dinghy and it was then that a boatman appeared with a rope that they tied to the burning hulk. After towing the flaming wreck into the bay it sunk beneath the waves and we thanked our lucky stars that fire had left us unscathed for a second time. All was peaceful until the local disco got going. At midnight the children woke screaming as a visceral boom roared through the boat, rattling the rigging, throbbing in our chests, prompting Friday escapes to islands where the waves soothed our sleep. On exploring Tortola's northern flanks we could not resist anchoring off a tiny sand cay, a cartoon desert island with a single palm tree. Swimming ashore we frolicked in the waves as they lapped against that minimal land form; the sensual sea and guaranteed solitude favouring us with an afternoon of irresistible intimacy.

The island of St John became a favourite destination. We walked the coast to the newly constructed Mongoose Junction with its enticing cafes and shady verandas that referenced the traditional Caribbean style. On one occasion Roger the Rogue invited us to an open-air performance of chamber music, generously risking the children's interruptions. However, they listened enthralled by the sounds and the sight of the sun setting over the sea. Having heard there were pre-Columbian petroglyphs on Saint John's eastern side we sailed for Saltpond Bay to follow a maze of tracks to rocky outcrops where the Taino people had etched their images. Sam led us home, intuitively aware of his surroundings, choosing the correct direction at every fork of the trail. We awoke to devotional voices drifting over the water and saw that a congregation had gathered for a beach service. Music moved us beyond earthly things and it seemed that living in harmony with nature made us more receptive. Vivaldi or Bach accompanied breakfast and as I practised yoga on Hornpipe's curving deck, my spirit soared with Faure's *Stabat Mater*. While we painted, Stravinsky's *Pulcinella* pirouetted about the anchorage, forever bonding his music to that time and place. I recall leaving Billy alone on Hornpipe and rowing home to the glorious crescendo of a Beethoven symphony to find him listening, completely entranced.

When Monday dawned we woke with the sun to sail back to Road Town for work and school. Keeping up appearances was challenging, especially when Sam, who was too busy talking to think, walked into the harbour. And then we were offered a small luxury that made a big difference. When the yacht broker who had tried to sell us Molly Bloom offered us the use of his shower, I wondered whether guilt had prompted his gesture. Or was it a bribe to counter our knowledge of his immoral assessment? Situated in a remote area of the dock, the shower was both clean and private, and as the abundant water splashed over me I felt reborn. Then something distracted my indulgence. Focusing beyond the frothing water I met the curious gaze of two black guys peering around the door, inches away. An ear-splitting shriek erupted from the depth of my primordial being, a howl that ricocheted around the tiled room, projecting them into the narrow alley beyond. Slamming the door I re-locked it, for what that was worth. And as I gathered my wits they shouted, *"Whyat oooman, we gon come bak in der an fuk yoh nah! Whyat laydee we gon get yoh!"*

Having already opened the door they could do so again! What could I do? No one would hear my shouts and I was trapped in the tiled room, a sitting duck! With each lurid threat, their bravado built. My mind raced at survival speed. An escape in the dinghy would be too slow. There was only one option. Grabbing my towel, I quietly turned the key. In a breath, I slipped out and bolted down the alley, bursting into the pub, wearing just a towel. To the barflies, I was just another drama queen. After a glance, they resumed stories of another boring day in paradise, yellowed fingers clutching listless fags, flaccid arms with beer-can extensions. They barely missed a drag or swig on my account, so why was I ashamed of my dishevelled appearance, as if I had invented the whole thing? The guys were found, skulking in the alley, and I was told they had been reprimanded, that they were "*Usually good boys!*" I was escorted to the boat and it was only later I wondered what would have happened if I hadn't screamed so loud and run so fast.

After the shower episode the broker offered us a dock berth and ran a telephone connection to Hornpipe. While stepping from the boat onto the wharf was convenient it was one step closer to a vacuous society that lacked the integrity to enjoy their days in the sun. David continued crafting furniture, but his enthusiasm had waned and what had once been rewarding seemed superficial, "*The mindless hours of sanding and finishing hold little for me, whereas I get excited working out on paper new ideas and designs.*" Robin and Diana needed their home for themselves, so David moved back into the little workshop behind the clinic, and although his skills were way beyond a local's capabilities his days were tainted with concerns about working illegally. Then something happened that increased our anxiety. I was visiting David when a skinny black girl came running up the steep street and before I knew it she had caught hold of my arm and pierced me with desperate eyes, whispering "*Help me, hide me, help me please.*" In a flash, Tattersall's gardener, Clarence, was there, the girl's hand in his as he dragged her into the undergrowth beyond the workshop. Clarence returned, looked us in the eye, calculated our silence as, in that moment a police Land Rover screeched around the corner and came to a halt. Four burly officers jumped out and ran down into the clinic, up into the workshop, questioning, searching. While we loitered like tourists, Clarence faded into the scenery, then, fearful of becoming involved, David locked up and we walked home together. Next day he learned that the girl had arrived illegally on a cargo boat, that Clarence had smuggled her home in his car. After brightening Clarence's nights, she moved on, but when Diana's cleaning girl heard the story she added, "*Dat boy's disgustin yo nah!*"

Illegal immigrants sometimes surfaced as they worked their way along the chain of Caribbean islands towards a better life. The underclass of Puerto Rico aspired towards a future in the Virgin Islands, Santo Domingans dreamed of moving to Puerto Rico, and a Haitian's only hope was escape to Santo Domingo. Haiti's resources had been pillaged for easy profit, her land destroyed by erosion while her starving people paid the ultimate price to immoral nations who exploit those at the bottom of the food chain. In equal measure, wealthy British, American, and European citizens who avoided paying taxes for their countries' schools and hospitals had generated a social climate that made cheating acceptable. The economy of the British Virgin Islands was founded on corrupt practice, with Tortola a modern day *Treasure Island*, profiteering from managing the money of greedy investors and tax evaders. And while we grappled with the discomfort of working illegally, our accountant friends never considered how their overseas banking practices impacted on the poor and helpless.

Billy's party WT

Ten years before, while I was teaching in Jamaica, I visited Haiti and followed the Corpus Christi Carnival through the streets of Port-au-Prince. As I surfed a wave of revelry I marvelled at how safe I felt amidst that crowd of masked dancers never realising that this was a society sublimated by a dictator. The procession concluded with a huge bonfire, and as dawn flushed the sky those night demons shrivelled to ashes, to be reborn in my sculptures and teaching projects. Amidst Tortola's Christian festivals, reggae's subliminal message of sex and salvation reassured us that the Caribbean culture was alive and well. We dressed and paraded at Halloween, Billy becoming a clown, Sam a wizard, myself a black cat. I created pirate and superhero birthday parties and on celebrating Billy's third on Hornpipe's deck, I made a Hansel and Gretel cake decorated with coloured flowers. The event involved party games and the safe passage of his fourteen small friends, for despite Sam and Billy's extraordinary life I was determined they enjoy all the trappings of childhood. And though our children never demanded toys or a more comfortable life, my desire to give them everything is a demise of every parent.

Maybe the Caribbean Carnival inspired Sam's production of Shakespeare's *Henry V,* that he directed in the summer of the new millennium. His actors' extravagant costumes created from car parts referenced contemporary punk culture, with motor vehicles representing horses. The dramatic chorus metamorphosed into a rock band that pounded out Shakespeare's rhythmic phrases from a rampart of the multi-story carpark draped with flags emblazoned with the *Fleur De Lys* and *Union Jack.* William starring as a proud Dauphin with an Aryan shock of bleached hair, presented another opportunity to heroically rip off his shirt in a play rampant with brutal fights. Courtyard cobbles resonated to the ringing clash of metal and William addressed the Dauphin's stirring soliloquy in praise of his horse, to a revving motorbike, *"When I bestride him, I soar, I am a hawk.... It is a beast for Perseus. He is pure air and fire."* His front wheel pawed the ground before he roared away, epitomising the spectacular riot that went on tour, performing a dawn show outside the municipal park gates of New Zealand's Stratford. William's act paralleled his rebellious years, an era when he owned a car that was as battered as a tin can that had been kicked down the road, when the brothers inhabited a classical student flat where they held abandoned parties, climbing on the roof to sip cocktails, suspending themselves on wires that stretched over the street, sharing their lives in a nurturing relationship that Sam affectionately describes, *"Billy with his sports car dented and scraped. His many words of wisdom to a dumb brother who always goes out with the wrong girl. Billy the fantastic flatmate, brilliant actor, and loving brother."*

David completed an enormous table and twelve chairs for Robin and Diana and they took advantage of our presence with a trip to Europe. Matthew's cot had been moved into an alcove outside their bedroom, but while in residence we laid out a huge mattress in the vaulted dining room and one evening David sat with his arms around the children reading from *Where the Wild Things Are.* Three golden heads clustered together eagerly anticipating his words, *"So let the wild rumpus begin,"* at which they would bounce on the bed, shrieking with joy. All of a sudden the phone rang, *"Hi Linda, it's Diana, how's it goin'? How's my little boy?"* *"He's doing fine,"* I said, *"would you like to talk to Matthew?"* I passed the phone to a happy little boy, but the minute he heard Diana's disembodied voice speaking from a city an ocean away, he flipped. His Mom was unbearably out of reach. And as Matthew sobbed inconsolably I tried to tell Diana that her son had been perfectly happy, that these were his only tears in three weeks of fun.

Near the end of our time in the house, our friend Marilyn arrived to find our circumstances an extreme contrast to the storm buffeted cottage where we had lived as peasants. She wrote in her journal, *"This place is like something out of a Hollywood movie. Dave and Linda are looking after this house for the owners and being paid for this as well as caring for their little boy Matthew. Billy and Sam are really beautiful children. Met Linda at the school – working there in the heat must be a test of endurance. I feel so wiped out and lethargic in the heat all the time. This evening Linda made an enormous paella after which I insisted she refrain from washing up and I said rather blatantly, 'Dave and I will do it' which was clearly me taking a dig at Dave since he's done no cooking or wash up since I've been here. I immediately found myself feeling guilty typically enough. I'm sure he feels he has other things to do at times like varnishing furniture or cleaning the swimming pool. I know that on their voyage it seemed difficult for Dave to take equal share of cooking because of pressure of work on the boat. I'm probably too quick to be judgmental about how other people organise their lives and Linda doesn't openly complain about this."*

On Robin and Diana's return we set off for Puerto Rico with Marilyn describing our altercations, *"A trip to Spanish Town to check out immigration. Dave nearly bust his hand trying to repair motor and Linda rowed off in a huff. Things a bit gloomy. However, we all cheered up as we left with beautifully gentle winds for a night sail to Culebra, off Puerto Rico. This was not to last long. A dreadful swell was met as we got out to the open channel. A sudden urge to go to bed overcame me, but I was awake to hear Linda take over Dave's watch and her terrible struggle with sea sickness. I awaited my watch with fear and trembling as the motion in the cabin was making me feel horrible even lying down. When it came, it was not as bad as I'd feared but general sickness came in constant waves. Just gripped the wheel legs firmly apart and stared at the compass trying to avoid looking at the heaving grey swell looming up and down all around boat. In fact, worst thing was keeping eyes open. My first real seasickness so think I've started to overcome fear of it just a little. Dave made breakfast - a heroic deed as the motion was still appalling."* Hiring a car in Puerto Rico, we visited the tropical rainforest of El Yunque where a lonely local invited us into his mildewed house to drink beer and discuss the constant rainfall. Clouds blanketed the valley as we drove up through forests of giant trees that disappeared into the mist, their trunks clad in mosses, shrouded with epiphytes. There was an artistry in the shafts of sunshine that painted the leaves and ferns with an emerald glow. A musical harmony in the piping tree frogs and perpetual rain. The children jumped in puddles, opened their greedy mouths to drink of the jewelled droplets, and when our hearts were soothed and sanctified we drove on.

After a stop at the antique remains of walled gardens and cobbled courtyards of the Taino, we drove across the dry plains of Caguana and it was already late when we inquired about a place to stay. We were met with blank stares until at last a positive response saw us following a shuffling proprietor along a dismal corridor to a nest of filthy rooms and old mattresses. I tried to forget those Jamaican hotels, with their crisp white linen and views over the turquoise sea. Although it was a trivial desire I longed for my children to enjoy that luxury and had bought them new pyjamas for the occasion. Following our adventure, we sailed back to Tortola for Marilyn's departure that led her to write, *"Billy and Sam seemed genuinely sad I was going. I adore them and will miss them badly. Billy gave me wonderful kisses as I left, and Sam was all morose. We joked a lot about them coming in my bag etc. Linda and I had a long chat about trials and tribulations of living on boat, assertiveness, and sexism."*

Marilyn's observations were valid, however the challenges of living afloat demanded that David and I worked at what we knew best. Our unsolvable issues went underground to emerge later and when Prue revealed that she was pregnant I was offered the option of running the kindergarten, matched by Tortola Joinery inviting David to become manager of their machine shop. Though tempted he believed that we would find work in other places, that having broken free to sail the world it made no sense to stop half way *"My real relationship with this nature/life is a creative one, it has to be used. I wish to celebrate beauty and life and not to do so would be a sin against myself and life itself."* We had accumulated funds to last until Australia and I knew we should take advantage of that hard-won independence, but whenever I thought of the long passages ahead I was filled with dread. I never mentioned this to David but he must have known my unspoken fear. I knew he would be horrified if I voiced my fantasy of splurging on a trip to *Mickey Land*, the fabled Disney World of Billy's dearly loved mouse. And while David longed for the open ocean, the challenge of making landfalls in new places, I wished only for Sam and Billy's happiness and safety.

Over the months of preparation I completed a quilt of fabrics from garments I had worn when pregnant and adapted Sam's cot cover into a wall hanging that filled our cabin with memories. David made a more effective tiller and wind vane that cleared the cockpit of cluttered ropes, but our biggest task was replacing the corroded water tanks. Despite aluminium being associated with Alzheimer's disease it was the only affordable material and somehow we squeezed the new drums through the hatch and into the bilges. Remembering Billy's nail incident David set up a ham radio for long distance two-way conversations, and I attended a First Aid course and purchased a do-it-yourself book featuring horrific photographs of emergency operations. David took up Robin's offer of operating on his appendix. Unlike my ragged scar that gave the impression a knife thrower had aimed, missed, and had another go at removing the acute gangrenous appendix that almost claimed me at thirteen years, David's cut rapidly faded to a delicate wrinkle. Doctor Tattersall generously amassed a supply of medications labelled with precise instructions, and along with those essentials that saved the day on numerous occasions, we remain eternally grateful for the opportunities Robin gave us. On hearing that Queen Elizabeth had awarded him an OBE for services to the British Virgin Islands in *Surgery, International Yachting, and Community Work*, we agreed the honour was well deserved.

David and I needed to find crew but tales of boats being stolen for drug smuggling made us wary. Most victims were thrown overboard, where they simply disappeared, however a friend had survived to tell his story. After becoming suspicious of his crew he managed to check the couple's gear before setting sail, and to his horror he found duplicate copies of the boat's ownership along with his passport, faked with the man's photograph. On deciding that an advert in the British Yachting Monthly would be a safer option we stated that in addition to sailing, our crew must be willing to share domestic chores, child care and expenses. Marilyn met with two serious applicants and felt so positive about Helen that, when the more experienced man backed down, we decided to manage with her alone.

When I suggested to Sam that we go to school to farewell his teacher he was scared the headmistress would punish him, so I went alone to pick up his books and accept Miss Bowrey's present. She cried on hearing of Sam's fear but sometime later he wrote her a bubbly letter about his adventures with sharks. Then, just before Christmas, the new kindergarten teachers took command, destroying the boat and playhouse, fencing the children like zoo animals. While Prue and I had treated those kids with love and respect, wiped their bottoms, dried their tears, they had empowered me to teach again. For, on returning from Jamaica, my attempts at controlling the street-smart London pupils had resulted in humiliating lessons when crayon warfare took over. Following the ineffectual principal's suggestion that the PE teacher deal with problem kids in the boxing ring I managed alone. My heart reached out to my suffering students, a wafer-thin girl whose mother refused her food, the African boy who cowered beneath the table after nights walking the streets for fear of a drunken stepfather. And when a vicious girl yelled, "*What's the point of doing wot you say, our last teacher went mad, the one before topped 'erself; 'ow long you going to last?*" I said, "*As long as it takes!*" But I knew that projects using craft knives might cost more than pride, and at the end of that heroic year I accepted a transfer to a supportive school. There my students painted friezes and sculpted life-sized figures and I established my reputation as an innovative, inspiring teacher.

With Robin's house complete, David found a job converting a fishing boat into an outdoor bar for a Virgin Gorda resort. The children played as he worked and we often borrowed the resort's Boston whaler to buzz over the waves to Necker Island where a mansion was being constructed. As we gazed over the sparkling sea we imagined how it would be to live and work there, making furniture for Richard Branson. However Hornpipe was wasted swinging on her anchor, so we finalised our plans and celebrated New Year of 1984 at the Bitter End Bar, never realising this was the first link in a chain of events. When the throbbing reggae beat roused Bouncer, he dropped ashore to where guys with spidery hair were grooving a move. "*Dey man, am Rastafari*" the locals said. "*Wonky webs,*" quipped Bouncer and then he saw Linda's bizarre black hair, "*Natty dreads!*" he cried, "*She da goddess, I'm sailin wid da ship!*" And so it was that our stoned spider committed to yet another ocean passage on the good ship Hornpipe, bound for the South Pacific.

LOW IN THE WATER

"Full fathom five thy father lies,
Of his bones are coral made:
Those are pearls that were his eyes,
Nothing of him that doth fade,
But doth suffer a sea-change
Into something rich and strange
Sea-nymphs hourly ring his knell.
Hark now I hear them, ding-dong, bell."

Ariel's song from The Tempest, William Shakespeare

On the twenty-fourth of January Hornpipe crept away from Tortola, avoiding customs for fear of being charged duty. Following a last night at St John's we continued to Red Hook, St Thomas, where David swung the compass while we visited Coral World marine park, the children running from tank to tank talking to the captive fishes, reading aloud astounding facts about their underwater world. As always, they were inseparable, Billy doing his best to keep up with Sam, so that on a first encounter their sun-bleached hair and lithe bodies gave them the appearance of twins.

We sailed for Culebra with David and I managing to pole the jib ourselves, finding time for an afternoon of windsurfing before sailing on through a powerful wind with black squalls. It was a relief to drift on a gentle evening breeze into Fajardo's Isleta marina, and while I prepared a welcoming dinner, David travelled out to Puerto Rico's San Juan airport to meet our crew. But as he scanned the arrivals he saw no one to match Helen's photograph. When a middle-aged woman with tight curls constrained in a headscarf confronted him with a, *"Hello, are you looking for someone?"* David's heart sank. Helen's haughty stance had blinded him to her presence and as he loaded her three bags and two huge suitcases into the taxi he tried to hide his foreboding.

Maybe it was Helen's air of entitlement that gave her away, indicated she always came first. Once she had filled the spare bunk and wardrobe with more clothes than the sum of all our personal possessions, Helen told us about herself; how, after raising two sons, she had bravely seized this opportunity to change her life. While we ate, Helen questioned the idea of a cooking rota when, *"Opening a tin of sardines is quick and cheap."* And why share food expenses when she was helping our family to sail around the world? As for the children, Helen had been there and done that. And so it went; on and on. Our advert and letters stating our expectations had been ignored. Helen's correspondence communicating her willingness to accept our terms and embrace a family's cruising experience had been a sham. This was our first discussion and things were unravelling; what would Helen be like at sea? Maybe she had believed this trip would open the door to her new life, had chosen to ignore our conditions, thinking, *"I will cross that bridge when I come to it!"* David and I lay in bed urgently whispering, finally deciding that whatever Helen's reasons for misleading us, we must honour our part of the agreement.

Fortunately, the haul out was routine, just a few worrying patches where the previous paint had not adhered, and after covering them with epoxy pitch we primed and finished off Hornpipe's hull with anti-foul. Meanwhile Sam and Billy were exploring their surroundings and on hearing the dock workers speak Spanish they tried to imitate what they thought was a gobbledygook language. The security guard *Policeman Looey* laughed when we explained what was happening and maybe our kids would have learned through this method for they both went on to master several languages. But communicating with Helen was not so easy, with every conversation a confrontation.

After locating the best supermarket, we caught a bus and rode a wave of hyperactive Puerto Rican music to Fajardo's *Cash and Carry*, to find that prices were considerably less than the Virgin Islands. So began our biggest shopping expedition ever with Sam and Billy racing around, filling a stack of boxes. That afternoon we hitched out of town in search of nutritious wholemeal flour and brown rice, discovering traditional Spanish snacks of corn nuts rolled in chilli, sesame bars in gooey syrup. After buying enough food for a year we wondered how we would ever eat it all. The following day two trucks arrived and the fun began as we piled boxes on the foredeck, where the children gleefully ripped them apart, tearing off labels with gusto, while a bikini clad Helen worked on her suntan while marking tins which David and I listed and stowed. On discovering yet more bilge space I returned to the supermarket, to total an expenditure of two thousand five hundred dollars. Throughout the preparations, Helen had challenged every action. She described herself as a *"liberated woman,"* however it appeared her source of empowerment was taking advantage of us. Her stubborn nature wore us down and while I suspect that she considered David *an easy push over*, me an *up-tight bitch*, we had no alternative but to take her to Panama. Going it alone was too dangerous to contemplate and Helen's attitude might improve on the way.

Finally, our freshly galvanised anchor chain was delivered and after filling with water and fuel we farewelled friends and motored to Isleta marina, resolving to never go shopping again. On Saturday February the eleventh we set sail, dodging the shoals of Vieques, and next day we broke new ground as we sailed along Puerto Rico's southern coast. Despite Hornpipe being four inches lower in the water, heavy seas, and thirty-five knot winds, she felt strong and stable, but following a tense week of arduous preparations, we were unprepared for ocean conditions. As a series of squalls hit, our downwind pace accelerated and having foolishly set off towing the dinghy we were unaware of exactly when it broke its painter. David instinctively realised its absence but scanning the wide ocean stretching to the hazy shores of Puerto Rico appeared futile. At last we located the slightest deviation amongst the waves and as David manned the sails I steered while Helen stood at Hornpipe's stern pointing towards that blip. Dropping canvas, we looped around to retrace our path and follow a man overboard procedure. But where was the dinghy? Helen had become disoriented and lost sight of it. Amidst the distractions David's sense of direction had prevailed and after spotting the floundering hull we maintained a more vigilant watch, and as Hornpipe came near I leapt into the sea and swam a rope to the upturned hull. The event illuminated the trials of locating and retrieving an object at sea, that despite the advantages of landmarks, a full crew, and fair weather, we had almost lost out. With a sigh of relief, we anchored behind the mangroves of Bahia de Jobos where David took a break from arguments about who did what, clearing his head as he flew over the waves on the windsurfer.

The following day we motored up to Salinas where David bought a fisherman's anchor while I tried to locate someone to blitz our cockroaches. After a long sleep, we sailed fifty miles along the coast, running under a poled jib, with the dinghy safely stowed on deck. The narrow entrance through the reef into La Parguera was reputedly difficult and though I had more faith in Obelix than wind power, when David said, *"With this wind we should be able to sail into the harbour!"* it was too late to argue. While we habitually sailed to maintain a readiness for mechanical failures we were ominously close and despite wanting to play it safe I nervously acquiesced. Helen's inexperience rendered her inept so I helmed while David adjusted the sails and once through I was pleased with myself; until next time!

David had rowed ashore in a search of fresh fruit and vegetables when two men in suits identified themselves as drug-detectives, and requested to come on board. He was justifiably anxious for although we had no interest in drugs we had heard of stuff being planted, that in American territory a boat could be impounded and its owners imprisoned if the smallest amount of ganja was found. The detectives said they had become suspicious of Hornpipe's movements when we made a number of stops after clearing customs in Fajardo. As we talked the children played and they eventually left, after extracting a token penalty to justify their time. We had anchored in a breezy spot beside an enclosed bay, renowned for its phosphorescent plankton that thrive in waters fringed with mangroves. Motoring into the still circle the dinghy gently rocked and as the ripples dispersed the darkness intensified and we saw that our oars were coated with sparkling star dust. Swimming at night was questionable so I waited as David slipped into the water to dive beneath the silken surface and reappear as a comet, streaming with shimmering incandescence. The children clambered overboard, floated, clutching the dinghy, before launching loose with thrashing limbs to fly through the water, their bodies glistening with stars, illuminated in ethereal light. Then David indicated that it was my time to venture into the limpid liquid, to dive beneath that cosmic ocean as a moonbeam in the glittering night, and when the mosquitos took over we returned to Hornpipe.

The following day we set sail for Mona Island that conveniently lay

on our route to Santo Domingo
and Panama. The weather in the
notorious Mona Passage might allow
us to anchor beside the limestone
island that had been inhabited by
the *Taino* and *Arawak* people; had
heard that stone tools dated three
thousand years BC had been found.
Once David had rigged the Aries
directly to Hornpipe's new wooden
tiller, the self-steering took over, and
by five o'clock we were anchored

Sam LT

off Mona Island. When the island ranger motored out to suggest that
we would find it safer inside the reef we complied, and despite David's
doubts, motored into the narrow entrance only to realise the folly. It was
only Hornpipe's capacity to turn in her own length that saved her, when,
after bashing coral on every side, we withdrew. The following day David
rowed ashore with me swimming alongside the overcrowded dinghy to
avoid straining a faulty rowlock. And on hearing the children's discussion
on the probabilities of me being eaten by a shark, and Sam's optimistic
comment that it didn't matter, *"Because we've got Helen now!"* it seemed Sam
had figured that life would be easier without his mother telling him what
to do. But this was not the reassurance I needed.

On landing, Helen wandered away and we set off along a trail under
the crumbling cliffs when to Sam's delight he spotted a large cavern,
and while we relished the shade and admired the stalactites he crawled
through the tunnels searching for skeletons and goblins. Although the
island's interior remained frequented by five foot iguanas and wild boar,
we saw only goats and when the novelty of exploring caves wore off we
returned to where a group of Puerto Rican hunters were drinking away
the afternoon beneath the casuarina trees. The children ran ahead to
introduce themselves, *"My name's Billy and I live on that boat,"* and the hunters
suggested we join them, commenting that they hadn't believed their eyes
when they saw someone swimming ashore, *"Through all the sharks!"* That
on realising it was a girl they figured that, *"A shark would never bite a beautiful
woman!"* No one realised how much I needed their compliment.

In the diminishing light we saw Hornpipe rolling in the heaving swells, swinging in the gusts. But despite thinking that Helen would arrive at any minute there was no sign of her. Our yacht looked so far away and as the day faded we wondered how we would get home before dark. Mona Island stood alone in hundreds of miles of ocean and we were afraid of the consequences if an offshore wind got up as it often did at dusk. We didn't trust the holding ground and feared that at any moment we might see Hornpipe slide away. It would be dangerous rowing the overloaded dinghy through the pass to the open ocean, where if the wind proved too strong, we could be swept away. Surely Helen must have heard our shouts, seen us searching. At last she appeared, sauntering along the beach, saying that she had fallen asleep, unaware of how late it was. Then, despite our fears, we had no choice but to row out through the pass, David bending to the oars while I prayed the rowlock would hold. Expending all his strength he slowly clawed the dinghy upwind through the deepening darkness and somehow we reached Hornpipe, drunkenly wallowing in the heaving swell. We clambered on board, overcome with relief. David's arms burned with the arduous rowing, we were emotionally drained, but our family was safe.

While it was irresponsible to delay us after dark in an exposed anchorage we could not blame Helen for being ignorant of this. However, her stubborn defiance made it inevitable that other situations would occur. Despite concerns that the strengthening wind and rising swell might force a night departure, we slept and sailed for Santo Domingo the following morning. Just four miles into the trip the wind ceased forcing us to return for another rolling night by the beach before embarking on a gentle cruise when we sighted our first whales, and hooked a ferocious barracuda that we ate despite our fears its flesh might be poisonous. As the sun set we rounded Saona Island, off the southeast tip of the Dominican Republic, and from there we sailed west through a peaceful night to enter Santo Domingo harbour the following afternoon. It was obvious that cruising yachts seldom visited the filthy commercial port, but Helen, who had spent the trip sunning herself in her rainbow bikini, appeared oblivious to her surroundings. Her scanty attire was culturally insensitive and as five uniformed customs officers wearing hobnailed boots clambered over Hornpipe's rails, David told Helen to get dressed. When they departed a gang of security guards with shotguns and rifles gathered to stare through the windows; there was no escaping the intimidating sound of them hissing to attract my attention.

Over the previous days, as David and I worked and sailed, Helen had watched with an air of superiority. Her refusal to help clear up after the trip resulted in a blazing argument. When the urge to throw Helen, her luggage, and Barbra Streisand tapes off the boat abated, we resolved to tolerate her company as far as Panama, from where she could fly home or board a boat bound for Tahiti. Though she could afford alternative options, we dreaded sailing alone. We wondered how Helen had fooled Marilyn's circumspection and why the experienced yachtsman had backed out after their meeting. Had he looked into Helen's cold eyes and known he could not endure another minute in her presence?

Helen went her own way, leaving us alone to explore Santo Domingo's decaying villas with their encrustations of limestone and stucco that had been the capital of the Caribbean. Since Columbus first claimed Hispaniola for Spain, the island had passed through the hands of the British, French, pirate bands, and rebellious slaves, to eventually be divided into Haiti to the west and the Dominican Republic to the east. Within a massive stone museum we discovered relics of an era of conquistadors, of history portrayed as a lie, romanticised horrors beyond compare. However, the armour, galleons, and pieces of eight had awakened the children's curiosity and my memories. That thrill of rubbing shoulders with Egyptian mummies, a bronze Degas of a little ballerina alongside a fossilised pterodactyl incarcerated in a rock. Of how I had walked Leicester's sunken pavements imagining Roman soldiers marching into our damp land, unknowingly stepped over the secretly buried remains of England's last Plantagenet king when boarding the bus to Cosby.

One afternoon I took Sam and Billy to Santo Domingo's zoo, wandering the parkland looking at animals that were contained in compounds surrounded by deep ditches. David had remained to catch up on jobs and after enlisting an eager lad for the task of filling our gas bottle he ticked it off his list. Shortly after, the boy returned with a customs officer who revealed that a permit was necessary before the gas bottle could leave the harbour. So David set off on a trail through Santo Domingo's flag-hung corridors of power, passed from one bureaucrat to another. Letters were typed, stamped, and signed, hours ground by as he stood in queues at the pleasure of other officials who, shaking their heads, sent him in diverse directions. David longed for the process to reach any conclusion, and finally, after three typed letters and the signing of as many forms as one would deem necessary to purchase a house, the gas bottle was permitted to pass through the gates of the port. Eventually, when the entire afternoon had been taken up with this first-hand glimpse into the frustrations of Dominican life, the farce concluded. Now, all that David had to do was to find an establishment able to fill the bottle with gas.

That evening while enjoying dinner in a little cafe with red gingham tablecloths, we met an interesting couple. Beatrice, a French sculptor, and Jose, a Dominican painter, invited us into the jungle of their creativity. The paint splattered courtyard, penthouse, and rooftop was alive with forgotten colours and textures, peopled with Beatrice's plaster figures. As we talked art, sailing, and Santo Domingo we began to feel sane and when they invited us on a trip into the countryside we postponed our departure. The following day we drove north through rolling pastures and fields of sugar cane that had been forest a decade before. On stopping to wander a path beneath tall trees that shaded a scattering of huts, the locals directed us to where an old woman sat in the doorway of her tiny house. Chickens roosted beneath the bed where she had slept all her nights and as she talked Jose interpreted and tried explaining where we came from. When he said that we lived on the ocean she asked, *"Is it as big as our river?"* She had never seen the ocean. That day we had travelled further than she had through her whole life and when Jose described what the ocean was to us she listened with interest. Then she blessed our passage across whatever she imagined that ocean to be.

Journeying on we stopped for a simple meal and swam in a river where a cluster of women were washing clothes. Two men on horseback offered us a ride and then David and I were cantering along a dusty road and into a sleepy village to be beset by a gaggle of grimy boys. Galloping away we left them with memories of the day the crazy gringos rode into town. After completing the wonderful day with a cheap cafe meal we returned to find a British container ship, the Norbrit Faith, docked behind Hornpipe. The crew welcomed new conversations and the children's playful ways. We were soon exchanging books, eating their food, filling the washing machine again and again. English accents sounded foreign in that incongruous setting and as the sailors became more and more drunk the cook insisted I accept egg powder, tins of herbs, and boxes of cake mix that came complete with weevils. The free provisions were graciously received, the speckled cakes didn't taste so bad and, after all, weevils were a traditional component of ship's tucker. It was interesting to observe the crew's cramped quarters devoid of windows or character; to realise their perspective of foreign lands and people were gleaned from the underbelly of the world. And although they had recently voyaged around South America, the company they kept and the commercial ports were much the same as any English dockyard.

Having given up on asking for Helen's help we had no option but to take Sam and Billy along on our trip to the market. Where the grand old building's pillars and arched roof portrayed the crumbling opulence of a bygone era, the beggars that crowded the market's stone steps conveyed a timeless poverty. A child hobbled on bandaged leprous limbs while another leered at Billy and Sam, his face convulsed in laughter. Averting my gaze from their sores I circled my arms around my children and sought refuge amidst the tables heaped with produce. David dashed away in search of fruit while I bought a box of vegetables, and taking up the vendor's offer I tucked Billy in his pushchair behind his stall. Sam remained as I joined a queue for ice cream, paid and returned. But where were the children? Billy's buggy seat hung slack and the stall holder opened his arms in an empty gesture. Of course, they would be with David.

When David appeared and I saw that he was alone my heart stopped in horror. Our children were gone, gone, gone! Desperately, feverishly, I darted this way and that, my heart throbbing as I ran hither and thither calling their names, scanning that underworld beneath the trestle tables where a child could become lost in labyrinthine layers of sacks and boxes. I thought I glimpsed their innocent faces amongst the forest of shoppers. Had they crawled under the crates of vegetables? Were they playing in the toppling pallets or behind the pillars marbled with grime? I imagined terrible scenarios. Could they have wandered into the street? A crowd obstructed my view, the humidity was nauseous, the crush intolerable, our search futile. Then, of a sudden, with the lightest touch, the boy with the laughing face caught my attention, gazing up at me, intelligent eyes in a face that was beyond his control. And, with gesticulations and incomprehensible mutterings he led the way, pushing through the crowd, ever in sight, just beyond reach. On nearing the entrance steps I heard trucks hoot in the street, and there on the filthy ground, at the still centre of that storm of hurrying bodies, was the boy with bandaged limbs. He was playing with Sam while beside him stood Billy, cradling his Mickey

Mouse, surrounded by even more ragged kids. Our children had made new friends, they didn't see the danger, disease, and dirt; the trailing hands of beggars reaching to touch their fresh faces. Sunshine illuminated the scene, dust particles shimmered gold in the gloom. Our eyes opened in humility and gratitude as in that brief glimpse of another world we forgot the separation between us and them.

That momentary lapse coalesced into sinister visions; the guilt that is integral to being a mother. We were still fragile when Beatrice and Jose took us to the opening of an exhibition of carnival masks at the Museum of Dominican Man. Cultural performances accompanied impressive displays that parodied the island's savage history. The horrors of Columbus and subsequent colonisers came to life. That legacy of violence and plunder was enacted in *Latigos'* thwacked snaking whips that split the air, while hideous *Diablos* and *Cojuelos* with hooked noses, bared teeth, and twisted horns battled with hoards of villagers who thrashed the unwary with bunches of inflated cow bladders. It was all too much and satiated with this vision of hell we returned to Hornpipe where the British sailors invited themselves on board for farewell drinks. At last they left, fighting their way along the quay, leaving one of their number asleep in the cockpit.

In the morning he and his ship had gone and we were in the midst of breakfast when our friends arrived with a plan. That day Jose drove us west along a river valley and high into the mountains. There we left the car and on negotiating the loan of a donkey, wove our way down a narrow track with Sam riding while Billy skipped ahead, squealing in delight. Little huts perched on the steep hillside and it seemed that the locals subsisted on whatever would grow on their steep clearings of fruit trees, coffee, cocoa, and vegetables. After buying a basket of fruit and vegetables Jose led us to a river that tumbled over rocks into deep pools, and while an audience of small boys watched we ate our picnic and soaked in the cool, clear water before starting the uphill climb with the children sitting together on the donkey.

Our preparations involved David spending a morning carrying tubs of fresh water to fill our tanks, adding purifying tablets to counter dreaded diseases. Meanwhile I cooked a special meal for Jose and Beatrice before a visit to the natural history museum. There it was the educational tableaux of animals and a skeleton of a giant whale that captivated Sam's imagination. The sophisticated collections at the modern art museum were compelling, but I was contending with a stomach upset so I wended my way home. On departure day I untied Hornpipe's warps and pushed off from the filthy dock, waving to the guards and hangers on who had observed our every action. David steered for the open sea where a light breeze blew us past Puerto Palenque on a close reach. And as the sun set the wind settled to an easterly.

By the following noon we had cleared the Alta Vela Rock and laid a more northerly course for Panama to avoid the discomforts of sailing directly across the waves, predicting that as we drew near the wind would curve north east. The Aries was working efficiently and a routine of three-hour day and four-hour night watches allowed us the optimum sleep. As Hornpipe romped through the swells we set the fishing line and reeled in the Walker log that had spooked the fish on our Atlantic crossing. We soon hooked a shimmering mahi mahi, with mirrored scales of iridescent greens, yellows, and turquoises, mottled with subtle blue spots. After two hours of scaling, gutting, and slicing we had enough fish for three spectacular feasts starting with fresh ceviche marinated in lime, followed by steaks and finally a curry. My stomach was still weak so I stuck a Scopolamine patch behind my ear and as the nausea subsided I tried reading, but the text tangled in zig zags and I could barely interpret the helm's compass rose. Kindergarten teaching had drained my patience with my own children and the motion made Sam and Billy reluctant to begin their schoolwork. I needed to replenish myself, but there would be no respite with Helen manipulating every situation.

I would carry that authoritarian burden of teacher mother throughout Sam and Billy's childhood and it was only natural that their rebellions would be directed at me, that William, who had been exceptionally close, would become a detached adolescent. While excelling at the arts his fascination with the mysteries of life would lead him to a Bachelor of Science degree in genetics. On choosing a career at Genesis laboratory in Auckland William rapidly discovered that monitoring minute organisms in glass tubes under artificial lights bore no resemblance to his initial interest. However, he achieved some notoriety playing goalie for his Genesis football team. After an all-night party the gang dragged him out to an epic day's tournament on Waiheke island where, after saving every ball, William's victorious team-mates carried him onto the ferry to sleep his way home. Billy's football experiences in the Bay of Islands had given him plenty of practice. Playing a defensive role in his school's losing team had trained a brilliant goalkeeper. Meanwhile Sam never stood much chance of scoring in the over-sized charity shop boots I had stuffed with newspaper.

David's dawn patrol on our third day at sea gave opportunities for a star sight that proved rewarding when the fix gave a precise location that tallied with our dead reckoning. When his noon sun sight was fifteen miles out David returned to his calculations, determined to locate the discrepancy, and as Hornpipe lurched through the heavy sea he came closer than he had ever been to seasickness. Helen was out of sorts from sleepless nights, perhaps because she did nothing to tire herself. Our designated roles made for a tolerable relationship, however the problems remained. Helen's criticisms were the jealousies of a bitter woman and while her monologues gave nothing away we assumed she was divorced, that the proximity to our family had caused her to reflect upon regrets. The impasse reminded me of that magnetic power to attract and repel that thwarted my closeness with my mother, but lacking a primitive family bond there was nothing to build on. Helen was determined to get her Caribbean cruise with sailing lessons thrown in and despite us explaining that yachts charged big money for that sort of deal she bestowed her assistance as one contributing a favour. If we had been wealthy we might have dismissed her contribution to food and fuel, but what angered me most was that our vulnerable family carried the burden of a hostile passenger. Oh, Gerry and Catherine, where were you now?

That night on my watch I noticed a ship coming closer, repeatedly flashing a light at us. I roused David, who shone a torch upward to illuminate our sails and indicate that we were a yacht. On making radio contact we learned the container ship was en route from Barbados to Jamaica; the human connection heightening our sense of security. By our fourth day we had established a comfortable course towards Panama and with the settled conditions Helen contributed by teaching the children simple tunes on her recorder. I was grateful for her input and Billy's response initiated my resolve to maintain his passion for music. At midday David communicated with the watch officer of a passing ship, The Pegasus, and after expressing an interest in navigation the officer explained how he used tables to calculate the approximate meridian passage and altitude of

Venus before setting his sextant to scan the horizon for the planet. David was impressed by his practice, reassured when he endorsed our position, and before signing out, the navigator predicted a light easterly toward Panama.

Although the winds were not favourable it was good to be informed but as Hornpipe squeezed her course south she lay broadside to the seas. Despite making good progress the lunging sideways lurch wore us down and, in desperation, I had chosen Scopolamine's double vision, headaches, and unquenchable thirst over nausea. By our fifth day the wind had eased but not the heaving swell and erratic waves. Every so often Hornpipe broached, sending a huge body of water bashing against her port side, shooting high in the sky to fall as heavy rain. A mean hit projected the cassette drawer to the floor, spilling music tapes everywhere. Amidst the turmoil, the children continued crashing their cars and clattering Lego to a ceaseless commentary and when David tired of their chatter I tried to establish schoolwork. Sensing my vulnerability Sam set to provoking Billy, who broke into ear splitting shrieks. As Helen embraced yet another opportunity to undermine my authority David escaped to the deck commenting that the kids were worse than on our Atlantic passage.

Hornpipe had become a fizzing pressure cooker of personal dynamics. But as always it needed no more than a subtle wind switch for it all to change. With the Aries working and the children occupied, I felt the urge to do something! So, I made a cake. It was a crazy idea in a sloppy sea, when the previous day's waves had claimed three plates, a cup, and a baking dish. However, the coffee cake survived many a slip and after icing and sprinkling it with chocolate buttons we gathered our crumbs of congeniality, congregating in the cockpit for a civilised tea time. And when a particularly vicious wave sloshed seawater over the proceedings David exclaimed, *"There comes a point when you can only laugh,"* as he hurled the soggy remains at me. The kids didn't get the joke and Billy began howling while Helen dissolved in hysterics, relishing the sight of us fighting. All in all, the slapstick silliness released some tension; a brief truce before we reverted to our set course.

Between dawn and dusk Hornpipe sailed herself but, as always, the wind was fickle around sunrise and sunset. She was easier to manage, the self-steering was working, and I had found a solution to my seasickness. Having been spared the persistent sail changes of our Atlantic passage, David was considering managing without crew on our voyage across the Pacific. Despite the heavy sea, Hornpipe had consistently covered a hundred and fifty miles each day, but the vigorous pace was nerve racking for the one who would have to mend any damages and as David watched the whisker pole bend he fretted that a stray gust might broach the genoa and smash that vital item. At dusk the wind backed and eased. The sky became overcast with Hornpipe gently rolling through a sea, phosphorescent with stars that ignited in a twinkling flash as they skimmed past to slide into the black beyond.

Our sixth day dawned with a light wind switch to the north, setting David to fiddling with the self-steering. For the first time on that passage we hoisted the mainsail, to drop it on finding the Aries could not cope; neither of us thinking of reefing it to maintain balance and speed. Growing tired of the children's tantrums, I tried a new trick. A behaviour chart featuring my cartoon of us standing on the boat, with stick on faces, a happy face for cooperating, an angry one for being obstinate. We all joined in with David the first to be awarded a naughty face as he struggled to cook dinner. The chart brought about an immediate transformation and I wondered why I had never done it before, but it was easy to miss the obvious when the rigours of sailing overwhelmed my body, mind, and spirit.

David caught the briefest moment between clouds to shoot the evening star and moon for a fix that indicated Hornpipe's position just ninety-five miles from our destination. He calculated that if we maintained four and a half knots we should reach the port of Cristobal the following day. But the idea of running downwind in darkness, heading towards an unfamiliar, badly lit harbour entrance was daunting, and premonitions of having to stand off shore in rough seas and strong winds made our speed feel turgidly slow. The morning dawned overcast, rendering star fixes impossible, but when dead reckoning indicated we could reach land that day we hoisted the mainsail for extra speed. David and I hand steered to avoid a broach, and as visibility shrunk to ten or twelve miles we scanned the murky miasma, aching to sight the soaring mountains that lay within reach. A break in the clouds allowed David a fix – it was not accurate, and although a second placed us fifteen miles from land, some twenty-five to our destination, Panama remained a mirage. Despite the buzz of traffic on the VHF and ships passing close by it was still incomprehensible that land was out there. As David's tension built, Helen's scornful criticism added pressure. At last he sighted a vague outline approximately twelve miles away, and with the assurance we could make it by nightfall David went for a sleep. I remained, standing with feet braced on the cockpit seats, elevated to a height where I could see over the cabin, under the goose winged sails. And as Hornpipe surfed the swells downwind, reaching eight or nine knots in the rising wind, Panama's valleys opened with a welcome.

By the time David woke, Cristobal's breakwater was in sight, and before long we had left the choppy Caribbean in our wake. Turning into the harbour we made for a designated area where yachts from Ireland, South Africa, Holland, Germany, France, New Zealand, America, and Austria were anchored. David rowed over to the South African yacht, to discover they had met Hornpipe's previous owners on St Helena. While two years and an ocean had passed, there were many similarities in their stories of maintenance, crew, and financial problems, and in the telling the difficulties became enlightening, even funny. We watched a procession of gigantic ships cross the harbour to be devoured by the land and while waiting to be processed visited the yacht club for a luxurious shower and refreshing drink. Fumigation was required for any boat that had visited Hispaniola, the island of yellow fever, and while this solved our cockroach problem Bouncer was not happy. He had just climbed on deck for his daily jog when he spied men in white overalls spraying deadly fumes, *"Bother!"* he thought. *"Just when life on board was hotting up with those exotic stowaways zapping and buzzing through the tropical nights. Just as my fitness caper to keep up with that cute little limbo spider from Santo Domingo was paying off."* Bouncer camped out and on crawling home for breakfast he met with carnage. His heart was broken. The carnival was over, his only option celibacy, *"Oommm,"* hummed Bouncer as he cleaned up the mess, *"Before enlightenment spin a web. After? Whatever!"*

David made trips ashore, rowing the miles when our Seagull outboard died. His first impression of the American continent was a trip to the bank to pay the fumigator, who insisted on accompanying him, saying that Colon was teeming with muggers and thieves. As instructed, David waited in the taxi, hugging his passport to his chest while his colleague watched from the street corner. At a signal, David ran into the bank to hurriedly complete the transaction before a quick getaway. His return to the yacht club coincided with the arrival of a huge bearded hippie in heavy walking boots, who responded to David's flippant, "*You look like you just walked from Alaska!*" with an, "*Ah hayve,*" as the hairy man dropped his rucksack on the pier. Having walked, skate boarded, and hitch-hiked the distance, he was hoping to board a boat bound for Tahiti. I can still picture Big John's narrow eyes and heavy brows beneath a brimmed hat that concealed a balding brow. However, he appeared honest and was probably our only chance of finding crew. But as David wrote in his journal, "*What we really need is some happy jokey lad who can jolly us along, because Linda and I are both a bit serious.*"

LT

After fulfilling the same requirements as those for a super tanker, Hornpipe was ready to transit the Panama Canal. In the process David had rushed around numerous offices, signing forms in triplicate, amounting to sixty pieces of paper. Then at dawn on the eleventh of March two trainee pilots arrived to assist our passage through to the Pacific Ocean. Having agreed to tow Intxea, a tiny twenty five foot yacht with no motor, her charming Spanish Captain would help line handle along with Helen and Big John. After tying Intxea alongside Hornpipe we motored towards the far side of the harbour, with the two yachts rolling alarmingly. On reaching the sheltered channel our boats steadied and from there we followed a Japanese tanker up to the Gatun locks. We entered the lower lock in the company of a tug and as soon as the lock keepers had thrown down four heavy lines with knobbly monkey fists to catch and hold, the slimy metal doors clamped shut. A loudspeaker crackled an incoherent message and water swirled around our boats, lifting us on a rising surface. Meanwhile, the line handlers pulled in slack, maintaining an equal tension at bow and stern to hold our yacht in the centre of the channel. By this effortless means, Hornpipe climbed the eighty-eight feet of the three locks with Intxea hanging on her skirts. The process reminded me of a canal boat holiday with my parents, an Easter escape, after my mother's breakdown. Mum steered while Dad and I heaved the heavy wooden paddles to open the lock gates before dragging the unwieldy boat through the channel. Bonded by our exertions we were resting beside an open field when in a glorious epiphany: two swans flew from the sky to settle close by. I drew them in flight as they spread their wings to dry in the glowing light, never dreaming those ethereal birds would inspire my first public sculpture.

The expansive view from the top of the locks revealed troughs of water descending behind us to where a tanker waited. It was unnatural to see the horizon below, to float high above an ocean we had so recently sailed. Turning our backs on the Atlantic we motored on into the vast Gatun freshwater lake and headed for the locks that would lower us into the Pacific. The scattered islands of verdant trees had once been mountain peaks and despite the mahogany forest being swamped for seventy years, skeletal stumps still protruded from the shallows, with some of them sprouting leaves. The area's military significance to America had foiled our requests to stay a few days, however our pilots directed us to a buoy where, lulled by lapping waves, we slipped off the radar into a peaceful world.

The absence of that rhythmic thrum of sails or engine roar was palpable; the tranquillity and verdant foliage a mirage. Surrendering to the mellow fluidity our gaze softened. Occasionally an incongruous tanker swung into view, only to disappear amongst the maze of islands. We swam in the silky liquid and lay on the deck embracing that momentary bliss in our individual ways. The pilots fell asleep under the dinghy, David and John dozed off, and when Sam and Billy joined Manuel in his miniature boat I went below, moving with ease in the still galley, cooking up an enormous chili con carne to feed all nine of us. When it was ready we ate, relishing the still silence. Although it would have been heaven to linger in the idyllic surroundings, to wash everything we possessed in the endless fresh water, it was time to set off, with Intxea and Hornpipe tied together, balancing our Genoa with her mainsail, scudding along at six and a half knots. Sam and Billy crouched alongside Manuel, watching the waves speed past, trickling their fingers in the ripples, enjoying the view from a different perspective. Hornpipe would never again seem restricted, but though Intxea's tiny interior was no more than a bed with a few possessions strung to the walls, Manuel was content with his simple home and diet of rice and fish.

When the lake merged to a wide channel with grassy banks and hanging trees our silent slide shifted focus and we reluctantly dropped the sails to crank Obelix into action. After Gamboa the channel narrowed into the Gaillard Cut (now known as the Culebra Cut) with its tumbling waterfalls, rocky cliffs, and mountains beyond. As we waited for an enormous Japanese tanker to negotiate the Pedro Miguel lock, we seized an opportunity to fill our water tanks and take a hurried shower. On the arrival of a slightly smaller tanker we motored into the lock with the great ship edging in behind, the mechanical mules inching it forward until the colossal bow loomed over our deck. So began a slow, exacting descent with our companionable giant squeezing inexorably closer at each lock. Helen had abandoned Hornpipe to flirt with the tugboat men who had the advantage of not understanding a single word she said. Our descent took three hours and light was fading when, on reaching sea level, we passed beneath the arching span of the Pan-American Highway. There we were greeted with an unmistakable musky aroma we had almost forgotten in the Caribbean. After dropping our pilots at the Balboa yacht club we motored to the far side of the shipping channel where, on recalling the significance of that tidal aroma of stagnant seaweed, we found a deeper place to anchor.

Daylight revealed the vast Pacific, an ocean of possibilities. And although we needed to complete essential preparations for leaving, we spent a quiet day recovering. When Helen's incessant talk became too much, David dodged the colossal ships in the channel to motor her ashore. There she caught the train to Colon where she intended boarding a boat that would take her to Tahiti. Although David had stressed his back hauling up our anchor, the wind was irresistible and he released his tension with fast windsurfing, until on inadvertently lunging for the gunwale he strained a ligament, generating a debilitating backache. John and Manuel took turns massaging David's neck, restoring his body for the challenges ahead, but when the men set off for the city my anxiety reached fever pitch. Panama had been described as a hotbed of violence and our gringos' golden skin, bushy beards, and patterned shirts labelled them tourists, ready targets for muggers. Although they towered over the locals, David's hobbling gait proclaimed his vulnerability. John's lumbering stride and ponderous speech indicated that life had washed over him, but having made it from Alaska he surely couldn't be as dozy as he appeared.

Next day the children and I joined them, boarding a rickety bus with coloured streamers flying from its windows. As we drew near, the city revealed its shambling huts with rotting timbers and rusty canopies, cracked pavements and cheap American stores. Amongst the boards of lottery tickets and crowds of street sellers, a boy displayed a few items on an orange box – individual cigarettes, a canned drink, scissors, and a towel. A small enterprise that sustained the life of a child, whose ancestors had been lured to Panama with hopes for a better future. One of a racial mix of Indian, Chinese, Latin, and African origins who had toiled in terrible conditions, given their lives to building the canal we had passed through in one day.

On climbing down from the bus David and John went in search of charts while my first stop was the toy shop where Sam and I secretly searched for Billy's birthday, lovingly weighing the cost of each present against the pleasure it would bring, planning for an event, an ocean away. Then on to the market with the children clinging to my dress while I clutched my packages and purse. I had no concern about us being singled out as tourists. My brown skin, black hair, and worn dress merged with the diverse ethnicities. Stall keepers greeted me in Spanish and I could have been any harassed Panamanian mother. We slipped unseen through the crowds, gathering vegetables and fruits until, loaded like a pack horse, all but our bus money spent, we wended our way back to the depot. As we waited for the bus Sam asked why I was sad and his comforting observation shattered my defence. A longing to share my worries overwhelmed my composure. Sam was so mature it seemed as if he had been with me forever. I forgot he was just six years old and before I knew it I was explaining my fears about keeping everyone safe, regretting passing on my anxiety.

On arriving at the yacht club, we found David and John drinking beer in the sunshine and, having been denied their freedom for the past weeks, the kids made the most of the grassy space, spreading their arms like aeroplanes to run and throw themselves on me with happy giggles. I watched their glowing faces and abandoned bodies. Billy jumping up and running away, racing towards me with arms outstretched, experiencing that wonderful reunion, again and again. He could not stop this game of running and returning, following each separation with a jubilant reunion. His running was pure joy and we were swept up in that affirmation of meeting each other, becoming as one. Though the tense weeks had coiled me as tight as a spring, my children's love had saved me. The intoxicating joy of Billy's love purged my fear, and I drew that moment as it had seemed to me. My little boy runs towards me, and in a glorious instant I throw my arms around him like a circle around the sun. That day would define my boys' symbiotic relationship – Sam would advise me as a friend, Billy's affection heal my pain. And that was how it would always be.

LT

"To my children: Touch curled hands, press kisses on soft skin. Look with love and a wish, hold this time in your heart."

Once David's back had recovered he enjoyed striding along Panama's shambolic streets, the massed energy of that pioneer city. Unable to afford the yacht club's fifteen dollars a night mooring fee we had no choice but to anchor on the far side to run the gauntlet through the channel. We were aware our dinghy appeared as no more than a blip on the radar of those gigantic ships that carved their inexorable course through our route to shore. On one occasion when David and John were motoring home with the temperamental outboard, they spotted a container ship in the distance, and estimating the time needed they powered ahead. But on reaching midstream the Seagull died. While the juggernaut continued its irrevocable course, ploughing up a menacing bow wave, the men grabbed the oars and paddled for their lives. Somehow they gained ground, and as they slid into the surging wake of the super-tanker their pounding hearts echoed the thud, thud, thud of its throbbing pistons. When they told the story I visualised their race against the juggernaut, our little dinghy bouncing along its hull, their inert bodies tumbling in the turmoil. With that image haunting every shore trip it was best the children and I remain afloat, but when David visited Colon for a tin of paint he took them along for the ride. As the train left Balboa station, Sam and Billy leaped around, jabbering in excitement, high as kites, and as it gathered speed they rushed from side to side trying to see out of both windows. They chugged past the American Army camp, through luscious jungle and the lake we had sailed over and it was dark when they returned, tired and relieved at having avoided Helen. After clearing customs and purchasing a nautical almanac we were more than ready to leave, and while it had become an unspoken agreement that John would crew with us, we thanked our lucky stars we had found someone so helpful and natural around children. Manuel had remained tied alongside, enjoying the free food and companionship and before he sailed I gave him a huge tin of dried milk to supplement his sack of rice. Casting his last dollar to the wind, it fluttered away on the breeze that would blow us all across the Pacific. Then, with no money or responsibilities, Manuel abandoned himself to the elements.

GOING BANANAS

That evening of Thursday the fifteenth of March rewarded us with enough wind to hoist our drifter and slip past the tankers that waited in the outer anchorage. Sailing by night, dawn saw us amongst the Perlas Islands and when Contadora appeared out of the haze we motored closer to anchor off an incongruously opulent resort. Tall trees cast impenetrable shadows over a golfing green scattered with deer and peacocks; the bare branches of those awaiting their spring growth dropped faded flowers upon manicured lawns. Beyond the cultivated enclosure a dense jungle canopy attracted black tailed golden eyes that screeched raucously, while in the sky an abundance of pelicans, boobies, and frigate birds flew back and forth. The children had found swings to play on, so I practised yoga while the men strategised about bagging venison for supper, however, their talk was all bluff and on returning home empty handed we set off for the more natural island of Chapera.

At that time of year, the prevalent wind blowing from the Caribbean over the Isthmus of Panama sweeps away the surface water, creating a vacuum that sucks up the cold Humboldt Current. Our first swim in the Pacific came as a shock and we soon saw that the nutrient rich sea swarmed with fish and multitudes of turtles and rays. Swirling ripples indicated the presence of sharks and after seeing them leap clear of the water we were not so sure about entering. The tide raced back and forth and, where in Caribbean waters we had anchored close to a shore that barely changed, the gulf's seascape was transformed by the tide. That first night was full of surprises, starting with a warning bump from below, and by the time we had gathered our wits Hornpipe was well and truly grounded. John's dramatic *"Get the women and children into the skiff,"* addressed at everyone and no one, evoked the script of a theatrical shipwreck. As the tide swirled past I rushed around, closing ports, securing falling objects, anxiously preparing for whatever occurred. David estimated the level would drop just three or four feet, which was just as well when the sea floor turned out to be slabs of rock. Billy and Sam slept on, oblivious to the drama, their recumbent bodies inching up the wooden walls of their bunks, and while it was disturbing to see our yacht heeled over with her mast listing sixty degrees, her demise presented a golden opportunity. Lowering himself into the sea David set to scrubbing away the oily residue of Santo Domingo and as Hornpipe's angle increased we remembered Tormentil's embarrassing escapade on the Maryport mud.

Following our grounding, we chose to anchor further from shore, accommodating the twenty-five foot tides with a lengthier stretch of chain that created a different hazard when the boat swung into the shallows or out into the fast-flowing channel. John and David started using the windsurfer as a platform for exploring the underwater world and although they saw sharks lurking in deep water, the predators seemed disinterested even when the men speared a large fish. Our new crew willingly shared every activity, and his strength was a powerful attribute, especially when grappling with anchors and sails. John had become one of the family, and despite knowing almost nothing about him, except for fantastic tales of a daughter named Moose, of times when they had hungrily wandered meadows grazing on wild clover, we trusted him with our children's lives. When he pitched his tent ashore we put ours beside it for the children to use as a den, and after the restrictions of sailing and cities they played all day on the beach, never noticing the sandflies. One exciting night they camped ashore, with John close by. Waking to total peace, David and I lingered over that momentary lull in the action. When Hornpipe's maintenance could no longer be ignored we set to grinding the deck, cabin, and cockpit, sanding rusty spots until they shone, spending a last frantic day painting the deck from bow to stern, racing to complete the task before the sun set.

A longed-for beach day washed away the struggle and stress, rust and dust. The humidity sheltered us from the sun, and nights were so still we were awoken by the soothing cooing of doves. However, David felt that we should move on while the winds were still active in the Gulf of Panama. So, after hoisting our drifter we set sail, and with assistance from the tide and odd bursts of motoring, reached the southern end of Isla del Rey. On rowing ashore for fresh fruit, David and John swamped the dinghy in the surf and then a local informed them the village of Mafafa was three miles further along the coast. After an early start I lugged a big bundle

LT

of washing to the stream where I was met with a group of girls who eagerly carried and helped bash our filthy clothes against smooth stones. Laughter and song crossed all boundaries and while I relished their help and infectious joy, they gleaned intimate revelations about our lifestyle.

David had left Sam and Billy playing with the local kids while he sought out the village store. At his requests for yucca, bananas, plantain, sweet potatoes, pineapple, and limes, eager boys ran in every direction and with his list complete he and John set off for a jungle spring to fill our twenty-four litre water containers. As they staggered back to the beach children passed them, balancing similar loads on their heads, and when David put his down a smiling boy picked it up to carry, in addition to his own. After topping up the tanks, David and I met at a shack bar and were enjoying cold beer and a tune on an old jukebox when a man cried, *"El niño."* Following his gesture, we saw Billy, running full pelt, pursued by a band of kids. David gave chase along a dirt path between bamboo and tin huts. On catching up, Billy threw himself on the ground, sobbing uncontrollably. And as the inquisitive children gathered around he touched David's beard for reassurance. Billy had bolted in a panic; but where was Sam? Our fears abated on seeing him, brandishing a stick, posturing a heroic stance against another gang, and after leading our kids back to the beach they frolicked in the swirling waves, where the locals were too afraid to venture.

On his return to the boat John had bought a bargain stalk of bananas and another of plantains from a local in a dug-out. Using my initiative, I had independently purchased a stalk, and faced with a scarcity of other fruits, David had settled for three. After tying them along Hornpipe's stern rail she looked like the banana boats I had drawn as a child. That evening John revealed he had scored some pot at the village and, swallowing our phobia of American coast guards, we became gently stoned while listening to Keith Jarrett's *Koln Concert*. We valued our own perception of the world and neither of us needed drugs to shed inhibitions, enhance our imaginations, or discover an identity. One inebriated Christmas my dad had promised my brother and I fifty pounds if we never smoked before reaching twenty-one. That was a lot of money back then and my dad wasn't a generous man, so I valued his offer and used it as a credible excuse. By the time I reached maturity I had no desire to take up the damaging habit. I made it through Art College unaware of the benefits of inhaling, and when joints came my way, nobody noticed I was blowing out smoke. While I assumed pot was overrated, my wild dancing and eccentric clothes gave the impression I was high as a kite.

The first time I smoked ganja was in Jamaica. The convent school teachers found me out, *"You're not inhaling,"* they said, and showed me, as you would a child, saying, *"Breathe in as you take a drag, then hold your breath."* This was something I could do! Drawing the deepest breath, I held the stinging smoke in my lungs. Next time the joint came around I felt a tectonic shift as my brain rotated through a whirling panorama of images from a time when I worked at a shelter for London street kids. Morphing into a heroin addict I stumbled along grimy streets desperately seeking a fix. As I ran onto the balcony the horrified group restrained me and, in a lucid moment, I saw a nun plead, *"Please don't tell Sister Mary I was here."* The psychotic waves lasted three terrible nights and days. I spent them inscribing books for prize giving, and as the cloistered room expanded and contracted my addled brain clung to the task. The nuns marvelled at my diligence and I wondered whether I had lost my sanity. They worshipped effigies of tortured saints, a Madonna with a bleeding heart ringed with knives, but all I knew was myself and when the kaleidoscope of my mind settled to a familiar pattern I resolved to never repeat the experience; I had enough going on in my head.

A light breeze sprung up as we departed Isla del Rey on our voyage through the lethargic doldrums to the Galapagos Islands. The wind freshened with dusk and remained strong as we raced around Punta Mala, dodging ships. Dawn saw Hornpipe flopping and floundering in the irregular waves from the confused conjunction of the Panama and Costa Rican swells. The day loomed inexorably long, starting with Sam's "*I'm bored with reading, drawing, and Lego.*" I regretted that we had too few resources to fill the endless hours and recalled a childhood of days that were never long enough, when imagination could build a castle from a chicken shed, transform a branch of an apple tree into a horse. Meanwhile my children were imprisoned within a cramped boat, their bodies, minds, and spirits rebelling against the ennui and discomforts of sailing.

While latitude was usually easy to plot, David's daily fix proved inaccurate due to the challenge of bringing the sun's orb down to the horizon from a position almost directly overhead. He eventually settled for the easier option of determining our exact location from his dawn star sights. By afternoon the children had settled into a freely flowing cycle of activities, drifting back and forth from the saloon to the aft cabin, inseparable as always. Despite demolishing a whole loaf of banana bread, the vast supply had not dwindled and our leaden stomachs were synonymous with the humid atmosphere. Hornpipe drifted through a night garlanded with stars, an ocean twinkling with phosphorescence, and the occasional flickering flash of lightning indicated that the doldrums had caught up with us. When David briefly caught a sight of the moon and Vega his calculations revealed that despite our diligent tacks we had progressed a mere twenty miles during twelve hours of darkness. Our cruising life demanded a practice of *aparigraha*, the yogic practice of acceptance. But knowing and doing were different matters. Surrendering to nature's whim was challenging for David, whose complete involvement in sailing and navigating created an attachment to the outcome.

I awoke at six to the children's happy voices and a favourable wind that lifted our spirits and carried us through the day. When dusk gave way to the heavy clouds and static air of the doldrums, we dropped the sails and woke Obelix. We took turns to steer through the twelve hours of darkness that conveniently divided into four-hour watches, giving each of us an eight-hour sleep. Steering would have been tedious without our music tapes that lent meaning and magic to those solitary hours. A fresh south-westerly sprung up at dawn, and after hoisting our canvas John sailed Hornpipe through a rainbow, into a squall. As the first raindrops fell through our open hatch David and I leapt out of bed to collapse the bimini and attach a hose to the concavity. The ease of setting up the ingenious adaptation and the sound of abundant water gushing into the tank filled our cup; and as the rain lashed down we washed everything, including ourselves.

Scattered clouds frolicking on a blue sky seemed a sure indication of trade winds so David swung Hornpipe onto a starboard tack, hoping they would curve towards the southeast as we drew near the Galapagos. As the day progressed our consecutive logbook comments expressed an homage to the much-maligned banana.

> *"Do bananas make good bait?*
> *Who needs fish with all these bananas!*
> *Ah, the banana, the fastest travelling plant!*
> *It's travelling fast through my gut!*
> *Going bananas, HELP!*
> *There are more waves than bananas in this world."*

We ran a competition to see who could transform the greatest number of bananas in the most original way. Racking his brain, David created a cunning concoction, mashing and mixing the yellow perils into a tin of condensed milk and chocolate syrup scavenged from the bilges. His banana fool fooled no one and though Sam was never a fussy eater the pudding tipped him over the edge. As an impoverished student, he would survive art school and avoid debt by managing on less than twenty-five dollars a week. At that time Sam would have consumed any alternative to his frugal fare of rice, as long as it was not yellow and ready wrapped.

John often took Sam and Billy up on deck, to tell them about Kodiak bears in Alaska, or his childhood on the Pacific's Marshall Islands. We watched their golden heads intently listening to every detail, little hands abstractly stroking John's beard as he fabricated the story of his life. By the time he began his eight o'clock watch our family were hunkered down together and it was comforting to drift into sleep, gazing through Hornpipe's open hatch as an aerial view of stars and planets swung back and forth with the motion. Sam lay in his bunk observing the phosphorescent water flow past his porthole, causing David to reflect, *"We all have these things we remember. One of mine is night time driving down to the south of England watching the sodium town lights slip by. How much more romantic than all these is Sam's watching the sea and stars slip by from his little home out in the Pacific Ocean. At the moment, he is learning some of the constellations. Lucky child!"*

Sam's path to becoming a storyteller would not be smooth. To further his academic career he bravely returned home to teach *Theatre History and Design* at The Eastern Institute of Technology's *Performing Arts* department. In a situation reminiscent of school on the boat, Sam researched to keep one step ahead of his students, who said he was the best teacher ever. His studies primed him for his prestigious *Master of Fine Arts* at the University of London's Slade School. But first, to earn the exorbitant fees and living expenses, Sam embarked on a teaching job in South Korea, where he spent months never hearing a word of English. Apart from refusing to adopt his colleagues' practice of beating the unruly with bamboo sticks, Sam embraced the culture. The huge disruptive classes were captivated by Sam's masks and puppets and he became a *Pied Piper* to his students. On one notorious school camp, coach-loads of kids were driven to a country lodge, and once there the teachers began drinking. Wandering down to the river Sam came upon forty or fifty unsupervised children. Dreading the consequences of his co-workers' neglect he spent the afternoon on patrol, saving those who drifted into deep water. Thinking it was all part of the fun they clung to Sam's curly hair, giving him no choice but to dive under, like *Moby Dick*. After dinner, the drunken teachers partied on, and when Sam discovered students with no place to sleep he gathered cardboard packaging in which they huddled for warmth; the escapade proving that my son was responsible, and capable of anything.

Our trip was proving less demanding and more predictable than our Atlantic Crossing. Some days seemed to last forever while others passed unnoticed amidst the routine of cooking, cleaning, navigation, school, and play, but where Gerry's sparkling wit had been a lively catalyst, John was subdued and serious. He and David had become a dreary, all pervasive male presence. They responded to the boat's motion by slowing to a somnambulist pace, moving with the tread of great ponderous beasts. At other times they resembled climbers, maintaining a balanced stance as they circumvented a tricky route. Meanwhile, I was trying to acclimatise, fluttering around Hornpipe, tripping on toys and ropes, encountering every sharp edge, a butterfly in a jar, battering its wings on glass walls. My body was covered in bruises, my mind consumed by the powerful Scopolamine I dared not go without. Sailing exacerbated our strengths and weaknesses, and while David was caught up in a rewarding adventure, my intimate space had been breached by John's disturbing hints, his expectation that I should be shared along with our quest. A lack of opportunities to behave as a couple compromised my relationship with David, and with no affectionate words or touch to dissolve the distance I sought solace in domesticity. My endeavours became a ceaseless disruption that set me apart. There was no escaping John, and while our family could not manage without crew, I must deal with the problem.

The children's irrepressible joy appeared oblivious to everything. They spent days drawing or inventing stories about the crazy characters that inhabited their minds. One afternoon I mixed another batch of playdough as David helped Sam construct a paper bird and Billy made snowflakes, sprinkling glitter everywhere. After shaping squashy objects we washed away the mess with a splashy game. David began writing a *Navigation for Dummies* book, testing his explanations and diagrams on my addled brain. The complex calculations were all too much for me. Nightmare visions of my infant school's brittle stacks of slates returned, scrawled with a trickery of white chalk, of days rubbing those mystical mathematical symbols into whirlwinds of dust. I had spent hours sorting shells from sagging cardboard boxes. But where the chipped cowries came from, the prowess to calculate their numbers, I never discovered. When my high school mathematics teacher begged me to give up his subject, I could not predict that I would someday depend upon those skills. I felt like the poor girl in the fairytale who had been locked in a tower to complete the impossible task of spinning straw into gold. And this was when Rumpelstiltskin appeared, with a proposition. Alas; there would be no such help in my time of need.

Bouncer was hanging out below decks when John stumbled into the galley and started spooning green leaves, sugar, and cocoa into a bowl. Bursting with curiosity Bouncer dropped to the bench, and slurping up a dollop of the mixture, wandered on feeling somewhat legless. Sam remembers that when John presented a plate of misshapen crusty cakes he felt betrayed that he was not allowed even one, and while it would have been churlish to refuse John's hash brownies, David and I were stupid to accept. We rarely drank alcohol, choosing to keep our wits about us, particularly at sea. The pot we had smoked had been no more than mildly relaxing, and assuming that baking would dilute its potency we ate the cakes. They tasted completely benign but how wrong we were!

Once the children were asleep we left John on watch and went to bed, feeling mildly bubbly until out of the blue, David announced that he was *"going down the road to post a letter"* to his mother. I convulsed with laughter at the surreal suggestion, but as my giggles subsided and I saw our children softly sleeping, oblivious to the danger, I fell on my knees, pleading David to stay. Goaded by my reaction he mercilessly teased me, leaping to his feet, holding aloft the imagined letter to post in a fantasy letterbox. And my confused mind saw him stepping lightly over the lifeline, his body momentarily suspended in the moonlight, before disappearing forever. Although aware that my big boy's antics were an act, the emotional agony released paroxysms of laughter at my gullibility; the absurdity of it all. The cakes squatted in our guts, evil gremlins controlling the craziness. Whispered persuasions proved futile, tears and despair to no avail; eventually the cycle of madness and remorse subsided into sleep, but the crazy laughter of the madwoman as she tried to restrain her clown still echoes in my head. While frivolity seldom has sinister implications, our extreme lifestyle came with severe consequences for those who lost control, and I regret that foolishness and its potential to have destroyed those we loved.

After the evening antics, David and I slept soundly and woke feeling relaxed, as never before on an ocean crossing. It seemed the druggie doldrums had also passed; a gentle breeze caressed the sea and the sky was brilliant blue with a clear horizon that predicted trade wind sailing. So, after dousing Obelix, we hoisted the sails to cruise through the day with the helm perfectly balanced, Hornpipe swinging to a voluptuous dance, her mesmerising bow wave sliding away. We in turn surrendered to the ocean, with David studying navigation for survival while I moved through the confined boat, finding spaces where I could stretch into yoga positions to be rewarded with a euphoric vitality made happier when David joined me on the deck.

Later, when David was steering, Sam sat behind him on the cabin roof and shyly asked if he wanted a massage. For a long time, his little fingers caressed David's neck and shoulders easing an encroaching headache and once again our family went to bed together, to watch Sam gazing through his porthole chattering and chuckling to himself, drifting asleep with the water swishing past. Unfortunately, Billy was not so happy. His attempts at equalling his older brother caused self-perpetuating fights and Billy came off worse when competing with Sam, who was nearly three years older. As Sam's abilities escalated, Billy's sweet innocence eroded. He dissolved in tears whenever we tried to control his behaviour, and when John shared stories with Sam he excluded Billy, bluntly stating that he was a baby in need of his mother; a rejection that hurt a little boy who desperately wanted to participate in the world of men. David and I had also been influenced by our family circumstances. He had thrived on being a first-born, and the responsibilities he assumed following his father's death nurtured an influential leader, while from the first I had displayed a second born child's independent spirit, a rebelliousness that was a desperate claim for attention.

David felt it was inevitable that the younger sibling would be less pleasing, and confessed to thinking, *"He'll be better when he's older,"* denying the fact that Sam was also advancing. Would Billy always be one step behind Sam? I valued my sons' differences, and was in no hurry to see my youngest outgrow his natural development. I knew how it felt and consequently treated our children as equals, avoiding undermining their individuality by referring to them as 'the boys'. Billy's uncontrollable screams reminded me of my attempts at keeping up with my older brother; how our preoccupation with which of us our parents loved most was met with a, *"You're both as bad as one another."* It felt so unfair and I regularly left home carrying my basket and sooty bear, giving up on reaching the end of the garden. Trailing my brother's gang I pushed a wheeled donkey across rutted fields, making dens in ditches, finding bottles with the dregs of what we believed to be whiskey, downing the filthy liquid in a drunken bravado. When goaded with a, *"Bet you wouldn't dare,"* of course I would. My parents had brought me up with gender free expectations and a competitive determination that made me willing to do anything for some attention. Too naïve to know better I climbed trees, leapt from haystacks, and endured games that involved pins in fingernails or sitting on a metal bucket set over a campfire. Being left out was far worse, but when adolescent protuberances asserted an unmentionable sexuality my brother and I were thrust apart forever, and while he became a computer technician in semi-detached suburbia I chose the life of an artist and free spirit.

Dawn of our fourth day revealed a high cloud cover that rendered it surprisingly cool, considering we were only a few degrees from the equator. The freshening wind required we reduce sail and after breakfast we continued on a port tack. The sun's position directly overhead made David's noon latitude fix difficult, but he somehow managed a few shots that vaguely positioned us twenty-five miles north of our dead reckoning. With dusk the wind died and as dark clouds spread a blanket over the sky we dropped the sails and motored in search of a more favourable current and wind. However, the haze intensified and we awoke to a gloomy dawn with no stars to guide our way. Hoisting a sail, we found that the wind had backed south, southeast. Hornpipe had found the trade wind and she was soon romping along under full canvas. It was all action on board with John tying rat lines up to the lower spreaders. When David climbed aloft he described the sensation, *"Like flying through weightless space, turning back a bow wave of thousands of galaxies and stars."*

On previous passages, we had habitually worn safety harnesses to ensure against an inadvertent slip and seeing David throwing caution to the wind, balanced high above Hornpipe's deck, filled me with dread. The speed of our downwind flight exacerbated my concern that a freak wave or gybe might topple him off his perch. I visualised David's flailing body thrown overboard, and remembering our dinghy incident off Puerto Rico I imagined a futile struggle to retrieve him. How would we manage, bereft of a captain, husband, and father? I thought about our questioning children, the hopeless voyage without David's skill for finding land. My tears and persuasions were futile and by the time he climbed down I was sick with anxiety. On challenging David's stance he accused me of denying his freedom, and while this was our first argument about that questionable liberty, it would not be the last.

When David achieved an accurate noon fix, it revealed we were two hundred miles from Genovesa/Tower Island. Having heard rumours that the Galapagos restricted stays to three days, we hoped to anchor off the uninhabited island to prepare for our Pacific passage before our official arrival. As Hornpipe heeled to the wind her motion steadied, the breeze chilled, so I found David's denim smock, remembering how he had last worn it in the North Atlantic. Sam spent hours drawing Tintin cartoons, his single confident line encapsulating their characters. While he needed no encouragement, Billy's persistence stripped our responses of genuine enthusiasm. He was as physical as was possible in our cramped space, doing monkey hangs in the cockpit, throwing himself into yoga, blowing raspberries on David's skin and exhausting us with the usual battle about tidying up toys. As the light diminished he and Sam competed to spot the stars, recognising and locating Sirius, Capella, and Canopus.

The following day was deceptively cold with a clear sky and burning sun that made us aware of how dependent we were on the awning. As Hornpipe scudded over the calm sea we sheltered in the saloon, engaged in a science experiment, *"Fun with Magnets."* When the midday sight indicated that Tower Island was further than expected, our hopes for arriving that day were squashed. Later, when David's evening star fix positioned us nearer than his noon prediction, we dropped Hornpipe's jib to avoid a night landfall. The stars were brilliant and as David steered he kept Canopus between the jib and mast while consulting his charts to identify the Southern Cross and False Cross. During our eight day passage the varied wind had been accompanied with confusing waves and currents. That moonless night was no exception. At first Hornpipe happily drifted at four or five knots under her mainsail alone, and when the wind dropped we climbed on deck to increase sail. No sooner had we settled to sleep when it freshened, demanding that we decrease our canvas, and as the wind dropped, we hoisted our bigger sail. When it finally died, we woke Obelix, and after an active night that would have required no more than a tweak to a roller furling rig, David was up before dawn for a star sight. And as the sky filled with light, John climbed the mast to shout *"Land ahoy!"*

There, just ten miles to the west, lay Tower Island. After expectations of an extinct volcano cone rising from the ocean, Genovesa's grey smudge surprisingly condensed into black cliffs sprouting fuzzy vegetation with flocks of frigates, boobies, petrels, and swallow tailed gulls wheeling overhead. Hornpipe's eight-hundred-and-fifty-mile passage through the doldrums had passed in just eight days and as always David was the most surprised that his skilful navigation had come to fruition; for despite his competence he never believed land until it appeared on the horizon. As we rounded the south-eastern point of the island we hooked our first sizeable fish until it dived under the boat snapping our line, leaving us disappointed that since leaving Panama we had lost three expensive lures and caught just one small fish. When the engine faltered our hearts stopped; then the mechanical hiccup that was probably no more than a flake of dirt in the diesel cleared itself and at last we entered a flooded crater surrounded with the island's rocky crescent. Despite appearing impossibly deep for anchoring, a magical spot revealed itself in the north-western corner of the secret lagoon that reminded me of childhood adventure stories. When David dived to check the anchor he was surrounded by scores of enormous fish, so John swam off, intent on catching dinner, to return empty handed saying that the spear-gun lacked power.

After tidying the boat, we went ashore to a clamorous reception. The island had never known predators, so birds were everywhere, standing on rocks, nesting in the scrubby bushes, and flying overhead. We wandered wide-eyed amongst creatures so tame that our approach caused no disturbance. Swallow-tailed gulls regurgitated whole squid to feed their offspring while magnificent male frigate birds sat in regal splendour, engorging their throats like red balloons. Little Galapagos mockingbirds and Darwin's finches hopped over the rocks, and on walking up to a booby resting on a rock with its head tucked under its wing, the sleeping bird never stirred. Iguanas sunned themselves, their skins camouflaged against the crinkled black rocks, as brilliant red crabs ran hither and thither gregariously flaunting their zingy colours.

The beach was backed with cliffs on which were painted the names of boats and dates of their visits, and while walking through a rocky gully we were astounded to see John conversing with another man! There had been no sign of human habitation and having heard that the Ecuadorian Patrol Boat rarely visited we had hoped to pass unnoticed. As we shared our beach picnic with the young biologist he explained that he and a colleague were studying the finches and mockingbirds, and after assuring us we posed no threat to the environment he suggested we disappear for the afternoon while the cruise ship made its weekly visit. We reluctantly returned to the confined boat and motored out of the bay to hide behind the northern side of the island, where the cliff precipitated to more than a thousand fathoms. Switching off Hornpipe's motor we drifted, becoming increasingly restless as we waited for dark and the lights of the cruise ship to fade into the distance. We returned, escorted by dolphins flashing back and forth, squeaking and squealing, leaving a glittering meteorite trail as they dived to the depths.

The sheltered crater and sandy beaches of Tower Island were a safe

Galapagos gulls LT

playground for the children, a perfect place to unwind. Diving into a winding salt water gully we sought the sunlit surface of a small pool. Then on climbing a rocky promontory to a bay where the water teemed with forty or fifty sharks we shuddered on remembering our earlier dives. David and I windsurfed the fickle winds that sent us skimming with a fragment of a song, *"Skipping over the ocean like a stone,"* playing on our minds. And when I sailed over a huge shark I desperately clung to the boom, gripping the board with my toes, praying the wind would not drop and leave me wobbling. David had a similar experience when, seeing he was on a collision course with a shark, that a change of position risked a fall, he gambled on the sensitive creature avoiding his passage. And at the last moment it calmly ducked underneath him. Being adventurous he could not resist sailing beyond the bay, to know, *"That intense sense of freedom and release of being out so utterly alone, so free of everything, dependent only on the wind."* As he drifted on the gentle breeze David saw a turtle circling below, a shark lurking in the distance. Inquisitive boobies flopped into the water, floating nearby, nervously observing him with heads quizzically cocked, webbed feet spread, ready to paddle away. And before returning, David sat watching the sun on the waves, shards of light piercing the depths.

The island offered unique opportunities for drawing its wildlife. As an adolescent I had been blessed with the ability to render the characters of the wriggling schoolchildren, the soul and faceted features of an old miner, ruddy from carbolic and alcohol. While that demanding connection between eye, hand, and mind has been proved to be one of the most demanding brain activities I had discovered, the extreme observation brought about a meditative experience; a dialogue that intensified as I became absorbed with those feathered muses. On drawing a pair of frigate birds, the preposterous male inflated his scarlet throat and spread his wings with a dominant gesture. Scribbling at speed I portrayed beaked faces with eyes that gazed upon me with an all-pervading wisdom. A night heron stood grey, stiff as an old man in a raincoat, while swallow tailed gulls preened themselves to be presentable for their portrait. It was a privilege to observe their precise features and staccato movements and I stood for hours, blinded by the savage sunlight, drawing in a fevered frenzy, fixing those images on my page and memory. When we passed on our way these birds would continue living to an eternal pattern, while their transient images would grace an exhibition in another place and time.

One morning we awoke to the sounds of a large yacht anchoring close by, and being unsure of the situation we delayed going ashore. On rowing the children to the beach a guide informed me we had no right to be there and should leave for Academy Bay. Fortunately, the yacht soon left, but having decided to avoid further confrontations we sailed for the island of Santa Cruz on the evening of Friday, April the sixth. Random currents and a thick haze made dead reckoning uncertain, but despite the dawn being submerged in clouds David somehow caught a quick fix on Jupiter and after plotting our position he realised we had passed over the equator during the night. There was no time for pageantry, with David immersed in the complexities of navigating through the pea soup fog, John and I helming and managing sails; but I remembered photographs of my father's ship *crossing the line*. The traditional rite of passage featuring his captain attired as King Neptune, wielding a trident amongst a bevy of *greenhorn* sailors cavorting as Hawaiian dancers and mermaids, while amidst the morass of boyish faces was the laughing father I had never known.

David was preoccupied with juggling calculations and plotting our course when a colossal rock loomed from the mist, giving him *"The scare of his life."* Although Rocas Gordon was exactly where David had calculated, he had expected a low slab awash with waves. We hesitantly continued rounding the vague coast of Santa Cruz and on reaching Academy Bay the Port Captain explained that the fog was ash from a volcanic eruption. Then he asked, "*How long would you like to stay?*" And having expected just three days we were overjoyed when he offered us fifteen. Then we rowed ashore to the tiny settlement of straggled shops along a dusty dirt road, a shallow inner harbour with a fishing boat hauled against the dock. While Sam and Billy joined the local children, swimming and jumping from the steps, we watched from a café. On hearing of an English woman with a son of Billy's age living in a house overlooking our anchorage I introduced myself to Georgina, who insisted I return with my washing. While her machine churned through our dirty clothes the children played. Georgina was married to a local fisherman and glad of the oasis of girls' talk that helped us comprehend the incomprehensible behaviour of our partners. And as we hung the washing out to dry, we shared our fears, hopes, and dreams for our children.

The following day we stopped a Camionetta open truck, paying a few cents for the ten mile ride up to the tiny village of Santa Rosa. The road climbed a thousand feet, the landscape transcending from arid coastal scrub and cacti, to vast plains and forests of ash, sycamore, and hawthorn carpeted with bracken. At Santa Rosa, we parted company from John who said he intended walking up to a lookout. We guessed he would probably spend his day smoking dope under a shady tree and although David would have preferred a vigorous hike up to the three-thousand-foot crest we planned riding horses in search of the giant Galapagos tortoises. Our steeds knew the way and it was soothing to sway at an equestrian pace, with Sam and Billy holding on behind. After some time the silent forest opened to a sloping plateau of lush grassland that looked towards the brittle sea and relentless horizon. But when our horses started to trot, Sam and Billy complained about the uncomfortable wooden saddles and once again I was torn, between their limitations and my husband's thirst for adventure. David had given his all to reach these exotic places; he longed to explore and wanted to share the experience with me.

The transition to parenthood had been challenging for David, and where parents often shape their lifestyle around family, his sincere love of our boys was at odds with his desire to immerse himself in the wild. David believed that freedom was the vital flame in our relationship;

that Sam and Billy must fit into our ventures. And as he anticipated another rare opportunity slipping away, David made a stand. Yielding, I agreed to settling the children beneath a shady tree; to go looking for the giant tortoises, our horses plodding along an overgrown track, prickly hawthorn tearing the jeans we wore for the first time in two years. When the way opened to a muddy swamp we came upon a colossal reptile that retracted into its shell with an ominous hiss, remaining like a boulder that had rolled onto the path. Further along we arrived at a clearing where tortoises were wallowing in shallow ponds with yellow warblers and vermilion flycatchers fluttering overhead. But my mind was elsewhere, regretting giving in to Billy and Sam's discomfort, wishing they could see that wondrous sight. When we started back the horses bolted at a wild canter through the bush. It was only after gaining control that we noticed how the path appeared unfamiliar and realised they had followed a different route home! As we gazed over the wide plain the sight of so many spreading trees was bewildering. Each one was identical to that tree where we had left our children and as I searched for some landmark I felt sick to my stomach, knowing that I was completely disoriented, that they were helplessly waiting. However, after speculating for a while David turned his horse's head and urged it through the undergrowth. I followed, as his infallible sense of direction and astute observation led us straight to that one tree where we found Sam crying and Billy comforting him, saying, *"I told you they would come back."*

Together again, we started for home with David and I walking, the children riding like cowboys. When we encountered tortoises lumbering along the track this somewhat appeased my terrible guilt. Back at the café Billy, relishing the euphoria of having appeared tougher than Sam, drunkenly swayed around the bar, swigging a Coca Cola with his red cap rakishly askew in a performance that earned him the name *"Billy Bottle."* Then we hurtled downhill, riding the Camionetta's dust cloud. As the red sunset darkened to night our friendly stars appeared, but memories of that day would linger as a warning, that a momentary slip in a million cautious actions could spell disaster. Torn between relationship and children I carried my responsibilities like a ball and chain, forgetting how to laugh, anticipating danger everywhere. David resented anything that impaired his freedom with discussions leading to arguments and silent impasses. Meanwhile our children had developed an empathy beyond their years. They instinctively understood the load we carried, respecting David's role as provider, mine as a carer, Sam manifesting this with concern, Billy showering me with affection. They were inseparable friends and together we were four parts of a whole.

Hornpipe's maintenance and preparation consumed us; David and John dived to clear the hull of weed and barnacles, ferried water from a hotel across the bay, heaving the containers onto the deck to fill the tanks. My economical size rewarded me with excursions into the bilge, wriggling naked between the metal struts to patch the auxiliary water tanks. When the gas bottle we had supposedly filled in Santo Domingo ran out after two weeks' use we learned that local fittings were different, our hot dinners numbered. We eventually splashed out on a new cylinder and regulator. Then, following a foul afternoon fixing the forward toilet that had jammed with its sea-cock open, David considered it a blessing to have discovered the ticking time bomb in port. Spending an evening with shipmates from the yacht Ballerina of Cork, Clodagh, rascally Dermott and Alan, their crew, spoke of longing for the sun to sink below the yardarm so they could crack a keg to liven up card games on those endless ocean passages while we wondered if we would ever know the luxury of boredom.

One afternoon we walked out to the Darwin Institute where various species of giant tortoises lumbered through the rocky terrain of walled compounds. These living sculptures had weathered many generations, and two oldies peered out from shells carved with a graffiti of dates and names. David and I sat drawing Pepe and Antonio and when they disdainfully withdrew their quizzical heads we saw two girls approaching with knives. Without hesitation I grabbed a stick and as I advanced they slunk away, no doubt intending to return when the crazy foreigner had gone. The giants continued masticating the thorny cacti and rubbery leaves with their toothless gums, while in a nearby shed baby tortoises were being reared to revitalise the population that had neared extinction due to them being a conveniently packaged food for passing ships. When a small one toppled onto its back, helplessly waving legs and head in a futile frenzy, the children ran for the caretaker, to be rewarded by being invited inside the pen where they relished the infinite pleasure of sharing the world of those little creatures.

That evening, David and I visited a local bar where, fending off drunken salsa dancers, we discussed our imminent voyage, speculating on managing four or five weeks at sea, acknowledging that our lack of

Galapagos tortoises LT

communication had caused conflicts on previous trips, that the confined conditions exacerbated issues that remained comfortably dormant in ordinary circumstances. David resolved to talk with John and we hoped he would understand our need for personal space, that fishing trips in the solitary wilds of Alaska had prepared him for a long ocean passage. On Sunday, John valiantly offered to look after the children and we set off for a rare day alone, clinging to an open truck before clambering off at Santa Rosa to start up the long road towards the volcanic craters. High above, stunted trees and craggy rocks snagged the sky, while below, the land descended through a haze of avocado, mango, and banana orchards to an arid shoreline scrub. Succumbing to a virus I slept while David trudged on to find two enormous craters littered with boulders, ringed with cliffs; his dream of climbing a peak for a view over the island thwarted by the impenetrable foliage. On his return we ate our picnic under a tree, relishing a silence that was only interrupted by birdsong. Returning for the truck we crowded amongst the morass of swaying bodies. A drunk threw his arm around me and although I shrugged him off he lay amongst the sacks of bananas, clutching my leg.

Monday was taken with packing, shopping, and visiting immigration for our clearance. As the officer glanced through Hornpipe's papers he laughed, "*Why your boat, this name?*" he enquired. Following my hesitation, he looked long and hard at me, making a character assessment. Then, with a charming smile he explained that in his language, pipe translated as penis and horny meant sexy, "*So! You are sailing the ocean on a horny penis!*" he laughed. "*But it's a sailor's dance,*" I lamely replied as the charming official rolled his eyes and raised his arms in despair. Leaving him laughing I reported back to the *Horny Penis*, relieved that amidst the distraction there had been no mention of Tower Island. We recalled how we had scorned our yacht's name and the musical notes that decorated her stern, for by then we had started to identify with Hornpipe's whimsical logo, and had even painted our oars with her jaunty motif.

Then it was time to leave our new friends. Georgina came over for sad goodbyes and after supper we motored out of Academy Bay, hoping to find a quiet anchorage where we could spend a few nights before embarking on our most remote passage. At dawn we found ourselves unexpectedly far south of the island of Isabella, returning with Obelix mangling Sibelius' atmospheric soundscape. Drawing near the steep incline of petrified lava we speculated on how the fiery turmoil had surged into the sea and on assessing the volcano's towering cliffs John expressed his certainty they could be climbed. Sighting a boulder beach, we dropped a lead line to estimate the depth. Immediately the water bubbled with fish and on pulling the lead weight from the water we discovered that it was pitted with tiny teeth. So we replaced the line with a bare hook and, one after another, pulled out three large fish, catching dinner in the space of a minute. After dropping the anchor David dived into the eerie water to wedge it amongst the stones, harbouring no confidence in its holding. Then John, who had swum to the beach, returned with his usual tale of lobsters, turtles, and groupers waiting to be caught and for once we believed him.

Ashore, a boisterous swell crashed against formidable black cliffs that ascended to an almost vertical slope of jagged scoria and scrub. I admit to a secret relief that the volcanic terrain was so obviously inaccessible, knowing that anything less would have prompted an expedition. By the time we had eaten lunch the wind had gathered strength, blowing us towards the hazardous lee shore, and after motoring around the coast searching for shelter we committed to a tiny inlet. However, we had underestimated the katabatic wind that surged down the mountain, forcing Hornpipe into the enclosed bay. A fearful realisation swept upon us. The bay was utterly remote, the wind a savage beast. The circumstances could prove catastrophic. Would Obelix have the power and momentum to complete Hornpipe's turn before she was blown onto the ragged rocks? Inches and seconds separated us from disaster as David somehow swung Hornpipe around and out of the treacherous bay. It was foolhardy to remain and our departure could no longer be avoided, so when David said, *"Let's go!"* we hoisted the sails and scudded away at a cracking seven knots. Sam remembers how he was busy eating a carrot, carefully dissecting the outside to reveal the stalk of its inner core. When someone said, *"We are leaving for the Marquesas,"* he felt surprised, but back then life was unpredictable so he thought nothing of it.

Skipping Over the Ocean

"What are we in the infinity of ocean and sky?
A small baby at the breast of eternity."
Johanna Adriana Ader-Appels

Sleeping LT

Hornpipe surged forward, purposefully climbing the crests, dipping into the troughs of a great southern swell. The children continued their games, asking only, *"Where are we going now? Fatu hiva! Okay!"* Any reluctance at leaving was lost in our hurry to batten the hatches and tie down the dinghy before the light faded. It was April the sixteenth, 1984, and our passage across the Pacific Ocean had begun. By dusk the wind had become inconsistent and although we replaced our number two genoa with the drifter, its flop and bang eventually forced us to abandon sailing and motor through the night in search of the trades. A virus had hit; it was a volatile mix when combined with diesel fumes and before long I was throwing up. On David's watch he struggled to stay awake as his brain, lacking mental or physical stimulation, automatically shut down and he inevitably fell asleep and drifted off course. When a morning breeze found us we hoisted the sails and established a daily routine but by nightfall heavy alto clouds darkened the sky so on finishing John's soup we reefed the mainsail and switched to the number two genoa. I stood watch with the rig balancing the tiller until a wind increase forced me to wake the guys to drop the genoa and continue with the main and staysail powering us through a restless night.

The following day everyone was quiet and withdrawn, apprehensive about the passage that had barely begun. Having shifted from the airless forward cabin, John's comatose bulk inhabited the navigator's berth and on waking he succumbed to Hornpipe's violent pitching, crashing to the cockpit floor. The children continued their magnet experiments, then John pitched in with a biology lesson featuring rabbits. I was grateful for his help and the Scopolamine patches that were keeping my sickness at bay. The bird and sea life had diminished except for storm petrels, foreshadowing rain squalls that rendered an opportunity to wash the salt from our hair and bodies. With a degree of foreboding we entered our second Good Friday at sea. It was a day for curling in a bunk with a good book but the Scopolamine blurred my vision, so despite heavy waves pounding the hull, splashing into the cockpit, I started making hot cross buns. David managed a morning sight before a squall obliterated the sun, then the weather improved and by evening we were running off the wind on a comfortable course. Despite being sick and pale Billy persisted in scrabbling amongst the Lego, searching for pieces of a castle, suffering it repeatedly, tumbling down, bashing on to the bitter end. He finally conked out, to wake desperately in need of love and reassurance while, to Sam's disgust, he had to sleep in the forward bunk with the leaking hatch dripping whenever Hornpipe shipped a big wave. Though it only affected the starboard bunk we feared there was nothing we could do if the weather deteriorated.

Although a dusk wind increase saw us racing along at seven knots, on the cusp of being over-canvassed the squalls had spun us out of Good Friday without mishap. I woke feeling refreshed, to a sea painted that penetrating blue only found on the furthest reaches of the ocean, and after scurrying about helping the children make Easter nests and presents, we moved the clock back giving us an extra hour and time to consider our commitment. While the awareness there was no way back filled our minds, since our hasty departure we had avoided mentioning the totality of our circumstances. It was reassuring when David's noon fix revealed that during our previous day's run we had sailed a hundred and sixty-five miles and the sight of our brave little line, venturing from the Galapagos into the immense Pacific, had made enough headway for us to embrace the reality of where we were.

The ocean was an unforgiving place for the vulnerable. Having exacerbated his sore throat by resting in a damp corner of the cockpit, David commenced a course of antibiotics. John was suffering indigestion while I combated the bug along with nausea and worries about Billy who was congested with fever, seasickness, and diarrhoea. Sam was the only fit one amongst us, having dealt with the virus before adjusting to the ocean. As night fell he enjoyed the wind in his face, falling asleep in the cockpit. When David carried him to the forward bunk he marvelled at the beauty of the sleeping child's serene body, "*Such deep love. It's there too at occasional moments in daytime when one can momentarily penetrate the external onslaught of noise.*" And though his comment implied that our children were demanding, it merely reflects the confined circumstances that amplified their presence.

Easter day began with Hornpipe romping along and Billy throwing up over the back-cabin steps. At the sight of chocolate eggs and presents he made an immediate recovery and then Sam read him his Captain Pugwash book before immersing himself in a new Asterix adventure. They spent hours colouring rainbows with felt tip pens, enjoying space in the saloon which had become habitable following John's return to the forward bunk. As the wind dropped we opened the ports to refresh the interior and shook out the reefed mainsail to goose wing with the jib. John took the first watch while our family went to bed together and on David's shift he wrote, "*I watched the two boomed sails sweeping and gliding together like two great beating wings, dark against the fading sky, a great bird, swooping along.*"

By day our yacht's relentless rolling and tumbling absorbed all my energy. Caring for the children was a marathon and by the time the sun set I was shattered, yet all I would have achieved was two loaves of bread. I naturally adopt supportive roles and during the following years David and I would develop a collaborative relationship. I often assisted him, accompanying him to the 2002 Milan Furniture Fair where he exhibited *Body Raft*, *Reed Light* and a floor hammock called *Sling*. On meeting William in London we washed the contents of a broken bottle of tequila out of our sons sleeping bag and he revealed that his nose had suffered a similar fate while travelling the States. Meanwhile, Sam was funding his theatre design studies with work at Sadler's Wells, along with a play project for inner London kids. As Sam described helping them film their *The Lion, the Witch, and the Wardrobe*, he reminded me that a generation before I had helped artist Bruce Lacey create a sculptural playground for East End kids. I recalled him at Exeter Art College wearing a green fur coat, a garment sprouting cress seeds, how when the term *performance art* was coined, Bruce commented, *"It finally explained what I'd been doing all my life."* That back then I never guessed my son would choose a similar path.

Having settled into our ocean passage we established a routine two hours of morning school with afternoons free for the children to play. The environment was a source of inspiration, our boat a teaching resource, and on pinning a world map beside the toilet Sam quickly learned the names and locality of most countries and their capitals. Our sons would share flats in both New Zealand and London. There they collaborated with friends in creating *Mobiles*, a short film about relationships in an age of cellular technology. William slept through the final scene, his muscular body featuring as a battleground where armies of toy soldiers rampaged. A year passed and after our return to Milan we anticipated a holiday with our boys in Italy's coastal mountains. Sam arrived to share our squalid room at Giuseppe's, a hotel where one ate breakfast with the upstairs plumbing dripping on the cornflakes. Then an incomplete Trubridge clan gathered at Milan's Stazioni Centrale, *waiting for Billy*.

William had sent a postcard from Honduras, telling of his latest venture. That he had taken up freediving, spontaneously following a whale shark into the depths, returning to the surface, his lungs bursting. His descriptions of solitary evenings spent in peaceful meditation indicated that he was discovering himself. Although William was beyond my reach he had been constantly in my thoughts and every day I dedicated my yoga practice to him, prayed that he still lived. As we awaited his appearance, we hoped and held our breath. My heart was pounding when he condensed out of the crowd, laughingly late. *"You bastard!"* said Sam, as he hugged his brother. And we echoed that, loving him the more for the fear that had flooded our being. Then we caught the train to Linguiletta where we walked, talked, and absorbed the history of those deserted mountain villages; ventured into caverns where their communities had sheltered during the war. Although William was on a new course he knew exactly where he was going and one misty dawn he and Sam meditated in a ruined fortress, sharing the deep connection that had replaced their childhood games.

It is said that a yogi should choose to be born into a family with sympathetic attitudes. Billy and Sam would continue practicing yoga and when William started freediving he asked my advice, and so began his unbroken routine of the highly advanced technique of *nadi shodhana pranayama*. He continued his quest, travelling south to attend the legendary Italian freediver Umberto Pelizzari's transformational introductory course. On resolving to pursue a freediving career, William noted that Umberto's *Manual of Freediving* was only available in Italian, and despite having no knowledge of the language he offered to translate and publish the book in English. William spent that solitary winter translating the book, gaining a fluency in Italian that enabled him to teach freediving in Italy. He had remained in the beautiful Sardinian town of Santa Teresa di Gallura, maximising his savings while writing a futuristic novel and training for freediving. During those days a simple tune playing on the bells of a nearby church entered William's consciousness. Music has a unique power, and a handful of repeated notes may provide a lifeline to hang on to through arduous training sessions; life's challenges. Becoming aware of how his mind lingered on the resonant singular notes, stimulating a yearning for the next to fall, initiated a visualisation of slower sounds that adapted into a technique that lowered William's heart beat in preparation for diving.

During the first week of our passage we had covered one thousand miles, a third of our journey towards the Marquesas. Life on board danced to a lilting rhythm. Gentle waves rolled under and away, days slipped by and the ocean deepened to a miraculous blue. The children accepted whatever

came their way, only asking, *"When's the next island?" "Three weeks." "Oh."*
And then they returned to their sketches of robots and monsters. Billy
had developed a steady hand and eye for colour while Sam drew sights
he had observed, revealing a sophisticated perception in his rendering
of the tortoises at Academy Bay. Resisting using the Scopolamine I
was free of the parched mouth and blurred vision that accompanied
the hallucinogenic drug. However, an anxious need to prepare for the
unpredictable set me whirling, a domestic dervish, in perpetual motion.
I found no rest and as I strove to control the uncontrollable I interrupted
the ambiance of the elements. Eventually I sank into a siesta, avoiding the
temptation of a sleep that would lead to headaches.

The hot, wet environment made clothes an irrelevant encumbrance. It
was simply easier to be naked. We did not consider our innocent bodies
erotically charged and were unashamed of them. While garments
attract attention to what lies hidden beneath, they would have provided
a physical separation from John. Although of similar heights, David's
athletic body was ethereal compared to our crew's barbaric physicality
– qualities that exposed salient differences in their personalities. I felt
remorse for the cloistered privacy of my soul that found John intrusive,
his proximity repulsive. As children, my brother and I had barely noticed
gender differences until puberty divided us. Embarrassed by my emerging
breasts I tugged at my jumper to conceal the bumps and when my brother
persuaded me to sketch bikini clad girls, the significance of those drawings
that he hid in his room were beyond my comprehension. One sunny
school day, I had encouraged my friends to shed their shirts and before we
knew it we were summoned to the headmaster. Our naive responses, *"It's
rude to show our bodies and we might catch cold or get sunburn,"* were typical of
that inhibited era. However, the headmaster's introduction to sculpture
had encouraged my emerging creativity. Selecting a promising student he
drew our attention to her pertinent breasts and bottom, demonstrating
the body's proportions while we immersed ourselves in shaping our
lumpen clay figures, unaware of our intuitive sensuality. Sometime later
the little figures mysteriously disappeared and the headmaster was sacked
for being familiar with the girls. While this introduction to the human
form and the innate character of clay would influence my creativity, it
was my mother's comfortable Mother Earth body that led me to choose
the archetypal female as a recurring theme. She had made no bones
about finding my androgynous frame disappointing, saying *"You are a little*

girl," implying that I was not a real woman, never knowing that I am eternally grateful for the gift of motherhood and a body that dances and defines my impish spirit.

Early one morning we sighted three commercial fishing boats and as they drew closer we saw petrels and shearwaters diving to feed on the tiny fish that followed their wake. In an instant, a flying fish spun from out of the ocean to strike John on his back. Being hit by one's breakfast was a sure indication we were in rich fishing grounds, so he baited a hook in hopes of catching a mahi mahi. We had all withdrawn into our separate shells, with John revealing little of himself except that he had started keeping a journal. I still felt threatened by the intimacy of his benign presence, the absence of anything to define our separate relationship. He seemed to expect more from me, perhaps a shared physicality, but I was not part of the deal and a hint of any contact froze me into an ice maiden. I went about the daily chores guarding my privacy in as prudish a way as possible without a stitch of clothing to hide behind. However, it was impossible to avoid squeezing past John's naked body when we met in a doorway. Sam would reflect upon his child's view of the world: the disconcertion of encountering John's bits at eye level and David's memory of seconding John when hauling the anchor with *"His loose balls hanging out of his scrotty shorts,"* had been an *in your face* moment. Although we shrank from such unsolicited contact, it is probable that John relished random intimacies and, though grateful for his assistance, I recoiled from thoughts of what would happen if David was lost overboard.

At sea, food has a greater significance, and when the gas bottle ran out we thanked our lucky stars we had invested in the new regulator. Transforming raw ingredients into nourishing food was vital for our health and John willingly contributed to the cooking rota, creating Mexican tortillas with an authentic sauce. Pancakes were a fun diversion, with their tossing and turning adding an unpredictable edginess, especially when synchronised with wave action. We were dispatching a lacy light batch, saturated with treacle and lemon, when John cast a disparaging comment, *"Thayet's naht a payncake, thayet's a crayep! Ahl show you a payncake!"* Following his promise, John spent an afternoon plundering our store of flour, bran, dried fruit, molasses, and spice, mixing copious amounts of glutinous batter and liberally splatting it on walls and floor. We waited expectantly as a pungent aroma billowed from the galley. At last, true to his word, John slapped a slab of something healthy and heavy onto the table, making his announcement, "*Nah thayet's a payncake!*" The "*payncake*" was certainly wholesome, but like its maker it was dense, solid, and there was just too much of it. While John's culinary creation could sustain a fisherman hauling nets from the freezing seas off Alaska, it was a liability on a sailing boat in the tropics. In a future era, the grotesque culture of our world's dominant nation would evolve a term to quantify the *payncake's* Olympian investment of sugar and carbohydrate. But we had never been *super-sized,* and our tummies were inadequate to the task of digesting that gastronomic abundance, the excessive flatulence involved. Eventually, overcoming qualms at the cultural violation and waste of vital resources, we hurled their remains at the hungry ocean. However, John's *payncakes* would remain forever lodged in our memories, as they had in our stomachs.

While I refused to admit our dependence on John, the following day he would prove himself more than worthy of his berth on Hornpipe. The wind had evaporated with the sunrise and once again we were wallowing in light air with the sails thudding and crashing, becoming irrevocably worn. David and John decided to change them for our old set, and while I steered downwind to reduce the rolling they stripped Hornpipe of her canvas. Then, seizing an opportunity for a refreshing swim David lost no time jumping in and grasping the rope he had slung in our wake. John had climbed the mast to scan the view from the spreaders and I was preparing Sam and Billy, stalling until the situation was safe. On seeing a creature rising and falling behind David the kids shouted, "*Turtle, turtle!*" He was dropping back along the rope to investigate the shadow in our wake when John's voice boomed out, "*It's not a turtle, it's a shark! Get out of the water!*" And with a boundless alacrity David sprinted along the rope and up the Aries, where from a safe perch we scanned the translucent water. Where seconds before David had clung to the rope we saw the streamlined form of a predator. That foreshortened blob rising on the waves had looked like a turtle, but we had been so wrong. John's dismissive phrase, "*trolling for sharks,*" that he used to describe the fun of being towed behind a boat, took on a sinister significance. For out in the open ocean lone sharks are hungry and less inclined to take an investigative bite – more likely to lunge at their prey. We surmised that the oceanic white tip shark had been following us, living off our refuse, that it was probably responsible for a lost lure and teeth marks on a mahi mahi. Maybe we should have thanked John's *payncakes* for its sluggish reaction to live bait! However the close shave was not one to be repeated, but to be written in the children's journals. For having saved David from a killer shark, Big John would go down in Hornpipe history as a hero.

Following lunch, we wrestled the bulky sails from the locker at the foot of our bunk, and after dragging them up the steps into the cockpit it was *"Old sails for soft winds,"* a release from worrying about the decent ones rotting in the sun. Having inflated the children's dinghy before the *swimming with sharks* episode, I dragged it onto the foredeck where they happily played in a tiny puddle of ocean while we lay on deck watching the stained sails flop, flap, and limply hang on the mast. Although we adults longed for peace and personal space, the children needed to let off steam, and when John took his irritability out on them David recognised himself in the sharp comments, was reminded that Sam and Billy had never chosen to be there, that they helplessly bore our emotions. John had no concept of a child's capabilities and despite generously listening to Sam's chatter, he expected him to participate in the physical work of sailing, calling him *Little Lord Fauntleroy* for being idle. While most boat tasks were too exacting or dangerous for a six year old, as our kids became more able Sam was often too absorbed in his own world to be distracted by nautical practicalities, and it would be Billy who chose to hoist the sails and drop the anchor.

The epic day drifted past without further event with the log entries: *"Fluffy summer clouds to our stern,"* and *"Willing the clouds to produce wind,"* expressing our obsessions with the weather and the futility of wallowing along with the sails' crashing and thudding. However, the gentle motion presented opportunities for me to find cardboard animals for Billy and space rockets for Sam, which he spent days cutting, colouring, and assembling, giving them fantastic names and flying them around the boat. After battling every battle, our children had come to trust and recognise their dependence upon each other. They had learned that there was *"No satisfaction in cheating,"* that playing the game mattered more than winning.

When I grew tired of doing most of the cooking David created an unbelievable meal of spring rolls with sweet and sour sauce followed by a chocolate mandarin concoction. Though I appreciated his effort I believed that John should have stepped up, for despite the previous day's incident, I still failed to appreciate that tolerating our crew was the price we paid for our safety. Hornpipe was too small for confrontations but I confess to having fleetingly caught a comment in John's journal, *"If only Linda would lighten up all would be perfect."* What he wrote saddened me. Although I resented our crew's slothful ways, the catalyst for my negative attitude was John's dominant male presence, his dogmatic declaration that Americans carried the beacon of a moral code to the rest of the world. When he claimed to be a prophet, a potential patriarch, I was appalled. Perhaps all this would come to pass on his arrival in the Marquesas, where he imagined himself surrounded with supplicant women. John's ideological sense of superiority confounded me. A man of stature announces himself through humility and charisma; John had neither.

Friday the twenty-seventh of April was a perfect day for sailing. Hornpipe's drifter gently pulling her along as she hung, suspended between the ascendant sky and infinite depths. Engrossed in the changing patterns of wind, clouds, and waves, we hardly comprehended our incremental drift across the ocean. Hornpipe's position appeared unchanged, as if she were no more than a theatrical invention, a toy yacht bobbing on the cardboard waves of a popup book. We had dared to glance into that great beyond, and aware that land would only eventuate from our constant endeavours and ability to endure, we plotted our position on the chart, secure in the knowledge that our collaborations with the moon, sun, stars, and planets would show us the way.

Imprisoned in the chaotic nucleus of my family I was often too busy to consider the wonders of the ocean. The days were never long enough, the Dan buoy needed mending, bilges bailing, mainsail runners replacing in the track. All must be operational for that time of need. Self-expression was low on my list or maybe I was afraid of slipping into that everlasting void. Yet, one tranquil night watch, with Hornpipe sliding downwind on a silken scarf of Indian ink, I became mesmerised by the sight of our moon sailing on her sea of night, illuminating the clouds with a silver touch. And I found myself breathing with the ocean, painting by the flickering light of the Tilley lamp, identifying the depths with colour, scribbling into the edges of waves, soaking the pages with paint and salt. I could barely see what I was creating but one image led to the next as I greedily grasped for more, losing myself in that absolute suspension of time.

Having come a long way from the homely muddle of Redthorn Cottage, we had reached the very centre of the Pacific Ocean, with the nearest

"Sailing on her sea of night" LT

land Easter Island, twelve hundred miles to the south. While the wind and waves had been steadier than on our Atlantic voyage, memories of sailing from Tortola towards St John, *"Trying to kid ourselves that we were setting out for the Pacific,"* seemed long ago and far away. Each day had led us steadily onward to this furthest point on our longest passage. That morning, David experimented with the sails, to see if Hornpipe would go fractionally faster if he adapted our storm jib into a flop sail under the boom. When it came to rigging the outhaul, John climbed out along the boom and sat there dipping over the waves. As the additional canvas caught the wind, we hoisted the staysail, creating a corridor between the drifter and main, and the guys felt a tremendous satisfaction as Hornpipe swept through the water with grace and efficiency. There was cause to celebrate our halfway point, but little enthusiasm from the reluctant adults whose greater need was for personal space. While John confessed he had always been a loner, that he usually walked out when he had had enough of a situation, an ocean passage allowed no such opportunities for escape; when things got tough in our relationship or circumstances, we had to carry on and make it work. John retreated to the galley while we daubed ourselves with paint and danced around the deck flaunting our zany bodies. Washing it off was even more fun, with the kids releasing their suppressed energy in a wild frolic and the party completed with cheese straws, chocolate crisps, and a game of charades, with the kids simulating every animal they could think of, and many that Billy invented. The day culminated in a magnificent sunset when, with the flop-sail obscuring the view, we climbed up top to sit on the upturned dinghy, watching the sun disappear in a blaze of colour.

By Saturday the wind had become stronger, returning to the south-east, making us hope that the high-pressure system had fled. After the complexities of resetting the stay-sail and gybing the genoa, we were racing. Having abandoned routine school lessons I was engaging the children in topics of interest and finding that despite the lack of other stimulus, they were learning and questioning everything. Billy was engrossed with numbers and reading while Sam drew maps from the atlas and talked about stars, places, and people. On alternate days, I gave them a new book from my hidden store and with everyone occupied David woke Obelix to charge the batteries that powered the lights and ham radio. When the pistons pounded an irregular beat, suggesting a clogged pipe, he stopped the motor to overhaul the system. On starting up David was about to congratulate himself on a good job when he noticed that the temperature gauge had climbed way above normal. Returning to the engine room he grovelled for hours, before he noticed salt water leaking from the pump, indicating a broken shaft seal. Troubled by his diagnosis and lacking tools for the job, David called it a day.

With nightfall the wind backed and dropped, compromising our course but with no motor, wind, or energy we had no choice but to stand our watches coaxing the Aries through the light winds. David's frustration alleviated when he made radio contact with a man in Pennsylvania. Previously he had listened, unable to talk or transmit, hardly knowing what to say, but despite the poor connection he was overjoyed at the knowledge that in an emergency we might be able to communicate. On waking to find that the drifter had torn from luff to leach, I spent my day sewing it with assistance from John who broached the subject of *"building ma'self some noo shorts."* Repairs on his old ones were well overdue but I was not volunteering; John was already too close for comfort and I was not that generous. At sea, one thing leads to another and so it was that when David returned to the turmoil of the engine room he found the pump had frozen tight. After spraying everything with WD40 he left it to soak overnight. Though uneasy about using the petrol generator at sea it was our only option for charging the batteries. Then, immediately after starting it up, the generator abruptly stopped. With a volley of curses, David climbed back into his private hell to discover a blocked fuel line. The mechanical repair proved more exhausting than a storm when, during his attempt at fixing it, a quantity of petrol leaked into the bilge, creating major concerns that if he so much as switched off the engine room light, an electric spark might ignite the fumes, blowing Hornpipe sky high!

Amidst the distractions I had neglected Sam and Billy so I took them on deck to read what I had written the previous night, which in turn inspired Sam's story of two men on a raft who had forgotten about waves when setting sail from Cape Horn to Antarctica. While he had been inspired by his geography lesson, my tale was of a little bird that had visited during my watch: *"Early one pink and lavender dawn, a bird the colour of the clouds came to take a closer look at Hornpipe. She flew around calling, 'chirp, chirp, what are you doing with these little children so far from land?' Hornpipe replied, 'Swish, slosh, flip a flap, and have you followed us from the Galapagos, hoping to get your portrait painted?' They resolved their differences by dancing together. The little bird circled Hornpipe's swaying mast while she rippled her sails and dipped her boom in time with the waves. Then a small star peeped from behind a curtain of clouds. Being a special star she would perform in the theatrical menagerie of dawn, but not content with one dance she lingered, wishing to curtsy again. The clouds framed her sparkle, the dewy dawn mingled her colours in a magical mist before hastening to welcome the haughty sun, who was taking his familiar path through the sky. 'Why do you always go the same way Mister Sun?' trilled the cheeky bird. 'Why not take a twisting twirl around the mast with me?' sang that little traveller as she flew away over the seas, following a pattern birds have always known. Hornpipe waved and chuckled. 'Only I am free to go where I will. To fly with the wind filling my sail wings, as I carry the children curled, safe and snug, inside my hull. What fun we have. I can hardly wait for the next island, to see them plop like noisy pebbles into the water and surface with an explosion of bubbles, to feel their little feet running around my decks as they shout and laugh. For how quiet and still they have had to be, out on this great ocean.' Then Hornpipe became silent as the clouds cried, 'Look at us now. We are a steam train, puffing through a blue skyscape. See how the wind has transformed our trucks into a helter, skelter, fleeting, fleeing, fantasy flock of fluffy sheep.' 'Enough!' cried a giant thundercloud, his shout swallowing them up, capturing my mind. Meanwhile, inside Hornpipe the children stir from their golden honeycomb of sleep, and as another noisy day begins the fantasies fly away. My limbs tingle and the sky of my mind is rubbed clean of pictures."*

TO BE PACIFIC

"All my longings are to be
Where waves are no longer sea
But land's sweet curves to enfold me."
Linda Trubridge

David would claim that the first of May was the worst day possible. It began at that vulnerable time of waking, when on John's dawn watch the mainsail abruptly gybed, demanding we combat the tangled sails. The poignant reminder of our Atlantic disaster was another warning we could never relax our guard. Once the mainsail was sorted, the Aries started tormenting us with its habit of wandering off course, and amidst David's attempt to wrestle the *"useless contraption"* into submission, I took the helm. His response to such problems began with heartfelt curses followed by attempting to distance himself in hopes that time might erase the difficulty, but our close proximity made it impossible to detach ourselves from such situations. We could not stop the boat to take a break, or send the children outside to run around the garden; I could only soothe and support David, but whatever I did was never enough.

On his return to the engine's water pump David found it totally jammed. At land, parts could be borrowed or bought, advice sought, but at sea he bore the burden of fixing Hornpipe's mechanics alone with limited tools and no replacement parts. It appeared futile to free the mechanism and the thought of sailing through the Pacific Islands without a motor was daunting. David lay on the cabin roof while I massaged the congealed tension that gripped his shoulders and neck; felt him escape into the mesmerising sea and endless sky. On revisiting the engine room David noticed oil seeping through a breather hole, and not along the pump shaft as he had previously thought. The potential resolution of what had seemed an insurmountable problem supported his claim that time provides a solution, and although his philosophy was rarely a winner in our relationship issues, it was a relief to have Obelix up and running.

As the day wore on the disasters melted but as we ate supper against the backdrop of a vivid sunset, John said he smelt petrol and once again David descended into the hell hole, to find that he had forgotten to replace a small washer; that a drip from the fuel tap had filled the tiny space with highly combustible petrol fumes. As we prepared for another night without lights the Aries began compromising our course, but following some fiddling the mechanism appeared to be working. Then with a resounding crash the boom swung across with a shocking force that shredded our nerves, wrenching the preventer, and almost snapped the stanchion to which it was attached. David had done all he could to avert the barrage of breakages, but the gremlins had won; and as he stormed off to bed I collapsed in the cockpit.

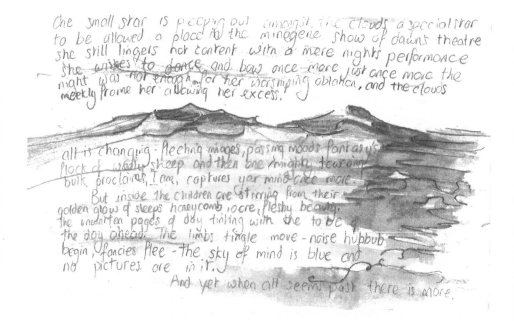

Wave hills LT

This was not the freedom David had promised himself. John was no help and carrying the total responsibility of navigating and fixing things was all too much. After weathering my husband's emotions, I longed to be anywhere but on the ocean dealing with life-threatening problems. Escaping into my journal I tried to paint and ended up writing, *"The heaving sea drives me crazy, sails flutter, paints run, and the sky changes again. Words cannot describe the clouds' colours, the light of the spirit."* David's dawn patrol gave him space to shrug off the battleground of the previous day, to establish a new rhythm. The inactivity of steering was his opportunity to speculate on the malevolent forces that had conspired against him, to seek a rational explanation for problems that had assumed a planetary scale. Drawing comfort from the infinite stars David wrote, *"A moonlit sky is a less wondrous sight, more like daytime. The stars need no thoughts – it is enough just to look and their beauty slowly fills you and uplifts you."*

The children had also learned how to escape their predicament. Sam had become a prolific reader and books filled days that were bereft of stimulus. Despite my concern that Billy was too young to read, he desperately wanted to share his brother's world. Imitating Sam's actions, his finger following the black squiggles on the page, he made up the story, speaking quietly to himself, or very loud, so that everyone would hear how well he could read. When I intervened, Billy said, *"I can do it myself,"* and he obviously considered the processes of learning completely irrelevant, thinking I was holding him back with my simple silly books. On the Atlantic, Billy had been a delightful, easy going toddler while Sam had acted the demanding child. Both were as strong willed as their father and accommodating their conflicting needs consumed my dwindling energy. Images of the lost nail, the despairing mother adrift on the endless ocean, an empty pushchair in a crowded market, and identical trees upon a vast plateau, haunted me then and now. A reminder that I must remain alert and aware. But show me the parent that has not, at some time, relaxed his or her vigilance; does not the pursuit of absolute safety present more sinister dangers? The addiction of digital games and sedentary lifestyles create children who miss out on life.

Back then it often seemed I was the only one conscious of our extreme predicament. Our children were unaware they were living an adventure, but in time they would pass on what their nomadic life taught them; not least the determination they applied to everything they did. When

William started freediving I realised that nothing I said would deter him from his quest to achieve a world record; that our parents must have felt the same when we told them we were going sailing. Although I was deeply fearful for William, I could not protect him and my only means of dealing with the anxiety was to embrace and understand his passion. In choosing to make freediving the subject of my research for a yoga qualification, I dispelled my ignorant fears and discovered its relationship to Yogic philosophy: concluding, that all humans strive for transformation; our spiritual need is greater than self-preservation. While a woman may find fulfilment and self-realisation in giving birth and rearing a child, a man's worth is too often measured through physical and aggressive endeavours. However, these instincts can be converted into actions that develop an inner strength and balance of body, mind, and spirit. For example, those who become involved in freediving, rock climbing, and surfing often discover that what began as a physical communion with nature evolves into a spiritual journey.

As the wind gathered strength we replaced the old sails with the dependable newer ones and, on noticing that the topping lift had wound itself around the back stay, we hauled John up the mast to sort it out. Half the morning disappeared in the operation. Soon after, while John was dozing on watch, a Japanese fishing boat passed without him noticing. I thought the close encounter would encourage his vigilance until, for no good reason, he abandoned the tiller, allowing the bow to swing into the wind. With a violent crash the boom slammed across in a savage gybe that strained the preventer, tore the stanchion, and smashed the bimini, catapulting a cushion into the sea. I can see the arc of the inconsequential cushion as it met the jostling waves, and how, in the blink of an eye, it had disappeared in our wake. The mishap reminded me that when sailing downwind the speed of Hornpipe's transit and the time it would take to change her sail configuration to tack upwind, would be too slow and disorientating to locate a floating object.

I watched David prepare for the noon sight, saw him release the sextant from its battered case, prayed that he would open the wet weather locker and reach for the red and yellow harness that lay beneath a muddle of jackets. He passed by the locker, but before he could step out of the cockpit I was there, timidly reaching out, saying, *"Haven't you forgotten something?"* And, docile as a dog, I offered the harness. But nothing would persuade

David, and as he braced his back against the mast and prepared for the fix, I shuddered and turned away. In my mind's eye, I see him hold the sextant high, throw his head back to capture the sun in its mirrors, bring the orb down to the horizon. David's complete focus allowed no quarter for self-preservation and without a harness there was no provision for that miscreant wave, a momentary lurch that could throw him off balance.

On our Atlantic crossing an anarchic attitude had allowed everyone to contribute their opinion and though I accepted that a ship must be controlled by her captain, this gave my husband a hierarchical advantage. David and I had conflicting perceptions of danger and while he felt that going on deck was the equivalent of a walk in the park, I could only imagine the consequences of one fatal slip. And the faster we sailed, the greater my anxiety. While David's refusal to consider my request appeared to display a lack of concern for his family, his only thought was that I wanted to restrain his freedom. He despised my 'psychological obsession,' saw my seasickness as a lack of appreciation of the wonders that surrounded us, considered me a fussing mother who should have stayed at home. The presence of our children in dangerous circumstances inhibited the fun-loving person David wanted me to be. My knuckles gripped tighter with each navigation sight. As Hornpipe's speed increased my stomach twisted in a knot leaving me quivering with emotion but pleadings, prayers, and sleepless nights were to no avail, and although I knew our characters were compatible, that we truly loved each other, I felt utterly alone. David was behaving like a rebellious teenager but there was nothing I could do or say to change his mind, to harness my Bear.

David and I were so close, and yet we appeared to inhabit separate planets. Before we met, while I quenched a thirst for travel and adventure, David had built a house and established skills. His transition to parent and provider had fuelled a yearning for freedom. The liberated women of my generation had paid the price of expectations that we could do anything and everything, with our men saying, "*You think you are our equals; go on and prove it!*" Throughout my life I had tried and failed to keep up with my brother, boyfriend, husband, had brought it upon myself in my choice of partner and lifestyle. My limitations were as much a safety issue as my husband's obstinate stance on the harness was symptomatic of the responsibilities he carried, and no matter how I improved, David would always exceed my strength, experience, and knowledge. And without him we were all lost at sea.

The problem was a conundrum. There was no one with whom I could share my concern; no friend to advise, my need to communicate denied. And when alone, the comforting words of hymns and prayers returned as uninvited, yet welcome guests.

> *"Breathe through the heats of our desire*
> *Thy coolness and thy balm;*
> *Let sense be dumb, let flesh retire;*
> *Speak through the earthquake, wind, and fire,*
> *O still, small voice of calm!"*

Seeking support from deep within myself I accessed an inner world that I could enter whenever I chose. On those intense night watches when waves pounded Hornpipe's hull I escaped to the life I had left behind. And while maintaining the course, my mind meticulously visualised every detail of a familiar scene, conjuring up family, friends, and chattering gossip I would have abhorred in real life. I imagined setting a table for an afternoon tea, and other claustrophobic gatherings that distracted my mind from the immense solitude. Then, as certainly as a feather pillow brings comfort and sleep, the terror passed.

On another occasion, I recalled a family visit to an old couple who lived on a farm near Cosby. After my brother and I had eaten our fill of cakes and relentlessly played *Over the Sea to Skye* on the parlour piano, we negotiated the yard's pungent cow pats and steaming beasts to walk the frosty lane home, under a sky sprinkled with stars. My mother knew all the constellations and we were filled with wonder when she gave names to those tiny points in that infinite space. One summer evening we watched a barn burn in a fiery conflagration, returning home to a rice pudding that, forgotten in the excitement, had cooked to perfection. The trees of that copse remaining stark and scorched in memories that I plundered at my ease to recreate the security of days when, longing for adventure, I set off skipping down the patched concrete road that led from the settlements into Cosby. Familiar windows winked at my passing. Dark passages opened to allotment gardens and the telephone box where I had made furtive phone calls to a boyfriend, a coin for each minute. Here was a house curtained for a birth, there a wall that had served as a train, a horse or bridge over a crevasse. Pausing, I gazed into my school playground where bottles of warm milk still curdled in crates, crossed the road to avoid the newspaper shop's delivery boys as they spat frothing spit and gobs of gum into the gutter. When a fight spilled into the filthy alley I hurried from their curled fists; still menacing after all those years. Church bells clanged and a spiritual magnet drew me towards those ancient walls that echoed a cold flame of unnamed desires as I recalled the teenager who, with nowhere else to go, had found solace there. How had she become a mother alone on the sea, viewing memories of her evolution from girl to woman through a lens that layered every building, puddle, and plant with nostalgia?

I often imagined what Rachel, Rondi, Jan, and Naomi might say, how their gentle presence would transform the solid male company into laughter and light. As a teenager, I had attempted to emulate Rondi's mysterious moods, but my enthusiasm always got in the way. She and her sister Jan had shared my schooldays and at weekends I rode my bike from the settlements to their council house, my long black coat and hair flying in the wind. Scuttling upstairs we created extravagant garments, plaited braids, painted henna on our hands, and wailed with Joan Baez. Clothed as Macbeth's three witches we hitched to Stratford where we bought standing tickets to be enthralled by every gesture and costume. Their Yugoslavian mama had welcomed me into her family, telling of how she had fought with the Italian resistance while her husband slumped in an armchair, heavy as the granite he hauled at the quarry. And all to feed and clothe his beautiful daughters as they blossomed from girls to women. Potatoes were often the only fare at the Crick house, yet every Friday Sid biked home with a fresh red rose for his wife. My father's toil before the humming turbines was typical of the drudgery those men endured after the war. But my generation had broken free. Rondi abandoned her typing pool and fiancé to join me on a creative path. Forever united, the sisters married on the same day, to live in a stately house that emulates the Italian villa I always imagined for them.

While I had found a way to transform those dark nights of my soul, if taken to an extreme such escapism could become a psychosis; however, delusions were my least concern with seasickness and Scopolamine addling my mind. I never asked myself what comfort Sam and Billy sought. My childhood happiness had rested on an absolute belief in my parents. But my background had been predictable, while Sam and Billy, lacking friends, relatives, and an all-powerful god, had only their infinite trust in us. Without some form of creative fulfilment, Sam's intellect would be adrift, a ship without direction. On completing his Slade Masters course, he returned to his former home in Northumberland with the intention of making a short film. *The Harvest* opened onto a foreboding landscape that framed a bereft woman inexplicably screaming into a hole in a ploughed field. The scene cut to a dark interior where a man beat the woman in a way that implied generations of brutality. One sees her vent her anguish into the barren soil, returning again and again until, finally, the earth cried back with a great wail of misery. While Sam had created the film as a taster for his full-length feature, *The Circus of Errors* would require financial support that only a reputation could generate. Sam eventually translated his script into a play that won second place in a Pacific radio drama competition. The story of twin brothers, enslaved to the tyrannical ringmaster of a travelling circus, featured performing cows, clowns, and gymnasts, and is set amidst a sinister landscape that taints the proceedings with an inevitable doom. We could only wonder why Sam's imagination had spawned those surreal characters caught up in that obsessive cycle of good and evil.

When the early morning mists cleared on the fourth of May they revealed towering banks of cumulus, Hornpipe surging along under her goose winged genoa and mainsail, her tightly sheeted stay sail swinging her back on course whenever she pirouetted on an irresistible wave. Our passage had become a blur of ceaseless days and solitary nights of perpetual motion, when it seemed nothing mattered other than our optimistic line of crosses extending towards the Marquesas. With just six hundred miles to Fatu Hiva, we should soon be there. A quiet calm prevailed, with the kids settling into school work after a session drawing shipwrecks and aeroplane crashes. David had bravely returned to the engine where, after spreading epoxy putty over a vent in the water pump, he bodged the remainder into holes in the dinghy. The real test would be when the engine had run for long enough to build up heat, but so far so good. I pottered about the galley making a chocolate cake to celebrate the anniversary of our meeting; despite David having no recollection of the date, he was always willing to eat a cake.

The day's haloed sun was followed by a watery sunset that predicted a change of weather. A wave thumped the hull, sparkled for a frozen moment, and fell as heavy rain upon my naked body. The wisp of a crescent moon appeared, and as lightning flashed across the sky silver waves reared from the void; stampeding horses with foaming flanks, leaping and tumbling, galloping away forever. Dawn revealed a transcendent sky and brilliant blue ocean. Then, in a moment the mood changed, as the wind veered, compounding the swell into lumpy waves that threw Hornpipe off course. David's frustrations with recurring mechanical failures were compounded on discovering the batteries were desperately low, that despite our using the Tilly lamp on night watches, they could barely sustain the fresh water pump and stereo. As his mood congealed to a seething aggravation with the Aries for wandering off course and irritation with John for being such a dull lump, I couldn't help but speculate on the chances of retaining our sanity if we continued on to Australia.

When Hornpipe danced in harmony with the Aries we were all free. While I baked bread, I helped the kids with their schoolwork, maximising our limited resources to create a relevant education. We had invented cartoons of a fictional French friend, *"Henri meets Sam and Billy,"* to familiarise them with the prevalent language of the Pacific, and had begun studying the creatures that inhabited their ocean environment. While Sam and Billy absorbed every scrap of stimulus their unrelenting needs drove me on with as much determination as Hornpipe's straining canvas. As we neared our destination I wrote, *"I grow weary of always having a trick up my sleeve. I long for a beach full of surprises, for that stillness, that nothing happening unless one voluntarily chooses to set one's limbs in motion. Here, everything is active, sundry items sway hypnotically from side to side, books slither over tables and pots fall from cupboards. Going with the roll, I resist the thrust and brace my muscles against the lurch that throws me at the walls; tuned to the tension of rigging and sails I remain alert, a tiger ready to pounce."* Becoming infected by the proximity of land, the children erupted in noisy games, and when we introduced Scrabble to subdue their craziness I never imagined that some thirty years later they would play a computer-generated version, maintain a daily connection from opposite ends of the world. On sharing my anxiety about William's challenging life, Sam said, *"Well he's still alive because he just sent through his latest Scrabble move, and he's winning as usual; the bastard!"* Nothing had changed, my boys were still competing but as always it was the game that mattered.

For safety's sake, we had chosen to cross the main shipping routes at an oblique angle instead of running with them, but as we drew closer to our destination we set a course directly towards Fatu Hiva. On Sunday the wind moved south and we decided to make haste with hopes of making a landfall on Tuesday. After gybing and setting a weather helm against luffing, we endured the same lurching reach as those first days of our passage. The voyage was ending as it had begun, with a violent twisting motion; the fluctuating wind filling our nights and days with sail changes. David increased his navigation to maintain a greater accuracy and on crossing a line from a moon fix with a sight from the noon sun he tried to explain the process to our crew. John's slow wits still mystified us and after deducing that long-term drug use had vacated his brain we wondered whether it would be easier to teach our children to navigate.

With an increased speed Hornpipe had covered a hundred and fifty-two miles on a run, but land couldn't appear fast enough for David and, seeking space and solitude, he took himself off to the fore deck to fix the broken anchor windlass. Since straining his back in Panama, David had needed John's help in hauling the anchor and chain from the depths. When we travelled on alone we would need a functioning windlass. It would have been useful to have my father's skill in making new parts from raw metal to repair his ship's engine, for John was no help whatsoever. Even at shore we lacked the funds to buy more efficient machines or to pay a mechanic and David was forced to fix all the problems himself. He took none of the delight that he had when mending the boom, and from the safe distance of the cockpit we heard him braying at the frozen cogs. As the tempo of his blasphemies built to a crescendo it became obvious he had lost the plot. Eventually he abandoned himself to bashing the *"Useless heap of crap"* with the crowbar and by this method and madness, he somehow freed the internal cogs. But in the battle some threads had broken and when the wind died David was too tired to steer his watch.

The following day our noon fix revealed we were just two hundred and twenty miles from the Polynesian Island that Thor Heyerdahl had written of in *Fatu-Hiva*. My granddad King had left it to me, along with Darwin's *Origin of Species* and recordings of Beethoven's Ninth Symphony; they had played a significant role in my evolution. And as we came within reach of the Marquesas I began cleaning the boat while David reassembled the windlass only to discover that a vital shaft key remained at the bottom of the bucket, decreeing another torture session.

Over the course of our passage we had united with the elements, accepted their savage power; sunrises and sunsets had burned trails through our hearts. But what would remain of the all-consuming rituals and routines of those remorseless days and solitary nights, that purity of body, mind, and spirit? Our boys had learned to make the most of every circumstance and Sam's casual comment, *"When we arrive in Fatu Hiva, I'm going to take the cars onto the beach to play with them all day,"* made me realise how sensitive he had become. As a diversion we held the first and last *Hornpipe Sports Day* with Sam, Billy, and John the main contestants. Attached to safety lines, they raced to the bow, bashing knees and toes on winches and deck cleats. Boredom was forgotten in an insane lemon and spoon race with the ocean an unpredictable competitor that delighted in pitching the athlete into the rigging. After jumping around in sail bags we completed the self-destruction with a water fight. Miraculously our injuries were minor, apart from the skin on Sam's nose which he sacrificed in a contest to push a Smarty along the deck.

When David's dawn star fix and noon sight revealed that Fatu Hiva was just sixty miles away we decided to push on in hopes of a sighting before dark. Sure enough, at four fifteen John soberly announced, *"I think I see land!"* and there was the faintest outline of a mountain sloping to the sea. As usual David was surprised at his accuracy, for if just one factor in his navigation had lacked an increment we could have potentially hit an unforeseen coast or wandered aimlessly over the ocean. A sailing boat responds to ocean currents, wind, and waves in a similar way that a hiker avoids canyons and cliffs when climbing a mountain, so locating an eight mile island after three thousand featureless miles was an amazing accomplishment. And though we longed for land, we lacked nothing; however if our tanks had run dry we would have been thirsty because none of the ocean squalls had yielded water.

Hornpipe sped along and by the time the sun was low on the horizon Fatu Hiva's misty mountains filled our vision. We chose to hand steer a course south of the island where, with the moon to light our way, we could seek shelter before it became completely dark. And as the sun set in regal splendour John and David shackled on the forty-five kilogram CQR anchor in readiness. While they slept I stood watch, gazing up the black rockface that ascended to moonlit meadows, hovering above the rippling sea. A land of shadows and mist, beyond the realm of mortals. After waking John I went below, to dream of walking those magical mountains. I became a bird swooping over the ridges and valleys, looking down on our boat's flickering gem of light; and in my memory those images remain, more poignant than any visualised walk through my past.

John roused David to a tremendous wind funnelling down the gigantic Pointe Tataaihoa. Stunned by the sight of huge waves and a broken sea crashing against towering cliffs, David seized the wheel and sent John up to gybe the sails. As they rounded the petrified cascade of black rock the wind completely died, so they dropped the sails and woke Obelix. As they passed the village of Omo'a, the moon sunk beneath the horizon and, despite having Hanavave's Bay of Virgins in their sights, powerful gusts hurtling down the crags made it too risky to venture closer. The sea was calm so the guys decided to shelter offshore with John opting to sleep on the deck. The night was frothy with expectations. Were we there, or was it a dream? It felt like the night before Christmas; yet the sun would rise on a more spectacular day.

Dawn still slumbered when we stumbled on deck to be greeted by the sight of mountains condensing out of darkness. As we watched, the golden light revealed colossal buttresses and craggy profiles that towered ever higher. Senses that had wearied of the endless ocean, eyes that had grown accustomed to flowing waves gazed up at jagged escarpments that crested against a brightening sky. Land was a vertical amongst horizontals, a static upon the kinetic sea. The passage of time and travel had washed us clean. Hornpipe had brought us to that moment and as she rested, drifting upon the silky

"Land was a vertical among horizontals, a static upon the kinetic" LT

water, we luxuriated in the morning's mellow tranquillity. What more could we ask than to silently watch, overwhelmed with the glorious sight. And then, in a moment, there was more, so much more! The sky filled with a glowing arc of vermilion and purple as a sudden shaft of sunlight beamed through a cleft in the ragged ridge, renting the mountain asunder, spilling in golden cascades that poured down the mossy cliffs, painting the hidden valleys and waterfalls with jewelled light.

And I wonder: had they silently amassed in the valleys of the ocean, gathered in the sleeping mirror of the sea, waiting to herald this dawn? For in that heartbeat, as the sun awakened the primal depths, aquatic angels moved amongst us, their breath filling the silence with sensual sound. Dolphins were everywhere, diving, leaping, splashing, surfacing, welcoming us to Polynesia with a rapturous homage; an ecstatic journey's end. Out on the ocean it had seemed we were destined to sail for all eternity, and yet those travails had led us to this waking dream. Light and land had appeared, the living waters pulsed with luminous creatures; this truly was the creation. Inadequate words drifted away as we watched, transfixed in wonder. Then, as silently as they had arrived, our dolphin friends returned to the inky depths.

ALONE

"The conditions of a solitary bird are five.
The first that it flies to the highest point.
The second that it does not suffer for company,
not even of its own kind.
The third that it aims its beak to the skies.
The fourth that it does not have a definite colour.
The fifth that it sings very softly. "
St John of the Cross

Windless sails and a calm sea rendered Hornpipe's deck open territory for the children; how they appreciated those forgotten freedoms of jumping, climbing, the space to act out their fantasy games. There was no hurry, and on motoring towards Hanavave we surveyed an enticing boulder beach fringed with palm trees, a rocky citadel with ramparts of vertical vegetation that hid verdant trees in secret ravines; shadowed gullies carpeted with vivid ferns. Those dizzy peaks and pinnacles appeared to fall from the sky to probe the depths with gesturing fingers, and even when Hornpipe almost touched the black volcanic cliffs there was still no evidence of a sea floor. Following weeks with no visible definition of our place on the planet, no sensations but those of the sea, every sight, smell, and sound of land was beyond belief. Polynesia already enthralled us, yet we had not set foot ashore. When an outrigger launch sped into view we waved ecstatically at the smiling crew. Our first sight of the island's inhabitants was excitingly significant, while to them we were just another of the yachts that came and went, birds of passage forever on the move.

As Hornpipe motored into Hana Vave Bay our senses were overwhelmed and, after dropping our anchor, we rowed ashore to where a dozen brightly painted outriggers were hauled up on the black sand beneath a towering buttress. Stumbling onto the beach we shuffled crabwise, dizzy and dazed with Billy as puzzled as when we had arrived in the Canaries. A woman, clad in a patterned *pareau*, with flowers in her black hair, emerged from a garden and took us to meet Matthias, the village elder and Gendarme. Matthias showed no sign of enforcing his authority when, after advising us to clear customs in Hiva 'Oa, he gave us a sack of gigantic grapefruits and a lawn mower part to fix. Then his beautiful daughter led us into the house, where a great ream of matted bark cloth infused the gloom with a mysterious earthy aroma. The magnificent cultural creation with its stylised foliage and mythological figures was the first *tapa* we had encountered, however with no funds and every conceivable space on Hornpipe taken, it would have to remain a memory.

When John began playing his flute, Matthias produced a harmonica, hesitantly feeling for common ground in their musical tastes. After a while we wandered away, following the stream, often gazing up at the rocky pinnacles that filled the sky. The air buzzed with fecundity and every turn of the path was a revelation, each flower a source of delight. Tangy grapefruits quenched a deeper thirst, and when we came on a pool shaded with luscious foliage we ventured in to wash off the salt and frolic in the zingy water. Shrimps nibbled toes and our skin tingled with forgotten sensations as our senses awoke after weeks of confinement. We returned, Sam skipping along chattering gaily, while Billy was withdrawn, often disintegrating in tears. The afternoon passed as we lay on the grass in the shade of the outriggers, laughing and singing with a group of young Polynesians who happily allowed me to draw them.

Despite having no certain plans for the future, as our distance from Britain had increased thoughts of returning receded. Fatu Hiva was the furthest we had ventured from urban society, and our voyage on would be a regression towards

LT

203

so called civilisation. There was no way back and as that memorable day drifted into dreams of dolphins leaping in the tingling air, flying through the depths we slept as never before. Waking to the aftermath of a three-week voyage we rowed ashore to embark on a heap of washing, with the children eagerly hanging dripping clothes on a communal line. Then we scrubbed the mass of goose barnacles and green slime that was growing on Hornpipe's waterline. Ballerina of Skellig arrived after a twenty-four day passage, along with a family on a French boat that, adrift for eighty-two days, had resorted to eating dog food (but spared the hound), while the vessel's garden of encrusted weed and its lack of a defining bow or stern appeared as devoid of direction as its owners. The *Ark's* angular hull was typical of other home-built boats that had been fabricated from steel or concrete in the Gaelic back yard. Such yachts bore evidence of their creator's interactions with new skills and names that suggested their owners' characters. Charivari, or *higgeldy piggeldy*, was a rusty barque from which a tribe of scruffy children erupted like jack-in-a-boxes; while the pink exterior of Oiseaux de Passage, *migrating birds*, revealed a hypnotic interior that reflected its enigmatic occupants, whose invitation for tea led to philosophical discussions on art and the romance of sailing.

Although David and I were freed of the routines of cruising, our days were anything but cruisy. John had become intensely annoying. He contributed nothing and we considered sailing on to Hiva 'Oa just to be free of him, and often found ourselves glancing over at Ballerina, where Alan, their crew, was always busy with something. David and Alan dived for fish and lobsters with little success. However, within the rocky recesses they discovered chocolate brown leopard cowries, and brought them back, marvelling at their glossy patterns. When the children found more washed up on the beach they started a shell collection. One moonlit evening we wrapped our torches in plastic bags and while I watched for sharks the guys dived into spooky caverns. On Saturday afternoon we escaped John's static presence for a family walk, following the river through meadows where copra had been stacked to dry amongst the palms. Further inland, dense copses of mango trees spread canopies of shade and mulch upon the earth. While Sam and David clambered over boulders and tree trunks, Billy and I remained, drifting in the stream. On climbing higher, they saw waterfalls cascading from vertical cliffs, columns of peaks towering to the sky, and when they returned we wandered home through the gathering dusk.

On our last day, David took a break, scrambling up the rock face to the right of the anchorage, finding a way amongst the thick grass and guava bushes that covered the outcrops. As the going became hazardous David realised that retracing his steps would be impossible; that a fall would mean certain death. He was committed to going up and remained stuck for a long time before continuing, using tiny indentations as hand holds, making moves that relied on balance, agility, and confidence. Remembering the climbing rule of maintaining three points of contact he eventually reached the top with knees wobbling, heart pounding. There he sat watching the activities in the bay, Ballerina setting sail for Hiva 'Oa, Sam and Billy playing on Hornpipe's deck. Then he turned his gaze inland to where a new road was being blasted through to the village of Omo'a. As usual David wanted to continue, but lacking food and water it was time to take the longer, safe route down to the bay.

Thanks to Matthias' leniency we had remained in the shadow of Fatu Hiva for five days. He gave us a supply of bananas, oranges, and pomplemousse, and requested we claim that Hornpipe had only just arrived in Fatu Hiva. We clinched the deal by giving him a ride to Hiva 'Oa and following sad farewells we were rewarded with a fast downwind sail. By dawn we were weathering squalls and rolling waves as we ate breakfast in Hiva 'Oa's exposed Baie Tahauku (Atuona Bay). After rowing Matthias and his ten sacks of oranges to a small freighter that would transport him to Tahiti, David set off on the two mile walk to Atuona village. A lift took him along the dusty road to the small habitation that lay beneath a range of purple cliffs and black clouds. The Gendarme, who had spent his morning checking in American yachts, gave a sigh of relief when our Captain spoke French and after explaining the complexities of entering French Polynesia, David wrote a request to our bank in Haltwhistle - to guarantee that on reaching Tahiti we would pay a bond, equivalent to the cost of sending our family home. Then David visited a shop awash with yachties where on comparing trips he discovered that Hornpipe's passage of three thousand miles in twenty-one days amounted to the fastest that season.

The following day we all endured the long hot walk to Atuona, with John carrying his rucksack and skateboard which he stashed behind the quay. Amongst the yachties making extravagant purchases was a bunch of pretty Californian girls in frocks and shorts. As we shared sailing stories they bemoaned the ordeal of cooking for the first time, one of them saying that after two months of marriage she longed to return to mommy and daddy. I had hardly spoken when she interrupted, *"Hey your voice is cute. Guys, come listen, speak some more!"* Searching for words I mentioned that I came from England, to which she asked, *"Say, what language do they speak there?"* My laugh faltered on realising she was deadly serious. I felt like a curiosity from outer space, but what planet was she from, and how had these lost souls crossed an ocean without a corner store to stock their shelves, a television to fill the vacuum? Most of the American yachts were equipped with gadgets and while I could not help but covet their roller furling rigs and navigation aids, if their technologies failed they were sunk. When the girls' conversation turned to concerns about tarnished silverware and damp linen I realised it was pointless mentioning my anxieties and wandered off, grateful for the interaction that had made me aware that I was more able than I knew.

The artist Gauguin had lived in Atuona, visually recording the islanders' culture and spirituality that had flourished in the Pacific before seafarers and missionaries brought the diseases and religion that almost destroyed their civilisation. While criticised for his sexual deviances, Gauguin's sins were modest compared with the priests, who tainted the Polynesians' instincts with guilt and shame. Gauguin recognised the people's enduring innocence and portrayed them as archetypal holy figures. His journal, *Noa Noa, a Fragrant Exhalation*, speaks of them with reverence: *"They dream, they love, they sleep, they sing, they pray and I see distinctly even though they are not there, the statues of their female deities. Statues of Hina and festivals in honour of the Goddess of the Moon."* For all my life I had admired the earthy power of Gauguin's sensual women and there I was on those shores, hibiscus flowers in my hair, a colourful *pareau* wrapping my spare form.

Despite John's attempt at persuading us to sneak him into French Polynesia to avoid paying his bond, we had abided by the legal requirements. Maybe that explained why, after paying back money he owed us, John melted into the crowd, never saying goodbye, leaving us wondering whether he would achieve his dream of staying on in Hiva 'Oa, earning a living fixing the lawn mowers of the lovely vahine in exchange for bed and board. Then we bought baguettes and indulged in the most appreciated ice cream ever, and had hardly set off on the long walk home when the children found a baby chick, lying, panting beside the rough road. They took turns carrying it, stroking its yellow down and urging it to live but, sadly, the chick was destined to die in its cardboard box.

Following what had felt like a life sentence, we were free of John, and once David had made a last trip to check out of Hiva 'Oa he winched up the anchor while I started the motor. The water pump reverted to leaking so we cautiously motored around the western corner of Pointe Teaehoa, whereupon fresh breezes and showers set us sailing, and collecting water, leaping around the deck, frothy with soap, teeth chattering, wrinkled as frogs. We had a rendezvous with a welder who we hoped would repair Hornpipe's broken stanchion, but as we drew near Serge's yacht with its perky cockerel weathervane we saw that he was busy fixing the American boats. The Ballerinas were there and as the children attempted to paddle their inflatable dinghy ashore they invaded our friends' sacrosanct happy hour with laughter and howls. Eventually I dropped them ashore, where despite being bitten by sandflies that the locals called no-nos, they became immersed in an endless game. Days drifted by as we waited in line, only to find the welder could not fix our stanchion, and when we next met Serge at a supermarket in Mo'orea, I didn't immediately recognise the welder who had abandoned his dungarees and helmet for a g-string.

During spare moments David and I windsurfed, with the mountains of Hiva 'Oa and Tahuata providing a spectacular backdrop. He dived with the Ballerinas, and while they searched in vain for large fish and lobster, David claimed enough small ones for a meal before the scavenger sharks moved in. On our return, I patrolled while he shot two red glass eyes, which Sam almost lost as he scaled their slippery bodies with his fingers. David and I suffered another barnacle session, diving and scrubbing upside down, finding it impossible to avoid the inadvertent gulp of toxic blue residue, gliding to the surface with lungs bursting. I only lasted a short time, but David had expended all his energy and later, when he became terribly sick, we suspected the poisonous anti-foul and excessive time underwater.

David was still exhausted when we sailed on a gentle breeze towards the north-western side of Hiva 'Oa, and as we drifted a tuna tugged our line, but even as we anticipated a welcome change from tinned food, the fish slipped away. Beating against a fresh north easterly we rounded Pointe Kiukiu before tacking under a formidable rocky buttress into Hanamenu Bay. On rowing ashore we came upon a herd of wild horses grazing under shady trees beside a palm thatched house. A gushing spring fed a pool, overhung with hibiscus flowers and palm fronds that slashed the sunrays into flickering light. Slipping into the silky water we soaked until the sun left us alone with the bugs. On returning home to an unappetising shepherd's pie we sighted an outrigger being paddled by two ragged men sitting amidst a pile of fish. The skinniest held a raw fish like a sandwich, beaming with shiny eyes as his carnivorous teeth chomped through scales and bones. Was it his snack's unmistakable shape and the proximity to its natural habitat that made the man appear barbaric? Shocked at our gut reaction we wondered whether the anonymity of tinned food had fooled us into forgetting that the flesh in our pie had once been a living creature. And when the fishermen handed us four red groupers we eagerly set to preparing a more wholesome dinner.

When David remained debilitated we speculated on the possibility of fish poisoning, finding it strange he was the only one affected. Going ashore, we came across a French family swathed in copious garments and when the woman described her no-no scars, we assumed that she was particularly susceptible, possibly paranoid. An onshore wind kept Hornpipe free of sandflies and the beach bugs hardly bothered us, so we set to scrubbing our washing followed by a vigorous game of volleyball. On exploring the valley we found overgrown stone platforms, paths, and terraces surrounded by citrus, papaya, and bananas trees and after returning laden with fruit Billy set to fishing with a crab's leg. When he caught a little black tipped shark we cooked and seasoned it with fresh limes, completing our hunter gatherer meal with a papaya salad.

Having heard of an idyllic valley we sailed around the coast battling a current and headwind, where it seemed the further we tacked, the more the wind swung against us. We must have travelled at least twenty miles to achieve nine, but at last a purple headland and crinkled ridge came into view. When squalls obliterated the cliffs we hastily dropped the mainsail to motor past a huge rock that our antiquated chart described as the negro's head. Tired after the vigorous sail we hastily anchored near an old pier, to be tormented through a wakeful night with the chain rumbling in the gusts as it wrenched itself against the coral. Rowing into Hanaiapa Bay we found an exquisite village of colourful houses with immaculate gardens. Two girls were sweeping dead flowers from a black boulder platform and they said that it had been the foundations of a marae, with carved plinths and a palm frond roof. While most Polynesian monuments had been lost to the jungle, this site had been maintained for ceremonies, however the bay's population had been depleted by disease and most had moved to Atuona or Tahiti.

As with other ancient habitations, the village gave us a comforting sense of returning to an era of grace, and this prompted a fantasy in our separate minds, of how lovely it would be to come upon an old tea shop. Magically, as if to order, an aroma of freshly baked cake drifted on the still air and as we neared a tiny house rain began to fall, reminiscent of an English summer holiday. Although the drizzle ceased minutes later, it was an excuse for two smiling women to beckon us in, to clear a space and place before us steaming hunks of rich yellow cake fresh from the oven. We could only wonder at the power of our wish. And as we gazed around the frugal room, entranced by its worn, cherished items, rickety chairs and cupboards that stood in saucers of water to prevent ants from invading their dank interior, we tried to express our gratitude with wordless smiles.

Polynesian girl LT

After saying our farewells Sam and Billy ran ahead as we started up a path towards Atuona that wound between hedges of hibiscus. An occasional stream trickled over the track, breadfruit trees and coconut palms leered above the fecund greenery, and we picked a pomplemousse and ate it beneath a tree, the sharp acidity cutting through our thirst. We wandered home with the children racing ahead, safe in the knowledge they could come to no harm. Beside the marae a little girl waited with a gift of fruit and when others came running we wondered at these generous people who had given us the warmest welcome we had ever encountered. Then we noticed an elderly couple seated on the platform, and on seeing the man's hideously deformed legs we were shocked on recognising the parasitic elephantiasis that had devastated this society, to witness the hideous disease that had blighted those beautiful people in this seemingly abundant valley.

Long before the dawn of Billy's fourth birthday we heard the kids jibber jabbering and eventually Sam came to ask, "*Can we wake up now?*" Billy was overjoyed at being the centre of attention as he opened the presents Sam and I had bought in Panama, along with fishing kits and a hand sewn bear rucksack. Our boys shared their toys and clothes but Sam preferred grotesque monsters to Billy's cuddly animals, and he had lovingly chewed the nose off his Mickey Mouse that I made the subject of his celebratory cake. After fishing and a futile dive for lobsters we went ashore to seek out the incongruous Hanaiapa Yacht Club, where on reading the guest book "*Garden of Eden*" and "*paradise*" comments, we added our contribution, that although the wild Marquesas and its generous people had won our hearts, the humidity was oppressive and the diving murky. No sooner had we returned to Hornpipe than we were punished with a violent storm, and as the rain lashed down we frantically collected water while the bay became a slurry of foliage that emanated an earthy stench. That evening the copra boat arrived and we climbed a rope ladder to a cabin packed with passengers, goats, and a horse. However, despite delighting in that authentic glimpse of island life, with no ice cream, beer, or petrol it seemed that even paradise could not grant our three wishes.

Having spent two weeks in the Marquesas we decided that taking turns looking after the children might present opportunities to explore, create, and write. Despite sharing their entire lives, Sam and Billy were amazingly tolerant, but the sense they would benefit from a degree of separation prompted David to walk up the valley with Sam, leaving Billy and I to enjoy a peaceful time alone. While the *Winkies* were outstanding students I was unrelenting in my standards, and where David was a novelty playmate, I carried the responsibilities. That legacy of mother/teacher would continue to influence our adult relationships, and on returning from London to resume his master's degree Sam needed advice, but not from the mother who had told him what to do when he was a child. His tutor embodied a similar maternal persona and in confronting Sam's intuitive creativity she defined his suspicions of academia. While recognising my sons vulnerability I felt certain that further study would add depth to his concepts. Eventually Sam capitulated and as he shed his worries he gained the authority of one who speaks on a world stage.

The extreme circumstances of our nomadic life had immersed us in circumstances that demanded a total dedication of body, mind, and spirit. Was it that ability to exclude all other stimulus when focusing on a task that led our boys to excel in their chosen fields? That lifestyle contributed to Sam and Billy's symbiotic relationship, making them two parts of a whole. Their inquisitive minds forever explored new ideas and although Billy's left brain logic contrasted with his brother's intuition, Sam's academic studies served to balance his creativity. Billy recalls his childhood years with respect and appreciation, *"As a toddler learning to swim and snorkel from our yacht Hornpipe in the Atlantic and Pacific Oceans, I learnt by trying to emulate my parents and keep up with my older brother, Sam. However, the lessons that have enabled me to become a better freediver have mostly been learnt out of the water. I see them now, as a kind of string of Aesop's fables that make up my life, and continue to do so. The nearer lessons are invisible, still in the process of assimilation, while those at a greater distance are familiar and well-defined."*

When David and I became concerned about our dwindling resources we decided to make a move. Following an early sleep we set off at midnight, slipping out of the bay, passing the rocky head, indigo against a starry sky. After sailing north west to clear the island, I slept, leaving David on watch, with Hornpipe rolling along at a leisurely pace, bound for the island of Ua Pou. At dawn, we gybed and poled the jib onto a starboard tack and were soon roaring along, assisting the Aries by leaning into the rudder. From our perch on the aft seat, Hornpipe's deck spread before us, with Ua Pou's colossal pinnacles looming out of the haze, while apart from those basalt pillars the island appeared flatter and drier than the other Marquesan Islands. After speeding past Motu Mokoe we lowered the jib and gybed the main to anchor amidst a flotilla of familiar yachts that were bobbing in the shelter of Hakahau's breakwater. Unfortunately, following our demonstration of sailing prowess, David wedged the stern anchor when rowing it out in the dinghy, and as he jumped into the water to clear the tangle he tried to ignore the critical eyes assessing his performance. Venturing ashore we found that a sports festival and dance party was underway and as we wandered we noticed how many locals were bandaged or marked with scars and suppurating sores. We were horrified to learn they resulted from a virulent blood poisoning carried by the no-nos and, hearing that in extreme cases the infection entered the bones, leading to amputations, we resolved to take more care, particularly with the children.

After our night at sea we were too tired to remain long, leaving our explorations until Sunday when we visited the town bakery with its beehive oven constructed from river boulders. Then Sam, Billy, and I spent a gentle afternoon while David explored and found a remote bay where he threw off his clothes to swim in the tumbling waves and lie on the hot sand, watching lizard like fish crawl from the surging swell. He determined that after clearing Customs we would all go there, and on asking the Gendarmes about buying petrol they generously filled our can. An entry in their records caught our eye. A familiar name was listed amongst the crew of Yacht Kaya, which had arrived on the twenty-fourth of April after a non-stop passage from Panama. While the woman from hell was too far ahead for an encounter it seemed our nemesis still haunted us. Gathering a picnic, we set off along a sandy path to Sam's chattering, *"What could we do there? We could...we could...we could...Wake up mind!"* Rounding a bend we came upon a stand of purple convolvulus turning their elegant heads towards a golden beach. The no-nos had set up camp so we lit a smoky fire and built a driftwood shelter where we ate our bread and soup with streaming eyes. Then David and I emulated the wizened old men, playing *boulle* with coconuts, while the children splashed in the waves and built dams to divert the sea from the primitive hut, never leaving the water long enough for their bodies to dry. Finally, we trailed home with two little figures trudging behind, Billy so sweet in his bush hat, with his bear rucksack a happy hitchhiker on his back.

Having anchored Hornpipe close to the shore the children were able to come and go as they chose, always in sight, whether frolicking in the waves or searching the rocky ledges for the tinkling arms of sea anemones. David watched out for them when I set off on my own adventure, following the stony coast road to the west before turning inland. There I gazed across a vast valley to where the menhirs towered thousands of feet over the jungle. Breaking new ground, I tramped through scrubby bushes, heading for the monolithic rocks, and was wondering whether it was wise to continue when a storm of wasps darted from the bushes, savagely jabbing. Shocked by the ferocious attack, I sunk to my knees, flesh stinging, dizzy with venom and fear. Then turning my back on the soaring spires, I staggered to the road and hobbled home with tales of impenetrable castles guarded by ferocious dragons. The following day David set off for the pinnacles, to be delayed in his quest by a friendly family who invited him to their Ascension Day feast of dried octopus, starchy taro, and cold beer. Destiny had prevented us reaching those ethereal peaks and as we set our sails for Nuku Hiva they evaporated in the mist as though they had always been a dream.

The relaxing sail and gentle breeze dissolved into calm and as we motored into Taiohae Bay the lush coastline and dark wall of mountains appeared both breathtakingly beautiful and gloomily foreboding. After setting two anchors to hold Hornpipe steady in the swell, we wandered around the small town that is the administrative centre of the Marquesas, finally indulging in ice creams to quench our ever-present longing. Discovering that we had arrived for another festival, we hurried home to allow Sam and Billy a sleep before rowing a mile to avoid the waves that surged onto the beach. On joining the crowd of *vahine* with black hair falling to their waists, polished skin glowing in the dark, the fragrance of frangipani garlands became overwhelming. As the drums grew persistent the traditional dance performance began with the frenzied, undulating bodies yielding a glimpse of the sensual Polynesian culture that had enticed the sailors who first visited the islands. The percussive beating of sticks on hollow log drums was enhanced by wistful songs, and when the band began playing schmaltzy western music we were surprised to find ourselves amongst the couples clasped in ballroom embraces. Amidst the wild activity Sam and Billy clung to their chairs bewildered by the gregarious, gyrating children, and when the locals began drinking beer at unaffordable prices we set off home, the thundering drums pounding in our ears.

A pattering of raindrops through the hatch was a refreshing wake up call, until the heavy clouds opened to stain the bay with the rich ochre of Nuku Hiva's soil. A large cruising yacht, Cyclone, had sailed in with an Australian couple on board, accompanied by two boys. Following a brief introduction Jeremy rowed over with two-year old Tim and while the older boys read books and built space rockets, Billy alternated between entertaining Tim while keeping up with the action. David took our gas bottle to the storekeeper, who overcame the problematic fitting by ingeniously tipping gas from his cylinder into ours and despite the transaction taking hours it was a relief to have enough fuel to last until Tahiti. The Marquesas had been an inconvenient place to live aboard, with an ever present swell creating rolling anchorages and problematic shore landings. We were ready to leave but we had heard of a perfect anchorage on Nuku Hiva's eastern coast, so we decided to give the islands a last try, hoping that Anahō Bay would live up to expectations.

Although all was quiet as we sailed within the shelter of Taiohae, we soon hit fresh winds and heavy seas, suffering a hard beat towards Tikapo Point where a sudden gust blew out our old jib. On rounding Cape Matauaoa's imposing cliff that

Papaya tree LT

plummeted hundreds of feet down scarred red rocks to where Hornpipe tossed in a turbulent sea, we sighted two pinnacles gazing down, looking exactly like Henry Moore's *The King and Queen* that stands at Glenkiln Estate near Dumfries. Running off downwind we gybed our mainsail and jib before turning beneath the headland flanking Anaho Bay. There we drifted on puffs of wind into the anchorage where, able to relax my guard, I inadvertently distracted David, as with a stomach-turning crunch we hit coral. Fortunately, the smash was no more damaging than bruised pride and paint. After the Marquesas' exposed black beaches, Anaho Bay was a serene crescent of white sand and shady palms that swept up to dark forests and towering rocks. A luxurious breeze flowed over the low isthmus from a bay we had passed when sailing along the east coast. The western facing hillside was a mass of verdant foliage with indigo shadows, reminiscent of Gauguin's paintings, while the ochre grass of the eastern slope suggested the textural brush daubs and slashes of Van Gogh.

For the first time in the Marquesas we dived in a translucent seascape, swimming with colourful fishes that patterned the ripples with flickering light. On exploring the beach, we discovered that even in that far-flung place, the French government had laid water pipes with taps. Half a dozen tourist bungalows were hidden amongst the trees; on peering into their frugal interiors we speculated that anyone who could afford to travel to that remote location would expect a more sophisticated, insect free abode. We watched an old woman as she wove palm fronds to repair a roof and heard that her once thriving community had become reduced to seven. Further along the beach we came on a small chapel with a sandy floor, built in the style of the other dwellings, with rows of tree trunks for seats and a stone slab altar covered with a white cloth. Incongruous religious prints, revealing ghastly anatomical details, shadowed the purity of jars of flowers; a humble wooden icon in an alcove touched our hearts in an unexpected way. And there being no one to sell us fruit we gathered the bananas, citrus, and papaya that lay rotting in an abandoned orchard.

Bundling up the kids to deter the no-nos, we dropped them ashore to play while we scrubbed Hornpipe's topsides and hull. On scraping around her ports we discovered two broken window catches that made us fearful of meeting heavy seas on our forthcoming voyage, and we had barely finished painting the first of six coats of epoxy when a huge rain cloud loomed overhead. As a vicious gust wrenched the anchor chain around a coral head it became vital we ease the pressure on the links. But our starter batteries were flat and so we spent precious minutes tormented by the howling wind, straining chain, and pounding generator. At last we had the power and as the rain lashed down David motored into the gusts while I washed everything on hand. Then we anchored further from the reef and warmed ourselves with hot cocoa.

We had become friends with the incongruous owners of a homebuilt wooden boat called Full Circle. While Sheryl was a timid southern belle, Mike had hinted at doing time inside a Mexican prison with stories that would slowly unfold. One night he and David went scuba diving, searching the moonlit coral heads for the ever-elusive lobsters. Then to Sam and Billy's delight Cyclone sailed into the bay and the children drifted back and forth between the boats, often staying overnight. One Sunday we all walked over the isthmus to the eastern beach of Baie Ha'atuatua, climbing palm trees to gather nature's fizzy drink. Waves were pounding the white sand and we threw off our clothes and ran in. Only after feeling painful stings did we notice the bluebottles littering the high watermark, and when a fog of no-nos besieged our succulent skin we hurried home.

The next day David dropped me at the head of the bay to follow a recently cleared zig zag path up through coconut plantations. The rampant jungle had already swamped the stone walls that bordered the track as, crossing a ridge, I gazed down on the anchored yachts and felt an intoxicating lightness on realising that for the first time in years I had no need to be concerned for anyone but myself. On entering a dark wood, the track became slippery with a mulch of glossy mango leaves. Streams tinkled and I joined their singing, skipping song as they joyously flowed downhill. Hearing cockerels call and the hum of a generator I slowed my pace. When the ground levelled I came upon huge blocks of hewn larva overgrown with ferns; the entrancing remnant of an ancient, abiding culture. And as I hurried into the present a happy sound of children emanated from a school painted with murals. Then the way opened to stone houses surrounded with hibiscus hedges and a white wooden church with red topped steeples standing in a field sprinkled with crosses. But I had already been gone too long so I started back, leaving Hatihe'u Village for David to explore.

After retracing my steps David had set to drawing an old waka outrigger, when a young lad proudly showed him the *tiki* sculptures he had carved. Then, becoming curious about what lay beyond the mountainous ridge, my man started along a twisting path bordered with palms that slashed the light into shadow spears. Despite a glittering noonday sun, it was cool beneath the trees. David walked on, following the track that looped over hills and gullies flanked by a tangle of wild fig, mango, and bamboo. Eventually he reached a high point where a great hole had been blasted through a ridge to create a new road with spectacular views towards 'A'akapa, Controlleur, and Taiohae Bays. The air hummed with insects and birdsong; frigates, swallows, and swifts undulated on the breeze, bringing the dramatic scene to life. David sat for as long as the day allowed, gazing towards brooding crags where waterfalls plummeted into dark chasms. Starting back with a relaxed energetic rhythm he was soon overcome with hunger and on reaching the village he asked a copra worker if he would open a coconut. As David gulped the thick milk they chatted and swatted mosquitos and when the man invited him for tea in his frugal house he talked of managing on a menial wage which he was obliged to exchange for expensive commodities; about retaining Nuku Hiva's carving heritage, which was reputedly the finest in Polynesia. When David learned that the man's wife was an artist, he gave her his drawing pad which resulted in reciprocal gifts of bread and fruit. Eventually he stumbled away on weary wobbly legs and as he crossed the pass the grey gloom of night engulfed the bay where, despite knowing David's habit of stretching every experience to the limit, I was relieved on hearing him whistle from the beach.

Those days were bathed in mellow serenity and we were our most relaxed since leaving the Perlas Islands. Birdsong greeted the dawn as we slumbered, barely awake, lulled by the swinging boat that slowly revealed the ever-changing landscape through our window. And as the first rays of light gently caressed those framed images of land, sea, and sky, we longed for each moment to last forever, knowing that just as those fragmented views would slide away and seldom return, the tranquil days would also pass. It was important that we used the full moon to light our way to the Tuamotus and so we set sail on a boisterous passage back to Taiohae. There we found that another festival had decreed everything closed except the new Catholic Cathedral, carved with biblical scenes, interspersed with animals, birds, tiki – even a skull-and-crossbones. And so it was we decided to visit Daniel the sculptor.

On disembarking from the beach, the Marquesas dealt their final blow with a huge wave that swamped the dinghy and cast us upon the shore. Once we had salvaged our packages and wrung our clothes we tried again and made it through the waves to sail for Hakatea Bay where David hoped to obtain a block of wood from Daniel the carver. As we passed beneath the towering cliffs that guard the narrow entrance, I began preparations for going ashore, only to discover that my purse, holding an equivalent of a hundred dollars, was missing, possibly lost in our capsize. After debating the financial disaster, we decided it was unsafe to delay our journey with a return and we rowed ashore with a hope of exchanging goods for fruit and wood. The village appeared abandoned except for an old couple hobbling on elephantiasis thickened legs, but they directed David to Daniel, and after swapping a spoke shave for toa and miro wood, he returned to where we were soaking in the freshwater pool. By the time we beat a retreat, our flesh had been savaged by swarms of no-nos.

SEA OF DREAMS

"I have a relationship with the depths
they beckon me beyond my means
cold dark vacant pressure
forever night, endless dreams."
William Trubridge

David cranked up Hornpipe's anchor and after hoisting her sails we aimlessly flopped in the disturbed waves until an errant breeze blew us out of the bay. Hakatea's brooding cliffs briefly leered at us before dissolving in torrential rain. But the treacherous land did not intend letting us go without a struggle, a cauldron of black ocean frothed beneath us and as the sky ominously darkened to Indian ink the squall hit. It seemed a bad omen. I dreaded that first solo ocean passage and as we scrambled to drop our genoa I whispered to David, *"Should we go back?"* But although he shared my apprehension David deemed it best we confront our demons – that we exploit the light of the full moon to aid our passage to the Tuamotus. So, at six o'clock on the thirteenth of June, we set a south westerly course, on a broad reach towards Manihi Atoll.

Hornpipe twisted and tossed in a turbulent swell and once Sam, Billy, and David had filled their bellies with hot stew they fell asleep, while I steered us through the violent squalls with the bright moon my comfort and companion. On waking David, we dragged out the staysail and after balancing it with the main, the Aries held a true course. Appreciating the price my partner paid for that precious gift of sleep, I curled into my bunk and abandoned myself to the sensation of inhabiting the body of a great creature, of traveling sinuously through space and time. And back then I found enough comfort in that transcendent visualisation to feel safe, even when there were plenty of concerns.

During that night, the squalls dispersed, but dawn's thick cloud made David anxious about the exacting navigation needed to make a safe landfall in the Tuamotus. Those atolls, with a name that ominously translates as, *"the dangerous archipelago"* are barely higher than a palm tree and identifying them is notoriously difficult. Manihi's pass flows with a rapid, unpredictable current rendering it impossible to motor against its outgoing tide of six to ten knots. And while it was vital our arrival coincide with slack water, fickle winds made predicting our speed a lottery, though hopefully, if we could make an average of a hundred and twenty miles a day, we would reach the pass at around noon on Sunday. Despite that commitment to circumstances beyond our control, the number two genoa was pulling well, and as the wind eased I slept while David helped the kids build a cut-out castle with knights and yokels. Then our fishing reel spun, and on landing the yellow fin tuna we marvelled at its sleek shape, the deep blue of its back, its shimmering belly of iridescent greens, mauve, and orange. And while the tuna represented three delicious meals, with evening upon us the fish must be gutted, scaled, and cooked, navigational sights taken and plotted, the children organised for bed before darkness fell.

"The bright moon, my comfort and companion" LT

There were other concerns: that last trip ashore to bathe in the freshwater pool of Hakatea Bay had afflicted Billy with terrible no-no bites that had developed into huge boils on his buttocks, knee, elbow, and thigh. Billy's misery seemed a high price to pay for a playful soak, and it was awful to observe his torturous struggle to avoid kneeling or sitting. We had seen how the Polynesians were blighted with sores, scars and amputations resulting from ulcerated bites, and as my fears escalated I started Billy on a course of antibiotics, bathed his bloated abscesses with poultices, gently applied pressure to drain the poison. While those moments of agony brought relief, I was reminded of the Atlantic nail, that once again I was abusing Billy's trust. He was a golden boy, caring and affectionate, constantly hugging me and on one occasion purposefully kissing my head saying, *"I'm going to put a kiss on your brain so you can think about it."* And as I watched him through a feverish night I willed the infection to pass; dared not think of how it would have been without Robin Tattersall's medicines.

Although the antibiotic rapidly took control of the situation, my maternal anxieties were with me for the long haul and they would surface when William began freediving. During his first winter in Sardinia he had eagerly anticipated the summer only to be foiled by severe sinus infections, exacerbated by his broken nose. Tormented by the ocean's proximity he tried every remedy, consulting a wizened Sardinian witch, to no avail. All that William cared about was that the season was wasted. He will never know whether that suspension from diving provided more opportunities for the vital dry training that expands and flexes the lungs, avoiding the damage that would blight other freedivers, and result in the death of a close friend. Meanwhile the frustration only increased William's determination. Each evening he walked to a secluded cavern in the sea cliffs and there he practised his pranayama and meditation, with the breath of the wind and the sight of the sea nourishing his spirit, deepening his resolve.

David's career was flourishing and after teaching a design workshop in France we set off to visit our son. Taking a ferry from Marseilles to Corsica we walked the island's ancient tracks and slept under the stars on craggy mountain tops. The island resonated with the raw music of passionate people and on visiting a prehistoric village I felt deeply connected to that ancient culture. Travelling on to Sardinia we luxuriated in the turquoise sea and climbed the gargantuan boulders of Capo Testa. William had replaced isolation with a relationship that was consuming his happiness. He was enslaved by financial burdens, plagued by his sinuses; yet despite that crazy pool dive costing him dearly, adversity was teaching him the restraint that would protect him through his extreme challenge. Each of us showed our concern, with David manifesting his love in practical support while Sam's presence helped resolve William's relationship. My son's gallant endurance reminded me of my father, whose life lacked acknowledgment or reward, and I invoked his sensitive spirit to help William through his crisis.

On our second day, the weariness of sailing alone became apparent so we switched to three hour watches to avoid either of us being awake for too long. The children fizzed with needs that must be fulfilled before they became bored or desperate and I buzzed around teaching and cooking; my taut face revealing an exhaustion I could not disguise. David's body ached from the violent momentum and as he prepared his noon fix he became overcome by the cooking fumes. When his calculations indicated we were two hundred and twenty miles from Manihi, he became concerned that we might arrive around midnight of Saturday/Sunday. Following hours of deliberations about the wind and speed David confirmed that the salient time for entering the pass would be between two and four o'clock on Sunday afternoon. Hanging off a low-lying atoll, in darkness, at the mercy of wind and uncertain currents, would be extremely dangerous, so we decided to reduce canvas and after hooking on our harnesses David and I clambered on deck to triple reef the mainsail. It was then that the winch shattered, splattering greasy parts all over the deck, and as David tried to reassemble it he found that the attachment that held it together had been lost in the chaos, and when the plastic sheath from the reefing pennant disintegrated, he despaired of the arduous task of fixing the mechanical instruments, made worse by the potential of losing or breaking irreplaceable components.

The children had mellowed and when the wind dropped we all lay down for a siesta; enjoying a quiet afternoon in each other's company. When David's dusk star sights revealed our position, a hundred and ninety-five miles from Manihi, he realised that our pace was now too slow to reach the pass by Sunday's slack tide, so we carefully shook out the reef. After dinner Sam stood his first watch, checking the compass and looking for ships from the safety of the cockpit, his only problem being telling the time for waking us. The night passed peacefully and David was taking a star fix when he noticed the triangle of a sail just ahead. The yacht remained at the same distance as he spent the day regulating Hornpipe's speed, taking navigational sights every six hours until, on locating the beacons of Manihi and Takapoto, he was reassured we were on track. My day was consumed with repairs on the drifter and helping David navigate so apart from supervising school work I had neglected the kids. After dinner I steered with the drifter gently whispering, the brilliant moon illuminating a clear horizon. On waking David, he took a moon fix to calculate our position as thirty-four miles east of Manihi; a distance that given an erratic current could decrease to a dangerous ten miles or less before dawn. It was foolhardy to continue sailing so we dropped the drifter and lay a-hull. Neither of us slept and when a dawn star fix indicated we had drifted to a position twenty-six miles from the north-eastern tip of Manihi, an additional fifteen to the pass, we hoisted the mainsail. At nine o'clock, shortly after spotting our companion sailor, the slight smudge of an atoll appeared on the horizon.

Maybe the tide had turned, perhaps it was the dying wind, but most likely it was the sight of land hardly changing with the passing hours that seemed to slow Hornpipe's progress. Our planned arrival at slack water became increasingly unlikely given that the tide would begin flooding into the lagoon around two thirty. The turgid progress and uncertain schedule made David irritable; the Aries couldn't handle the steering and neither could he. But I was strong on mindless endurance so I took the helm, and as we closed on that singular strand white sand emerged from the sea with palm trees providing textural variations on the colour green. Manihi was a curious sight after the Marquesas' brooding mountains. It was hard to believe that this atoll was older, that the volcano that once dominated the centre of that ring of coral had, over millions of years, eroded to nothing – that Fatu Hiva would also subside into the ocean, leaving no more than a lagoon surrounded by a coral reef.

The wind decreased, and on turning to parallel the coast we dropped the flogging mainsail to continue at a walking pace, with the drifter balancing our genoa. At eleven thirty David went for a sleep, leaving me steering with the land serenely gliding past and on waking he pondered whether we could reach the pass before the tide became too strong. Would we even get there before dark? Persisting, we had nearly rounded on our companion's red and yellow sail, when they gave up, and soon after the complete lack of wind gave us no choice but to risk motoring the last five miles to Passe Tairapa. Drawing near the break in the reef we spotted houses and a wharf to the right of the pass and as that panorama of the inner lagoon opened to enfold us it seemed that everything was under control. However, as we entered the narrow gap, Hornpipe surged forward. Rushing to the bow I saw the depth rapidly decreased revealing coral to port. The sun bouncing off the surface of the lagoon obscured whatever lay ahead and to starboard. All was lost in flickering ripples and eddies. I helplessly hoped that David knew where he was going and was unaware of his struggle to maintain steerage and see past the sail bags and awning. The tide had taken control and David's gesturing, "*which way?*" was lost in a sickening crunch as Hornpipe swung onto the coral.

As our yacht, home, and beloved companion lurched onto her side, waves threatened to engulf the deck and at that moment, David vented his frustration with the accusation, "*You're hopeless! Couldn't you see the channel, the V of disappearing water, the shallow bottom? I would rather be up there on lookout but I know you could never handle the boat, you'd just get in a useless flap. Surely you ought to have learned more after two and a half years.*" Shocked into panic I scuttled below to shut the hatches and ports while our stunned children watched the waves splash against Hornpipe's deck. All seemed lost, when above the rushing water, I heard voices and a buzzing outboard. Rushing to the cockpit I saw a launch crowded with gesticulating Polynesians. After securing our halyard they powered away, hauling Hornpipe's masthead, healing her over to free the keel. And as David motored with the exhaust pipe spluttering we swung off the coral into deep water.

Stunned by the disaster and unexpected salvation, we waved to the launch and silently set off across the lagoon. Although the reflective surface hid what lay beneath, the coral heads were marked with stakes, easily avoided. By five o'clock we were safely at anchor where, dissolving in despair I sobbed in the cabin. David dived to review the damage, and it seemed Hornpipe had suffered no more than a few scratches. Our relationship had fared worse. A lifetime of struggle had culminated in that confrontation; every word had cut my heart. Before the incident I had thought that David and I were successfully working together, that despite the stormy start and Billy's bites we had managed the challenges, that I had played a vital role. All those positives had been obliterated by the disastrous conclusion and David's opinion, that after all my years at sea I was hopelessly dependent upon his knowledge and skills. I had failed and my lover and companion thought me worthless. Crushed and fearful that my children could suffer the consequences of my inadequacies I wondered whether I should leave when we arrived in Tahiti. But where could I go and what about Sam and Billy?

After David had let fly at me, he realised that the situation did not really justify his wrath, however he said nothing because he believed that lessons should be learned before a more serious incident. While he knew we should have studied the chart and discussed the procedure before entering the pass, David had been swept along on a tide of exhausted distraction. The crisis had exposed my partner's hidden feelings, had revealed that he underestimated my contribution. David was unaware that when he vented his anger against the weather and inanimate objects, I countered his volatile emotions with composure and endurance. And amidst the hubbub of life he often overlooked the vital role I played in teaching the children, sailing, and managing the boat. My crime was somewhat mitigated when, a day later, we saw a yacht slew around at the same place, with the crew spending hours winching themselves free of the coral, and hearing that one of seventy two yachts to have grounded in that season had been skippered by the famous yachtsman, Eric Tabarlay, was a pardon of sorts.

Life continued and the issue went underground as we explored the lagoon. Although there were none of the elk horn or sea fans which require a flowing current, our anchorage was surrounded with coral outcrops that ascended from the depths to culminate just below the surface. Pulling on masks we swam through crystal water, experiencing the sensation of flying high over a sandy sea floor. Diving down we investigated grotesque pinnacles and grottos lined with velvety red and yellow polyps where parrot fish grazed. Sunbeams pierced the depths, saturating our vision with a luminous light that revealed turquoise clams, porcelain shells, and plume worms with twisting tentacles. Groupers were everywhere and David shot one for a sumptuous dinner, and sometime after finding a hoard of giant oysters we realised they had been placed there to cultivate black pearls. Becoming chilled I often returned home leaving David towing Sam and Billy's little dinghy, which they climbed into when they had had enough of diving. The sheltered lagoon was a safe place to explore the underwater world and they began venturing alone in search of cowrie shells and sea urchin spines, however they preferred shallow water, having been frightened by a book about the movie Jaws. Further from the boat we saw black and white tipped sharks and on one occasion when diving alone, David was purposefully followed by a large one that was attracted by a coral graze on his leg. And although he had heard that the species was docile, he clambered onto a coral head until it swam away.

William would pursue a life in harmony with nature, and on our second visit to Sardinia I practised meditation and pranayama with him on his favourite rock overlooking the ocean. One afternoon, David and William paddled a double canoe a kilometre out into the bay, where his son jumped in and dived down to lie motionless on the sea bed waiting for a fish. When David paddled ashore William continued diving alone. After a fruitless hour he made one last attempt and at thirty metres he sighted a huge fish and from that moment it was certain they would be united in death or glory before the day was over. Though they shared the same economy of movement, William's breath was used up, even before he went for the kill. The death was mercifully quick but the battle was yet to come with the surface high above and the enormous fish exceeding his size and weight. Hugging the lifeless body William started towards the light; stretched beyond endurance he somehow reached the air. Then began a slow swim as he dragged the fish on that last long passage to land.

When David returned, we walked to the piazza and sat over a drink, watching the sky deepen to purple and vermilion. Then, as we wandered home through streets of pastel houses, we witnessed a spectacular sight: a gargantuan beast was labouring uphill. As we drew closer we saw that this was not one creature but a man, bearing a great fish upon his back. The limp tail dragged the ground. A monstrous head hung over the man's shoulder, their gleaming, sinuous bodies met, spine on spine, melding in a barbaric fusion of hunter and slain, human and fish. He walked on bare feet, spear in hand, glistening skin echoing a slippery silhouette that bled into the dying orb of the sun. The man-fish was a sight from mythology. Those last rays illuminated the faces of those who observed his weariness; how he appeared to carry the whole world upon his back. And then, as the light touched his profile, we saw it was William, that while we lingered in the tavern, he had battled the monster and had somehow returned from the depths. We watched and wondered at his endurance, fell in beside him as he staggered home to throw the fish upon the ground to complete the task, crouched in a pool of sodium light, a scene reminiscent of the punk Dauphin of Sam's production of *Henry V* that sharp clash of metal on stone, the sudden flow of blood as blade cleaved flesh from bone. This fish was the resolution of a hidden goal: while Umberto had speared large fish, William's previous catches had been unworthy of comparison and, willing to die in the task, he had somehow survived his rite of passage.

Familiar yachts arrived in the anchorage; an American family on Primavera swapped a mask and snorkel for food, and Klaus Stortebecker on his enormous aluminium yacht told us of how a woman had sued his charter company and travel agent to win a settlement of forty-two thousand dollars for a sprained ankle that healed in three weeks. Meanwhile, Hornpipe's inevitable maintenance escalated into fixing the generator and revamping the saloon, galley, cockpit, and stairs. When the kids blundered into the sticky varnish and fell down the absent steps we encouraged them to play at the exclusive resort, and one evening David and I splashed out on a cocktail and beer, wishing we could afford a meal at the plush restaurant. Concern about our dwindling funds had generated attempts to trace the lost purse, but despite regretting the money that would provide food for hungry bellies or vital mechanical parts we eventually gave up on the dodgy phone connection to Nuku Hiva via Tahiti.

Our anchorage was enclosed by a narrow margin of land, clothed with shimmering coconut palms that merged into a mirage of sea and sky, and although waves washed over a narrow spit, nights were so still the stars were reflected in the lagoon. One evening while out for a walk we found ourselves enclosed in a tangle of bushes and palms that had fallen during the recent cyclone. Land crabs were everywhere, defiantly waving pincers before scuttling into holes that pock marked the ground. When Billy and I set off home, David and Sam followed a path cleared by the copra farmers whose smouldering bonfires and stacks of split coconuts were dotted amongst the naked trunks. They returned with a bundle of fronds which David attempted to weave into a hat. And as squalls deluged us with rainwater I embarked on another washing day, taking time off for windsurfing. While David improved his technique, my lack of proficiency was masked by the novelty of being a woman who windsurfed and when Primavera offered the use of their board and rig we put aside our primitive gear. Given a fast board, strong wind, flat water, and a captive audience, I performed tricks, holding the boom with my neck and doing splits while bending backward until my head skimmed the waves.

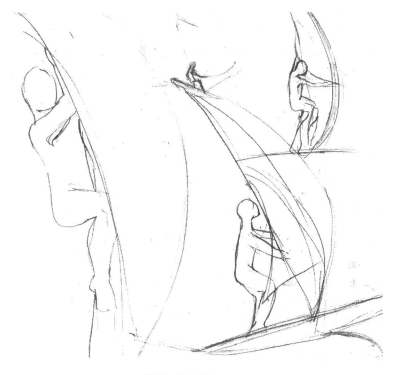

Windsurfing LT

When the time came for sailing on we heard the yacht Magic would also be taking advantage of an eleven o'clock slack tide to negotiate the pass and sail to the nearby atoll of Ahe. Since Magic had also gone aground on entering, they had nervously set two anchors, and the sight of them blundering around trying to retrieve them was strangely rewarding to David, whose pride had been scorched during our misadventure. While Hornpipe's bedraggled flag hung limp as a rag from her backstay, we had noticed Magic's plummy English crew diligently raising and lowering their ensign at dawn and dusk, respectfully standing at attention throughout the ceremony. That morning David couldn't resist temptation. When they devoutly unfurled their Union Jack he seized our cronky fog horn and piped a volley of croaky notes that trailed into a squawking screech; and as heads swivelled to his rousing rendition we collapsed in the cockpit, laughing hysterically.

Hornpipe followed Magic to the pass, where a local launch came to assist. After watching the yacht hurtle through the tide race, we seized the moment and beckoned to the locals. Carlos jumped aboard and seized the tiller while his father went up front to guide Hornpipe through the shallows. The coral looked so close and the water was running fast when they said *"That's it, you're through,"* and leaping into their launch they zoomed away leaving us to swirl through the pass. As we whizzed past the wharf we saw mothers sitting beneath a shady tree, little children playing marbles in the dust; the homely scene making us wish we could have spent more time in that authentic place.

There was little wind on the open sea but after setting the drifter and genoa, Hornpipe managed three knots, tailing Magic as she motored drunkenly towards Ahe. When a bank of black cloud emerged from the horizon, we dropped our drifter with David noting the time, course, and speed in case we lost sight of land. However, the squall delivered no more than a shower and a welcome wind that sent Hornpipe surging along Ahe's north coast, her sails filling like the graceful wings of a swan while Magic paddled through the troughs, an ugly duckling powered by a lumbering motor. My relief at clearing Manihi's fateful pass had been replaced with the nervous anticipation of entering Ahe's lagoon, but I busied myself with the accumulated chores. David enjoyed helming, maintaining a respectful hundred metres from the shore; searching for a break in the featureless palms that would indicate the pass at the lagoon's north west corner. Seeing Magic's waddle lessen and her skipper climb into his dinghy for an inspection, we gathered our sails and, firing up Obelix, headed towards the entrance that was reputedly wider and deeper than Manihi's pass. Having decided that I would helm while David observed and directed from the pulpit I stood, feet braced upon the seats, cautiously approaching the standing waves that indicate the centre of the channel. In a moment, we slid into the lagoon, and breathing sighs of relief we hoisted our canvas for the four-miles to the village of Tenukapara on the southern side of the lagoon. As we sailed we heard the American boats coaxing Magic into the pass, and as the light faded we joined the gathered yachts that were sheltering behind a small reef.

The following day we rowed ashore and ran into Ari, the chief who told us how a recent cyclone had washed away all the houses, breadfruit, and citrus trees. Initially the wind had hit from the south, switching to the north when the eye passed. As five foot waves swept over the atoll the community huddled inside a concrete hall, and while only one person had been hurt, all that remained of their village was a barren three hundred metre strip and a scattering of palm trees. The government had provided materials with the provision they would be removed if not used immediately, so the lagoon resounded with hammers and saws as the islanders constructed flimsy tin roofed hardboard shacks to replace their traditional houses. On enquiring about buying vegetables I heard that all the people's shady gardens had been destroyed, that their shop was barely a cupboard with a few tins of corned beef, sugar, and flour, which explained why a man with a headache paddled out to ask if I had an aspirin. The one surviving building was a house on a small island to the east of the village that Bernard Moitessier had built five years previously. This French yachtsman, philosopher, and environmentalist had been set to win the *Golden Globe*, the first single handed non-stop around the world race, when, abandoning his circumnavigation he rounded Cape Horn for a second time to continue onward to Polynesia. Moitessier pursued his deeper affinity with the ocean, writing, *"I no longer know how far I have got, except that we long ago left the borders of too much behind."* And seeing his simple pole house lovingly constructed from local materials we felt connected to this free thinker who had practised yoga on his yacht.

Four yachts remained when the American boats headed to Tahiti for the *Bastille Day* celebrations. John and Joyce from Seattle had invested everything in their immaculate yacht, building and stocking Walkabout with home dried vegetables and fruits. But they missed their friends and John, who suffered from glaucoma, could not use drugs to counter his extreme seasickness. While the French couple on Charlie Brava were self-contained, Benoit and Martine on their home built yacht, Chrysalis, told us their plans to work and make babies in Tahiti. They lavished attention on Sam and Billy, who pored through their treasure trove of French comic books. One afternoon Ari took everyone diving, towing a large plastic tub for the fish. Although David was shivering after twenty minutes, he learned much from watching the Tuamotuan's technique of extending one arm, with the other alongside the body, working his nose against the mask to equalise and reach a depth of twenty-five metres. There he waited and when a fish swam past he shot it with a long wooden shafted spear and on surfacing tossed the fish into the tub after first breaking its neck.

Although David returned empty handed, after tea and cake on Hornpipe the gang donated a grouper and parrot fish for our dinner. Apart from the copra industry the islanders farmed oysters for pearls. Twice a year an itinerant Japanese circulated the atolls to culture the oysters, which the locals supplied, paying two dollars each to the expert who opened them and inserted a small white sphere of shell; a task that amounted to four minutes of easy work. Those oysters that accepted the culture took two years to grow a grey misshapen pearl around the intruder. However, when Ari and David dived over the racks of shells, they saw cultures scattered on the sand and he expressed disgust at the *"no good Japanese"* who had forced the oysters too far. After gathering the little white balls Ari returned them to the expert, demanding he repeat the process.

Sam and Billy spent hours playing on the beach, searching the shore for shells, wearing sunhats and plastic sandals to protect their feet from the sharp coral. We had taught them to watch out for poisonous stonefish and a dangerous cone shell with delicate patterns. They returned with stories of what they had seen and a renewed enthusiasm for that microcosmic world. Although maintenance jobs severely restricted our space, if we did not keep up, Hornpipe would deteriorate beyond repair, so we set to grinding the blistered cockpit sole and engine room hatch. No sooner had we finished than the sky fragmented into alto level mackerel patterns and although we hurriedly finished that first coat and erected Hornpipe's awning, water sloshed onto the vulnerable paint. During the night, powerful wind gusts stressed our anchor chain that had wrapped around a coral head and the following morning the radio buzzed with talk about the storm. On hearing how Full Circle had battled two days of headwinds to achieve sixty miles, that Cyclone was somewhere north of Mo'orea with a blown-out mainsail, a broken engine, and two sick crew, we feared for our friends. I ventured out to gaze at the colossal waves that surged over the outer shore and they reminded me of how vulnerable we were, that the unpredictable ocean could crush us all, if it chose. *"When I gaze into the shimmering waves, sending up sprays of crystalline light, I turn away in awe, lest the sea's wild horses hypnotise me with their tumbling, tumultuous, beautiful destruction. I know I should let go and allow myself to be saved but I am afraid I will be consumed by their power."*

Our month amongst the Tuamotus had been dominated by *howlies* that seemed to follow a ten-day pattern, making us wary of timing our departure. While we had learned that an atoll offers scant protection from waves that build over the fetch of the lagoon, coral heads also created problems when letting out extra lengths of anchor chain. Stories abounded of yachts weathering six foot swells and sustaining huge damages, some heading for the open sea. We were fortunate that an inner reef to the southern side of Ahe's lagoon protected us from the forty knot northerlies. And it was a perfect windsurfing wind. Despite our size difference we used the same gear. I was massively overpowered but wow did I go! One afternoon David windsurfed to the far side of the atoll, where on wading out along a strip of rock it seemed he was walking on

On the beach LT

the sea, hovering in the sky. There he stood, watching waves pounding the pink coral, feeling tiny in that infinite space.

Due to our delayed departure we were invited to the wedding of a couple who had returned from Tahiti for the ceremony – the first on Ahe in ten years. Their Mormon religion prohibited dancing and drinking liquor, however it was lenient about sexual freedom and the twenty-year-old bride was the mother of three children, with her eldest already five. The couple led a procession to the church, where, after lengthy incomprehensible monologues and a musical performance on homemade instruments, the final speech welcomed us yachties. Early the following day the villagers set to cooking a feast, two pigs and a sheep, roasted on spits; five gallon drums of rice, sweet potatoes, and beans bubbled over fires. Who knows where it came from and who would eat it all? I donated some Puerto Rican snacks and while our kids politely passed them around, years later Sam would write, *"Linda gave the last of the sesame bars away at that wedding in Ahe. Suddenly everyone was eating them. I wonder if some islanders remember, as I do, their sweet taste, and seeing cheeky children happily sucking on candy that I had always thought was being saved for me and Billy."* Small deeds have a big impact and a mother's sins are never forgotten.

While the Tuamotuans prepared the feast, I sat drawing amongst a crowd of children. David wandered off in search of palm fronds and soon all four yachtsmen were sitting in a circle exploring ways of weaving a hat. The rafters of the Marie had been decorated with cowrie garlands but where we had expected traditional mats, trestle tables were spread with white cloths. As we feasted the women filled our plates from overflowing dishes and then a band played while, as a special dispensation, the couple danced in a western style before attending church to absolve themselves of the sin. The uncompromising religion denied the islanders any form of self-expression so there had been no joining the dance, but at this point the village matriarch, Mama Fana, who had seen our yachtsmen's attempts at weaving hats, set to teaching them. Having raised ten children and given birth to twenty, she knew how to assert control over the men who obediently fiddled with the reluctant fronds. It was there that David successfully wove the first of the many hats he would construct on our passages amongst the islands. While his skill would remind those who had lost the art, David's knowledge of three-dimensional weaving also influenced his ground-breaking range of lighting designs.

Having hoped to depart with the French boats, we were delayed by David's stomach upset. Before leaving, Florence on Charlie Brava bought one of the patchwork bags I had sewed on our passage, encouraging me to make more to sell in Tahiti in hopes that the meagre earnings might subsidise a meal or two. When the Walkabouts rowed over to relay a radio message that our purse had been found in the Chinese shop in Nuku Hiva, they stayed for dinner and Mahjong. Despite our plans for an early night, we were drawn into discussing the cruising lifestyle, and when Joyce and John revealed how years of preparation had dissolved in a disappointing reality, the knowledge of others' challenges was perversely comforting. At last we found ourselves in bed but before drifting off I realised that following the overhaul our generator remained on deck, that it would be vulnerable on our forthcoming voyage, that the altered magnetic field would compromise the compass. So we dragged ourselves out, and after charging the batteries and heaving the generator into the engine room we resumed a sleep fraught with anxiety. Rising at five thirty David attributed his aching body to the disrupted night as, with just enough light and wind, we motor-sailed across the lagoon on the course Ari had given to accommodate a lack of markers. Although I was a bundle of nerves, once we had bounced through the tide race my worries diminished.

After setting the sails we ate breakfast and despite the disturbing prospect of failing to clear the atolls before dark, the wind increased as soon as we had passed Ahe. The atolls lacked defining features and good visibility was an essential for navigating our way through so we maximised our speed and accuracy, by hand steering the course towards Arutua, from where we could follow the coast to slip between the atoll and Rangiroa in daylight. David carefully considered every decision and took note of landmarks in case clouds obscured the sun and when a radio forecast mentioned an upper trough of thundery showers preceding strong winds from the south west our concerns increased. But we were sailing faster than expected and shortly after lunch we saw a line of palms on the horizon that rapidly defined as the scattered *motu* of Arutua Atoll. After goose winging we followed the shore, rolling along on a gentle breeze and though black clouds were building as we rounded the atoll's western point, they dissolved. Kaukura lay to the south east and Makatea was close by, but they were unreachable in a night sail; with our course clear of obstructions, we could sail directly towards Tahiti.

Sam and Billy had left us alone to manage the boat, which was just as well; I was seasick and starting a period and David was feverish with the onset of a tropical flu. We settled the children for the night, and as the sun set behind Rangiroa a huge silvery moon rose beside us. David fell asleep soon after supper, but having forgotten to reel in the fishing line it suddenly whirled out with an enormous fish in tow. After hauling in the tuna, we threw it on the cockpit floor feeling almost as helpless as the fish. Then I stood watch and filleted the bounteous flesh while David slept into Friday the thirteenth of July. Sailing in the Tuamotu Archipelago would make any sailor superstitious but I had fortunately failed to register the date and rarity of this auspicious occurrence when coupled with a full moon. Bravado became trepidation when David woke with extreme pain in the toe he had gashed on the coral. And though the wound had appeared fine when I bandaged it, on unwrapping his foot I discovered a substantial infection surrounded with wet, dead flesh. The sight was too much for David, his face drained of colour and as his eyes rolled away he crumpled in a faint. I caught his fall and held him close as his consciousness returned. David came around feeling helplessly overwhelmed. After consulting our medical book, the true cause of his aching limbs, fever, and swollen lymph glands became obvious as we identified a red line advancing up his leg, a symptom of the virulent blood poisoning that accompanies advanced staphylococcus.

David's sore toe   WT

For the second time that month we gratefully turned to Robin Tattersall's antibiotics. David sat with his foot elevated, giving orders, and although we were not set up for single-handed sailing, the day passed without further drama. The wind retained a steady fifteen knots and when a brief rain squall caught the slices of tuna I had laid out I consoled myself that the sea air was probably too humid for them to dry. Sam and Billy were sensitive and when their noise invaded the peace we reminded ourselves they needed to let off steam. Hornpipe was sailing an efficient broad reach and when a lack of the predicted westerly current set us too far south for Tahiti we decided to avoid Teti'aroa atoll by continuing until we could make our approach from the west. Although the predicted weather system seemed to be moving slower than expected, high-level clouds gathering from the south west indicated that a storm was brewing and on estimating we were still a hundred and ten miles from Papeete, we remembered how Full Circle and Cyclone had battled to make half that distance in two days. As the sun set we wondered whether the wind would last long enough for us to reach Tahiti before it died or turned against us.

Fortunately, the easterly wind remained strong and the miles steadily ticked off. After a midnight sight of Jupiter and the moon David decided to square our course downwind, towards Tahiti. Resetting the rig required both of us, so David limped onto the rolling foredeck, protecting his toe and screaming when it brushed an obstacle. The day dawned with just enough visibility to claim a sight of the moon and Achernar and on calculating the fix we discovered the favourable current and wind had propelled us to just ten miles from the island. Although the trough's evil black clouds blanketed the mountains they momentarily lifted to reveal the sloping silhouette of Tahiti Iti to port, with Tahiti illuminated against the hard horizon. Once a squall had passed with little effect, we relaxed our guard. I was steering as another heavy cloud approached and when a vicious blast hit Hornpipe hard on her port side it backed her sail and buckled the whisker pole. Thunder roared, a ferocious wind howled, and driving rain soaked me as I leaped to the deck. Concerned about losing sight of land David took fixes from every visible feature and recorded our position between every downpour. As we sped towards the treacherous finger of Pointe Venus' unmarked reef at Tahiti's northern tip, the squalls became persistent. It was an immense relief when the light momentarily broke through the morass, revealing towering mountains shrouded in indigo clouds that could have been scrawled with charcoal. We were never so grateful as when Hornpipe creamed around Pointe Venus, her white sails pulling us towards the most romanticised island ever.

Having preserved our engine for fear of the cooling system faltering we could at last motor through Papeete's pass. As the modern port revealed its shiny spherical fuel tanks and breakwater, some of Tahiti's mystery dissolved. Against the quay, thirty or forty yachts jostled for space; after tiny islands, it was fascinating to observe cars flowing along a boulevard and sprawling buildings that climbed the hills to mingle with the mist. It was so easy to motor through the still water and as we passed the airport and opulent hotels with lawns sloping to the lagoon, Sam kept up an excited commentary, *"Ooh lovely tropical grass, I want to roll and sunbathe in it!"* When the Channel De Fa'a'ā opened to Maeva Beach, he recognised a familiar yacht – it was Cyclone! The children were delirious with joy and as we motored alongside, Jeremy and Tim's heads popped out of the hatch. Once we had anchored, the family rowed over in their dinghy, Big Belly, to tell their story and present us with a bowl of fresh fruit and salad. Anna and John told us how, after blowing out their mainsail, they had spent days struggling to make headway, that when their engine's water pump faltered, they had nursed it through the flat calms. They took the children away to play and stay the night. Then the storm set in; visibility dropped to a quarter of a mile, thunder and lightning roared around the mountains and the wind boxed the compass. It poured all day and as we cleared the debris of the trip we kept repeating how lucky we were to have made it in time. Although our passage from the Tuamotus had taken little more than two days, the infection and exacting navigation had exhausted David. His legs felt like lead and he ached all over, so after supper we went to bed and slept for eleven hours.

We awoke to complete silence, to drift in dreams, recovering and discovering ourselves. The nonstop pressure of sailing and parenting had abated, everything remained in the order we had left it the previous night; there were no fights or surging waves, the boat was a vacuum of peaceful stillness. When we went to collect Sam and Billy everyone was having such a good time that they were invited to stay. So we caught *Le Truck* into Papeete, speeding along a crowded road beneath lush breadfruit and palms. Everywhere was shut, including Tahiti Tours, where our mail awaited, but on wandering to the quay we found it a home from home of familiar faces and yachts, including Full Circle, Primavera, and the one hundred and twenty-foot racing yacht Sayonara, last seen in Tortola. And tucked beneath her bow disguised as a sailing dinghy was Intxea. Manuel sculled over in his inner tube and tarp dinghy to tell his story; that on leaving Panama he had headed to Cocos Island and Salinas in Ecuador followed by the Galapagos. From there he sailed to the uninhabited Marquesan island of Eaio and on arriving in Tahiti the officials had allowed him to stay while he repaired his yacht. Then, lacking the money to pay a bond, he had checked out – but a tiny Spanish boat taking cover while circumnavigating the globe could easily pass unnoticed amongst the flashy superyachts.

After buying a few food items from the market we wondered where our money had gone and decided we must either find work here or hurry on to find work in Australia before the cyclone season commenced at the end of November. David and I made separate trips into Papeete, riding the truck in the dewy morning to the pulsing beat of *tamure* drums. Enquiries about the lost purse revealed it had been passed to the Gendarmes, but before it was returned it prompted a radio connection that fortuitously led us to a potential job on nearby Mo'orea – a retired American couple who, having built a contemporary house, were in need of furniture. After six months of travel we could only stop if we had an income, so David telephoned the Morrisons to arrange a visit. Then we plodded the streets in search of parts to repair the whisker pole, our latest casualty, the winch that had collapsed on approaching the Tuamotus and the engine's water pump that had worried us since the Marquesas. On hearing of a wind generator for sale, we dipped into our funds in hopes of it providing a means of charging our batteries and conserving the petrol generator. After extracting three thousand dollars from the bank we paid our bills and bond, relieved that despite an expensive return to civilisation our yacht had sustained relatively little damage over six thousand miles and six months of sailing.

Hornpipe had proved herself, and of all the boats we had seen, none would have suited us better. Our arrival in Tahiti presented a fresh start. Would this promised land help us rebuild our relationship? While I could not have managed alone, our voyage from Ahe to Tahiti had shown we were a balanced team. Although we live in a society where couples separating is normal, David and I shared an expectation we should deal with our difficulties. Our passages were of my choosing and while nothing and no one is perfect, when the storms of life blow hard it is better to stay with the ship than to jump in a life raft.

THE SHADOW OF THE SHARK'S TOOTH

"When I was a young boy
My mama said to me
There's only one girl in the world for you
And she probably lives in Tahiti
I'd go the whole wide world
I'd go the whole wide world
Just to find her."

Reckless Eric

From Maeva Beach we could see white horses breaking out at sea. Near the reef, we watched majestic waves topple in a foaming mass just fifty metres away and although we breathed the salt spray and felt their thundering vibration our dinghy barely moved. There was hardly a breath of wind within the sheltered bay, and David was gloomy at the prospect of motoring to Mo'orea, but we hadn't gone far along the mirrored lagoon before a breeze sprung up. We rapidly sailed the fifteen miles to Mo'orea's pass into Cook's Bay and after dropping our anchor on the white sand, we cleated the wind generator to the deck. While I hauled up the propeller David held it still. When it was safely overhead he let go of the huge blade. Then, as a beast released from captivity, it whizzed into a roar that felled me to the deck. Rushing inside we watched the meter climb to twenty-four, twenty-five volts. Action – Electricity – Lights – Whoopee! Previously, evening activities had been conducted by the dismal glow of a hurricane lamp, and Sam and Billy were thrilled with the prospect of being able to read in bed. But as the wind increased, the whirling vibration intensified, and it took courage and coordination to lower the spinning propeller before it self-destructed or decapitated us.

On that first day David set off to visit his potential employers: Dick, a retired gynaecologist, and Mary, who wrote articles about interior design. While cruising the Pacific they had fallen in love with Mo'orea, and after buying land and building beside the lagoon they snorkelled over the coral in the way most couples take a daily walk in the garden. Being

Hornpipe sails into Oponohu Bay to anchor beneath Moua Roa   LT

immediately intrigued with David's album of furniture, the Morrisons borrowed a bandsaw and emptied their garage to create a workshop, and after anchoring closer, beneath Oponohu Bay's Shark's Tooth Mountain, David bought a moped to transport him to their house in Ha'apiti. We would be allowed to stay in Mo'orea on condition that our children go to the local school, and on meeting the headmaster we were told the only time westerners, *popa'a*, had attended Papatoai school, it had not been a success. However, he assured me that our children would be free of the negative attitudes that the French colonisers aroused.

On the eve of Sam and Billy's first school day we set the alarm clock, and so enthralled were they by its ticking that they went to bed early, speculating on what it was saying, eagerly anticipating it ringing. Sam's dreams featured the clock, that became a space invader, a robot, a bomb about to explode. Waking long before the event they lay in silence bottling their excitement and when it rang, there was a shriek, a cheer, and tumbling footsteps to bring the news, *"Mummy it did it!"* as they enacted its shrill trill and how they had jumped in their beds, farting in surprise! There was no end to their descriptions of the clock, its tick and tock, the orgasmic ring as it accomplished its purpose. Many dreams would be shattered by that raucous herald; as barely surfacing from sleep I prepared breakfast and rowed the kids ashore. Lazy fishes came and went within the lagoon and a friendly dog waited on the beach; an aroma of wood smoke lingered in the dewy shadows and all was still but for cocks crowing and pigs rustling in the undergrowth. My walk to the school bus was accompanied by two alarm clocks, tick ticking as the kids impersonated that jaunty march through time. But on future mornings I would have to urge them along, never relaxing until we sighted that small group beneath the mango tree, those last-minute scuffles as the children gathered posies for *Madame*, before the brightly coloured bus whisked them all away.

After running back along the road, I rowed home to pick up David, and after dropping him on the beach he unlocked the moped and buzzed along the shady road beside the lagoon, passing through tiny settlements, breathing in a fragrance of flowers and ocean breezes. Although the authorities were unaware that David was working, we were comforted by knowing the locals were unable to make fine furniture, and that we would spend our earnings on the island. David visited a Tahitian sawmill and familiarised himself with local timbers, while Dick and Mary encouraged him to design in a tropical oriental aesthetic that complemented their house's Japanese style. They delighted in seeing their furniture evolve from discussions over coffee through to the final revelation. At the end of each day the three sat over cold beers, sharing a wise and wicked sense of humour as they watched the sun set through the lattice of palms that framed the lagoon.

Since setting off from Tortola my sphere of activity had shrunk to a few yards, and though I cherished Sam and Billy, this was the first time since their births that I was not responsible for their wellbeing. I returned to the empty boat and there I sat, adrift in dreams, listening to the silence as memories of all those days when I had needed this space and tranquillity washed over me. A warm moist breeze swept down from the forested flanks of Mo'orea's peaks and pinnacles, the palms stirred. Then, despite a desperate need to replenish my creativity, I squandered that freedom on domestic chores. In the late morning I climbed to Hornpipe's deck and hovering on a blue mirror aboard my solitary home I opened my arms to begin my yoga practice. Embracing the sun, I breathed with the wind and waves, flowing from oblations to vigorous warrior asanas, and inversions - dancing in the light and dedicating my yoga to those I loved.

Who knows what filled Sam and Billy's day as they made that brave step into the unknown? As traveling children, they had learned to reach out to others and although it was difficult being the only non-Tahitians, all communications were in French which the locals were also learning. The kids rapidly developed a fluency, with Sam reading French comics and translating conversations for me. Creativity became his secret weapon as he appeased bullies with drawings of robots, and one day Billy told me he had recited a poem, *"Petit Poisson Rouge,"* at his *Maternelle's* assembly. On arriving home hot and tired, they played in and out of the water, foiling my attempts at getting them to tidy their muddles and by the time David appeared I was ragged and fraught from the squabbles. Following dinner and a bedtime story I took another shot at navigation. However, whenever I opened my special book with its imposing title, *NAVIGATION: very hard!* my mind froze and as David repeated the complexities of taking sights and calculations that translated to a position on the chart I wondered if my brain would hold true when paralysed with seasickness.

Billy's *Maternelle* was a homely environment where the teachers provided their children with toothbrushes and healthcare. One afternoon I found them sleeping on mats in an open *fale* and while the education was limited we continued helping our kids with their reading and writing. Sam's teacher explained how he spent his time, *"He is always doing something. You see him and his friend sitting together, go closer and you see that Sam is drawing him."* One day his school went on a trip to Papeete, and at dusk they returned still singing, their headmaster jovial as ever. Knowing nothing of Polynesian tradition Sam had lacked a flowered crown, until a mother stepped forward, having found space in her heart for one more after weaving them for her nine children. With no words to express my gratitude I made a cake, and a child led me to an earth floored hut with partitioned beds, all beneath a single roof. As the families gathered my offering appeared to diminish. And after embraces and tears they let me go, but not before gifting me a woven basket of fruit.

Sam and his friends wore crowns of flowers ST

On one occasion the local kids came to play, in what became a nerve racking experience when I realised none could swim. To those Tahitian children, Hornpipe was a palace and as I rowed the crowded dinghy ashore I grasped a sentence of irrepressible chatter, *"C'est plein de jouets!"* It's full of toys! For the local kids, spare moments were taken up with chores and they had no possessions, so when Sam told me that a friend was getting a bicycle I guessed it was a fantasy. Our children had forgotten their playroom in Redthorn Cottage with its shelves of books and floor awash with cars and trains; that on venturing outside they had become frozen and muddy within minutes. While we had reduced their toys to a box of Lego, a bag of animals, and cars, the beach and lagoon was a playground where they could invent a multitude of games. They treasured small things, created their own entertainment, drawing animated cartoons accompanied by dramatic dialogues, *"Here comes spider man, he's driving a truck, but he crashes down the mountain and falls into the sea. Now a whale pulls him to the surface."* Storyboard sketches that bubbled with verbose commentaries, *"Here comes a wave, hold on Sam, it's flooding the boat. Oh, no we're sinking!"* Seldom bored, they never asked for more, but sometimes I scrummaged in my rag bag to augment their battered animals with bears, a puppet octopus, moray eel, and a zoid with a bobbly tail.

Inanimate objects transformed into fantasies and Sam remembers playing in a canvas cavern of sail, an amorphous bubble of light that thrashed at its restraints. Such games nourished our children's imaginations, prepared them to be innovators and leaders. Sam's performances would develop from a similar methodology, as in April 2005 when he briefly returned to London to collaborate with friends from his time at the Slade. His theatrical troupe, *The Playground*, created and presented their first production, *The Restaurant of Many Orders*, at Saddlers Wells. It began as a response to the inhuman practices of detaining and torturing political prisoners at Guantanamo Bay and Abu Ghraib, through the guise of a traditional Japanese tale of two naive huntsmen who, coming upon a tavern in a forest, eagerly anticipate dinner. Mystified by the lack of customers they are hypnotised by the mesmeric mime of two sinister waitresses who lead their victims towards a gruesome demise. The production demonstrated how Sam's academic studies had boosted his instinctive creativity and the performance earned him outstanding results for his Master of Arts. Sam's concept would metamorphose into a cameo presentation at the *Prague Quadrennial*, where, after painting the individual face of each participant onto a papadum, he toasted it in a microwave, twisting their image into a grotesque caricature. The queue to Sam's booth grew as, one by one, his audience wandered away, nibbling the edges of their papadum masterpieces.

Apart from Hornpipe's upkeep, food was our only expense. I sought economical ways of using local produce, cooking papaya and breadfruit, boiling fruits into jams and chutneys, husking and grinding coconuts to supplement muesli, biscuits, cakes, and puddings. One day I hitched home with a twenty kilogramme sack of flour, somehow heaving it onto the boat. My quest for wholemeal flour led to my persuading a chef to grind the wheat I had bought at a store, only to discover the gritty grains were used as chicken feed. Supportive tasks were time-consuming and I rarely stopped. And while I secretly craved acknowledgement I tolerated the drudgery because I knew that neglect would compromise our health and wellbeing.

Hornpipe lay at anchor opposite a small *fale*, occupied by an androgynous couple whose sylph bodies appeared sexually transparent. The way they lay languidly entwined, lean limbs mirroring the other, preening their clone's long golden hair, had made us assume they were twins. Their romantic mystery would be forever associated with the cruise liner, Queen Elizabeth 2, that anchored in Oponohu Bay. We rowed along her colossal hull, gazing up her towering topsides, awed as ants; yet, when this dinosaur ran dry for want of fuel, Hornpipe would still be sailing the breeze. On that morning of the liner's departure a launch motored over to the *fale* and the enigmatic couple climbed aboard, clad in elegant attire, a final glimpse that whetted our curiosity. Sometime later we learned they had been found dead in each other's arms. Maybe the money had run out, perhaps they had lived an opulent life while they could. But as I bathed in their garden grotto decorated with flowers and shells it seemed their spirits still danced in the golden sunshine and sparkling water.

Having thought that Dick and Mary were the only English speakers on Mo'orea we discovered Jean, an artist whose one room *fale* stood in a field surrounded by horses. She cooked us curries and showed us her painted portrayals of Tahitian life. I reciprocated with a Hornpipe dinner and Jean, timing her arrival to savour the sunset, hailed us from the beach an hour earlier than anticipated. It was kamikaze hour on board as I dashed from galley to sunset glow, glossing chaos with chatter, desperately gulping a snatch of wine when David surfaced, smutty with oil following a hellish session in the engine room. And although Jean had appeared oblivious to the kids' crescendo of toilet activity, I resolved never to ask anyone to dinner ever again! We kept a windsurfer board permanently polled out from Hornpipe's hull, a floating play platform that could be easily released for paddling ashore. Because David expected the children to behave like responsible adults, he asked Sam to *"Just tie the board up,"* never thinking to check the knot. Next morning it was gone and a week later a Polynesian family paddled past on a flotilla of canoes and rafts towing the board, loaded with firewood. When David tried to explain, they appeared confused – their need was greater than ours and the law of the sea deems that salvage belongs to the finder, so he relented. Soon after, a dinghy washed ashore and after watching it for days we eventually tied it off Hornpipe's stern, thinking someone would claim it, but no one ever did. Around this time we met a group of windsurfing professionals, and on showing interest in their new F2 board they offered to sell. David and I could not believe our luck, or the power of the board, as we shared the exhilaration of catching surf breaks at the pass, describing those happy go lucky times, *"We have found an immense vitality and an invigorating purity."*

The Polynesians embraced communal living and our family had become part of the scenario. David rode his moped along the leafy road to cries of *"Papa de Sam, papa de Billy,"* and no one questioned when I washed our clothes with the women at the water pump or helped prepare a school feast along with the other mothers. One evening we watched a screening of *Mutiny on the Bounty* that was presented for the locals who had participated in the historic reenactment. On running into a group of New Zealand Māori preparing their waka for a return voyage, I noticed their stories were told in the spiral tattoos that enhanced their faces and muscular bodies and it made me curious about the culture of Aotearoa.

The Tahitian women's abundant hair and strong features needed no adornment, but subtle messages were conveyed by the placing of a single flower, which for special occasions were woven into luscious garlands. Men and women, young and old, wore the brightly patterned *pareau* that adapted to every shape and event and could be wrapped around the body in various permutations; the women hoisting it high when fishing or dropping it to their waist when hot. Traditional garments are comfortably timeless and I had worn my Palestinian dresses, African *kaftans*, Peruvian *ponchos* and embroidered blouses from Mexico with no concept of how insensitive it might be to appropriate another culture. As a child, I had embraced the theatricality of dressing up for a village parade in my grandmother's yellow *kimono* embroidered with a silver dragon, wearing a red chrysanthemum in my hair. My generation had proved that clothes could be fun. We had broken all the rules, abandoning wasp waists and matronly bosoms for miniskirts and trouser suits, had flirted with gender issues, flaunting capricious bodies, and painting childish freckles on our faces. With nothing to wear, I spontaneously transformed a shirt into a dress, sewed a skirt from a scrap, wore PVC hot pants one day, a floor length *sarong* the next. Maybe I was seeking an identity. Forever free from following fashion, I morphed from cute to mysterious, and as my hair exploded in an inky blot my parents despaired of me finding a husband.

David's mind was consumed with creative ideas; oblivious to trends he spared no concern for appearances and wore whatever came to hand, only discarding his clothes when they were beyond repair. Our one drawer and tiny cupboard was sufficient for all our garments. The tropical warmth clothed our bodies and softened our features. Alone at home I abandoned everything, so it was fortunate I was wearing shorts and a shirt on that rainy day when the intruder called. David had rowed the dinghy ashore leaving it for me to swim over and collect. I was in the galley chopping vegetables and hardly registered the soft thud as it came alongside, until I became aware of a presence, of someone blocking the light. Looking up I saw a man in the doorway and heard his, *"Amour! Amour!"* falling as a plea from his lips. In an instant I was screaming, *"Allez vous en!"* the foreign words springing from my lips more readily than my own tongue as I advanced, knife in hand, eyes aflame, blind with rage. With stumbling feet the Tahitian hit the water and swum for the shore, my screams a pack of dogs at his heels.

Following this invasion, I was wary of being alone on the boat until the substantial diversion of David's Aunt Julia. Having invited herself, Julia appeared with a jolly, *"Hello dawlings. I won't be any twuble, I'm just beach combing!"* Prior to this the authorities had ignored our presence, but when a police patrol boat investigated we attributed this to her previous stopover at the home of Tahitian activist Bengt Danielsson. Although secretly supporting the fleet that sailed for Mururoa to protest nuclear testing, we could not afford to associate with events that would jeopardise our opportunities to earn and survive. The Pacific had experienced more than its share of nuclear fallout and Dick had revealed that, as a ship's doctor, he had witnessed atom bomb tests on Bikini atoll, showing us a certificate that affirmed his attendance in the jargon of an era that *Le Bomb* had changed for all time. As Julia graphically enlightened us about the AIDS epidemic, body piercings, and pornography, we feared for our children's generation. While her campaigns in support of abortion, feminism, and causes that reflected her personal trials and tribulations were enlightening, it was hard to understand how sexual liberation and emancipation had led to such problems, a cruel irony that we should hear all this on an island that had suffered the scourge of European colonisation.

Sam's first impressions of his Great Aunt Julia were as *"an intriguing envoy from a world we had left behind when we sailed from Europe."* She was happy to fill gaps in the Trubridge family saga, that David's forebears were of German Jewish descent; how his great grandfather William Keiffenheim had taken his wife's surname to avoid being associated with Germany. When Julia's father, Hugo Trubridge, abandoned a marriage and two sons to abscond with his offspring's governess, Ada Broad of Newcastle, the jilted wife refused him a divorce. Ada in turn would trick Hugo into fathering Tony, Geoffrey, and Julia; and in an era when being born a *bastard* was a social stigma, the family was forced to travel the Continent to avoid scandal. While Hugo frittered his wealth, paying prospectors to pan for gold, indulging his obsession with alchemical experiments, his children became fluent in several languages. They suffered the all-too-familiar tragedies of that era, with Tony killed in the war, Geoffrey, David's father, dying while his sons were boys, and Julia enduring the abuse that shaped her personality. David's family tree is a legacy to centuries of Keiffenheims, presented on a scroll several metres long, with a coat of arms at the top, while his mother's equally lengthy lineage of London Salters Merchants originated in Scotland. My family tree would barely cover the back of an envelope, however our stories are just as romantic. My father's grandmother was reputedly born of gypsy blood in the Cornish fishing village of Clovelly, from where her son, William King, eloped with my grandmother, Elsie, and though she was disowned for lowering her family's status, their frugal wedding photo shines with a love that abandoned all else, *"For she had gone with the raggle taggle gypsy, Oh!"*

On Julia's first morning, after the family had departed for school and work, she announced her intention of going for a swim. When I expressed doubts about whether she had the agility and strength to climb back on board, Julia dismissed me with a, *"Don't wowy abowt me dawling I'm a big girl!"* It happened in a flash. Casting voluminous undergarments to the deck,

Julia donned a yellow bathing cap and with a jolly, *"Tally Ho!"* she launched herself at the uncomprehending ocean. Her belly flop resounded around the bay and as a seismic wave rocked the boat, apprehension clouded my mind and I settled for an optimistic 'what goes down must come up'. Julia wallowed around pontificating on how she adored the ease of movement, the sensations of floating free of encumbering weight. Eventually, as if requesting help with an awkward zip she called, *"I'm rather tired dawling, just give me a little hand back up."*

While we were used to clambering onto Hornpipe with the alacrity of youth, Julia was considerably older and larger. First off, she tried our homemade ladder but, despite my best efforts, it twirled and buckled beneath her bulk. Seizing a solution, she described how she would just flop into the dinghy before stepping up over the railing. One didn't argue with Julia, so I set to countering her mass, clinging to the dinghy's rearing bow. Heaving and hoing Julia hauled herself half into the submerged dinghy, from where, seizing a bucket, she began bailing the infinite ocean. Julia was used to being in control, so she had no means of comprehending why the sea insistently poured back over the side. In her thrashing, Julia had become entwined in the fishing net; her marbled flesh shivered with exertion and as I set to untangling her, the situation became excruciatingly intimate.

A powerful current ran between Hornpipe and the shore rendering it too treacherous for Julia to swim and too far for me to drag her, clinging to the dinghy like a great barnacle. While resigned to accept directions, would Julia be able to make the coordinated moves that would save her life? Launching our steadier windsurfer I guided Julia onto the board, balancing her weight as she shuffled from supine to sitting. At last she triumphantly stood holding the rail. Then, before I could stop her, she leaned into Hornpipe's hull and made an impulsive step. The predictable occurred: board and boat parted company, Julia teetered to horizontal and hit the water with a spectacular splat! A yellow bathing cap cheerily broke the surface, *"Dawling I'm getting tewibly tired,"* Julia spluttered, and I could see that she was afraid. This was a catalyst for a certainty I did not possess. *"We can do it,"* I assured Julia and as she rallied I told her to follow my precise instructions. Climbing onto the board I braced to counter Julia's metamorphosis from whale to woman, amphibian to homo sapiens. Guiding her foot onto the window's ledge I entreated her to, *"Hold it there,*

Julia!" as in a twinkle I was up and over the rail, ready for the next move. *"Now, pull yourself up,"* I encouraged. But Julia was exhausted. It was now or never, life or death! Bracing myself I grasped Julia's arms, and ignoring her cries of, *"Stop! Stop! Dawling you're bwuising me,"* I hauled her up. Julia flopped over the railing, landing in an amorphous heap upon the deck. She rallied first, ruefully inspecting her bruises, berating me, *"You had no need to gwip me so hard, dawling."*

My back and arms burned with exertion, however Aunt Julia appeared undaunted by the escapade and the day after I was cooking in the galley when I heard a, *"Tally Ho,"* followed by an almighty splash. Buoyed by the swell, Julia's abandoned body floated free, her opulent bosoms bobbing on the waves. My heart sank, and I marvelled at Julia's belief that I possessed the strength and desire to save her. When Sam innocently enquired *"Aunty Julia, why are you wobbly like a jelly?"* she invited the kids, *"Go on dawlings have a pwod!"* adding, *"It's an education!"* for my benefit. And Great Aunt Julia's presence on board, or overboard, was enlightening in every way. While life had been cruel to Julia, she had retaliated in good measure, and her stories were littered with the havoc she had wreaked on those who had not obeyed. She had stretched a vague connection with my parents, using their home as a watering hole on overseas trips while they weighed the entertainment against her prolific swearing. Julia and Josslyn were polar opposites and their relationship following Geoffrey's death had been tainted with bitterness and blame. David remembers a Christmas visit, the brothers squirming when, after the Queen's speech, Julia floridly described the goings-on in the film *Last Tango in Paris*. His mother never forgave Julia for this or countless other occasions when Julia had delighted in embarrassing her.

Julia schemed and dreamed of us settling in Australia and over subsequent years she would spontaneously appear with her sleeping bag and collapsible cup, insisting that she was no *"twuble."* However, Julia's commanding *"Oh, darling, just do this for me,"* could not be ignored. She always needed more, much more, and when Julia became fanatical about dowsing, believing she had psychic powers, she railed against those who refused to accept her claims. Julia frequently appeared at our sons' student flat, expecting to meld into their lives, prompting Sam to write, *"Throughout our growing lives Julia has come and gone, passing through on some grand caper, leaving behind astonishing insights into her world."*

Following Julia's departure we winched the moped aboard and sailed to Huahini to meet Gran for Christmas. Accommodating three generations on a small boat was especially difficult given such a wide age range. On exploring the island, Gran endlessly compared the climate and beaches to Britain, trying to persuade us to return. While she forgave David's adventurous spirit, I had stolen her son and deprived her grandchildren of their British upbringing. She would gaze adoringly at David and turn to me saying *"Isn't he wonderful?"* And despite loving my husband, I hungered for that affection and admiration he brushed aside. I wished my parents could experience our children's lives, that we could afford a visit, forgetting that I had felt claustrophobic and trapped within their house, encircled in a mesh of roads. The Midlands was a world away; and what was life without the rhythmic pulse of the sea, sunshine on my skin and Mo'orea's mountain watching over us?

The reappearance of Mike on Full Circle came as a welcome diversion, as he completed his story of a drug deal gone wrong. After his capture in Baja on the Mexican Peninsula, he had been dragged onto a ferry bound for a prison across the gulf. When he spontaneously leaped into the ocean with a total disregard for sharks and armed guards, he did not reckon on the captain turning around to pick him up. Conditions in the Mexican jail were appalling, with a policy that a warder in charge of an escapee was forced to serve that prisoner's term. But somehow Mike tunnelled out, to subsequently dive on North Sea oil rigs, saving his five hundred dollars a day for building a boat to travel the world. At Huahini we met the Sealestials, a charter yacht crew of Captain Keith, a British lawyer turned vagabond, Caroline, his wife, an accomplished nurse, and Noddy, a young Barbadian with dreadlocks. On discovering that we had celebrated the previous New Year in the same Virgin Gorda bar we vowed to make it three in a row and before leaving they promised to visit us on Mo'orea. Then we sailed home under the gaze of our disapproving passenger. As usual the trip was challenging with Gran questioning how we managed longer voyages and she left us with a sense of relief, and disappointment, that her stay hadn't been much fun.

David started making a dining table for Dick and Mary and at weekends we made excursions in their Land Rover or drove our moped along looping forest tracks beneath wispy Casuarinas. We used it to transport us to open-air films in Papatoai, David ferrying us short hops so that no one spent long alone. One day we climbed up to the base of Moua Roa, along tracks submerged in leaf mulch, weaving amongst the flying buttress roots of towering chestnuts, slithering in the muddy diggings of wild boars. Although it was refreshingly cool in the ethereal forest, disappointingly there was no birdsong. But there was entertainment as the children daubed themselves with tribal markings of orange earth. The trail ended beneath cliffs shrouded in green algae and we retreated with a sense that Mo'orea's mountain was equally inaccessible as mysterious. One could not live in such a powerful place and not be deeply affected, and while I translated those wonders into yogic affirmations of breathing and being, David wrote *"We've both caught ourselves thinking recently what a terrible loss there will be in our lives without Shark's Tooth mountain there above us. Life here has been all and everything that we ever wanted."*

After sailing over to Tahiti's eastern coast, we anchored near the famous Papeari break, where we watched giant waves crash on the reef, marvelling at the surfers who risked lacerations on the jagged coral. One sunny morning we gathered provisions for a three day walk and hitched up a winding road into the mountainous interior. As the lush vegetation of the coastal meadows transcended to precipitous cliffs, it started drizzling and it was raining heavily by the time we reached the road's end. Reluctantly clambering out of the warm truck, we hastily improvised raincoats from rubbish sacks, donned our packs and set off along a shingle track beneath vertical faces that disappeared in mist. Rounding a corner, we encountered an oppressive grey vista; a murky basin enclosed by rubble slopes, shrouded in black clouds. Our vision of camping beside an idyllic mountain lake were wasted on that hostile cauldron. Boulders crashed down shale walls, the air was bitterly cold, it looked like Mordor and was no place for us. Turning our backs on the eroding wasteland we set off for a gentler world of sunshine, and as the road descended the climate miraculously transformed. The rain ceased and as we shed our rubbish bags, colours were invented. Sunlight glittered on leaves, dew drops burst in refractions of blue and violet and at sea level it seemed time had stopped: everywhere was unchanged. Had our escapade been a dream or a nightmare? That night we camped ashore, cooked pancakes over a fire, and frolicked in soft grass, appreciating warmth like never before. We wandered the grounds of the Gauguin museum, through rooms adorned with tableaux of the artist's paintings and sculptures, collected starfruit for jam and met the great tortoise that had seen Captain Cook's arrival in Tahiti. And just as the yoga position *paschimottanasana* emulates that creature's retreat from the world, the ancient amphibian retracted into its shell, emitting a hissing exhalation.

On our return to Oponohu Bay a replacement gas cooker had arrived packed in Styrofoam bubbles. Sam and Billy pleaded with David to let them play in the huge box and their anticipation escalated when he indicated there was a surprise inside. At last they were given the go ahead to dive under and amidst the foam bubbles; surfacing to compare notes, *"Have you found it yet?" "No, me neither."* David had not revealed what they were searching for, or that there was nothing there. We had conflicting ideas about truth and trust. David believed that expectations were the real deal and, following Julia's visit, there had been talk of a castle in Germany. While once upon a time his family may have owned a castle, in my pragmatic mind the fantasy built false expectations of a prosperity that wasn't there in our time of need. The castle was a facade but the idea allowed our children to dream and where I had lived too frugally to shake off money worries, their aspirations were unquenched by adversities. They believed they could do anything and William would commit everything to his freediving career. In 2005 he travelled to the Bahamas in search of the perfect place to dive and, despite rumours that devils lurked in the depths of Dean's Blue Hole, the spectacular site met his expectations. The Long Islanders were friendly, William found a diving buddy, and every day when he stepped from the shallow beach into the circular pool that drops to two hundred metres he felt a thrill of expectation. After swimming his float to the centre of the natural amphitheatre he released the weighted dive rope and began his preparations. With regular training, William's performance improved and he started planning a world record attempt at Sharm El Sheikh's mecca of freediving. But as the time drew near he became afflicted with a mysterious illness.

While in the Caribbean, we had heard of *ciguatera*, conflicting stories that made us cautious about eating tropical fish, until the Tahitians showed us ways of testing which were safe. But William had been a small child when we lived in the tropics and such discussions had passed over his head. Years later as he trained for the world record he reduced his living expenses by catching and eating fish, and on becoming stricken with a range of debilitating symptoms he attributed them to his extreme regime. When a friend described the effects of fish poisoning William immediately recognised the dizziness, fever, numb limbs, and tingling sensations of *ciguatera*. Following a drastic change of diet, his health started to improve. However only time would heal the incremental malaise and meanwhile the symptoms annulled the sensations of hypoxia and muscle cramps, making deep diving extremely dangerous. Preparation time was lost and William was still debilitated when he made his record attempt. Yet, despite the adversities, he managed his dive to eighty-one metres in the constant weight with no fins discipline but was unable to complete the surface protocol. During the dive the governor of Sharm El Sheikh had waited on the beach with a congratulatory medal which he presented saying, *"You deserve this for your effort."* Meantime, on the other side of the world, we eagerly awaited a phone call. William's voice gave us an indescribable relief, but where he had hoped to make a living from the sponsorship that follows success, the dive had left him high and dry with no money for another attempt.

Just when it seemed that nothing could stop the kid's headlong energy, Sam suffered a terrible bout of diarrhoea and fever. It was frightening to see him crushed by the sickness and when Dick advised me how to sustain Sam's electrolyte with fruit drinks and broth I was deeply grateful. While once again we had enjoyed the benefits of being employed by a doctor, it is heartbreaking that millions of children die from the treatable disease. Sam's tests revealed a bacterial infection and with medication he regained weight and strength. But we were becoming aware of other dangers and when a friend showed us his severely malformed foot from stepping on a stonefish his description of the agonising near death experience gave us a greater respect for the ocean habitat. One afternoon when swimming around Hornpipe I felt a surging ring of pain and saw a glutinous tentacle of a Portuguese man o' war circling my ribs. Hauling my body on board I slumped to the deck and crawled into the cockpit, gritting my teeth as heart racing muscular contractions gripped my torso. While I conjectured that a fragment of the venomous creature must have drifted over the reef to wash past Hornpipe's hull, the aching lash developed into a snaking red scar that remained for many months. On hearing that an American dentist was giving consultations from his yacht, I seized the opportunity of an affordable treatment. As I reclined in the cockpit he injected and operated a faltering drill, powered by his boat's engine. Reservations about the cleanliness of the operation turned to shock when the filling cost far more than the French dentist and on questioning the price, his

"I travelled from the United States to bring you dentistry superior to anywhere in the world," left me speechless.

When the Sealestials sailed into the bay, they were accompanied by another charter boat, Sheer Terror, with her crew of Paul, Jo Jo, Nasty Nick, and Polly, who were wearing wigs and animal masks. The insane introduction defined a kindred British humour and during subsequent dinners, films, and parties, we laughed until we ached. Our new friends included Sam and Billy in their escapades and excursions, like the time we all set off to climb the mountain, carrying ropes to scale the cliffs, to be fortuitously diverted by an idyllic waterfall. Those days were alive with innocent discoveries, such as Caroline giving the children apples. They had read about apples but had no memory of ever eating one, and they victoriously held them aloft before crunching into the exotic crisp flesh. It was a rare and wonderful treat when Paul on Sheer Terror bought them sweets, which they saved to offer the children they had seen sailing in on a catamaran. Their gesture was met with a stony silence which, unknown to Sam and Billy meant *"We're not allowed to accept sweets from strangers,"* and it was a sad glimpse of the suspicious world beyond our sheltered lagoon.

During those five weeks of fun the Sealestials, Terrorists, and Hornpipers became an extended family. They left with a promise we would meet again. When a friend who managed the Bali Hai avocado and grapefruit farm offered us the use of his house, we moved ashore. The land-lubber's life was carefree and spontaneous with space to dance and enjoy long showers, to sleep with the sound of crickets chirping and wind in the trees.

Wahine LT

On walks to the school bus Sam and Billy found grapefruits beneath the trees, shells on the gravel road. I boiled cauldrons of marmalade and set to decorating Hornpipe's galley, completing the renovations with our children's pictures. While so many cruising yachts were gloomy and squalid, ours was a bright haven, a home on the high seas. After making a quilt for Mary's grandchild, she gave me her sail maker's sewing machine, with a hand cranking mechanism ideal for sails and awnings – useful for smaller items. A local girl with a boutique in Mo'orea displayed my patchwork bags and when she said they had all sold, I went to collect my earnings. She promised that I would have the money, *"next time,"* and resolving to be more assertive I returned, only to find the shop boarded up. Imagine my grief when a neighbour told me she had left the island with many unpaid debts. There was nothing I could do. All those stolen moments, sewing on my night watches, had been wasted and once again I had failed to support my family.

Although David had produced fewer items of furniture than in the Caribbean, the experience of working for Dick and Mary had refined his aesthetic. They had allowed him to work without compromise, repeatedly saying *"It doesn't matter how long it takes, just make it how you think best."* And in response he had conceived and created unique designs. *"How often, if ever again, will I have such a rare opportunity? To my friends in Mo'orea I convey my profound gratitude. I would like to do for wood what the medieval cathedral builders did for stone. They elevated it beyond all seeming limits of its potential. They lightened it - they gave it a grace, elegance, and beauty that could only be done as a combination of artist and material. The sum surpassed the product of the two components. I see slender curving lines of glowing wood, seeming slight, yet with a glowing strength and structure derived from their symmetry, their sense of proportion, and their wood rhythm."* Choosing a local chocolate hued wood called *tou* with dust filthy as coal David melded flowing shapes into his most proficient piece. A visiting Frenchman who failed to see how the design exploited the use of hand tools, pointed at the chair, then the garage exclaiming, *"E made dees, in dere."* The tightly refined structure referenced Chinese Ming dynasty furniture David had seen in London's Victoria and Albert Museum, when perceiving their aesthetic balance had been a *"heart stopping moment,"* an inspiration that was surpassed when Dick and Mary showed him a book of photographs of Polynesian art and the life changing realisation we were surrounded by a thriving cultural heritage, entirely independent of western influence.

After David visited an American surfer who had married a local girl and become renowned for his beautiful sculptures he began a carving of my windsurfing head dip, writing in his journal. *"I am still a learner soaking up experiences and with time the summation of these will be put forth, recreated through my work, be that in houses, furniture, sculpture, whatever."* Our plan of settling in Mo'orea seemed attainable because of a legacy to Paul Gauguin: a provision that artists did not pay taxes. I hoped my explorative drawings might have a commercial potential and longed to manifest my creativity, to reflect the Polynesians' earthy beauty and that godly realm of Mo'orea's mountain. When drawing, I reached into the shadows that lengthened as children laughed, cried, and grew to adults; and though my concentration was often lost in a gaggle of wriggling children, those images and memories - the forever that flowed between us - remains a treasured possession.

While my journal dialogues were often outpourings of elation or desperation, others reveal meditative observations: *"Holding stillness in my mind, listening to the silence, so that when thoughts cease I might hear the pulse of the earth and feel it beating within myself."* In dreams I broke the shell that separated me from that child who had roamed free as a leaf floating in the breeze. Compelled to capture the kaleidoscopic patterns of clouds, the stars that spiralled in the cosmos, I found myself writing poetry:

> *Soft rain dimples the sea's counterpane.*
> *All is being, moving, dancing.*
> *Glowing microcosms responding to the fluxing moon,*
> *persistently doing what they have always done.*
> *How hard the waves smash upon the circling reef.*
> *Are they rising to surge over us?*

> *A bird arrow pierces the lagoon,*
> *enters that watery world of fishes,*
> *seizes a silver dart and ascends to the sky.*
> *Waves caress the shore.*
> *Mountains melt into the ocean.*
> *Birth, life, death; evolution occurring in a breath.*
> *And another bird plummets into the sea.*

Almost a year had passed since our arrival in Tahiti and as our time for leaving drew near we eagerly anticipated an arrival. News abounded of Britain's punk revolution and maybe it was the snappy lyrics of Reckless Eric that had galvanised Gerry's yearnings into an escape. On proudly showing him Hornpipe's wind generator, Gerry observed that it was turning despite a lack of wind, and we realised we had mistakenly set the batteries to power the propeller and not the other way around. Shortly after, Gerry bought a surfboard from a local, leaving it unattended on the beach, from where it was duly claimed. He valiantly participated in Hornpipe's overdue haul out, grinding, patching, and coating the hull with anti-foul. Meanwhile the children and I stayed with Mary and Dick, concluding their school year with Sam's chic young teacher giving him a book about the shells of Tahiti. I had made Billy patterned shorts and a floral crown for him to dance in the *Maternelle's* festival. As I helped the mothers prepare a traditional feast I saw him chattering and cuddling his friends as naturally as if he had grown up speaking their language. When the principal told me that the government perceived the Tahitians as a primitive race – that the locals did not understand her attempts at preserving their culture – I remembered her words and on a chance meeting some thirty years later she revealed that much had changed, that she is involved in navigating Mo'orea's traditional sailing waka.

Sam and Billy embraced every moment in a rapturous joie de vivre, leaping around chanting *"I'm so happy, I'm so happy."* The most precious aspect of our time in Mo'orea was how they had bonded with their Tahitian classmates. Few children would have coped with the emotional and intellectual challenges. I remembered Sam's sadness on leaving the Caribbean, and hoped they would find new friends, that wherever we landed, Sam and Billy would retain their accepting minds, free of racism and prejudice. Although I had the greatest admiration for my offspring it was hard to maintain a healthy equilibrium within Hornpipe's tiny space, and while we did not expect to always live afloat, the real issue would be fulfilling their needs. On reaching journey's end, we would have to decide whether to immerse ourselves in our own culture or return to the purity of tropical islands. Our voyage would test us all and, wishing we could remain beneath Mo'orea's mountain, sheltered within her circling reef, I wrote, *"I shiver with trepidation when I think ahead, knowing that I am no braver or wiser than before. Where do these wanderings lead us and why travel onward, either spiritually or physically, when what we search for is here, and now?"*

THE PRICE OF PARADISE

"Yes, to dance beneath the diamond sky with one hand waving free
Silhouetted by the sea, circled by the circus sands
With all memory and fate driven deep beneath the waves
Let me forget about today until tomorrow. "

Bob Dylan

Leaving Mo'orea ST

On motoring out of Oponohu Pass I sat at Hornpipe's stern, peeling potatoes, watching Shark's Tooth mountain melt into tears, sending out a silent wish for our return. Our voyage filled me with trepidation. The engine was already overheating, the stern gland leaking, but at last we found the wind and set a course towards Ra'iātea; and by dawn the island was in our sights. Entering the pass, we caught a sizeable mahi mahi, and after anchoring behind Moto Iriru, we walked the reef, splashing through the shallows to awaken any stonefish. Even at close quarters those hideous creatures convincingly resemble coral encrustations and, sure enough, we spotted two of them, squat as stones, deadly as vipers, lurking in a pool. As the tide flooded the lagoon we waded back to the dinghy, seeing their grotesque shapes in every step.

After a day sail to Bora Bora we prepared to voyage on to the deserted atoll of Suvarov. From there we would head for American Samoa, to stock cheap provisions before cruising through Tonga and Fiji and on to Australia, where we hoped to organise legalities and accumulate finances for our return to Mo'orea. Bora Bora's expansive lagoon was perfect for windsurfing and we relished a rare meal out, at Hotel Oa Oa. There I met a woman on a South African cruising yacht and while her two girls played with our boys in a gnarled *tou* tree we shared a mutual concern about safety at sea. On complaining about her children's disinterest in learning it became clearer when she talked of throwing their scribbles overboard. Why would a child or anyone engage in an activity deemed worthless? Although storage space on a cruising yacht was limited, as an artist I couldn't help but value all creativity, especially my children's, and in that situation my hoarding instinct had paid off. When she expressed a superiority to the generous islanders, her prejudices appeared particularly offensive and realising we had nothing in common I left to spend our remaining francs at the market. When Gerry and David had battened down the hatches we slipped our mooring with Sam giving a farewell blast on the fog horn while I wrote, *"Releasing our attachment to land is the ultimate experience of letting go; of giving ourselves to the ocean."*

Sailing out through Bora Bora's shallow pass, we picked up a favourable south westerly with a steep sea; after reducing canvas, Hornpipe was racing, with waves foaming along her hull. Though it was a rough, rollicky start, if we had waited another day we might have lost the favourable wind. David was ecstatic, but he was the only one! Both Sam and I were sick, Gerry and Billy sat slumped in the cockpit and even David admitted to feeling a little nauseous when he went below to make a cup of tea. No one was hungry and by the time Maupiti disappeared, the children were bedded down, the wind showing no sign of abating. David was in his element, leaning out of the cockpit, watching the phosphorescence shoot past, calculating the tensile strength of Hornpipe's rig, adjusting ropes to increase her speed until the jarring seas and fickle wind snapped an Aries line, forcing him to stand and steer.

By morning a huge swell was surging up from the south west and after shaking out the reefs and raising the genoa to sail a broad reach, I set to washing the dishes. I was trying to control my seasickness when Billy cuddled up to me in his sweet way, asking, *"Is this where the milk is?"* *"Not now,"* I said, *"But it was; do you remember?"* *"Oh yes,"* he sighed, reminding me that as a baby he could never get enough of the loving comfort that flowed between us. Sam's birth had awakened me to the wonders of motherhood, but when Billy joined the family my days overflowed and there had never been enough time to fulfil everyone's needs. By night, too tired to sit through hours of breastfeeding, I had climbed into the spare bed to snuggle with Billy and as he drank from me we fell asleep together. I would awaken to find him scrummaged beneath the duvet, and how he breathed I will never know. Our hearts had stored those golden memories, but since leaving that security I had become acutely aware of my children's vulnerability. Love had transformed me into a desperate creature, for although I would have sacrificed my life for my children, sailing had made me all too aware of my limitations and nature's supreme indifference.

As the frenetic motion eased, the children asked how long we would be at sea. Billy seemed to think the whole world was a succession of islands and maybe that was not a bad idea. Weathering the ocean had sapped everyone's energy so we abandoned schoolwork with Sam reading the log book while Billy slept. On hooking a small mahi mahi we set to preparing a feast, with David filleting, Gerry grating coconuts for cream while the children ate the raw flesh, all the time enquiring about fish, life, death, and everything else. After putting some fish aside for sashimi, I marinated fresh chunks of flesh in lime juice. Hornpipe was in a hurry and on clearing Motu One before nightfall the open ocean extended to Suvarov. Soon after dark the steering line broke leaving us no alternative but to helm through another night; finding it more uplifting to follow the stars instead of gazing into the compass. At dawn, we refreshed ourselves with a *pamplemousse* from the Bali Hai Farm at the foot of Shark's Tooth mountain, and after fixing the Aries and gybing the jib, Hornpipe was sailing a comfortable six knots, presenting an opportune time to bake brownies for a lunchtime treat. It was then I discovered Sam and Billy's head lice and set to on the formidable task of washing their hair.

When seasickness and our stay-at-home existence reduced my mind to nothingness, I found it soothing to recall sensations from beyond that wilderness of water. The children's chitter chatter ran through my head as I registered their pivotal point of happiness, the probability of them remaining content to scrabble in the Lego box. Since discarding our connection with land we had become attuned to the ocean's fluting tremor of wind and waves. As Hornpipe swung through the swells familiar sounds conveyed a hiatus of domestic harmony. That symphony of groaning ropes, slapping sails, and thrumming rigging commanded our attention. The steel doors fretting in their latches was accompanied by a staccato squeaking and squealing of hinges, a soft swish of coats in the cupboard. The percussive clang of pots and pans grew to a crescendo, the cymbal crash of a miscreant saucepan awakened the depths. Our logbook comments glossed over the chaos, creating order from the agonies and ecstasies of those days at sea.

Gerry   *"steering not so bad after all."*

David   *"Hornpipe spreads her wings and flies again."*

Linda   *"brownies, lice, and fish for supper!"*

Gerry   *"new moon ahead."*

David   *"watch too good to end."*

Linda   *"shortened watch – speeding!"*

Gerry   *"clock back one hour."*

David   *"pumping mast alarming!"*

Linda   *"two reefs at end of the last watch – broke a wind vane."*

Gerry   *"sailing beautifully + Walkman = great watch"*

David   *"Aries never worked so well! Better than me"*

Although David's calculations showed we had covered a hundred and forty-seven miles during our noon to noon run, a fight was brewing. He wrote in his journal, *"Linda was nagging me again about my harness. Why do I find it so annoying? It produces the same sort of reactions and feelings in me as similar things my mother used to do. Then it was the manifestation, not of a healthy giving of love, but a helpless and desperate dependency, a clinging suffocation that aroused pity and the need to break away. It reduced her stature. I couldn't love her as an equal free human being. My mother drove me away from her emotionally by this terrible imbalance. It's nothing like as bad as that with Linda. It's almost as if the harness becomes a symbol of physical attachment. At times when I am standing up on the boat feeling*

*her fly in exultant freedom across the ocean, the wind in my hair, the pure beauty of
nature all around, it can only be destructive and produce resentment at its insensitivity."*
Although Scopolamine blurred my vision I managed a scrawled response,
*"I also long to be up there with the wind in my hair, hate being the chains that bind
you, know that I am physically and emotionally more dependent on you than is healthy.
Though you have more experience than me, I think this issue boils down to whether
one wears or doesn't wear a harness, keeps watch at night or doesn't, because of one's
opinion about what is safe, and at sea mine is less than worthless. I wish there was a
way to eliminate my fear of sailing, but this would mean a compromise on your part.
I don't want possession of you or your soul. I love you and would hate to be searching
the empty ocean for you."* While I tried to be David's equal, sailing cruelly
manifested our differences. The Scopolamine was not helping and I
continued throwing up, with the drug intensifying my emotions. All hopes
of applying my navigation skills faded when I realised I could barely add
2+2 let alone calculate a sight. I wondered if David and I would ever fly
together as, unloved and despairing, I cried about nothing.

Sunday dawned to a huge swell and unrelenting trade wind. Hornpipe
was broaching uncontrollably so it was *all hands on deck* to substitute the
staysail for the genoa. David had enjoyed his watch and was paying
the price for having stayed an extra hour. He said that I looked awful
and no doubt I did, with my face stoically strained from nausea and
Scopolamine, muscles aching from countering Hornpipe's violent lunges.
The conditions proved almost impossible for a navigational fix and David
wrote, *"It's not often that we are on a crest of a wave with a clear view of the horizon,
nor does that moment last for more than a few seconds. Practice!"* His eventual fix
and calculations revealed a run of a hundred and fifty-seven miles, and
our position two hundred and sixty miles from Suvarov. There was no
respite as the kids bounced around seemingly oblivious to the perpetual
motion until Sam lost his temper at an object that spun out of control.
Their constant dialogue and hunger for interactions compelled me to
occupy them with an arithmetic game, and then David taught them
battleships, noticing how Billy quickly calculated the coordinates to find
Sam's hidden ships. This prompted a discussion about what they would
take on the life raft and after deciding there would be no space for their
shell collection Sam said, *"Well when we are on the reef like Robinson Crusoe we
will go back for them."*

On entering a new time zone we gained an extra hour and a later bedtime.

During David's watch he adjusted the sails to avoid straining the rig, and as the mast started pumping he woke Gerry to help him double reef the mainsail while I held Hornpipe on a close reach, and despite the extra pressure breaking the wind vane it was a blessing because, on replacing it with the larger spare, our course deviated only ten degrees. Hornpipe soared through the night with the niggling sounds of straining ropes and water sloshing in the sail locker keeping David on alert. The following day's noon fix rewarded us with a run of a hundred and forty-seven miles, and with a lighter wind and just a hundred and fifteen to go we gybed the sails and shook out the reefs. The air was horribly humid and when a bank of low alto cloud deteriorated to light rain we cautiously dropped the mainsail to manage under the poled jib. Once the front had passed, the sky brightened, and as the wind grew stronger Hornpipe picked up her pace.

Shortly after midnight we estimated that Suvarov lay just thirty miles away, too close to continue at speed. So, after replacing the genoa with the staysail, we waited for dawn. The violent rolling and Gerry's irritating sniffle kept David awake and as the sky lightened he rushed on deck, sextant in hand. Visibility was low, the sky overcast when, through a gap in the clouds, Venus appeared to reward him with a vital fix that positioned us twenty miles north east of our estimated position. Even David was confused as, doubting his hastily taken sight, he chose to believe the dead reckoning. And then there was nothing for it but to sail in search of Suvarov. Gerry slept while Hornpipe wallowed downwind to a soundtrack of slamming sails, rattling pots and clattering Lego. David became nervous when a series of squalls passed, and as the wind deteriorated to a whimper, he reached the limit of his endurance. The batteries were flat so he decided to motor, but just as he released the propeller brake, Hornpipe surged forward on a new wind and with it the sky cleared. David's most recent fix had placed us south of our destination and despite saying that he didn't expect land to appear before ten thirty, by eleven thirty he was looking anxious. So where was Suvarov?

When Gerry woke, he joined Sam and Billy who were leaping about the cockpit, peering under the sails, hoping to bag that first glimpse of land. As we approached a flock of birds, Gerry pointed to the fishing reel saying, "*We will now catch a fish!*" As predicted the reel whirled and we hauled in a tuna. David was levelling the sextant for the noon sight when

Gerry climbed the mast to announce, *"I'd better clear my throat for this....
Land Ho!"* And there, just eleven miles to the north, was the eastern tip
of Suvarov. Finding that pin prick in the ocean, hundreds of miles from
any land, was an amazing achievement. Even the slightest error could
have led to us missing the low-lying atoll and David was right in thinking
we should have reached Suvarov earlier. For having come slightly too far
south we could easily have sailed past and never known.

After hardening our sheets, we sailed a broad reach while hastily eating
a lunch of fresh tuna steaks. Even on nearing Suvarov's southern flank
there were few signs of the shallow reef except for tiny fragments of land
that hovered like mirages on the shimmering sea. These motu were all
that remained of the mountainous island that had eroded over millions of
years, leaving a ring of coral with a circumference of forty-five miles. As
Hornpipe rounded the atoll we took turns climbing the mast to scan that
conundrum of tranquil water amidst the wild ocean, with the silhouette
of a wrecked copra boat warning of a fate that awaited the unwary. After
drifting past Gull Island's wheeling birds that gave voice to the still day,
the wind died and we motored to the entrance to shoot through the pass
into Suvarov's lagoon.

After anchoring we all dived overboard and while David checked its
holding I kept my eye on a posse of black tip sharks. On surfacing we
found ourselves in the company of six cruising yachts. An American
couple rowed over with a welcoming loaf of fresh bread, but we were *"So
tired and excited"* after those four demanding days and nights, so following
another meal of tuna we all went early to bed. Suvarov had become
renowned as the home of hermit Tom Neale who, after visiting when his
ship briefly anchored there in 1945, had obtained permission from the
Cook Island government to return and live on fish, coconut crabs, and
garden produce. In 1966, a friend helped him publish *An Island to Oneself*,
and sometime after Tom's death in 1977, Suvarov had been declared a
National Heritage Park. The yachting community had continued visiting,
planting fruit trees and maintaining Tom's cabins and winding tracks. On
rowing ashore we found that his old shack housed a book exchange where
the children donated and discovered books to fuel their avid reading.
There were also tanks of washing water and gardens where chickens laid
treasured eggs, providing a yachting haven on one of the most remote
islands on earth.

When a depression hit with violent gusts of forty knots we abandoned ourselves to an exhilarating afternoon of windsurfing, but not before David had dived to fasten a fender that would prevent the anchor chain from snagging the coral. The clear water was populated with edible fish of all shapes and sizes and despite several sharks lurking at Hornpipe's stern the white tips were merely inquisitive. The greys were less trustworthy and on hearing they would attack a diver carrying fish, David and Gerry kept their catch out of the water to decrease the chance of them sensing its dying vibrations. However, when parrot fish and jacks are hit they give a cry, and on wounding a big blue parrot fish a pack of sharks instantly appeared. Gerry had become uneasy in the water and preferred line fishing, while David, having less patience, dived alone, cautiously moving on after each catch, returning with food for several days. Charles, a veteran of the Pacific, took the men coconut crabbing, teaching them how to reach into a crab's burrow while avoiding claws that could open coconuts and crush bones. One day David returned with a crowd of them jostling in the dinghy waving their claws in the air. It was not immediately apparent that he had secured the menacing creatures, and the sight of his legs spread, wedding tackle recklessly swinging at crab crushing height, would have given anyone the jitters. Although the crabs had a delicious coconut taste, they were not worth a ball crushing.

Anchored beyond the flashy yachts was a battered frog box with two children on board. The little girl appeared morose, burdened with the responsibility of looking after her toddler brother, but after shy glances Sam, Billy, and Chloe were soon chattering. Hearing Sam's flamboyant French, we knew this was the greatest catalyst for learning. Chloe balanced the boys' energies and they jumped up in the morning eager for adventure, returning at dusk, exhausted from roaming the reefs and shore. Never before had they been so independent. Like the tame kitten that turned feral after being released from a yacht, they ran wild, climbing the coconut and burao trees, building huts, digging a vegetable patch, and creating palm frond clothes and ropes. Shrieks of laughter echoed over the water and occasionally we saw them emerge from the jungle, caught a glimpse of one up a tree or hiding in the undergrowth, their healthy bodies and minds darting here and there, exploring, creating, playing without purpose, prejudice, or pride.

David and I relished our own company but without Catherine, Gerry was adrift, hanging around the boat. However one day he walked with the children along the reef to Whale Island at the north of the anchorage. We joined them there and as we ate our picnic, agitated tropic birds, noddies, boobies, frigates, and terns wheeled overhead, for amidst the prickly bushes, fluffy fledglings were awaiting their return. While we lazed in the sun, the kids built a den and cleared a secret pathway to a shrine where they laid the bones of a seagull. They dived in search of shells and in their imaginations discovered precious jewels; how could anyone improve upon their carefree lives? I wrote, *"We learn so much from seeing our children rejoice in this special place. They play all day and the day is never long enough."* As Brancusi said, *"When we are no longer children we are already dead,"* and his sculptures reflect the eye of a child that perceives the spirit in all things.

Beach kids LT

Suvarov was a place of healing and on talking with the other cruising women I found that we all struggled with our partners' differing perceptions of safety. Nell, the woman who had welcomed us, needed to talk: she casually enquired about our netting before mentioning a child, *"She often played on deck and while we were anchored off Ua Pou she fell overboard, before we could do anything Mazie drowned. It was never a problem until we lost her."* Although Nell told her heart-breaking story in a matter of fact way, her silent boat was awash with grief. Her yacht's cockpit and deck was completely exposed making the tragedy somewhat inevitable and who is there that hasn't momentarily relaxed their vigilance, risked the lives of those they love. But after I realised my mind had judged her in less time than it had taken her toddler to drown, I remembered that David and I had stolen moments to preserve our relationship. Every action has consequences and though our children had survived, memories of those lapses remain. Along with our Achilles heel of the harness and my navigation issues David chastised me for taking my responsibilities too seriously while I struggled to accommodate his free spirit. A friend of mine had said, *"After having a baby it's much the same except that the child is outside in the cruel world."* And it seems that while a man's life is lived, loved, lost as a matter of course, women remain the nurturers, life givers, and broken hearted mourners.

It was my protective impulse that compelled me to travel to Egypt in 2006, to witness William's second world record attempt at diving eighty-one metres in the constant weight with no fins discipline. After days of travel my plane descended into Sharm El Sheikh and as the first shards of dawn illuminated the desert the crumpled mountain ranges flared like cardboard lit with a flaming match. It was years since I had seen my son and as I stumbled from the plane I stepped out of line. A soldier shouted and raised his machine gun, but I was breathing the same air as William. A taxi driver drove me to his hotel, and then I was hugging my little boy, hardly recognising my son in the man he had become. I felt his fragility, saw that his emaciated frame and deep eyes needed assurances I could not give, knew that he had expended everything on this quest. And although I had no doubt he was capable of the task, I feared it would not be this time.

One evening William, myself, and his loyal safety diver Mike, travelled into the desert through road blocks requiring passports and persuasions to reach an oasis encampment where woven carpets were spread upon the dry sand. The day faded as we sat drinking syrupy traditional tea beneath a heavy sky. When I expressed surprise that William, who abstained from sugar and alcohol, had drunk three glasses his response *"Is it sweet?"* was ominous. I reached to the heavens with a silent benediction for my son, and my heart opened to his freediving friends whose spiritual depths shone through their gentle generosity. I knew I could only watch and wait while they held William's life in their hands, and when the time came to return through the black night of stars, I felt strangely at peace.

When security restrictions surrounding a bevy of Tony Blair's politicians, who were staying at a resort nearby, delayed William's dive, I lingered through those hot Egyptian days absorbing all I could of freediving. The judges quizzed me, *"What was your son good at when he was a boy?"* I answered, *"Chess, art, music,"* and they said, *"So, William's a sensitive artist. He's wasting his time, a freediver needs to be an athlete, a machine."* I swallowed my pride, and replied, *"William will bring a new dimension to free diving."* And when they mocked and goaded my son, saying, *"Keep this up, man, it takes a lotta tries to get a record; we're enjoying our holiday and you're paying the bill,"* my son took it all, but I noticed how he wore dark glasses in their company. And while they could not anticipate that William would prove himself the Renaissance man of diving, when a conversation revealed stories of our family's cruising adventure, their surprise turned to respect.

I found myself overwhelmed by that first encounter with freediving. On the morning of William's dive, I watched his slight figure enter the ring of spectators, a matador in his red and black wetsuit, shadowed as an omen by the female judge. My son's composure commanded a respectful hush from those watchers who stopped to gaze at this boy/man, walking silent as a

Diver LT

somnambulist, bearing his cloak of probable defeat. He strode with a stature worthy of a king and maybe he intoned the affirmation, *"When walking, walk."* I breathed to myself, *"It is not over, he has an affinity with the depths and one day he will succeed."* The rest was inevitable! William dived, knowing that he was no longer capable of returning from the depth he had reached when training in the Caribbean. On ascending he blacked out twelve metres beneath the waves. Watching at a distance I saw panic, heard anxious voices, feared the worst; then Mike dragged my son's limp body to the surface and administered artificial respiration. William regained consciousness and when all had passed my feelings condensed into words.

> *Today my son was led as a lamb to the slaughter.*
> *I heard his innocent breath curdle with phlegm.*
> *Saw the broken back of my child, hollowed in supplication.*
> *As did my father's before.*
> *Thoughts congeal into anger.*
> *Let them go, let them go.*
> *Stop – Breathe – Think – Act.*

William's friends, Nic and Mike, whom he described as *"Both beacons and mirrors,"* had travelled to his record attempt and they reminded me that my son had retained his integrity, that he would return to fight another day. Even the hotel waiters and gardeners treated William as a brother. They felt his agony, believed he should have succeeded, saying *"William's our hero!"* When had my son grown into this gracious person who, even at his most vulnerable, carried himself with dignity? Giving up was never an option and though William needed this world record to establish his freediving career, survival is dependent upon resources. When it came to travelling home, William could not afford public transport so he walked through London, shivering and hungry, longing for the comforting warmth of the Caribbean. And though I would have done anything to smooth my son's hardships, they would strengthen his resolve and dissolve his ego.

The soothing pace of Suvarov had seeped into our souls and made us whole. While exploring the jungle, I came upon a concrete platform built as a coast watching station. A roof, held aloft on timber stilts, created a sheltered airy pavilion with framed glimpses of the ocean. *"Each of us seeks a special place, a temple,* and here was an elevated stone square, an altar on *which I laid my offering of yoga,"* David wrote, *"It's her little place and while I need to motor off to remote corners of the atoll in search of utter solitude, she finds her peace here."* He immersed himself in the environment, making several trips to the atoll's northern corner where, cleansed by the sea and sky, he felt a *"Wild primitive excitement."* He wondered why that exultant energy was lost on many in the anchorage, who rarely went beyond their confined yachts, and the island log book's constant references to paradise made us question what it suggested to those who appeared oblivious to their surroundings. Many claimed to have chosen a nomadic lifestyle to escape the pressures of society and the territorial attitude of a sailmaker, who had set up business in Tom's refuge, made us wonder what might occur if we were all marooned on that tiny island! David had expected that a cruising life would inculcate its participants with a heightened sensitivity, however many were unchanged by their experiences. In a similar way I had been disappointed at how yoga practitioners were often unaware of its deeper nature, and it seems that paradise is a state of mind, that wherever you go, whatever you do, will be a heaven or hell depending on yourself.

One afternoon we wandered the wide coral ledge that separates the Pacific Ocean from the haven of the lagoon, the wild from the tame. Floating on the wind's breath, I saw myself mirrored as rippling sunlight, dancing on a kinetic surface. And as the horizon watched from every side, I squatted, naked as a beast, to pee in that pure water. The breeze caressed my skin. I became the sea and sky, an unborn thing, an amoeba without definition or trace. Evolving to human, I reached to the sky. The wind sighed a sorrowful song to the roaring waves, I spread my arms to inscribe the circumference of heaven in my flight. Then, for fun, I went a little mad, singing, shouting, circling my limbs in arcing waves. Was this my hand, touching, feeling? Was this sensation within or beyond? Had I shrunk to a microscopic particle or become a colossus clawing the sky, measuring the sun's pathways from eternity until that day? And when my troubles had evaporated, I followed my family home, feeling saner and more satisfied than I had for a long time. *"With all memory and fate, driven deep beneath the waves,"* I had forgotten about today until tomorrow.

That freedom was all the sweeter for its elusive nature, and although we wished we could remain on Suvarov, there were other islands to see, food and gas supplies to replenish. We planned to surprise our friends from Sheer Terror, who were heading for American Samoa so, after the children had enjoyed a last morning ashore, we hauled up the anchor, only to discover that the generator's fuel pipe was blocked. And after waiting for the wind generator to power the battery we departed to a fanfare of conch trumpets. Once outside the pass, Hornpipe shot away on a rollicking beam reach, flying over the waves at an effortless seven knots that prompted Gerry to write, *"Why isn't sailing always like this?"* Unfortunately, once free of the shelter of Suvarov, the sea became lurching and lumpy. Following new advice, I had made acupressure wrist bands to control my nausea, but they made no difference. As my sparkle drained away David, becoming annoyed by my vacant expression, wondered why he was the only one eating supper, with Sam vomiting after two mouthfuls and Billy, who craved fresh foods, avoided the unpalatable stew, saying that his tummy hurt.

Hornpipe surged on her way and when the wind increased it seemed we might reach Pago Pago before the shops closed on Thursday. On my midnight watch, the moon was up and a large comet streamed across the sky, shattering as it passed overhead. Then I slept, to be awaken by the children's excited cry, *"A fish, a fish!"* As I grabbed the gaff and knife, David swung the mahi mahi into the cockpit where it nearly flapped into our cabin before Gerry threw himself on its thrashing body that was almost my size. Replacing John's orange fishing line with a clear two-hundred-pound monofilament and using plastic squid lures had proved worthwhile and as preparations got underway for an invigorating *poisson cru*, Billy and Sam popped fresh chunks into their mouths while Gerry threaded slices on a line to dry in the sun. Meanwhile Hornpipe was surpassing her Gulf of Panama record with a run of a hundred and seventy miles. However, converging winds from the great Southern Ocean and a local sea were creating hideous waves. Capitulating to Scopolamine, I watched huge rollers loom from the darkness, lifting Hornpipe on surging mountains of water that dissolved in the silver moonlight with a final farewell splash.

Despite protesting that he spent sleepless nights lying in his bunk, Gerry appeared healthy. The children were alert as ever, but none of us had the energy to help them with school work so Sam occupied himself, constructing a model of a Wild West town before playing Scrabble and chess with Billy, regretting that since teaching him to play chess in Bora Bora he had never won a game. Billy saw moves others missed and how was Sam to know that his brother was destined to become a chess and poker champion. Billy also loved washing up, watching for when it was my turn, swishing the plates and cutlery in the bucket before carefully drying and organising them. They invented fantasy games, speculating on characters they created. *"Flash man was a Lego man dressed in red who liked cheesecake. He could fly and lift spaceships and when superman or batman got into trouble they called on Flash man."* And as an adult Sam would reflect, *"When I was little I spent most of my time trying to turn a very small space into a playground."* Our nomadic life taught our children how to transcend limitations, gave Sam the imagination and confidence to create original performances from unexpected circumstances.

After another outstanding run of a hundred and sixty-seven miles, we anticipated an early arrival in Samoa, but despite maintaining a northerly course to avoid Rose Atoll and the three Manu'a islands, the noon sight revealed our position twelve miles further south than expected. While the error could have resulted from erratic currents, inaccurate headings, or a compass deviation, it seemed best we continue on a heading south of Manu'a's outlying reefs and submerged banks. As the wind dropped, cloud formations predicting a front made it imperative we forge ahead. After setting Hornpipe's genoa and wing with her mainsail she picked up speed, as with hopes of sighting the island of Ta'u before dusk we peered into the gloom, believing we saw vague shapes in the hazy porridge. As the sun set David thought he saw a darker patch upon the horizon, wondered whether his imagination had conjured up the angle of Ta'u's three-thousand-foot mountain. When the incline became certain David set a course south of the soaring peak and by nine the island's luminescent haze was evident, six miles to the north. Calculating that Tutuila's Pago Pago lay seventy miles further, we held hopes of making a landfall early the following morning. But as the wind eased we became beset with concerns about a four-knot current off the island.

Despite his unease David slept deeply and when I woke him he was completely unaware of time or place, *"Watch, what watch?"* At dawn there was still no sign of Tutuila and when the island materialised ten miles further north than expected we assumed that a southerly current had swept us off course. We were setting our rig for Pago Pago when a violent gybe tore the mainsail, breaking the Aries block, so we rolled the sail onto the next reefing point and took turns at the helm. The rolling motion had agitated the sediment in our tanks, rendering it a milky colour with a terrible taste. The proximity of land gave an opportunity to purge the tepid water with Gerry pumping while, incapable of wasting a single drop, I collected it for washing our sheets. After motoring into Pago Pago harbour we waited a frustrating four hours for the customs officials; by the time they appeared it was too late to get our radio fixed. On hearing that Sheer Terror had been delayed, our plans evaporated. But when we wandered into town in search of fresh fruit and ice cream we met Pete, who had left Carlisle for a job at the tuna canning factory, and he welcomed us home to meet his wife Sue and four-year-old Sarah.

The following day the family drove us around Tutuila's cliffy coast, through banana plantations and communities shaded by deciduous trees. Empty gas cylinders hung at the village entrances that, when rung as a bell at five thirty, indicated that *palagi* foreign visitors must leave and prayers commence. Sa'uele village was a picturesque scattering of *fale*, with separate cookhouses. The dwellings were single rooms on raised platforms with coconut mat walls that were rolled up by day, allowing breezes to refresh the interior and its neatly stacked mattresses, linen, and clothes. While David and Pete set off to scuba dive, Sue and I sat on the beach watching the kids and talking about *home*. But boat living hardened me to Sue's loneliness. She had no understanding of the value of clean running water, of how I craved her secure existence, the space and time to fulfil my creative aspirations, how it might be to switch on the television and claim a momentary respite from my clamouring children, to appreciate them once more. Sam and I were grappling with our relationship and maybe he too was making comparisons. However, I saw only my own needs as, free at last, I wandered away to draw a group of children. Others gathered and an imposing man sat for me followed by sisters Siaosi and Fa'apisa who shared a page with brother Alatise. They appeared to have all the time in the world to welcome my presence, and as my eyes absorbed their features, my hands worked the graphite, striving to express their varied personalities. When a woman said, *"Many palagi come, they sit on the beach and then drive away!"* I realised I felt close to these people because their lives were similar to mine.

Escaping Pago Pago's noisy harbour we motored around the north-east coast to anchor in a deep bay near the village of Afono. Although our trip required the chief's permission he was not the *head hunter* the harbour master had led us to expect. Sarah stayed overnight and, while the kids played, I joined David who was drawing the lashed beams and woven roof of a round hut that stood on stilts over the sea. Within its shady interior three women slumbered on woven mats. It being *tapu* (forbidden) to do anything on a Sunday, they silently watched time pass, allowing me to share their company. The meditative drawing and soothing presence of those archetypal women blessed me with a real sense of Polynesia, and taught me more about these generous people.

Ami, the village spokesperson, invited us to return and the following day we drew and drew while our new friends talked and laughed. In the distance, we heard Sam and Billy's shouts as children chased a chicken, and when we were about to leave, the family produced the creature baked with bananas. On exchanging addresses the girls sang and danced, inviting us to live in their community, repeatedly entreating us not to sail away on the dangerous ocean. It was both touching and overwhelmingly claustrophobic and when they finally accepted that we must go, they prayed and gave us their blessing. While David and Gerry sailed alone Sam, Billy, and I walked the dusty track to Pago Pago,

Samoan girl LT

enjoying the liberation of going our separate ways, the thrill of running down the hill to see Hornpipe proudly sail into the harbour.

As days stretched into a week of waiting for our friends, we learned that the radio parts would not arrive before our departure. Fortuitously we met a New Zealand family on their wooden ketch Tern, and it was then we started considering their homeland as a destination. When Sheer Terror arrived, the revelries began, with an evening when all ten of us crammed onto Hornpipe, followed by a party at Pete and Sue's with the children watching cartoons as we danced with a forgotten abandon. I bought birthday presents for Sam, replenished our dwindling clothes from the cheap stores and loaded seven hundred dollars of food at half of Tahiti's prices. The children had begged us to take them on the cable car that crossed the bay from one peak to the other and Sam, who had stayed up late, puffed uphill while Billy was so excited he ran to the top, oblivious to the humidity. The spectacular view revealed a fleet of tuna boats with their distinctively high bows and sloping stern ramps, where they carried a boat for manipulating the nets. However, the rusting hulks of Korean long liners, a black slick and green slime oozing from the cannery, made us resolve never to eat tinned tuna ever again.

When a storm delayed our departure we docked alongside Sheer Terror and watched the yachts that had made an early start return with torn sails, and as the wind reached fifty knots we motored out to anchor in the driving rain. The anchor immediately dragged and then the engine stopped – along with our hearts! We were as good as kippered when, to our enormous relief, Obelix fired a thundering volley. Gerry freed the propeller that had been fouled by the anchor's tripping line and it was a lucky escape. Yachts were breaking loose all around and we were surprised when the Sheer Terrors came over for supper. While their captain admitted to grasping every opportunity to forget his relentless job, we could never have abandoned Hornpipe; she was all we had. Our Samoan family came into town to farewell Ami and load us up with two enormous branches of bananas. They all crowded on board for tea and when Ami's ferry to Western Samoa was delayed she stayed overnight, to return home when its departure was indefinitely extended. Finally, the wind abated and after waving to Sheer Terror, we blasted them with water balloons to avenge a previous attack in Mo'orea. Another boat joined the fray, hurling water filled condoms, and when the Terrorists ran out of ammunition the Hornpipers reached for their bananas. The two yachts parted company with Sheer Terror circling the island before heading north for Hawaii, while Hornpipe sailed south to Tonga. But when we made a brief radio contact to claim a victory, Jo Jo sounded annoyed, and it was then we realised our biodegradable missiles had been more messy than fun.

Once clear of Tutuila we met with a large swell from the south east and after motor sailing free of the island's banks, we hoisted the genoa to bear away for Tonga. On realising that our Sumlog was failing, Gerry dived to check it: he found a broken wire so we had to stream out our Walker log and abandon fishing. The wind had swung forward of the beam and as Hornpipe violently lurched to starboard her bow slammed into the waves, rendering the forward cabin untenable. A procession of squalls with erratic winds heightened the tension. Waves smashed the hull, slopping into the cockpit, however it was too stuffy to sleep with our door closed so we endured the occasional splash into our aft cabin. But at least we were sailing fast, with the genoa pulling hard, dipping its foot in the troughs. As the anemometer registered twenty knots the sails flapped in agitation. Something had to give and we were pulling on harnesses to go aloft and reduce canvas when the boom broke!

The smash held none of the drama of our Atlantic disaster. It appeared that the overtight kicking strap had exerted too much pressure on the rotting boom and after dropping the mainsail and securing the pieces we continued sailing under the genoa. Our party nights had exacted a toll and despite David escaping seasickness he was suffering a headache. Moving around the tossing boat required an immense effort but by the afternoon Hornpipe was sailing a steady beam reach under a clear sky. We had presumed that our course deviations were due to fickle currents but when the dusk star sight placed us further southeast than expected we started to doubt our compass. After supper, we left Gerry on watch and fell into bed with the problem unresolved. During the night, the wind dropped and backed so at first light we detached the mainsail from the broken boom and hoisted it to sail with a loose footing and, following the success of our adaptation, we released an extra reef for momentum. When the noon fix gave a location further south than expected we blamed the discrepancies on a compass adjustment we had made in Tahiti and compensated with a twenty-degree course adjustment. Hornpipe struggled with sailing dead downwind so when the goose winged mainsail and genoa proved uncontrollable we replaced the configuration with the drifter which made the self-steering manageable.

Ocean passages presented us with challenges most families never experience. We were all highly charged people and it was not surprising that our yacht was too small to bottle our energies. While at anchor we had the beach but at sea there was no escaping the children's natural exuberance and high spirits that were exasperating in the pervasive heat. Appetites had returned so I started cooking while Sam and Billy vociferously tackled their school work. David's headache persisted and we longed for a moment of silence, for it all to stop, and as the emotional climate reached boiling point tempers degenerated into a shouting match. I hated the way I interacted with my children; however, there was no choice but to keep on keeping on. During our stay in Pago Pago, Polly had taken the kids aboard a cruise ship that lay docked in the harbour, and seeing the stark contrast between that floating hotel's luxurious swimming pools and abundant entertainments had made them question Hornpipe's prohibitive space. Where previously our boys had comfortably compared themselves with their friends in Mo'orea, they must have wondered why Sarah had it so easy.

The evening rendered perfect conditions for a star sight that positioned Hornpipe just seventy-five miles from the nearest point of Vava'u. During David's midnight watch we crossed the international dateline, making a giant leap from Wednesday to Friday, completely annihilating Thursday the twenty ninth of August. The wind was lighter than ever, so he woke Obelix to ensure a daylight arrival and amidst the distractions of a strident Van Morrison tape and a seductive full moon he neglected the dawn fix. Despite compensating for the compass deviation, uncertainties about the course preyed on our minds and it was a huge relief when a slightly darker line upon the horizon condensed into the certainty of land. Hauling in the Walker log, we let out the fishing line and almost immediately a mahi mahi was bouncing in our wake, but as David made ready to swing it over the stanchions, he momentarily hesitated, sending the fish into a frenzied spin that dislodged the hook. Obelix soldiered on, battling a southerly current, the land reluctantly revealing itself, our luck turning when we caught two yellow finned tuna in quick succession.

As we cruised into Vava'u's sounds, I wondered how we would ever find our way out of that labyrinth. After days of rough seas and responsibilities, that inner sea was still as a lake, its shores benign. While Sam and Billy leapt around the boat, speculating on the shells that lay hidden in the captivating depths, we adults stowed the ropes and sails, casting glances at wooded islands and overhanging cliffs, spotting familiar yachts, including one with a pet marmoset monkey which swung through the rigging to delight the children. On tying to Neiafu's wharf, a huge man with a broad smile and a straw mat tied about his middle introduced himself as the customs officer. Gratefully accepting a cup of tea, he produced a crumpled photograph of a couple and a boat that had gone missing. It all appeared very sad, but at this point a dour immigration officer arrived who, refusing the tea, requested whisky. While we waited the Tongans became engrossed in an animated discussion centred around the photograph. They eventually explained, *"We make mistake...this people's very, very bad; they on yacht, they make bomb, we look for them."* Their broken English and our imaginations concocted a macabre scenario. But before we knew it, the sullen official had stowed the whisky bottle in his briefcase and clambered onto the dock, where he met Gerry, who after proudly presenting him with a tuna steak, was heartbroken when he learned of the demise of his whisky. And after pondering over the story of the missing couple, the boat, and bomb it seemed that a long finger of anarchy had reached out to touch our lives. But it would be sometime before the more sinister truth was revealed.

SALT, SWEAT, AND TEARS

"Warm caresses, smacking kisses,

They hug me so tightly now,

encircling this body that thrust them into the world.

I wait, arms wide for their noisy return.

Their tumultuous being, doing, and questioning.

And, when sleeping, a stupor of still limbs, softly breathing.

A gentle remembering, like sunlight comes creeping.

Of first smiles dawning; the joy of their living."

Linda Trubridge

During our time in Polynesia we had adapted to various landscapes. The peaks of Mo'orea's Moua Roa had become our spiritual home, and on those dewy mornings when I rowed the children ashore and walked them to school I had almost believed we would always live within that crescent of coral. On Suvarov we had shed many skins. The pulsing sun and infinite horizon had roused us to soar as giants against the sky. Samoa's stormy mountains had exposed the claustrophobic closeness of strangers; those days had escalated into a kaleidoscope of parties. And as we sailed towards Tonga the nebulous sea washed away those accumulated experiences, opened our hearts to new faces and places. Vava'u's maze of inland waterways was a safe haven where, in making yet another start, we would discover that more was happening than appeared at first glance. Over millions of years the subterranean coral of ancient seas had been pushed up to form a land mass that had subsequently eroded into Tonga's labyrinth of limestone islands. These islands lie along a fault, where the action of the Australian Asian continental plate riding over the Pacific plate continues to create active volcanoes to the west, the Tongan trench to the east.

A quest for fresh food took us from Port of Refuge along a road of pounded coral, past a slip where Chloe's boat, Kurma, was hauled out for a repaint. On reaching the centre of Neiafu we found a few colonial buildings including a general store, a coffee shop selling local jewellery, baskets, and sculptures, and a stall selling tomatoes, taro, and pineapples. The Tongan people embodied an imposing dignity. Their presence, clad in a chiaroscuro of black *lava lava*, topped with a golden mat emanating the fragrance of fresh cut straw, embodied the wholesome simplicity of a holy order. And in a land where a man must resemble a mountain, their statuesque forms claimed status and power.

After returning to Hornpipe laden with fresh produce I spent the afternoon at the Paradise hotel, where for a small fee we used their facilities. The children played in the pool and I set to work on the laundry while David walked out along a network of paths that crisscrossed an undulating causeway. There an old man sat in the shade of a mango tree twisting a rope from coconut husks, watching the pigs and children freely roam amongst his vegetables. That evening while sharing a banquet at the Vava'u Guest House we learned that Sundays were a rest day, with no activity permitted, except church services and self-reflection. However, David and Gerry had a boom to fix. Despite their lack of respect for missionary impositions they deferred to using hand tools to avoid provoking God. And on finding that the plug they had constructed in mid-Atlantic had swollen tight they spent the day chipping it out before shaping and fitting a new one from hard wood that David had bought at the wharf.

On hearing that the King of Tonga would visit the Vava'u agricultural show while touring his island domain we started early, with the children waving homemade Tongan flags, singing, "*We're off to see the King,*" and a less respectful, "*The King is in the altogether!*" Arriving at the parade ground we found the festivities in full swing, with stalls of vegetables, fruit, and woven mats set up, and though nothing was for sale until the judging had finished, David persuaded a woman to sell him a pandanus mat for my birthday. Intimidating police women ordered us into rows and as a brass band launched into the jaunty *Puppet on a String*, a cavalcade of army and police vehicles drove past with King Taufa'ahau riding a plastic chair on the back of a utility truck. His mighty girth was shrouded in the ubiquitous black garment and straw mat and the only indication of his regal status was the deference of his minions. No one was allowed higher than the King, so those making a move had to crawl. Billy was terribly disappointed having expected the King to be a magical person, while Sam observed how his round bald head and huge sunglasses resembled *Toad of Toad Hall*. After a lengthy speech, the King toured the grounds, waving from his truck throne, peering out from beneath a vast Mexican sombrero. But by then the event had become a Monty Python sketch. Apart from the ritualised clowning of Tongan grandmothers who mocked the band, the ceremony was devoid of cultural integrity. Colonisation and religious protocol had hijacked the island ways and as troops of girls with swaying hips and sinuous hands emulated a Polynesian dance, their ankle length dresses and mats reduced their movements to a staid parody. That evening Gerry visited a Vava'u bar where the hostile locals made him wonder whether they would act on their aggressive threats. Did they really hate foreigners or were they drunk? Gerry didn't remain to find out.

Tonga's King and Queen LT

Tiring of the crowded anchorage we set off for Port Maurelle to dive, windsurf, and catch up on boat maintenance. Although there were no yachts in sight our presence started a stampede and by the following day eight had anchored beside us. The locals had told us that the notorious Mariners and Swallows caves were situated on a nearby island and so we went looking for the underwater cavern where a young girl and her lover had hidden to escape the attention of a despotic chief. The island dropped off to a depth too great for anchoring, so we loaded the tubby orange dinghy we had found in Mo'orea with a picnic and snorkelling gear. A splattering of rain fell as we motored beneath cliffs overhung with foliage, and as we entered a narrow gap the sea became choppy. On seeing a cloud of flying foxes swarming against the sky we knew we were close and when they returned to the branches of an ironwood tree the children spotted the cavern's dark shape looming below the cliffs. After throwing the anchor onto a ledge, David took a big breath and disappeared into the black hole. He swam for some twenty feet of flickering darkness before surfacing in a round pool. Stalactites were visible in the light from the cavern's underwater entrance and the atmosphere emanated an eerie luminescence that was intensified by the rhythmic pulsing waves which caused the moisture in the trapped air to shrink and expand, misting and clarifying with the rising/falling swell.

David said that an eternity seemed to pass before Gerry's head popped up beside him and when they returned to the children and me waiting in the dinghy, Sam was very keen to go. I was relieved when Billy said that he didn't want to do it. This was an ambitious venture for anyone let alone a child and David spent a long time preparing Sam while keeping his anxieties at bay. Only later did he tell me of his fears of him panicking, trying to go back, or getting stuck. But when the time came, Sam dived without hesitation and I followed his elfin body, swimming down a few metres, making short tight strokes as I started along the dark passage. Sam had surfaced, proud as punch, and I scrambled out, lungs gasping for air, eyes trying to grasp the transient vision

Tongan dancer LT

as faces melted and clarified. We sat on a rock shivering, observing the fluctuating pressure of the trapped air – that basin of imprisoned ocean. I dared not imagine being stuck in the spooky chamber and knew I must leave before anxiety shortened my breath. There was no way out but to dive into that leering mouth and follow it to the daylight. Sam left first. Ignoring our advice about taking a deep breath, he paused in the middle of a babbling conversation, dived under, and was gone in a flash. Breaking my trance, I slid into the sapphire pool and swum into the light. On reaching the dinghy Billy said he wanted to dive but we were all too cold and tired to return and Sam sensitively remained silent about his accomplishment. His disappointment would fuel an immense determination that eventually saw William return to train for his world record freedive with the intention of claiming it on his home turf in Dean's Blue Hole, Long Island.

The wind was funnelling between the islands when, hungry and shivering, we started back for Hornpipe. David coaxed the outboard while Gerry frantically bailed and I deflected the waves with our diving flippers. We bent to our tasks and the gallant little outboard somehow managed the three miles to Maitaitunga where, on drifting into Swallows Cave, we found a space large enough to shelter a small yacht. There we hung on the azure water eating our miraculously dry sandwiches, gazing up through shards of sunlight at rococo stalactites that plummeted from the ceiling, and cliffs pocked with ledges where swallows nested. After motoring home, we went ashore to walk a grassy track to the village of Falevai, feeling conspicuous as we passed the seemingly deserted houses. Although dogs chased piglets and hairy pigs chased dogs no one took any notice of us until, on meeting a family collecting copra under the palms, a hefty girl deftly husked a coconut that David was fumbling with. And as the sun set we drank nature's cocktail and talked about our adventure.

Having decided to experience Isaiah's Tongan feast we caught a gentle breeze that lasted until Pangaimotu Island. There we anchored and rowed ashore to a narrow beach where our meal was baking in a Polynesian *umu*, earth oven, beneath the overhanging cliff. A band of fiddle, banjo, and guitar played while Isaiah's daughters danced in incongruous grass skirts they had created from shredded rubbish bags and then the food was carried out on stretchers of palm fronds. Once Isaiah had said grace we unwrapped a multitude of taro leaf packages to discover individual morsels of lobster, poisson cru, octopus, fish, spinach, pork, taro, cassava, watermelon, chow mein, and noodles in coconut milk. The green coconut water was more delicious than a fine wine; eating with our fingers added to the ritual and I relished every mouthful while Gerry scoffed his in minutes. After supplementing the big boys' rations I drew the giggling dancing girls before rowing home over a sea that reflected every star in the sky, through a silence so heavy it woke us from our sleep.

Sam would create his own notorious feast as, following the London premiere, he adapted his *Restaurant of Many Orders* to a New Zealand setting that portrayed the hunter characters as naïve colonials. His Wellington performance space emulated a restaurant with a concierge who sat the audience at tables laid with dinner settings. As the mysterious waitresses seduced and reduced the brash colonials to anonymous victims, a door swung open revealing a hooked carcass illuminated by a naked light bulb. A methodical stripping of identity and humanity, boxes of discarded spectacles and shoes, made sinister references to a holocaust. Eventually the chained hunters were submissively led along the table, with the waitress expertly slicing strips of bacon from the victim's mask, placing slithers on the audience's plates. While one person delicately ate the proffered meat, most looked on in stunned horror as the charade reached its grotesque conclusion. Sam translated his gastronomic creative event into the Italian *commedia dell'arte* style, and attended Italian classes to develop his language skills before touring venues in Rome and Florence. The performance concluded with the dancers rolling out a vast sheet of pastry to encase their victims in a huge pie reminiscent of Shakespeare's *Coriolanus*. And when interviewed on an Italian radio programme Sam was fluent enough to respond and explain his concepts in his host's language.

David and I introduced a feasting theme at a workshop for the Vitra Design Museum's summer programme at Boisbuchet in France. I awakened our students' creativity by leading them through yoga practices before encouraging them to reinvent the ritual of eating. The gastronomic feast culminated in groups traversing the opulent grounds, gathering to eat courses that related to the elements. The culinary affirmation of earth was a soup served in bread bowls with diners seated in a circular pit, warming their feet at a central fire. Wandering on to a castle courtyard they sampled crisp vegetables presented on ice trays to an accompanying sound feast of tinkling water – concluding with delicacies suspended in airy sky hammocks. The project encouraged us to present similar experiences in Tasmania and New Zealand where, after inspiring the participants with yoga and meditation, David led them into creative interactions with the environment, to inscribe patterns upon the earth with their bodies, construct with found objects and emulate the sensory stimuli of our sailing life. And as our students opened their eyes to nature, they developed a revolutionary new perspective on contemporary design.

With hopes of finding a secluded bay we anchored to the southern end of Pangaimotu. There on the sandy island of Tapana I practiced my yoga beneath the shady pines on their soft carpet of needles. A shelf of reef stretched before me, and there the children spent hours searching for shells. And while they only took those that filled a gap in our collection, they were so abundant we hardly spared a thought for the innocent aquatic life and its fragile ecosystem that would concern us so much in years to come. Despite our limited understanding of ocean ecology the lack of fish surprised us, but lobsters were plentiful and one day David found four, lurking on a ledge. Then, shivering from the current that surfaced from the depths, he headed into the balmy shallows where round coral heads were aflutter with turquoise fish, like humming birds on blossom. Hearing his shout, I saw him haul a huge creature from the lagoon. The triton's trumpet had died in the grip of a crown of thorns starfish. And it was a shock when we learned that the prickly predator was the perpetrator of the reef's demise.

David had hung the triton shell in the rigging where its contents slowly decomposed casting a dreadful stench over my birthday that occurred with memorable presents: a grass skirt, the pandanus yoga mat, and a horse ride. While there was only one saddle it did not stop us cantering along a narrow track through banana and taro plantations, riding high beneath shady palms with the sparkling sea beyond and below. When the Kurma family joined us in the anchorage, the children roamed free, inventing games that tested the boundaries, becoming screaming savages, beating a sea snake to bits. Sam had started talking about girls, saying he liked them best of all, meaning Chloe, and in a letter to his grandparents he wrote, *"I have a girlfriend at last."* And one day he said, *"I really want to marry Chloe when I grow up. But do you think she will recognise me then?"* Sam had started rehearsing how he would ask Chloe, but circumstances were conspiring to foil his plan.

Chloe's family must have been brave to sail their cumbersome boat on unpredictable ocean passages. Kurma's rusting hull rose high in the water like a submarine, revealing none of her secrets. It was surprising to discover that the interior of that floating caravan was as large as Hornpipe, despite her being ten feet shorter. The sight of a huge computer wedged on a shelf was as incongruous as an electric light switch on the wall of a cave. We had never known anyone with a computer and had no idea what the family used it for. I recalled a mechanical contraption that filled a room at the art college; how, after activating the beast, it printed screeds of crosses across spools of paper. And as its novelty waned I questioned the purpose of that technology, never dreaming it would change the world, liberate our creative expression, and replace David's chisels and planes.

When Gerry and David returned empty handed from their dive, we scrapped plans for a seafood barbecue and settled for roasting bananas and marshmallows on our beach fire. Fabian, Chloe's mother, sang a haunting song of how the sea had called her, of that baby girl who had changed her life, *"You make dreams and pictures in your songs, you are a clown who makes a mirage."* Although I barely understood, I empathised with her wonder. No words were necessary to fill the spaces in the darkness as the children danced around the fire waving sparklers, their leaping bodies splashed with light, shooting stars falling on the sand. Then Sam used his new torch to send a message into outer space, *"Hello up there,"* speculating on the reply, *"Hello down there!"*

Sadly, the Kurma family sailed away leaving us to fathom their mysteries, the dilemma of when Sam and Chloe would next meet. That night Billy was telling his Bear stories, about making a little house, a cooker, and a pen; about mixing ink and glue to fix a seat. One by one Billy created the details in his mind, speaking in his joyful little voice. What a sweet boy he was. Fabian's songs had reminded me of those simple, perfect times when my children were babies; before my authoritarian role as mother and teacher made me a target of rebellion. I remembered when love was all sunshine and dreams, of how Sam's first spontaneous smiles had grown into exuberant ideas. Would it matter if I shirked my responsibilities, allowed myself to laugh and have fun? But would Sam let me into his world? I recalled that before he was born I had dreamed of my baby; that he was more beautiful than anything I had ever seen. Perhaps, if I drew Sam, that double act of creative connection, mother and artist, would shatter our prescribed roles and allow us to forget the everyday struggles. And eventually it would be Sam who claimed that opportunity, drawing and painting a series of portraits that revealed more than I could ever convey.

Rust had broken through our yacht's cockpit and decks, and as we began another bout of grinding we welcomed Gerry's participation. When he made a trip into Vava'u to sell his paintings and blow the money on fags and beer, we squandered our time on back-breaking chipping, grinding, and sanding. Hornpipe's maintenance had undermined our relationship and despite having grown emotionally attached we considered whether it might be wise to sell her. As our living area shrank and sank into confined chaos, every action became fraught with tension. Losing my temper, then hating myself for those outbursts, I dissolved in a cycle of despair, crying myself to sleep. How could I expect Sam and Billy to respect my values when I could not control myself?

On completing the journal that had been my companion on the Atlantic and Pacific passages, I resolved to hide my tears behind a smile. It was a good intention but it had never worked before. While I craved David's support, he rarely acknowledged my contribution or talked of us as a team. And how could my partner understand when he had never experienced the everyday occurrences of a family? How could a man value emotions when he had learned to suppress his own? David's formative years had been almost entirely male oriented and while he had no means of empathising with my distress, I never realised how the shadows of his formal education and absent father influenced our relationship. I remember David's mother berating her husband's commitment to his students, bemoaning that her sons had been bereft of a family life even before their father's death. Considering the traumas endured in educational institutions, David appeared unscathed; but his lack of sympathy left me desolate and confused. When I tried to talk he remained silent. Would I ever know what David was thinking?

I decided to create an opportunity for a quiet discussion over a cup of coffee and, while all I needed was a word of encouragement, a reassuring hug, David's rational arguments provoked frenzied zigzags of anger. Driven to desperation I hurled my coffee mug at him, only to see it impotently arch over the railing, hit the water and sink along with my pride. David dived to retrieve the mug and suggested that I go ashore, do yoga and *"Get over it!"* I wished that I could. Tears would have served me better and although it sounds laughable, back then it was painfully sad. Having always been his own boss, David wasn't going to compromise for what he considered my psychological flaws and when he accused me of sabotaging his freedom, he failed to see how far I had come to meet his expectations. In turn I never realised the depth of his affinity with nature, how as a schoolboy bereft of loving care, he had sought his comfort in the mountains and ocean. Although the wilderness inspired me I also needed companionship.

Lurking behind every disagreement was the fact David was the only one fluent with sailing and able to fix Hornpipe's multiple eccentricities; persistent jobs that stole his opportunity to relax. His father's death had left him with an urgent desire to grasp his freedom and while he needed me strong and deplored my weakness, our demanding lifestyle exposed my inadequacies. It was a conundrum. We shared the deepest love for Sam and Billy – my husband and family were my all and everything, but I felt them slipping away. I sought comfort in the Bhagavad Gita's ancient text. *"In the dark night of my soul I feel desolation. In my self-pity, I see not the way of righteousness."*

Gerry returned and with the completion of Hornpipe's paint job she looked as good as new, and with space to move, my desperation passed. Since Chloe's departure Sam and Billy had been at a loose end, and it was on one of those afternoons when they were hanging around waiting for something to happen that we proposed they go for a walk. When their voices melted to silence we drew a deep breath and settled to work, relishing the continuity of unbroken thoughts. We had expected a quick return after a brief exploration of the beach, however as the day faded we grew anxious and regretted sending them off alone. Gerry climbed a hill and David scanned the shore, whistling and shouting their names, but there was no sign. I had started running up the rutted track when, illuminated in a golden glow I caught sight of two small figures trudging homeward. They chanted their adventures, of how they had walked and walked, following paths that wove through the jungle past shacks and gardens, how, hot and hungry, they had met a man in a hut who shared his meal and set them on their way. Intuitively orienting a maze of tracks, they had somehow found their way home. We had never imagined that Sam and Billy would wander so far and be away so long and although their presence was a proof of a maturity beyond their years, following the adventure we were more careful with our suggestions.

When it was time to move on, David and Gerry sailed alone, gently drifting on a north easterly breeze while I hurtled past them on the windsurfer, crisscrossing amongst the islands, on the most spectacular run of my life. Sailing Hornpipe required steely control but windsurfing was instinctive and free of responsibility. We met between Vaka Eitu and Lagitau Islands, beside a reef that dried at low tide. There the children pottered amongst the rocks and shallow pools, finding marbled cones, nerites, and a lovely textile cone. One night, with the moon no more than a silver wisp, David and Gerry dived the reef's outer cliffs, that plunged to great depths with virulent corals, sheltering colonies of small fish. They returned with five lobsters and, when a passing fisherman traded another, we could not resist. Although crustaceans had long been my favourite, with no fridge to preserve them I ate far too much. The orgy of eating resulted in persistent stomach cramps and as they became unbearable we scanned our medical books and identified the symptoms as intestinal colic from a protein overload. An enema gave instantaneous relief, followed by the phenomenon of a day off with David taking the children diving, returning with the biggest fish he ever speared. But this my boys ate alone.

After exploring the island and repairing our damaged mainsail we returned to Neiafu where Gerry embarked on paintings of yachts. After shopping and extending our visa we feasted at the Vava'u Guest House where we met an English couple, Jon and Lorna from Zephyr V. They were accompanied by a lone *Kiwi* clad in carpet slippers and raggy shorts, from an equally rough and ready yacht, Woodwind. As they hatched a crazy plan of salvaging a yacht we became intrigued. David recalled Dick on Mo'orea telling him of the fifty foot Manureva that had been wrecked on the Aitutaki reef. There she had lain, until Kiwi John bought her with the intention of salvaging her lead ballast, but on sighting the beautiful yacht he hadn't the heart to destroy her and had voyaged on to Vava'u hoping to persuade his friends to help him patch the wreck and sail it to New Zealand. Lorna and Jon had agreed to give it a go but as the evening unfolded we sensed Lorna's agitation and Gerry's interest. Although beating eight hundred miles to windward in a tubby boat, followed by a tricky salvage operation and a further one thousand eight hundred miles to New Zealand did not appeal to us, for Gerry this was an adventure.

While sad at his leaving and concerned about negotiating Fiji's reefs and the passage to Australia alone, we had to let Gerry go and over breakfast we told him that he should make his own decision.

Gerry continued his painting commissions, staying at the guest house, while we sailed to Hunga Island taking a stowaway with us. The children had adopted a tabby kitten that had been wandering the docks, but the rollicky beam reach and choppy sea was too much for their furry friend! First it shat in the Lego box, then it puked on the deck, but as we dropped anchor in the sheltered waters behind the island of Foelifuka the kitten became cocky, climbing the stanchions, bouncing on the Bimini and running along the boom. On taking him ashore he climbed the trees with bursts of frenetic energy that earned him the name Battlecat, however we knew he could not survive an ocean passage and that quarantine regulations would prevent us taking him into Australia. Those were homely days, as David prepared the boat for the imminent voyage, I fulfilled our food fantasies with chocolate covered digestive biscuits and croissants while the kids compiled an illustrated inventory of our shell collection. After lunch, they set off for the shore; Billy on his boogie board paddling his arms like a surfer, legs kicking like a frog as he towed Sam, who lounged in the rubber dinghy waving his paddle. Billy took such pride in his performance that he neither noticed nor cared whether his older brother was contributing. But on their return Sam donned his flippers to tow Billy.

Boys swim ashore ST

Several mornings later Zephyr V motored towards us, her decks laden with timber; Gerry at the wheel, sporting a stubbly beard, wearing a vest and straw hat. It was obvious he was going on the venture and had come to collect his things. After dropping his anchor almost on top of ours, Jon came aboard and proceeded to treat us like lackeys and when they stayed for a last supper he prattled about sailing boats while easy going Gerry turned the gall to humour. The following day we all went ashore to collect lemons and after another territorial bout we hugged Gerry and waved farewell. Although we would miss his enthusiasm and help on the ocean passages, we knew that Gerry's accepting nature would see him through, that with Jon paying his keep he would be richer for the experience.

There was a serenity to those mornings when David read until, sleepily surfacing to morning cuddles, I was born into another day. Sam's obstinacy had passed, along with my anguish. We had discovered a deep contentment, fallen into a peaceful rhythm that balanced our emotions, healing the hurts. There were opportunities to talk or make love in the afternoon, and we saw only the local fishermen, who used a cavern on nearby Foelifuka as a base, paddling past in outriggers and drifting home across the lagoon. David began going ashore to the shade of a palm tree where he wrote an article for the American magazine, *Fine Woodworking*. This synopsis of his life, with reflections on how cruising had influenced his creativity, initiated an idea for a book, however it would be many years before *So Far* came to fruition.

We had come together as a family and although we would not always live in isolation we had no intention of returning to a climate and culture that would confine our personalities. David and I considered sitting out the hurricane season in Tonga's sheltered islands, wished we could build a temporary shelter where we could spend time writing, drawing, and sculpting. The kids thrived on their routine of work and play but for a longer term they needed friends and the local school was not a viable option with classes taught in the Tongan language. Before the morning lessons they planned the afternoon; as soon as lunch was finished, they swam ashore, looping through the water like otters, seldom on the surface, dipping and diving in fluid harmony. Once there they spent hours building sand fortresses, tunnels and moats, exploring the pools and cliffs of coral, or searching for shells, ever loyal, always together. Days unfolded without interruption and teaching became rewarding, with my children absorbing ideas and information as naturally as breathing. I found a nourishing pleasure in reading my children the Pooh Bear tales. On coming to *"An enchanted place,"* where the little boy grows up and leaves his old bear and daydreams behind, I choked back sobs as I recalled my childhood, of stories around the fire on winter nights. Those glowing memories had formed the foundation stones of my life and I wondered what Sam and Billy would remember when they looked back in years to come.

My boys would come of age in an era and society where men chose self-destructive ways of proving themselves. While it is known that the adrenalin released in a stressful situation will trigger the flight or fight response, some people are more emotionally and physically able to live on the edge. My only means of dealing with potential danger was to maintain a constant readiness, that compounded into a hyper-vigilance that would haunt me in subsequent years. Scientists have discovered that risk takers have less dopamine inhibitors; that this factor makes them more inclined to test the limits of human endurance and more able to manage such situations. Though Sam tended to be cautious, Billy was driven by a need to surpass his older brother and it would come as no surprise when a DNA test revealed he is hard wired as a risk taker! No guesses are needed to deduce who he inherited that from. However, William has discovered an activity infinitely more rewarding than driving a fast car or numbing his brain with alcohol and drugs and he maintains that his considered approach eliminates the danger of freediving. While his plummet and ascent through watery space renders an experience free of attachment, William's eventual acceptance of using a safety lanyard reminds me of David's uncompromising response to wearing a harness; of his refusal to sublimate his freedom.

It was inevitable that I would try, and fail to restrain my wild boys. At any suggestion that our lifestyle was dangerous, David would repeat the phrase, *"You are more likely to be hit by a bus."* Fun and fear were inextricably linked, and maybe this was why David had taken Billy's hand to jump off the diving board in Tortola. When questioned he claimed that such frolics were liberating. But despite David's habit of pushing boundaries he was meticulous in his seamanship, careful in his work. It is no fluke that, following decades of cabinetmaking, he retains all his fingers. They are a tribute to his intense focus, and awareness through those seconds, minutes, hours, and years spent working with lethal machines. A whirling blade spares no regard for the absent-minded practitioner, neither does a mountain protect the hiker who wanders off track. The ocean is perhaps the most severe taskmaster, offering no shelter from the elements, obliterating all sign of one's passing.

Once when we were walking along a coral ledge we saw that Billy was diving into the pools oblivious to any hazards. When we explained the risk, Sam leapt out of the water with fear, and as though to prove a point, the very next day David spotted a big moray eel and shark in the same place. The incident made us aware of our children's vulnerability; that their happy-go-lucky ways created a potential for danger. Staying in the safe confines of the boat was never an option, so it was vital we taught them how to recognise and avoid problems. This was when *Mr Accident*, a sort of superhero, tripped into our lives, sacrificing himself to educate our children in the art of safety. Together we created a zany cartoon, *The Nine Lives of Mr Accident*, with the children drawing every predicament they might blunder into, including sharks, stonefish, poisonous shells, caverns, and cliffs, in hopes that a respectful awareness would help them avoid a disaster. One day David took them to the centre of Bracken Island and taught them to blaze marks to find their way home. The kids thought it great fun but when it was time to return, they hurtled in every direction. On further occasions when they arrived home with tales of being lost in the jungle, their very presence proved a point, but although Sam and Billy were safe in an island environment, they knew nothing about crossing a road or riding a bike.

Each day after lunch we had a compulsory siesta with Billy lounging naked upon the hard deck, shunning any suggestion he might be more comfortable on a cushion. Then he and Sam thundered about the boat gathering belongings, searching for lost things, concluding the commotion with two loud splashes, followed by a babbling chatter that merged into the distant waves. And as Hornpipe subsided into silence we felt the relief that occurs when a storm has passed, leaving a trail of debris in its wake. Their return was a reverse enactment and, as their cavalcade drew near, voices became shouts. They could not wait to tell their stories; *"Hey guess what we've got? Fish!"* and, *"Linda, Billy broke my stick and we built a hut."* *"No Sam, I want to tell it."* Their tumbling energy engulfed us; and we loved it. Our children were happy, healthy, alive with doing and being; I prayed it would last forever, that nothing would ever harm them.

After nine days sheltered within that flank of white with its flickering, flowing turquoise tide, we ran short of water and fresh food. We sailing on, through a patchwork of inadequately charted reefs, and wandered ashore at Ofu, where an old man helped David select a fallen log of *Milo* wood for a sculpture. On their return his wife opened coconuts and cooked us a fish while others helped fill our water tanks. Eventually, refreshed and regaled, we motored around to Kenutu Island on the eastern reef where, on seeing wild ocean waves erupting through a break in the rocks, we eagerly rowed over to clamber up an encrusted coral wall. And as we watched the relentless procession of waves smash against the reef we were reminded of our impending trip beyond that safe haven. Further along we reached a gap through which a huge surge swept over a coral ledge. The kids leaped up and down, competing with the howling wind, yelling battle cries, Sam bantering with the booming waves, *"Splash me, see if I care! Come on, try it!"* And if ever there was a sorcerer's apprentice it was he. One almost believed the tumultuous ocean might respond to that small boy and when his theatrical gesture was ignored, Sam reverted to chasing Billy through the primeval landscape. As we wandered away with our gaze focused on finding shells we nearly stepped on a big black and white sea snake that was slithering over the coral. Then, after gathering papaya and coconuts, we rowed home to Hornpipe, afloat on a mirrored sea of tranquillity.

Beach combing LT

The following day passed, with David and the kids working on their shell collection, Hornpipe gently rocking in that anchorage beside the reef, looking back at the green islands. Collecting had become a compulsion for the boys, who were entranced by the magic of turning over a rock to find a jewelled spiral or a crusty shape that might scrub up to reveal a treasure. Sam and Billy enthusiastically participated in the stinky process of burying the shells in sand boxes before a soak in caustic soda to dissolve coral encrustations and finally cataloguing them with Latin names. Bouncer came across the special box and was considering moving into a little porcelain house with a clever name when he saw Sam enticing a hermit crab from its lodgings, giving a little whistle to confuse the silly crab, before yanking him out and packing him off to a new home. Realising the claustrophobic grotto was a trap, Bouncer returned to his boring old web, happy to hang out in his hammock. Yes, this was the life; what had he been thinking of?!

After the smelly job the children paddled their boogie boards to the beach, Sam talking too much to care where he was going, Billy intent on improving his technique. They had become harmoniously compatible and we knew they would look after each other. As the sunlight waned they returned, Billy swimming underwater, his legs kicking a natural breaststroke, feet encased in the plastic sandals that protected him from coral and stone fish. Sam, who wore flippers, arrived first, and clambering into the dingy stretched out an oar to help Billy win his battle against the current. They emerged from the water, sleek as seals, eyelashes beaded with dewy droplets, silhouettes against the sun. Theirs was a relentless energy that churned through the days. We were either screaming at them to give us a break, laughing at their antics, or glowing with pride at their accomplishments. Once, when we asked Sam to *"Just stop,"* he ruefully replied, *"I wish I knew how!"* Sam's gangly limbs had outgrown his nervous system and since losing his two front teeth, he perpetually crashed into things and we couldn't help but call him *"Mr Accident!"*

Moving on, drifting under the mainsail and number one genoa, we spotted a white beach behind a protecting reef. On rowing ashore, we found a grove of deciduous trees where noddies and terns nested in branches at a height the children could reach. It became a game for them to climb up and return with the precious eggs, racing in front as we wended our way around the perimeter of the island, crunching through crackling leaves as galaxies of anxious birds wheeled overhead. They argued over whose turn it was to scramble up through the foliage, to claim the cream and brown egg in a hot hand, to return and recount their number, planning whether they should be made into pancakes or a cake. Though Sam often turned back, Billy was determined to get the egg whatever the cost. Sometimes he became stuck and we heard his sobbing cry, *"I can't get down."* And despite falling a few times, the jubilation of finding the warm treasure resting on its cushion of leaves, the care necessary to carry it down, pulsed as a drug through his brain. Sadly, many were unusable but their plunder and the anticipation of a feast surpassed all else.

On finishing our fresh food we supplemented our diet in ingenious ways. Billy grew bean sprouts, learning that five attentive days may provide a fresh salad; how replenishing a puddle of seawater could reward him with a teaspoonful of precious salt crystals that added a sparkle to our meals. Finding, growing, and hunting for food made us appreciate its worth, and on killing a fish we showed respect for the creature that fed us. All this gave us a sense of collaborating with our surroundings. One lunchtime we sat down to a meal of homemade yoghurt, cottage cheese, bread, and a green papaya and bean sprout salad with salt to season. That evening I created a memorable curry from cassava, green papaya, coconut, and fried breadfruit, along with a heart of palm salad, followed by a papaya dessert.

As night fell David anxiously scanned the sky with growing concern about an unpredictable storm. Clouds were building from the direction of the tiny lagoon's shallow pass and our alarm increased when we heard radio talk of a freak storm in Fiji that had ripped off roofs, spinning them a hundred feet high. However, our sky was sprinkled with reassuring stars and after a night dive we slept, only to be woken soon after by a rising wind and the sight of high alto cloud encroaching from the west. Worries that waves might render the entrance impassable kept us awake, calculating how to raise our second anchor, debating whether to leave or risk becoming trapped in the exposed place, where if Hornpipe's anchor dragged, she would instantly go up on the reef. At first light the wind generator was screaming. When David cranked up the anchor my heart was in my mouth and as we motored through the pass waves broke against Hornpipe's hull. Once clear the swell rolled her from side to side, slamming the dinghy into our stern. But once we had safely anchored in the shelter of Euakafa Island we could comfortably watch the weather deteriorate, the wind and waves increase.

Sam thrived on independence and that day he hatched a plan of exploring the island alone. On finishing school, he was ready with his art bag of pencils and a sketchbook. Hovering a while, he said, *"Linda, I don't want to bother you, but would you mind rowing me to the beach?"* And I was pleased to be bothered by his polite request. Later, Billy, David, and I went ashore to gather coconuts with Billy shinning up the palm trees like a tree frog. I was toying with the idea of Sam being lost when we saw footsteps heading along the sand to where he was sitting in the shade, so absorbed in reading his book, that he had not seen us. Everything was in order and an aura of maturity shone about him so we reverently tiptoed away, to avoid bursting in on his world. He would acknowledge us when he was ready. On greeting us Sam exuded a calm pleasure. He showed us his delicate drawing of the waves, islands, and sky; and was proud of his written reflections on being there.

> *"Here I am*
> *Here I am drawing, writing, while.*
> *While everything is happening.*
> *The waves are lapping lap, lap, lap, lap,*
> *Here I am sitting."*

The delightful episode reflected a choice Sam had made. He was growing up so fast and I was grateful that, although he sometimes acted like a buffoon, Sam was comfortable within his deeper self. We walked to the extreme point of the island where caressing waves had worn rocks into caverns and passages while other encrustations remained as brittle as when the liquid lava frothed into spikes. After husking coconuts, we returned with the bounty slung in net baskets. The sun was melting into a misty haze when we stopped to fell a small palm for its heart, continuing with Billy carrying it, emulating an Olympic weightlifter, Sam parading in front, brandishing a palm leaf flag. A subtle shift had occurred. Our kids had developed a respect and sensitivity for each other's needs, so when they went ashore with their notebooks, we avoided too much encouragement, allowing them to own their discoveries.

The following day was near perfect, with a magic that began even before I woke. Sam was up first, quietly tidying his and Billy's beds, moving through the boat, taking care and pride in his task. Billy took up the idea and as they worked through the jobs they rapidly accomplished an order I could never have achieved in their presence. There was nothing assertive or bombastic in their actions and after breakfast Sam requested that he wash up, which he did with my help in putting things away. Billy swept the floor and before long the boat was ready for school. Our children had ignored the jobs' chaotic potentials, avoided the fun to be found in sweeping the cat around the room, flooding the sink, or playfully hurling a wet sponge. They had chosen to enter our world, recognising this as a privilege, with no expectation of reward. At last we were pulling together as a family instead of David and I serving their needs. Sam and Billy's actions made us confident we could meet the challenges ahead and I realised how much pleasure there would be if we began every day this way, enjoying work and play, finding happiness in every moment.

After school, we walked onto the reef beneath the sheltering sky. There we delved under rocks and into pools, discovering the minuscule details of that vast seascape. Plunging in the ocean, we entered a hidden world. Sinking to the sandy floor we followed a shell's winding trail, before returning to that edge where the sky caresses the sea. What defines a human? An ability to tunnel into the earth, run on the land, or float in the ocean; to dive the watery depths, fly in a machine traveling through air, or explore the ethereal reaches beyond our planet? But where do we belong? Can we survive in any of these environments? We have entered outer space and yet we do not understand how consciousness arises. Sadly, we squander our sunshine days. Our versatility is our power, but we forget how to dance in unison with nature – that we are stardust, twinkling for a moment in a life golden with opportunity. Let us not become forever outcast from our mother the earth. Consider the dormant instincts that lie within us; our ability to move with strength, wisdom and grace, the potential that can be reached when we shed our limitations.

THE GOLDEN COWRIE

"As I drop down into the deep blue, I have to let go. I must let go of everything that attaches me to the surface and makes me human: light, sound, identity, and the need to breathe itself. First I swim, then I sink downwards, my body becoming heavier, lungs shrinking under pressure. I give myself up to the sensation as the ocean draws me into itself. I must not think about the coming ascent, which will be much more difficult than the way down. I cannot anticipate in any way that this free fall into the abyss will ever end. The crushing pressure silences my mind, and I fly into the night, a being without thought.

Now is the time! Now is the time to return to air, to light! This is the test! The extent to which I have dared to penetrate this twilight realm must be equalled by my desire to return to the element that sustains life.

There I will breathe the hungry first breath of a new-born child.

Breathe! Breathe! Breathe! Breathe."

William Trubridge

WT

On our return to Neafu news was of a visiting Australian cruise ship; a craft market being set up on Euakafa Island. Sailing there, I noticed our dinghy had broken free and was insolently floating away; by the time we had dropped our sails it was sneaking up on a small island. I swam to retrieve the escapee and after hoisting it on board we anchored and set up the windsurfers to exceed all limits in that powerful wind. Next day the cruise ship floated in the bay like a huge wedding cake. Tenders ran back and forth, ferrying pink and white Australians whose bulging bodies oozed an oily entitlement. We saw the Tongans openly laugh at one who was swaggering up the beach wearing little more than a g string but, sadly, they were dependent upon the vulgar tourists and would inevitably emulate their ways.

The shore had been transformed into a street of *pareau* covered stalls. David selected a chunk of sandalwood while the boys scanned the displays of shells with Billy adamantly stating, *"I think we should find them ourselves."* Sam was still eyeing them when the stall owner, realising he had no money, gave him a bag of little ones. I was immersed in drawing when an old woman asked what I was doing. And on explaining my desire to engage with people and places, her response, that there was no reason to do anything, that just being was enough, reminded me of the Yogic philosophy of *aparigraha/*acceptance and *samtosha/*contentment. The Polynesians lived in harmony with themselves and nature. And what more was there to life than to enjoy and cherish nature's bounty? Concern that change might sever a connection with their gods and ancestors resulted in every activity being conducted in accordance with customs. The islanders were afraid of the supernatural and, unused to being alone, they conformed to a group dynamic rather than individual initiatives. The artisan maintained a shamanistic authority, a discourse between the past, present, and future that invested the raw substance of the earth with a divine nature. A god may be angered if rivalled by a *tiki*, so it remained vital the voice of the stone, wood, or flax reveal itself without encroaching on its connection to the source. And why make a bird from a stone; can a stone bird sing? The Polynesian climate is benign; there is food for everyone and, while clothing is irrelevant, one might adorn the body with flowers, shells, and tattoos. They had no reason to strive for more. However, we had observed persuasive advertisements telling the locals that, to be happy they must buy stuff, making it only a matter of time before they forgot their traditions.

I wondered if following the Polynesian way of *being* would lead to a lethargic lack of purpose; whether a return to Mo'orea would squander our potential. Our ancestors' endeavours to survive the deprivations of their hostile environment had produced societies and individuals that asserted their power over nature, religions that despised human instincts. Our forebears had evolved technologies that distanced them from nature. Turning their back on the earth they had clothed their shame; hidden within houses embellished with the proof of their accomplishments. We too had built a house that protected us from the elements; had toiled to amass provisions and worked hard to safeguard our future. And when we realised there might be more to life we made a change. What would come next? Would we continue to serve our innate sense of purpose or was there another way?

After our brief encounter with *civilisation*, we motored to Ovalau and anchored in the lee of a small island. There we retreated into our shell. David typed his article, the children resumed schoolwork, and in the evenings I studied navigation, becoming confident that if necessary, I could find land. One afternoon our kids sculpted a walled city of tunnels and moats, a fisherman came by with a pail of sardines and another perfect day melted into the sunset. Billy had remained, playing alone on the irresistible sand, when a group of Tongans arrived in canoes. I saw an old man, bent in conversation with Billy and then he was sitting, a proud figure-head in a narrow dug-out with the old fellow paddling him around the bay. I watched them join the group by the fire, silhouettes against spiralling flames, waves breaking on the distant reef. The sky was flushed with pink and purple when the smiling, grizzled old fellow returned Billy. He had made his own friends and proudly told us he had been to a feast.

As the moon waxed we realised we must take advantage of the beneficial light for our passage through the Lau Islands. Reluctantly winching up the anchor we drifted into Neiafu, knowing the holiday was over, that our next stop would entail some serious earning. And as the time for leaving drew near, Battlecat sensed his fate and slunk into a dark corner. In a final, heart wrenching moment we dropped him on the dock and sailed away.

Battle cat WT

Needing to spend a few hours preparing for our departure we anchored in Port Maurelle, and ran into the renowned cruising couple, Lyn and Larry Pardey. On a brief encounter in Samoa we had found we shared similar values, so when they invited us on board their tiny boat we eagerly satisfied our curiosity. Their commitment to an ecological life had led to them dispensing with a motor, to depend on their sailing expertise and a huge oar to scull their boat away from danger. We also discovered they avoided compromising their hull by employing the bucket and chuck-it toilet. Their immaculate lifestyle did not include children so we had left ours at home and on returning to the chaos we felt content with our lot.

It was a perfect night for our overnight voyage to Tofua in the Ha'apai group and after clearing the deck and hoisting the dinghy aboard we motored along the channel towards the open ocean. As my man tidied the sails at the bow, I stood at the helm picking out the silhouetted islands in the moonlight, following the heading he had carefully lined up to avoid the reef. Although we had found the charts unreliable, when David glimpsed a coral head beneath the hull it was a shocking start to our lone passage.

Once clear of Hunga's southern banks, I remained at Hornpipe's helm, confident of the open sea ahead, and enjoyed time alone with the gentle wind and glittering waves. After I had dozed my watch away, David took over with expectations of a clear sea until we reached the volcanos. He was mystified when, soon after dawn he sighted Ofolanga Island ten miles to port, and on scanning the muddled information in the pilot, he found a vague reference to a current. Setting a new course we pulled in the walker log and let out the fishing line and after losing our first mahi mahi we soon had another fighting in our wake. Doubting we could get the formidable creature on board David swung it back and forth, until on his third attempt he slung it up and into the cockpit, where it twisted and spun in a frenzy. David threw himself on the fish and while I shrouded its head in a cloth he made the kill. As we approached the volcanic islands we gutted and sliced while Sam drew the land rising from the waves, a view that was unchanged from that which Captain Bligh and his officers had gazed on after being cast adrift in an open boat by Fletcher Christian and the Bounty mutineers. And later, thanks to Bligh's expert navigation and leadership, all his crew arrived safely at Timor in the Dutch East Indies.

The wind diminished and by lunchtime our sails were flogging so violently we had to drop them. Considering ourselves infinitely more fortunate than Bligh or the Pardeys, we motored the last ten miles to a choppy channel that separates the larger, lower island of Tofua from its neighbour Kao. A powerful surge was bashing against Kao's black cliffs that sweep up through wooded slopes to a volcanic cone at one thousand and thirty metres. Tofua's northern coast is also exposed so we followed the shore west, passing crumbling cliffs where recent falls, some with dust rising from the rubble, revealed rock strata that had been laid down during numerous eruptions. A lush undergrowth of casuarinas and jungle creepers overflowed the cliffs and when Sam and Billy spotted caves they speculated on the pirates and dinosaurs that lived within. When a white tree trunk came into view, with a man standing at the top with his open boat anchored below, we saw that it was a ladder for accessing the plateau.

The rolling was manageable so we dropped anchor and when David dived to check the holding, the unbelievably clear water and eerie round stones reminded him of Isabella in the Galapagos. Some thirty feet below he found Hornpipe's hook neatly balanced on a boulder, and after wedging it amongst the stones he spun to the surface. Figures appeared on the beach and a man swam out to welcome us to his island. John offered to show us his island and, on deciding it would be impossible to land our dinghy, we put our clothes in the plastic bathtub and swam ashore, pushing it through the water. A precipitous pile of huge boulders had been thrown up by violent storms, and even on that gentle day there was an echoing boom of the surge rolling stones together. John lifted Billy on his shoulders and we followed him, scrambling up the near vertical track to a breezy plateau from where we could see the ocean stretching to the shimmering horizon.

The fertile volcanic soil had attracted itinerant Tongans, who had planted the slopes with kava which they exported from Nuku'alofa to Fiji where the roots were used to make a soporific drink. This had traditionally been processed by young girls who chewed and spat the pulp into a ceremonial trough, from where it was handed around in coconut bowls in a ceremony that led to the participants consuming vast quantities of the murky elixir. John led us on a corrugated trail over ridges and ravines where Tofua's molten lava had flowed to the sea. Scorched trees thrust through jungle clearances where plots of root crops flourished, with fruit trees dominating the steeper slopes. On reaching the western tip of the island we slid down the path to a rough coconut palm shelter, where our friend lived in isolation, cultivating vegetables intended for his family. Kava roots lay drying in the sun and below this humblest of habitations a ledge of black rock fell away to white surf. John had almost no possessions: a machete and strength were his only tools, green coconuts his drink, vegetables and fish his food. We felt a huge respect for our new friend, who lived as a castaway to support his wife and children in the Ha'apai Islands. On our return, a group of Tongans hoisted our laughing children onto their shoulders to slither down the bank with perfect composure. Then John swum home with us, pushing a basket of produce, and while we sought out a spare diving mask, fish hooks, and some mahi mahi to repay his generosity, Sam regurgitated fragments of history he had read about the islands; mentioning Captain Cook's visit as though it were yesterday, inventing gruesome details, such as the natives eating the sailors, to make his story interesting. And after showing John around and sharing a teatime we made plans to meet the following day.

On waking, it was mysteriously quiet on Hornpipe. A note on the table explained everything. *"Dear Linda, we have had breakfast and have gone ashore to help John!"* We had lain in bed listening to the discussion that preceded the departure. It was mostly about who was going to jump first, followed with a *one, two, three, plop!* Wait for it…Peace! The children had found John in his kava plantation where, after helping, they all swam out, dragging a branch of bananas. While we ate cake and drank tea, John questioned us about Hornpipe. He obviously envied our ability to travel where we chose, to anchor off a remote island with all the comforts of home, and we could see he was trying to conceive a way of achieving this for his family. It was then we realised that in exposing our friend to a world beyond his means we had tainted his contentment. Having grown used to being the ones who scraped by, we found our new cultural responsibility very worrying.

John had wanted to guide us up to the volcanic crater but the weather was changing so, after a last dive, with David shooting an octopus and John revelling in seeing the underwater world, we cooked a feast in John's *umu*. As the sun set we ate, feeling enormously sad about leaving our dear friend and when we swam home in total darkness, Sam's mind flooded with images of sharks, sea snakes, and octopus. We awoke to the tumult of waves tumbling the boulders, a backwash violently rolling Hornpipe from side to side. Hastily waking Obelix from his slumber we started for Hokula village in hopes of finding shelter.

David and the children longed to climb the volcano, so despite a poor holding ground strewn with boulders I elected to look after Hornpipe. I watched my boys swim ashore, scramble out of the surf, and disappear into the jungle; imagined them stumbling up the treacherous lava towards Tofua's smoking summit. Then I enjoyed a rare time alone, and as I sat gazing across the channel at the raging surge pounding Kao's black cliffs, my mind wandered. If cast upon those ragged rocks, the cruel breakers would deliver the first blows, our minds would be consumed by a fight to survive, a knife would be a constant companion for hacking coconuts, killing fish, creating shelter and a canoe to escape. When a leviathan passed with a bevy of dolphins frolicking in her wake, I felt an overwhelming contentment and on realising it would be dangerous to spend a night in the exposed anchorage I began preparing for our passage.

After clambering over the boulders my boys had found a missionary lad waiting to guide our entourage up the volcano, and after setting off they came to the most perfect village imaginable. Tall trees sheltered the traditional round huts that were elevated on a grassy plateau, caressed by a fresh breeze. Beneath shady trellises women sat weaving pandanus mats before an expansive view of Kao. As they continued, the kids speculated on how far it was, and whether the rocks would be hot. And whenever they rested the lad said, *"Let's go, everyone!"* eventually helping Billy, who was stumbling behind. Sam said that his heart thumped so hard, that on starting up again he was immediately tired, but they kept going, with the thought that if they returned quickly I would also have a chance of climbing the volcano. At last they reached the five hundred metre summit. Beneath their feet, a steep slope plummeted through woodland to a freshwater lake that extended to a western ridge pocked with vents that belched smoke. Having expected a blazing cauldron they were disappointed by an absence of fire and brimstone, but on seeing a slag heap pointing a finger of solidified lava towards the lake, they named it *The Cracks of Doom!*

David would have walked further, however the children were hot and tired, so they sat with their legs dangling over the edge, sharing sandwiches and talking about volcanos. Then they looked out for a last time, at wind patterns on the water, a canoe fishing under Kao, and the distant islands of Niniva, Ofulanga, and Fatuhao. Returning was hazardous, with the slippery gravel rolling like marbles beneath their feet, but it presented no problem for the lad who spread his bare toes and slid down. When Billy ran after he was hoisted high to be carried, shrieking with laughter. Sam's sandals hurt his feet so he and David cautiously followed, to arrive at the village and find that school had been let out early to meet the *papalagi*, with Billy drinking his second coconut surrounded by giggling children. Although they would have liked to stay, David was anxious about the anchor dragging and when they hailed from the rocks I swam ashore and set off, leaving them to return to the boat. Billy fell asleep on the first seat he reached and, as Sam settled to reading, David looted our trading bag for a cap and t-shirt for the lad.

Finding the path, I hurried to the summit to be as impressed by the view as the fact that Billy had lasted the distance, knowing I would have succumbed to his cries of *"Carry me."* It was late, and when I turned to go back the slope yielded no sign of a path. There was no option but to bush bash through the prickly undergrowth. Somehow I found a way down where, with no time to spare, I launched my scratched and stinging body into the sea. By the time I had swum home David had fired up Obelix and as I motored into the wind to ease pressure on the chain, he cranked the anchor from the depths. Eventually he gave up on the winch and set to hauling the combined weight of anchor and chain; David's despair at the damaged links, ground to bare steel by the boulders, only matched by his torn, aching back.

After motoring clear of Tofua we set our sails to catch the breath of a south easterly towards Fiji. As a last wisp of dirty smoke from Kao's peak faded, the wind died and when we could no longer tolerate the flogging canvas we motored. And when the noise and fumes became too much we sailed until that was also unbearable. A waxing moon floated on an indigo sky and the warmth and tranquillity was a blessing; but the exertion had been more than David could handle. His torn back, the clattering engine, and tricky navigation made for a bad start. During our dreamtime on Tonga we had forgotten those taxing ocean passages, with their all-consuming helming and sail changes. Dawn saw me hunched over the wheel, David scanning the sky for stars, while Sam and Billy devised a way of climbing through their hatch into a secret space beneath the dinghy where, refreshed by a flowing draft of air, they devised an imaginary world. When the novelty waned, they hit on the idea of dragging clothes out of cupboards and drawers, putting them all on together. Then, smothered in hats, boots, and life jackets, with arms full of toy animals, they waddled around the boat, laughing and falling over until they became hot and seasick. Sam explained the perverse delights of their "*Mister Raggle Taggle game. That it felt so good when you took it all off and it was just plain hot!*"

Weaving a path through that treacherous area of ocean was unrelentingly complex. There was no room for errors and despite a clear sky and calm sea that was ideal for navigating, predictions of a trough with twenty to twenty-five knot winds gave us cause for concern. An inconsistency between our star and sun sight was also disturbing, with our chart showing a multitude of *vigias*, indicating rocks, shoals, or reefs, scattered in every direction. Although David was racked with headaches, he could not rest. Then, while standing watch on our second night, he suddenly grasped the source of those baffling navigational errors: that just before our arrival in Tonga, we had crossed the dateline and skipped a whole day, but had forgotten to change the day. David immediately set to plotting and calculating our previous fixes with the correct date, and when his figures tallied, they revealed we were nine miles from, and heading directly towards, a *vigia*. After waking me to drop the sails and motor clear of danger we thanked our lucky stars he had realised just in time to avoid a disaster.

While not officially permitted to stop at any of the Fijian islands before clearing customs in Suva, we decided to risk putting in to the southern Lau islands while we waited for the trough to move through. Although we had no chart of those islands the benevolent conditions allowed us to feel our way around the reef and as we entered the pass the fishing reel spun with a mahi mahi on the line. As we stealthily crept through the shallow entrance the glaring sun obscured whatever lay ahead, however the lagoon proved free of coral. After heading towards the cliffs of Ongea Nariki, we dropped anchor leaving the dinghy on deck, our sails unfurled, to support the excuse of waiting on a wind to take us to Suva. The arid island consisted of no more than a sparse growth of spiky trees on limestone cliffs that were formed of compacted coral recently raised from the ocean floor. It was late, so after a refreshing swim we returned to our floating home and fell into our bunks for a deep sleep.

Sunday the twenty-seventh of October was a wonderful day in a magical place. A soft light smudged the horizon and Hornpipe appeared to hover above the lagoon with her white hull flickering a phosphorescent glow. Only the black outline of a wreck on the reef and a distant blur of islands beneath motionless clouds indicated where the sea and sky met in that all-encompassing space. Abandoning ourselves to the sun and sea we found the lagoon was as warm as a bath, the surface glassy without so much as a ripple. Diving down our bodies cast shadows on the white sand, images met to frolic like water sprites and when the tide turned we drifted home on the swirling water. Sam and Billy spent their day swimming here and there, following the trails of cones, augers, and horn shells, spying on the fish as they went about their business. Eventually the dimpled patterns in the sand led them to where Hornpipe's shadow darkened the sea's floor. All too soon the sun sank into a mellow haze as, sated by our aquatic day, we ate in a daze, fit to burst with joy.

"We entered a hidden world" ST

The sea and sky had formed Sam and Billy's personalities and made them one with the ocean. Maybe it was inevitable that William would shape his life around his aquatic potential, establish a career in the element he loved. He wrote of his early experiences of freediving: *"Some of the most magical moments have come at the most unexpected times. It could be when I am just lying on a sandy sea bottom at ten metres, watching tiny fish come and go, and I realise that I feel completely at home in that setting: I have absolutely no urge to breathe or return to the surface, and I am part of the underwater world and its events. During this time, I feel a complete diffusion of my body into the water. The absence of any kind of stimuli (sight, sound, weight) combined with the slowing of my heart rate and thoughts mean that I lose any kind of physical reference. I'm not feeling or thinking, so that just leaves a sense of consciousness. I exist only as awareness. It is a very liberating experience."* On a brief home visit, William continued training, swimming underwater lengths at the Iona pool, holding his breath while walking our garden until he dropped, mentally preparing himself for being very alone and very deep. His dream required that he fund his freediving endeavours, become his own physiotherapist, nutritionist, and trainer. But despite committing all his resources William had nothing to show for his dedication. However, my trip to Egypt had given me an insight into my son's passion, that he must achieve his goal to claim a living from freediving. His humble acceptance reminded me of my father who, in an era when self-fulfilment was considered indulgent, had sacrificed his dream for his family, and on hearing this William wrote, *"It's interesting to think that there's a direct line of at least partial causality from your father, being stationed in Bermuda, giving you dreams of exotic faraway lands, leading to you and David taking the decision to sail away from it all, meaning I was a child of the waves and the depths, expressing it in freediving."*

The twenty-eighth of October was our wedding anniversary and, though we had planned to dine out in Suva, that simpler day was perfect in every way. David cleaned shells and I prepared meals for moving on, while the children swam ashore, to return bubbling with excitement, *"We found a rare shell, we found a rare shell!"* Sure enough, it was a special shell with the delightful name, *Precious Wentletrap*, and they were so thrilled they couldn't help repeating, *"I'm so happy we've got a rare shell, a precious wentletrap."* They watched intently as I hooked a baby hermit crab out of the tiny shell, setting it free to find a more common home. Then the delicate twist of white and pink was passed from hand to hand before being gently cradled in cotton wool and placed amongst the other fragile shells. Their dream of finding a golden cowrie – a shell that graced the ceremonial garments of Kings and the rarest found in our area of the Pacific – sustained a passion for the ocean environment that was worth more than gold.

After sailing across the lagoon, the wind died and, once beyond the island's lee, we hit lumpy waves that flopped Hornpipe back and forth with her sails crashing and thudding. Incensed by the cacophony David's mood cast a pall of gloom over the boat. But once free of Fulaga the wind increased and Hornpipe raced along at seven knots with her bow wave tunefully singing. As the sun set, the full moon appeared with the promise of a partial lunar eclipse and on handing the helm to David I climbed on deck to drop the jib and run under the mainsail alone. After pulling in the Walker log we hooked two mahi mahi; however, Hornpipe was winging downwind so fast they each escaped before David could reel them in. A wind shift delivered squalls and heavy clouds that obscured the eclipse and dawn brought an erratic sea with barely half a mile of visibility. Knowing that maintaining our bearings might prove tricky David and I hand steered to ensure an accurate dead reckoning. Strong currents run between the islands of Moala and Totoya so it was with relief when we left them in our wake, but as we continued ploughing our course towards Suva it seemed the cloud bank was shadowing our every move.

The coast of Viti Levu is lined with reefs and David had become increasingly worried about making our landfall at Suva. Sailing was an all-consuming routine, of steering, sleeping, and navigating, with David and I passing each other like ships in the night, with brief intermissions to eat the meals I had prepared, to read our children a story or share a game of chess while helming. While we harboured hopes of arriving soon after midnight, a strong current conspired against us. When David managed a late sight it gave only the distance from our destination, with no indication of how far we were to the north or south. As I steered he continued his navigational calculations and it was a relief when he managed a fix on a radio direction beacon. At two o'clock I picked out the lights of Suva.

David had drawn a detailed chart of Suva harbour, adding the lights listed in the pilot book to prepare for a night arrival. He felt it would be easier to identify the harbour entrance by its lights, but before we could use his map the day dawned. Despite the reef and town being clearly visible, we found the obscure landmarks confusing, but we eventually located the pass and dropped our sails to motor the last two miles to the Royal Suva Yacht Club. After immigration procedures, lunch, and a snooze, we checked into the yacht club to the greeting, *"Hornpipe at last!"* And as the secretary handed us a pile of letters, David saw that a final notice for a parcel was due to expire that afternoon. Jumping in a taxi he zoomed into town to arrive at the post office just as it closed. Our old yachting friend Reggie had sent us a spare impeller from England, and who knew what dire circumstance might require that part for our engine's water pump, that had so narrowly escaped being returned to sender? Amongst our mail was a postcard from the mother of my Tortola friend Prue, that explained why she had never responded to my letters. I learned that her baby son had been born with severe disabilities and that her troubles had compounded to a tragedy when her husband drowned. Prue was a survivor; she and her three children would return to New Zealand where she became a leading authority for Kindergarten education.

At last we could finalise the paperwork for our Australian residency and after a rag bag attempt to smarten up for an interview we learned that our permit would only be valid if we reached the continent within six months. Out of curiosity David visited the opposing consulate to find that New Zealand needed skilled craftspeople. Both applications required medical certificates so we hurriedly sought a superficial examination and reluctantly paid for chest X-rays. Rumour had it that, despite having purchased Hornpipe overseas, her Australian registration made us liable to pay a sales tax and import duty of half her value on arrival. The prohibitive expense and our lack of enthusiasm for visiting that vast eastern coastline, with its crowded marinas and venomous creatures, rendered New Zealand the better option. So we suddenly decided to sail for Aotearoa, with the intention of earning and saving for a return to Mo'orea.

Being reluctant to sail south alone, we posted an advert on the yacht club notice board. An American couple responded. Brad, who had just finished two years with the Peace Corps in Western Samoa, and Claire, an exhibition curator from Virginia. Despite limited sailing experience, both were enthusiastic about crewing for us. While in Suva we visited the library to sustain the children's voracious hunger for books. Reading added depth to their imaginations and there they found one I had loved as a child, *The Midnight Folk*, by poet John Masefield – a story of pirates, witches, and magical animals, that could have been written for Sam and Billy. The dusty Suva museum was another treasure chest of surprises, and I was marvelling at the feathered warrior helmets when Billy tugged my arm whispering, *"It's here, it's here!"* We found Sam, speechless before a rickety cabinet of ceremonial cloaks, gazing at a shell the size of a duck egg with a milky base and glorious honey dome. The children had so often discussed their prospects of finding this ultimate trophy, and there it was. The King's crowning glory, a golden cowrie, splendidly presented for all to enjoy.

While I posted presents to our families, David, in anticipation of seeking furniture commissions in New Zealand, printed a swag of expensive photos for a folio. He tramped the city seeking parts for the Sumlog and grappled with fixing the outboard which had never been the same since it had spun off its bracket and continued running, sucking sand into its system after hitting the ocean floor. Eventually he took it to a mechanic who, after replacing the spark plugs and fuel, miraculously brought it back to life. An ice cold shandy at the yacht club saved the day. Meanwhile Sam and Billy were watching countless films in the club lounge where, despite seeing *Octopussy* six times the novelty never waned. Another drama unfolded in the harbour, where, following thefts from cruising yachts, the police and yachties had started a nightly surveillance. Hearing shouts, we learned that six Fijians had attacked a group of yachties including our friend Andy from Jacaranda who, shaken by the violence, said, *"I'm a lover not a fighter!"* While the fracas was a shock after our quiet time in the islands David took his turn, patrolling the harbour with the policeman.

Escaping the city we travelled inland to Colo-i-Suva forest park where we picnicked amongst the pools and waterfalls of an old mahogany plantation and made another trip to a cultural centre with artefacts and recreated island scenes. On visiting a chief's house beautifully constructed with carved beams lashed with *magi magi* ropes of various colours and thatched with leaves, Billy lay down in its woven interior saying *"What a snug, cosy house, I wish I could live here."* We watched Fijian dancers presenting theatrical skits on an island surrounded by a muddy moat. Performances that involved men who, with much croaking and splashing, impersonated frogs to distract an amorous young couple. This was followed by a choreographed battle where they vigorously wielded their weapons with a fluency that captivated the children. And when we talked to the curator about Fiji's racial divisions that stemmed from the British colonial policy of indentured labourers brought over from India to work the sugar plantations, he predicted trouble between the traditional Fijians and those with western ideas.

Brad and Claire moved on board and once again we became an extended family. Though quietly sensitive in their forthright American ways, Brad hid behind his peaked cap and dark glasses, while Claire was a kindred spirit, a girl to balance my boatload of boys. They had travelled with every intention of experiencing the Pacific culture, but had found the yachting community rather insular, which was unsurprising when most were returning to civilisation on sufferance, with long lists of jobs to be accomplished. With the medical results, our Australian residency and New Zealand visa were confirmed and after spending a frightening six hundred dollars we couldn't wait to leave. Having planned sailing the forty miles to Kadavu for a few carefree days before continuing on to New Zealand, Saturday the sixteenth of November proved windy. We reefed the mainsail, but as we headed through the pass a thirty-knot wind hit hard. The waves were huge, the forecast ghastly, and we were soon soaked to the skin with Claire, Billy, and I all seasick. When it seemed unlikely we would make Kadavu before dark, we turned and hurtled back through the pass. After spending the remains of the day on the beach, we bunked down early in readiness for the three o'clock start that should allow time for sailing to Kadavu and diving the reef.

The sky was clear when we gathered in the cockpit, and as David cautiously motored past the beacons that mark Suva's reef, we found that, despite the flat calm in the anchorage, we were soon battling a fresh northerly. I took over, steering into a massive swell, while our inexperienced crew helped David wrestle with a second reef in the mainsail. On hearing water splash onto Brad and Claire's bunks I called David below to seal the leaking fore-hatch. Hornpipe was being driven along the edge of the reef when her rig exploded with a resounding bang! Though our foresail's luff still held, the canvas was bellying, fit to burst as I shouted, *"David, come quick, the forestay broke!"* David, Brad, and Claire scrambled to drop our mainsail, while I turned into the wind, easing the pressure on the mast as they fought the flogging genoa and snaking ropes. Somehow Hornpipe's rig held as, gripping her wheel, I steered into the wind and waves, fearful of looking up. But it was not over. In the time it had taken to tame the bucking boat, she had dropped back and, with no sails to power her, Hornpipe was helplessly rising and falling on a surging swell, just two waves from the reef. David leaped into the engine room and mercifully Obelix stirred, gathered momentum, broke into a regular rhythm, and when my man slammed our trustworthy engine through the gears, Hornpipe swung on her heel and headed away from the reef.

We all knew how close we had come to disaster, and as adrenalin broke the ice of our new relationship, shock turned to jokes about the close shave. With predictable optimism, I was heartened by the fact our near catastrophe had happened at a place where boat parts would be readily available. While I viewed the problem as a redemption from a worse fate, David felt the mishap should never have occurred. After motoring back to the yacht club, we hoisted our captain up the mast, where on retrieving the shattered toggle, he was amazed that the corroded stainless steel had held, that the seemingly insignificant breakage had not dismasted us. It being Sunday all stores were closed, so our best bet was the other yachts; however it was still very early. As the anchorage showed signs of life, David did the rounds, striking lucky when he found that Fandango had a toggle, and Sea Lark a pin. The rest was simple, and we woke from an afternoon sleep to see Chrysalide sail in with Benoit, Martine, and baby Chloe returning from a month in Kadavu. They told us their plan of Benoit sailing alone to New Zealand, while Martine, who was anxious about a long passage with a baby, would fly the distance. The following morning, when we made our third attempt to leave, there was ironically no wind. But after motoring into the lumpy swell, the breeze increased to fifteen knots and with Brad and Claire steering it was an easy sail.

The Fijian reefs lay deeper than those surrounding Tahiti and even when we drew close the only indication was a slightly brighter tone of water when, after dropping the mainsail, we ran downwind to round the Astrolabe reef before entering Kadavu's northern pass to anchor off Namara Island. Although the day had turned cold and grey, a swim was soothing and cleansing after the city. David rowed ashore, disturbing gangs of crabs as he collected a sack of coconuts and during the night torrential rain conveniently replenished our fresh water supplies. Claire and Brad helped with the chores, then as they pursued their own ventures we scrubbed the barnacles and weed that had grown thick on Hornpipe's hull. While it was wonderful to share my space with a girl I could relate to, being more used to forthright males, when Claire dumped out the silverware with the dishwater I abruptly rebuked her *"We're heading out into the ocean. Now get it right!"*

When Sam, who had become increasingly adventurous, set off to walk around the island we were unconcerned because he was usually sensible, but it was unusual that Billy chose to remain on the beach. Perhaps he anticipated the endless days at sea and was taking advantage of a last chance to be alone, but after a while we became aware that a man was sitting under the tree beside Billy. They talked for a long time and when

Sam appeared, the Fijian paddled them out in his canoe and came on board. While Pona had learned English working on a Swedish freighter, it was impressive that a chiefly man would respect a small boy, and choose to have a discussion with him. Unsure of what the procedure was, we hesitantly gave him the bag of kava Benoit had given us and, after graciously explaining the protocol of presenting such gifts to the chief, Pona offered to take it for us. And when he returned with a papaya we gave him some tins of corned beef. Tern arrived and the children spent their day on the beach making brief forays onto the boats. Perhaps Billy was intent on proving himself when he shinned up Tern's wooden masts in the same way he climbed palm trees. At this point Wayne came on deck and looked up at our son then across at us with a questioning stare. Billy shone with enthusiasm and, like the yellow sun he drew at the top of his pictures, he was a bright treasure. But he was unstoppable and if it wasn't this challenge he would think up something else. Despite us never comparing our boys, he constantly strived to keep up with and overtake Sam, unaware his brother was almost three years older.

Years later we would support William's dream of setting a freediving world record in Dean's Blue Hole. His friends Michael, Nick, and Mike, who had attended all his previous attempts, were there, but on the day of his dive the safety divers thought it was yet another training session. Only William's judges knew this was a record attempt, and in this way he avoided some of the tension surrounding the event. On April the ninth, 2007, William woke us with the news that he had achieved an eighty-one metre, constant weight with no fins, freediving world record, and following a rest day he took it further, diving to eighty-two metres and returning to complete a clean surface protocol.

William's hunger for success had been replaced with the contentment and elation of achieving his supreme goal, but tragically, French diver Loic LeFerme had died that day, following an equipment failure in a *No Limits* dive. These sensational stunts, in which the diver depends on a machine to reach the depth and return to the surface, attract large audiences and have led to a number of deaths. Although it appears that humankind's risk-taking urge becomes strongest during that transition from child to adult, a man's sense of worth is achieved through a rite of passage, while a woman encounters the more immediate challenges of childbirth and nurturing her offspring. Sadly, the equivalent transformation for a man more often involves aggressive actions that deny their innate sensitivity. However, a man's primitive warrior instinct could as easily be translated into creative or physical expressions. It could be positively employed in connecting to the environment, as seen in the recreational athleticism of rock climbers and freedivers, whose every move transcends a deep affinity with body, mind, and spirit.

Kadavu reminded us of the tranquil Perlas Islands, Manihi's lagoon, and the more recent Lau Islands. Deciding to take advantage of a last chance to explore the reefs, David and I set off, leaving Claire, Brad, and the kids on Hornpipe. On becoming aware of a pack of sharks circling close by we clambered back into the dinghy and ventured further over the glassy sea to the western reef. There, with Ono Island and misty Kadavu hovering in the distance, we slid into the limpid shallows to dive amongst flocks of minuscule fish, passing fat parrot fish browsing on purple polyps, following the rippled sand through a coral maze. Abruptly finding myself gazing over a precipice into an infinity of indigo, I hesitated, then taking a deep breath I spiralled down the encrusted cliff, falling towards velvet darkness. We wished we could linger in that deeper blue, but the pressure on ears and lungs sent us spinning to the shimmering surface, through water so clear it had no presence. Mesmerised by the depths, we dived again and again, into that silent void beneath the sea. Then we retrieved the spear gun from the dinghy and flopped into the water with a different intent. The scorching sun was high in the sky and few fish had chosen to venture out, however David persevered, hovering like a raptor, darting after his prey. And when he had shot enough for dinner we motored home through broken sunbeams.

Muppet Overboard

"Languid waves roll in,
With silver caps and blue robes
At the earth's feet to kneel."
Sam Trubridge

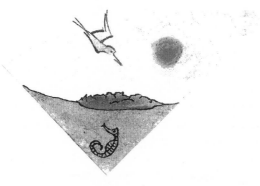

Farewell WT

As the sun set on that last perfect day we shared our barbecued fish with Wayne and Beth along with a reluctance at returning to civilisation. They set sail at first light but despite David being keen to take advantage of the fresh breeze our preparations took all morning. On leaving, a headwind forced us to motor through the Naingoro Pass, running along the south east of the reef, with David transcribing transit locations into course changes. Having become increasingly suspicious that our compass heading was some ten degrees out he checked its discrepancies while I steered and scanned the lagoon for uncharted coral. As one appeared beside our hull I wondered how many more lay unseen in our path. However Hornpipe passed unscathed and after three hours we came to the benign channel with gentle breakers on each side, and taking a last, longing glance at tropical islands we hoisted her sails and slipped through into open water.

Hornpipe was soon romping along, headed for New Zealand on a course of one hundred and eighty degrees. But setting everything in motion for an ocean voyage made for a hectic time with a crew that had no understanding of sailing. I steered while David fastened the engine brake, paid out the Walker log, set up the Aries, checked the navigation, bodged the leaking forward hatch, and pushed a pin into the faulty hinge of the forward port. No sooner had he let out the fishing line than we had a mahi mahi twisting in our wake and after a successful landing we set to preparing a feast. At dusk we feasted on *poisson cru* before commencing a routine of night watches, and with the moon in its second quarter, there was a welcome brightness in the sky. As Friday the twenty-second of November drifted into Saturday, David took over from Brad, who was listening to music on the Walkman, sitting in a lotus position on top of the aft cabin.

I came on watch to find the wind had dropped to ten knots. Hornpipe was whispering along barely holding her course; it was a beautiful day, but not for sailing. The filter we had bought in Samoa had failed to improve our tank water and we hesitated to drink the foul liquid. Our unquenchable thirst intensified with the sun's rays that rebounded around the cockpit with every slap and shudder of Hornpipe's sails as she wandered off course. While David longed for the perfect sailing conditions that he promised himself were normal, Claire lyrically enthused about the peaceful ocean. On listening to a Ham net weather forecast that a Norfolk Islander was broadcasting for yachts en route to New Zealand, we learned of gales around North Cape, of a front approaching from the Tasman sea. Being informed was everything. While David wished it would pass quickly, the tranquil conditions invested the day with endless potential. Sam helped me with the cooking and then he and Billy illustrated a message for Santa Claus which they pushed into a bottle along with marbles and a pencil, launching it at sunset, singing, *"We wish you a merry Christmas."*

The wind dropped and at midnight David cranked Obelix into action, but when I woke at seven the sea was a flurry of white caps. The twenty-five knot breeze from the north, northeast promised a magical day and once we had set Hornpipe wing and wing she flew over the waves. Inside her sunny saloon the children settled to their schoolwork. Billy made a little book of things he will do *"when I grow up,"* illustrated with drawings of him climbing a Mount Everest covered with palm trees, *"Diving for nis shells in the Philippines,"* and concluding, *"When I grow up I am going to be a king."* William continued to believe that anything was possible and in August 2007 he announced a freedive through the Dahab Arch wearing no more than a mask and swim trunks. At twenty metres a diver's weight sinks faster than an encumbered scuba diver so before starting he warned his safety divers that if anything went wrong they should just let him go. On the day of the dive William walked barefoot and then swam over the reef to the arch. After deep breaths, he ducked under and took a few powerful strokes before dropping to the Arch entrance at fifty-five metres. Then he began his thirty metre swim through the coral tunnel, turning to ensure he was through before heading for the surface. Maybe William remembered the unfinished business of Mariner's Cave, for on meeting the air he dissolved in jubilant laughter; the euphoria of being born into a world of sunlight.

By the time William visited for Christmas the media were taking an interest: in Canvas magazine's article titled *In the Deep,* Claire Harvey described him as *"Earnest and thoughtful, tall and lean, gazing into the middle distance."* She quoted his assessment of the risks involved, *"It's about the balance between life and death. I have to judge it exactly right so that when I turn around my desire to live matches precisely the extent to which I have dared to kill myself. It has similarities I guess to Orpheus on his journey into Hades, if you look back or show any kind of fear, then that will ultimately betray you. Freedivers do die, but just like in any other sport like mountain climbing, the rest of us still return to dance along that thin line, and in so doing taste our own existence."* William's reference to Orpheus and Eurydice had been inspired by his brother's incorporation of the myth into his presentation of Sleep/Wake. Sam's chance encounter with a sleep scientist had initiated an art/science collaboration and subsequent production that creatively suggests that the consciousness of sleep is closely equated to a time of death and transfiguration. As Sam began developing his conceptual performance I was reminded of his childhood projects that related to our voyage: taking pride in documenting sighting, drawing, and observing the sea birds that inhabited the ocean, propelling his imagination beyond Hornpipe's confines. Endeavours that were driven by a curiosity about life that continues to this day.

When Sam said he had not seen his Fraggle Rock Muppet for ages I searched high and low, and on recalling a last sighting of his zany friend watching a movie at the Suva yacht club, we concluded that Gobo had jumped ship. Then, as the fickle wind became too light for the Aries, David and I steered through what would have been a peaceful afternoon but for our boisterous kids' nerve jarring screeches. After finding them new books, silence descended on the boat with Sam wedged in his bunk, lost in adventures, while Billy read his *Little Red Riding Hood* before reciting the story word for word. While our single crews of Helen, John, and Gerry had needed our company, Brad and Claire's independence balanced the dynamics, and though Brad's silences were disconcerting, he was keen to learn. Despite the airless forward compartment, our crew had slept the afternoon away and when they surfaced we ate an early supper, as with a last glimmer of gold the sun disappeared over the horizon. We fell into our bunks with Claire choosing to serve my watch and Brad extending his as a recompense for their lazy afternoon. And although I was grateful for an extra sleep, David craved those solitary nights when Hornpipe surged through the ocean with no other care in the world.

Dawn's clear horizon rewarded David with some excellent star sights. Despite the day's brittle chill a voluptuous swell was rolling up from the south, transforming the ocean to a rippling blue field that sinuously undulated beneath our hull. I enjoyed a leisurely breakfast, imagining myself a passenger on board a cruise line and when the wind died we dropped the sails to motor. It was then we noticed how the sea's surface was blotched with a green scum: speculated on whether it was algae or volcanic dust blown on a breeze from Tonga. Tuna played beneath Hornpipe's bow and the sky was aflutter with tropic birds but our lack of progress was winding David tighter and tighter. Finally, he quenched his frustration in showing Claire and Brad the process of using the sextant, allowing the kids to experiment with a plastic one we kept on standby.

David's ocean encounter with the shark had made us wary of swimming, but the circumstances were too good to miss. So after electing a look out and throwing a line astern with a lifebuoy on the end, we ventured in, to find that the sea was thick with strings of eggs and baby jellyfish. Pilot fish made friendly advances and Sam and Claire thought they saw a seahorse. I hung on the surface never venturing far from home. The liquid essence from which we evolved was too immense for me to contemplate, but

David followed the sun's rays down, resurfacing with wide eyes. In the impenetrable darkness he had seen a pinpoint of light like a planet or a stationary gleaming eye. Although he could not fathom the mysterious entity, he described his experience, *"The brilliance of the distant underwater was brighter than any jewel. Rising, I was bursting up to the stars, hardly aware of breaking any surface."*

Climbing aboard with bodies and spirits cleansed, we continued motoring south and when the cockpit's reflected light became too much we stopped again. Despite the sea being considerably warmer Hornpipe's pitching designated that this be no more than a quick dunk, a refreshing dip that sustained us until a sparkling, fast moving object appeared on the horizon, a plane that roared overhead, blasting our panorama to pieces. After making radio connection David stupidly realised that he had nothing to say and when the pilot offered a navigational position he found himself briskly responding, *"With these clear skies we know exactly where we are."* Then after predicting calms for two or three days the RNZAF Orion pilot resumed his routine patrol.

Sailing to New Zealand WT

When ruffles of wind raised our hopes we hoisted the sails and after enduring hours of thumping and booming we added a Brahms violin concerto. And as the breeze evaporated the full moon cast her gleaming pathway over the sea. Before taking to our bunks, we furled Hornpipe's sails and roused Obelix to pound our brains into submissive sleep. I was on watch as dawn revealed a promising breeze. Hoisting the canvas, we hand steered through an uneventful morning that offered opportunities to catch up on numerous chores. After tightening the backstay, topping up the engine oil, and bailing the sail locker's bilge we were interrupted by the sight of a cargo ship, an indication of our proximity to the shipping lines. As she loomed closer David wondered whether her officer might be unaware of our presence and on calling up the Capitaine Cook III, they informed us they were transporting cargo from New Zealand to Fiji and Papua New Guinea. She passed at a few hundred metres, with Sam and Billy blowing a squeaky fanfare on our foghorn. That afternoon, while Brad and Claire slept, the children decided they needed airing and after patiently listening for voices they crept up with balloons, releasing them to spiral around the cabin with a manic *bwwuzzz*. They repeated the prank with Brad fighting them off, which was exactly the diversion they needed.

When the pitiful breeze died, we dropped the flaccid sails. Our day's progress had amounted to thirty miles and we were cold for the first time in years, but David's spirits lifted when the forecast indicated an imminent high. A sunset blush still lingered in the west as the huge moon emerged to paint the sky silver, purple, and indigo. Our children were tuned to sleep during the hours of darkness, to rise with the dawn, with late sleepers waking to the brittle rattle as they rummaged in the Lego box and argued over prized pieces. But that morning it was barely four thirty when Billy got up to play with the Lego and when he realised it was crazy early, he quietly tidied it away and sensibly went back to bed. Hornpipe sailed over a murky sea with school, navigation, cooking, and cleaning chores filling the morning. By afternoon the clouds had thickened to rain, but despite a frustrating week of little wind we were over half way, averaging a daily run of ninety-six miles which mostly consisted of motoring through the nights. On learning it was Thanksgiving in the States, Sam requested a holiday, but the calms were perfect for school activities and there was little else to do. As the wind died we drifted with David reading while I practised yoga on the deck with Billy joining in, before spending hours driving toy cars around the obstructions, making motoring sounds. Sam remained below, wearing the Walkman headphones shouting out Pink Floyd's school-kid anthem, *"Hey, teacher, leave them kids alone,"* never imagining that thirty years later he and David would find themselves chanting those words at a Roger Waters concert.

The restrictions of sailing had foiled many attempts at enlisting the kids' help with domestic chores. Billy often helped with the washing up, sitting cross legged in the cockpit, wiping every dish, stacking them neatly before carrying everything down to the galley. There he climbed onto the counter to carefully put the pots away in the cupboards. But on a wild sea these simple tasks became dangerous. Sam was a reluctant participant and we wondered whether his laziness was a rebellious response to Billy's desire to please. While Sam liked to be in control and initiate actions, he was gaining a huge sense of achievement from projects based on visual foundations. With no computers, video, or television to fill our children's minds they invented a fantasy world peopled with toy animals that metamorphosed into despicable characters; Bobby the monkey became a demon on a rocket ship, a pirate who enacted bloody battles and terrible tortures. Sam and Billy's creative resourcefulness entertained them through long days when land must have seemed a lifetime away, producing a treasure trove of drawings and stories that are a testimony to their lucid imaginations.

Billy alone LT

The sea had become lively, with dolphins leaping and splashing in the distance; black and white pilot fish darted beneath Hornpipe's bow. Birds swooped over the waves, porpoises flickered in the depths and the occasional Portuguese man o' war floated by. Yet, despite the rampant sea life, our pace was too slow to make our lure appealing. After supper we were discussing how the perpetual calm was getting to us when an unexpected breeze from the east set Hornpipe sailing like a stately swan. It didn't last long and once again we hid our disappointment in the darkness. Dawn's trade wind clouds and easterly swell seemed promising, but within hours the wind had dissolved in drizzle. While I steered David moodily helped the kids with their schoolwork. His total immersion in sailing lowered his tolerance of Hornpipe's faltering progress and after a week at sea he longed for action. I dared not say how I preferred the steady pace, that Sam and Billy thrived on the simple pleasure of those tranquil days.

After lunch, when the wind had again failed to live up to David's expectations, his gloom hit a new low, so I put on a Fawlty Towers tape and we laughed ourselves silly at the same old jokes. Brad and Claire disappeared for a siesta and David played chess with the kids while steering the virtually stationary boat. By the day's end the clouds had lifted, the wind was up and our spirits soared as we rode the gentle north-easterly. The high alto clouds dissolved overnight and after goose winging the sails and tidying the foredeck, our yacht was ready for action. When David's noon fix indicated we were two hundred and eighty-five miles from the Bay of Islands he calculated that, given a decent wind we might arrive in two days, just ahead of the predicted front. Hornpipe was bowling along at six knots, the sun sparkled on the waves, and David felt free for the first time on that passage. And yet a dark cloud had appeared on the horizon.

As Hornpipe's pace increased, my anxiety had surfaced like an undead zombie in a horror movie. How could I spoil the atmosphere by voicing concerns that our fast downwind pace minimised the odds of finding a man overboard? That every time David went on deck I visualised him tripping, falling, irretrievably drifting away? My imagination saw it all: Hornpipe's confused crew, grappling to restrain her flogging sails, the helpless heroine, yelling orders as David's head slid from view. I saw us turn to laboriously tack upwind through the pounding waves we had slipped over on our downwind flight. While amidst the panic we must keep that dot of a human head in sight. There were no landmarks upon that panoramic ocean; a speck would disappear in moments. We who remained would have to deal with all this, and the children's questions.

Most families never confront the extremes David and I had inadvertently chosen in taking up a cruising lifestyle. While he felt my anxiety indicated a lack of faith in his judgement, if anything, it was an admission of my own inadequacy. Yet despite those conflicts we worked well together. My instinctive grasp of subtleties balanced David's logic, and when he was desperate or weary, my stoicism carried us through. But everything was at stake on that battleground of concern versus freedom and although I tried to live in the now, these were our children, our lives, our home. I could not let go of my need to do and say something. As the miserable morning passed, David remained silent to avoid an embarrassing scene. It was such a shame! A little sympathy would have defused my anxiety; a small compromise could have bridged the gulf that separated us, but this dispute had become a matter of pride and we had lost our ability to talk or laugh about it. David wrote, *"A small boat on a long sea voyage is no place for highly charged emotions. I thoroughly resent both having my instinctive freedom fettered and the complete lack of trust in my own common sense and judgement."* Eventually I told David the sad truth, *"I don't want to go sailing anymore!"* And then he suddenly said, *"I've got a solution! We raise the lifelines; make them higher to prevent me falling overboard."* Although he had not backed down David had acknowledged he cared, and that changed everything.

While we drowned our altercation in loud music, Brad and Claire kept their distance. After Brad had spent the morning in the fo'c'sle, when Claire made uncharacteristic comments we wondered if they were also at odds, or empathising with our issues. Then somehow, we all brightened up. David and the kids worked off their reckless energy in a pillow fight and suddenly there was a mahi mahi on the line. After hauling it in we saw it was silvery, with pale viscose blood and a fatty layer beneath its skin. Most perturbing was the flesh that continued twitching half an hour after the fish had lost its head. And as Hornpipe rolled downwind at a reckless pace Brad embarked on a culinary feat, baking tortillas and pumpkin pie for a Thanksgiving dinner. Brad was obsessive in his preparations; rigging a support rope through the galley, bracing himself to roll the pastry; raising the sides of a dish with greaseproof paper to contain the sloppy mix. His extreme cuisine attracted Claire's comment, *"That's typical Brad!*

He never accepts anything." The result was an amazing feast and even Billy ate the pumpkin pie, never associating it with the soup he had refused at lunchtime.

When the front separated, with one half heading north to Fiji, the other south to New Zealand, Hornpipe spread her sails to fly wing and wing, through a day and night of consistent north easterlies. David's noon fix on Sunday the first of December positioned us one hundred and sixty-five miles from our destination. The sun sparkling on the ocean prompted us to take a cool sea water wash. Following supper Billy commented, *"Yippee, lots of washing up to do!"* and Sam joined in before we rounded off the celebrations with fruit juice and a secret hoard of chocolate. During the previous night David had savoured a few squares of an enormous chocolate bar. Then the bar vanished. We were shocked and surprised when our midnight thief's identity was revealed. Claire, who had fooled us all with her refined habit of using chopsticks in favour of cutlery, was mortified when we found out and on explaining the concept of saving treats for special occasions she said, *"I guess we can't just get more at the corner store."* Claire's charming honesty made up for the indulgence and we claimed a sweet satisfaction from reminding her of the misdemeanour.

The northerly picked up at dusk and after many changes we polled the genoa wing and wing. Hornpipe was sailing a good six knots and at two in the morning David's dead reckoning put us just eighty-five miles from the Bay of Islands. Every time he lay down his sleep was interrupted, so he stayed awake for the dawn fix, to be rewarded by a host of stars that remained long enough to locate our exact position. Hornpipe was hurtling downwind at seven knots and with neither Claire nor Brad able to helm without risking a serious gybe I hand steered through the morning. Despite the forecasted front the sun briefly appeared for a noon sight that set us thirty miles from the Cavalli Islands, forty to the Bay of Islands. And as a bank of cloud signifying the meeting of two air masses obliterated the possibility of sighting land, we recognised it as the fabled Aotearoa, *"Land of the Long White Cloud."*

When the wind dropped, we doused the jib, and as the cloak of cloud swept over us the visibility decreased to half a mile. We motored on through torrential rain and with the mainsail holding Hornpipe steady I launched into a huge pile of washing with Brad and Claire looking on, highly amused at my scrubbing, sloshing watch keeping. David slept and woke to brilliant sunshine that illuminated a row of fluffy clouds. After taking a sight he disappeared below to calculate our position, and as I draped garments over the lifelines I scanned the horizon one last time, to recognise the slightest hint of grey separating the sea and sky. *"Land Ho!"* I shouted, relishing the dramatic announcement that had conjured Aotearoa out of the ocean.

Soon we could all see that fragile line of hills collaborating with clouds. With the Bay of Islands too far away to reach that night, the Cavalli Islands were our best option. They could easily be missed and making a landfall after dark would be hazardous but with four hours of daylight and just twelve miles to go it seemed worth the risk. Shivering we pulled on the itchy jumpers our mothers had knitted and, as our toes tingled in the chill, we had no doubt we were too far south. The kids were fascinated by the unfamiliar garments and Sam was speculating on the delights of New Zealand when he was interrupted by the line spinning. He remembers how, after hauling the unfamiliar fish on board, we gazed at that envoy from the new land that was as brown as the water it inhabited, and though we diagnosed it as a sea trout we later learned it was a trevally. David had hand copied charts from Wayne's *Pickmere Atlas of New Zealand* and as we motored between the rocky islets he identified the craggy islet of Nukutaunga. The dank aroma and surging tresses of seaweed reminded us of seaside holidays, and the scene evoked the cliffs of Cornwall. Yet this relatively new land had been recently colonised. And while our passage resembled that of its Māori settlers who sailed the first waka, our system of navigating using a compass and sextant would have been familiar to Captain James Cook of the Endeavour. For the wind had blown us all to Aotearoa.

Most travellers arrive at a crowded airport that is identical to any other, followed by a journey that gradually reveals the cultural identity of a land and its people, until finally, the remotest and often most memorable place is reached. Our landfall in the Cavalli Islands had reversed that order and although we felt no desire to go further, we could not enter paradise until we had passed through immigration. Hopefully night would give us a breathing space to prepare for that official arrival. As we motored into Kikipaku Bay I stood at Hornpipe's bow, scanning the green water before dropping our anchor between two arms of rock within the shelter of a high island. Our passage was complete, and no matter what New Zealand had in store, I felt safe and secure. As the last golden rays caressed the hills we ate a special dinner of roasted fish before falling into our bunks, to rock in Hornpipe's cradle. But during the night David remained on alert, tuned to the whistling gusts and rumbling chain, dreading our anchor lodging under rocks and having to retrieve it from the freezing water. No one else was capable of diving deep to heft an anchor free and most essential jobs were contingent upon David's strength and expertise. This alone made him grasp the brief freedoms that came his way, rebel against being responsible for all our lives.

On that fourth of December 1985 we slept until the sun's rays illuminated the golden cliffs and copper water. It was as though that day was the first that ever dawned and Sam longed to roll in the meadow hills and dewy valleys of a land that glowed with the vibrancy of spring. The scenery was inspiringly beautiful, but the air was numbingly cold for bodies the tropics had pared of excess flesh, and while the children layered themselves in woollies, hats, and gloves with all the enthusiasm of a dressing up game, we prepared to sail on. The anchor came up readily and after we had hoisted her mainsail and genoa, Hornpipe flew wing and wing, surfing down the waves at a thrilling eight knots. The exhilarating ride silenced us, but Sam was intoxicated with words; after being starved of stimulus he boiled over with excitement, talking up the land and all he intended doing once he got ashore. Sam threw words into the air like a juggler, speculating about what we might find on our arrival, spicing his commentary with tales of headhunters and cannibals, addressing his outpouring at everything and anything. His endless torrent left us speechless. A seagull settled on the stern rail, and Sam was away again, *"Oh he's so lovely, let's have him as a pet, get some bread, hey seagull stay with us."*

The fresh north westerly remained true and, as Hornpipe raced along the coast that stretched north and south beyond our gaze, David commented that we could have been sailing the English Channel. At our moment of glory, Claire took a family photo of the children sitting wearing harnesses upon the cabin roof, David steering with me at his side. I was elated, enjoying the fast sailing with all fears of losing my man absolved by the thought that, if my muppet fell overboard, he could bloody well swim to the land! However, I knew that if anything had happened to David on this or any other passage, we would all have been lost, that this dark truth had been the real source of my anxiety and lack of self-worth. I was the muppet on our boat, for despite sailing halfway around the world I was still not proficient enough in navigating or managing Hornpipe to have got anywhere alone.

We had long since abandoned our tank water for the emergency supplies in our plastic containers and as the foul liquid became agitated Billy chose to stand by the sink, patiently pumping it all away. Two hours after leaving the Cavallis we rounded Cape Wiwiki, passing within the Ninepins rock that marks the entrance to the Bay of Islands. As katabatic gusts rebounded down Mataka Mountain, we dropped the poled genoa and hoisted our staysail for a close reach with Hornpipe healing in the squalls that whistled down the Kerikeri Inlet. There was nothing to indicate any difference between this end to an eight-thousand-mile passage from the day jaunts of local sailing boats. On passing Moturoa Island and Fraser Light, the houses of Russell and Paihia came into view and then we furled our sails and cranked up Obelix to come alongside Opua wharf. As the reverberations silenced to stillness, we stepped onto a land half a world from where we had set forth almost five years before.

Familiar boats were arriving by the moment and as we filled our tanks with clean water the children ran along the wharf to visit Carla and Ged on Tern, to learn that they had also motored most of the way, thoroughly enjoying the light winds. However, those cruising boats that had left a week before us had experienced fifty knot winds from the north west and a young man who had suffered severe seasickness had been hospitalised since his arrival. Knowing we could not bring vegetables, fruit, meat, honey, or seeds into the country, we had eaten all our fresh food, so while we waited for clearance we bought a huge tub of ice cream and sat in a circle, digging our spoons into the indescribably delicious, chocolate creaminess. The officers spent all afternoon on the paperwork, revealing the sinister truth behind the Tongan story of a boat and a bomb: that French secret service agents had entered New Zealand posing as yachties, to bomb and sink the anti-nuclear ship Rainbow Warrior. When the officer bantered about searching French boats for bombs, we explained that genuine French yachties were fiercely anti-nuclear and more likely to sympathise with the New Zealand government than their own.

That evening we moved the clock forward one hour and on that seemingly endless day it was still light at nine. Then we rowed Sam and Billy over to Pine Island, where they found a new habitat for their imaginary games before joining a boatload of cruising kids for a chaotic party while David and I hitched to Paihia's shopping arcade. There we were met with a questioning, *"So how do you like New Zealand?"* And after wandering from shop to shop, looking at what we would buy if we had the money, we concluded that we had been perfectly happy in Suvarov without purchasing anything. When a French yachting couple gave us a ride home, I realised the distancing effect of a foreign language made them oblivious to Paihia's faded colonialism that was reminiscent of an out of season English seaside town.

Before leaving, Claire and Brad cooked a special dinner, and when it concluded with strawberries and cream our kids thought it the most exotic dessert, ever. We had been lucky with this couple who said that sailing with our family, *"Had thoroughly altered their lives."* Brad had asked endless questions, methodically processed every scrap of information. Claire had gazed at the stars, absorbed the pulse of the ocean, and lived the dream. We had shared our home, philosophies, and tantrums. They knew everything about us and yet Brad remained inscrutable, Claire a mystery. We watched and waved when they caught a lift to Auckland, before flying to Indonesia and China. And every Valentine's Day an exquisite handmade card, bulging with fragments of poetry, stars, and the memorabilia of travels and love affairs, would arrive. And by the time we realised they came from Claire it was time for her to join us on another ocean passage.

THE LAND OF THE LONG WHITE CLOUD

"For Keith from Sam. Remember, they say. But what?
I remember chasing a dropped mask. Sinking. A fallen leaf, fluttering.
Disappearing into depths under your boat. Like my memories of you. Sinking
with time...I remember the blue. A toy car given me from your desk. It's still
here. In the box, we pull out for visitors' children. Your children."

Sam Trubridge

Alone again we anchored near the entrance to the Bay of Islands and walked through and up onto the clifftops that looked north towards the Cavalli Islands. It was an homage of a sort, an acknowledgment of our arrival in Aotearoa, at precisely the antipodal point of where we had set sail from Spain, half a world away. While this alone was testimony to our strength and endurance, it was not enough. We were holding on to a dream of returning to Mo'orea, and it would take time to appreciate this land of new beginnings, old ways, and cold winters.

While waiting to catch the tide that made the Kerikeri river passable, we anchored beneath Doves Point. I was taking Sam and Billy ashore when, on meeting a fellow Brit, our conversation revealed a mutual reason for leaving. Martyn expressed his droll disappointment that the doomsday prediction of nuclear war that had brought him to New Zealand had come to nothing, and before long our family was walking the winding path towards his cottage on the clifftop. Martyn's boyish appearance of a huggable bear had endeared him to an ever-changing cast of girlfriends, but he was also a renowned architect and sailor. As I made jam in his kitchen, David discussed work opportunities. Then we watched a powerful film about Colin McCahon, finding it enlightening to witness the New Zealand landscape through the eyes of its most famous artist.

On celebrating Christmas tied alongside an old square rigger named Breeze, Wayne of Tern told us of a couple who owned a workshop. As the year drew to a close we sailed to Dicks Bay to meet Brad, the American, whose expressionless face was framed with heavy glasses, and Bette his Swedish wife who earned them a living creating quilts. While our kids bounced on the trampoline, they proposed we winter in their co-owner's beach house in exchange for completing the workshop. Then, as we gathered around a blazing fire to see in the New Year, a Zodiac buzzed towards us. In the waning light three revellers stumbled up the beach holding aloft a bottle of champagne, shouting, *"Found you at last!"* Sealestials' Keith and Caroline had sailed from Australia's Great Barrier Reef to honour a vow made in Huahine; that we would complete our celebration of New Year together in three different locations. They had crossed an ocean to keep their promise, with Polly flying from Hawaii to share the fun.

Australia and New Zealand are seasonal destinations for yachts that follow the trade winds through the Pacific, with many of their owners visiting the South Island before sailing away like exotic birds of passage. While it would be some time before we could afford a car and a road trip, we retraced our arrival, sailing north to the Cavalli Islands and Whangaroa Harbour. There we walked through meadows of English flowers to an abandoned settler's cottage and climbed Okahumoko Rock to gaze over a scene that had witnessed many bloody acts – the presence of a breeze adding authenticity to a sense of times past. As a front moved through, I transcribed my Galapagos drawings into watercolours, while the boys constructed polyhedral models that they hung in the saloon. David never considered the significance of this project until, years later, when teaching a workshop in Perth, he playfully assembled a mathematical shape from plywood. On returning he riveted the pieces into a sphere and carried it into the house saying, *"What do you think of this?"* My initial thought was, *"Oh no, something else to clutter the house!"* followed by the obvious solution. When we hung it from the ceiling with a light bulb inside, neither of us saw it a design breakthrough or realised that the sculptural lampshade would transform our lives. David refined the form, William cut pieces on the bandsaw, the interest escalated, and Coral became the first of an ever growing range of kitset lights.

At the end of January we returned to Doves Point, where David helped a designer complete his racing yacht. The kids caught a bus to the Kerikeri school, where they found themselves well ahead of their peers. One weekend while anchored off Roberton Island, a battered boat swung past with a cheery, *"Gu-day,"* from those on board. It was Gerry who, after salvaging Manureva from the Aitutaki reef, had helped sail her to New Zealand. After a brief time together we went our separate ways until, some twenty years later, when he returned with his Danish wife and daughters. Gerry's shimmering underwater paintings had made a mark in Denmark, but he remained the same passionate surfer and fisherman. And, having been cared for by Gerry as his own, it is not surprising that Sam and Billy visit and maintain a lasting friendship with him.

Hornpipe's extensive refurbishment was a top priority, so following an overnight sail to Whangarei we stripped her of her mast and hauled her ashore. The battle of the rust lasted from dawn to dusk, with us keeping costs down by doing all we could. It was nerve racking exposing the vulnerable steel, knowing that excessive humidity or rain would wreck the job. Starting with ripping off the wooden toe rail we welded on a robust metal bar, followed by sandblasting the cockpit, topsides, and hull that resulted in three holes, including a substantial one in the engine room. After replacing Hornpipe's boom and adding mast steps, a swim platform, and higher stanchions, I resolved to never mention the harness again. The yard was a volatile environment, with booze nights when the workers broke into sing-songs and fights. By day the children attended a local school, sustaining cuts and bruises as they ranged around the dangerous boatyard. It was there that Billy proved his navigator potential, calculating the number of bricks in a wall, moments after entering a room. Meanwhile within our tiny saloon I was stitching lengths of toxic PVC for a commissioned awning. Then on April Fool's Day our gleaming yacht splashed into the harbour, the ripples reflecting her white hull encircled with the green and blue stripe that invoked the land, sea, and sky in what would forever remain Hornpipe colours.

Our elation was tainted when a letter from immigration refused David's request for a work permit, despite his endorsements of proficiency and portfolio of photographs. When pressed, the officer suggested he present our case in Wellington. The balmy autumn days were soothing but our escape to Great Barrier Island was shadowed with concern about the expense and outcome of the forthcoming trip. The children played in drifts of leaves and relished the independence of walking alone to a waterfall. One day we hiked up a winding forest path from Port Fitzroy to Lookout Rock and Cooper's Castle. And after I had succumbed to Billy's entreaties of *"Carry me,"* he and Sam pelted down the track beside the Kaiarara stream, showing no sign of tiredness after their fifteen-mile walk! Cruising to Smokehouse Bay we fired up a stove for a luxurious hot bath, that only a boat dweller would appreciate. Keith, Caroline, and Polly flew out from Auckland to spend a last weekend, walking to the Kauri Dam and returning for a traditional English roast. As we waved farewell to the Sealestials, we resolved to stay in touch. They returned to England, Keith to a law firm, Caroline to nursing, saving money for a cruising lifestyle with subsequent offspring Rory and Katie. It was Polly who told us of the tragedy. That Caroline had returned from night duty to find her children crying, *"Mummy, we can't wake daddy!"* Lovable Keith, husband, father, and sailor had died of a heart attack. Holding true to the future they had planned, Caroline moved her family to New Zealand, coping with the harrowing circumstances, giving her children more than enough love to replace their lost father.

While Polly took her *Wonder-Boys* on a blistering walk up to Lookout Rock and down to Okiwi Beach to experience the view at close quarters, we enjoyed a quiet day before sailing north to the Bay of Islands. After gleaning written endorsements from Brad and Martyn, we moored in the Kerikeri basin where Sam and Billy resumed school while David prepared for his immigration interview. As water nomads, we embraced the way of the warrior, however life had taught me that it was sometimes wise to conform. Eventually, after voicing my concerns about David expecting the officials to accept him *as he was*, wearing his ragged jeans and sandals, he accepted that, for the sake of his family he must borrow a jacket, shirt, tie, and shoes. David caught a bus to Auckland where he gathered references from craft galleries before riding the overnight train to Wellington. The interview went well and he returned with fresh optimism and new wetsuits to help us brave the winter.

Having grown up naked and free, Sam and Billy did not understand the cold, and when low tide in the Kerikeri basin exposed its oozing banks they saw the potential for fun and announced that they were going mud sliding with the gang. Gingerly stepping off Hornpipe's swimming platform they ventured onto the slippery riverbank. Then the yacht basin resounded to whoops of joy as abandoned figures hit the voluptuous mud. Elfin silhouettes slithered over the shiny shore; tiny footsteps left trails of indigo puddles. Briefly stopping to lather the slime into suits of black, the urchins curled like koru to bomb the river with resounding splashes that sluiced the monster, revealing pink flesh, wrinkly fingers, and goose bumps. Their game broke every taboo of clean, and only when the chilly evening mist settled over the river did they cease. I was ready for them, Hornpipe's stovetop steaming with pans of water and, after shooing them back into the river to wash off the worst, they wallowed in the fish tub we used for a bath. It had been worth it. But like them, I was made for the tropics. As a child I had been plagued by the freezing English winters and where sunshine would have cured my eczema and chilblains, Mum bound my limbs in bandages coated with pungent cold tar ointment. A built-up shoe balanced a leg that was longer, and I came last in running races, except for that day when the teacher gathered the children around to announce, *"Linda is the real winner of this race. She wins on effort!"*

Having made many friends, mutual trust led to employment and support. I had little to exchange, so I reciprocated with gifts of bread and preserves. But David needed a workshop and our family a house, so at the end of May we sailed to Dicks Bay to take up Brad and Bette's offer. The kids spent an hour on the school bus as it wound along the gravel road towards the historic village of Russell, and on their return they raced down the zig zag track to the secluded house and workshop that stood tucked into the cliff. Blackened tea tree trunks barred the view of a grey sandy beach studded with shells and Hornpipe weathering the waves further out. Although we relished the hot showers and glorious fires, it was bitterly cold in the sunless house and as the children struggled to settle into their third school Sam lost weight and began biting his fingernails. When a report informed us that his work was slapdash, I wrote to his teacher. Her curt reply concluded, *"Sam is allowing himself to be bullied."* While I had suggested that Sam emulate Michael Jackson's *Beat It*, boys were expected to fight. My son had survived an antiquated Caribbean education, had learned a new language to make friends in French Polynesia; so why was he being bullied in a village school? Sam never complained and I recall my parents enquiring if I was happy, that I always said yes! While I would have done anything to please them I had recoiled from requests of, *"A penny for your thoughts."* I wasn't selling any secrets and when I escaped into my imagination they called me a daydreamer. Where I had embraced my differences, Sam's accent and background made him a target. He longed to have friends, and all we could do was boost his confidence with beach football, building a hut, and cooking on a campfire.

Despite our need to earn a living, finishing the workshop took months. Meanwhile Brad blundered around and we noticed that it was Bette who cooked, cleaned, and provided for the family. Eventually David set up a workbench and we carried the tuck box ashore. This remnant of his boarding school days harboured memories of the Dykehead workshop and others along the way. Within its dark confines, Bouncer had strung a web to trap insects, and when the going got tough he had hunkered down amongst the planes and chisels. The huge hairy Caribbean spiders had intimidated him, Polynesia was overrated in his opinion, and when Bouncer sniffed the cool air, he wondered whether he had been magically teleported back to Northumberland. And my, how the children had grown! They were even making their own toys. He wondered if they would notice their old friend, and when he swung past they cried, *"Look there's Bouncer, he's been with us all along!"* Bouncer whistled a happy tune as he slipped through a splintered panel. And where one might presume a gigantic wave had hurled the box against a bulwark, spilling the contents into a frothing foam, with Hornpipe escaping sinking by a whisker, the truth was the tuck box had been the victim of an assault! Wood is a fickle media that twists, splits, and delights in fooling a cabinetmaker. The price of perfectionism is high and when a tricky piece of furniture drove David mad he lashed out at the tuck box. On other occasions I had saved his creations from a similar fate; however, David is a gentle, sensitive person whose rage is only ever vented on inanimate objects.

New Zealand was proving a difficult place to earn. We no longer had finances for moving on, and when immigration sent another refusal, I decided to promote my teaching qualifications. The Whangarei education office encouraged me to seek out a job before applying for a work permit. No sooner had I contacted the local high school than they spontaneously called me in to relieve a sick teacher in the art department. Hailing the school bus I clambered in with the students, who averting suspicious eyes avoided the *pākehā* teacher. Their abrupt voices conveyed a language of insults and commands and it was no surprise to learn that the previous generation of Māori had been forbidden to communicate in *te reo*, their own tongue. Disheartened and alienated by my colonial culture I remembered how my Polynesian friends had welcomed me as an equal. After teaching for two days, I filled in forms to claim my pay and apply for a work permit. Imagine my shock on receiving the education authority's formal response: that my criminal act of teaching without a permit rendered our family liable for deportation. Any thought of crossing the Tasman Sea during winter's storms was terrifying, so I followed the school's suggestion that I avoid prosecution by volunteering my wages. But my opportunity to earn a living had been curtailed, my confidence shattered.

Our immigration problems had most likely been exacerbated by our arrival on a yacht. Many travellers applied for residency just to extend their stay. We had also intended leaving, but as we weathered the bureaucratic doldrums our plan of returning to Mo'orea drifted away. Time would prove us worthwhile citizens, and when two men in suits made an impromptu visit, expecting to catch David smoking dope, they found him busy constructing a bed frame. Following numerous enquiries, medical certificates, blood tests, and X-rays we were summoned for an interview. Borrowing smart clothes and a vehicle we drove to Whangarei where we were ushered into the abode of the chief immigration officer. On scanning me up and down she blurted, *"You're not what I expected."* I wondered what surprise I had pulled on this interrogator who possessed a file on my family. Shuffling papers, Mrs Roach brandished my application in which the photocopier had rendered my suntanned face completely black. *"You look like an illegal Indian immigrant from Fiji!"* she said, concluding with, *"And I imagined that you were bigger!"* I was dumbfounded. It seemed that my birth certificate, qualifications, and testimonials amounted to nothing against an assumption based on my skin colour. I abhorred racial prejudice and longed to counter her remark with a rebellious, *"Well what if I was!"* concluding with the French onomatopoeic slang for her name. But I could not jettison my family's future, so I made a feeble joke, while wishing that I could *Blat* that Mrs Roach.

Following the confrontation we drove south, with the children chattering along the way like Australian Aborigines, singing up the land. Having known only little islands they had expected this one to end at Whangarei and were spellbound when the skyscrapers of that *land of Auks* rolled into view. As we drove over the Auckland Harbour Bridge they held their breath in a playful competition that pre-empted Billy's apnea practices. While David sought work, we visited the zoo, museum, library, and shopped with the kids' savings from their dollar-a-week pocket money. Returning home, we continued using Hornpipe for transportation, sometimes hitching a ride with Māori families who, understanding hard times, always made space amidst their babies and dogs. Hardly a day passed without a familiar yacht sailing into the bay, with birthdays an opportunity to set treasure trails. When Sam's friend presented him with a stuffed harrier hawk, the kids' cabin was the only available space, so that bird in flight joined the menagerie at the foot of their bunk.

I sewed a multitude of clothes and furnishings for Hornpipe, while David redesigned his Mo'orea chair, exhibiting it with a sculpture, jewellery box, and the earrings he had carved on our passages across the Atlantic and Pacific Oceans. Although we could not afford sentimentality, their price exceeded the perceived value and they remained unsold. No sooner had David established himself than Brad began building his house, blundering about the workshop; a liability around dangerous machinery and exacting craftsmanship. We had grown increasingly wary of his schemes and expectation that we should sort his muddles. Brad remembered only favours, forgetting we had earned every one; he knew that after months of building the workshop we depended on it to earn our living. The stress and frustration gave David headaches and every night I massaged his back and neck to ease the pain. But I could not alleviate his concern that his father's brain haemorrhage had happened at a similar age; thoughts that filled him with an urgent need to make the most of his life.

The children often joined David in the workshop, quietly working beside him. Billy constructed a fishing rod and Sam a wooden box canoe which he named *Ika*, the Māori word for fish; he paddled it around the bay when the sea was calm. Then he spontaneously glued and nailed off-cuts, constructing robot characters that he painted and patterned. Later ones hardly evolved beyond a nail in a piece of wood, before they were enlisted into the gang of freaks and armoury of swords, guns, and wooden calculators. Meanwhile Billy had begun methodically carving the first of his animal sculptures. *"Making wood carvings alongside my father in his workshop,*

I learned that the initial ecstasy of inspiration never lasts to the end of the task – often its energy was exhausted by the first gleeful hour of chiselling, then if patience and discipline didn't take over, you'd be left with a hacked-at block of wood that only half-resembled the intended camel/giraffe/whale. Watching him steadily work to create elaborate works, and an even more elaborate lifework, in the same way that he steadily devoured mountain ranges on our long hikes, I've witnessed the archetype of patience and discipline. Thanks to my father, I have never reneged on a training session, or quit when results were discouraging."

When the days became warmer, David's mother arrived for six weeks, and as usual occupied herself with knitting while observing us from a safe distance. Five years and three visits had passed since our departure and I longed for my parents to share Sam and Billy's lives. Hiring a campervan we explored the Hokianga and Ninety Mile Beach, soaked in the mud pools of Ngawha Springs, and visited Cape Reinga, where Māori believe their soul leaves Aotearoa on its return to Hawaiki. But the rebellious landscape offered few references to Britain, and Gran saw only danger in those happy-go-lucky times. She lived a lonely life and desperately desired our companionship, but we had precious little spare energy and were quietly relieved when she departed, leaving us to manage our problems alone.

One day we decided to test the six-person life-raft that had accompanied our passages across the Atlantic and Pacific. Carrying the Avon box into the workshop, we set it down and pulled the cord to inflate the raft, which dramatically burst free of its container, expanding with a gaseous hiss. OH WOW! Then, in a breath, it deflated. OH SHIT! What a sobering sight! We watched, frozen in horror, as the life-raft sank beneath the waves of our expectations, picturing our family treading water around that collapsing sack of rubber. Neither of us spoke as we silently processed the event, resolving to be better prepared in future. While the life-raft's pressure valves had corroded, its claimed six-person capacity was barely enough to house one, let alone a family. So we decided to build a dinghy that would adapt into a lifeboat that could be sailed. A local boat designer drew plans and after lightly stitching the foam core onto an upturned mould we covered it with layers of fibreglass and resin. We sanded the outside of the hull, then turned the floppy, fragile shell to start the interior and once we had fitted stringers, a wooden gunwale, decks, and bulkheads at bow and stern, she gained strength and integrity. David finished the details, while I painted our dinghy with her name Jolly Boat on the bow.

Although it had been a strange way to build a boat, Jolly Boat proved strong yet light enough for us to carry. On launching she gracefully alighted on the water, her clean lines echoing those of Hornpipe. She rowed well and once we had learned to co-ordinate our double oars David and I cut through the sea at a cracking pace. While he supplemented our provisions by diving for grouper, moki, and seasonal scallops, I netted flounders and trolled for kahawai. When I saw birds wheeling over agitated schools of fry, I jumped in the dinghy, and with a reel threaded on my leg I rowed through the bubbling water, dragging the line after me, repeatedly crossing the frenzy; throwing kahawai into the fish tub. However, I could never stomach using a knife, so I hit the fish with a stone, screaming apologies with every blow. I could not succumb to pathetic instincts with my family to feed, but untangling flounders from the net rendered heart stopping moments, when, even after bashing them to death, their bodies recoiled on the chopping block.

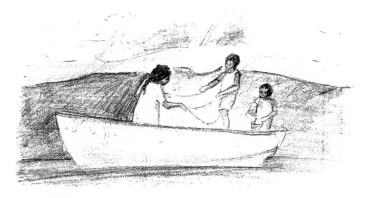

Fishing LT

When hoped-for commissions came to nothing, David desperately consulted the I Ching and, acting on the prediction, began making a dining table and chairs for Russell's craft gallery. With the pending arrival of the owners of the house, I rowed boatloads of belongings to where Hornpipe was anchored a considerable distance from shore. Almost immediately Harry and Kelly ventured out to discuss Brad and the circumstances to which they had unwittingly committed. But Kelly had no qualms about unloading her emotional baggage, leaving hapless victims untangling the bitter accusations. Having learned how words slice like knives, that emotional wounds never heal, we avoided becoming embroiled in their dispute. Meanwhile we wondered about the third owner of the workshop; a scrimshaw artist who was away sailing. Years later we would visit his unfinished house to find a Valkyrian hall of colossal timbers projecting over the bay. One pictured axes and clubs stashed in the hallway, fiery steeds tethered at the door, and although we never met we speculated on how he had fitted into that *ménage a trois*.

On selling their home in Russell, Brad and Bette moved into a tent on the beach and began building a house amidst the dense undergrowth. Set on unstable foundations, like Brad, it was only a matter of time before it would sink into the swamp. Following Christmas in the claustrophobic commune, we escaped to Deep Water Cove where we enjoyed a forgotten freedom. Taking Jolly Boat out on that first expedition, we felt her fly over the waves, bearing our family in her belly. After diving in the cavern of Piercy Rock, we walked to the lighthouse threading our way through dark manuka forests and over a clifftop path that spans the sea with a sky bridge. One morning we washed our clothes in a waterfall, the kids transforming the chore into a carefree comedy. On returning to Dicks Bay I tried to contribute to our finances by sewing fisherman's tunics and curtains, but the anchorage was beset with fickle winds and waves that swamped the dinghy. The wind was often too ferocious to row ashore with the shallow tidal bay leaving the dinghy high and dry or floating far from reach. The children accompanied David; Sam constructing more robots with Billy laboriously sculpting a giraffe, while Brad's gang of clumsy builders wielded planks and cut rough timbers, rendering the machines too blunt for fine furniture. Carving was the only feasible job so, amidst the devastation, David began his second sculpture, *Wind and Sea*, refining the wood to a minimum, until the light glowed through the stylised sail that met a free-flowing wave at a slender juncture. Their fragility made me nervous and when David sent his sculpture's away to the Wellington Academy of Fine Arts, I breathed a sigh.

Sam and Billy were a magnet to other boys and this was how we met the Iron Butterflies. The men negotiated a skill swap, with David fixing their yacht's cupboard doors, Ian reciprocating with heavy metal welding. In response to their attempt at converting us to their Baha'i faith, I taught them yoga, which would have been a fair transaction but for David's scepticism and my belief that yoga presents truths that prevailed before and beyond religion. As autumn faded to another dreaded winter, Brad, who was well-aware of our dependence, suddenly increased the workshop rent to a hundred dollars a week. Although he and Harry claimed they were setting up to make furniture, we had never seen them lift a finger to earn a living and it appeared they hoped to redeem their financial blunders by charging us an exorbitant rent. It was also about ownership and egotistical delusions about being our benefactors. Brad had enthused about attending a therapeutic workshop, where a crowd of lost souls were blindfolded and let loose to run around a paddock. While many had been injured in the resulting carnage, Brad said he had found the activity liberating, which left us wondering what purpose the exercise had served to one who metaphorically spent his life running around like a headless chook.

On the same day Brad doubled David's rent, the Academy of Fine Arts rejected his sculpture. In desperation, he took it to Auckland along with a sample chair, to discover on his return that the entire dining set had miraculously sold. But despite the breakthrough, David was gloomy at the prospect of another year trying to make ends meet. Though we had made little progress towards financial or legal security, a family on a nearby boat blatantly extolled the joys of living on a benefit, saying *"Why shouldn't society support us? We are raising our children to be exceptional people."* Although the couple enjoyed the luxury of time and security, we never saw their children play or swim. On showing us their illustrated map of a proposed world trip, enquiries about leaving were brushed aside and we heard that their only sailing experience, spent motoring from Whangarei to the Bay of Islands, had been traumatic. Like others on home built boats they were nervous about risking their enterprise on the high seas, and to our knowledge they still remain in the Bay.

When our neighbours commissioned David to make a range of conventional furniture for their Remuera house he was suddenly inundated with work, and on the strength of this we bought a 1967 Valiant Safari that we named Beatrice. Sam and Billy set to scrubbing their *new* car with a pride that was obliterated on our first trip on the muddy back road. The freedom of wheels was sweeter for five years' abstinence, the land exhilarating to eyes accustomed to sea vistas, and as David and I slid closer on Beatrice's bench seat she held us in her spell, humming over the hills with the kids jabbering in the back. But winter was upon us and despite friends who welcomed us for the the occasional hot shower, Hornpipe was inhospitably cold and I dared not contemplate the months ahead. Then, following Billy's pirate party, we returned to drop his friends off in Waipiro Bay and noticed a host of coloured flags flying over a house with a pointed roof and chimney stack. The bold proclamation that the owners were in residence induced us to bravely knock at their door, to tentatively suggest we house sit. To our surprise they were keen, on condition we renovate the exterior as payment. The very next day we signed an agreement with lawyer Don Ball and lost no time moving into Smugglers Point, filling the cavernous house with music from their classical collection, luxuriating in hot baths and a blazing fire.

Taniwha WT

We had struck gold. As we sipped coffee on the terrace that overlooked the sheltered bay where Hornpipe lay at anchor, we knew a profound sense of peace. Within that secure setting, we established a relaxed way of being. The kids spontaneously visited friends and when David returned from Auckland with a set of dog-eared books they played their first game of *Dungeons and Dragons*, throwing a dice to initiate and invent scenarios that overflowed into the landscape. Sam took charge, guiding them through the riddles of his creative mind. Morgan, with his *Star Wars* fuelled fervour, was a serious participant and while Ben often lost interest in the game's cerebral contortions, Damian would only accept a snack with a morose, *"Well then, I'll have to jog,"* which he did, on the spot beside the table. Meanwhile, overwhelmed by the action, Billy's strident voice pitched higher and higher until they could bear no more.

After meals David habitually immersed himself in a book or crossword, inevitably falling asleep, while I rarely stopped yet never seemed to achieve enough to merit a break. On two days I hitched, often walking miles, to earn a pittance at a Russell tourist shop. The money was gobbled up by our food bill, while with space and electricity on hand, I completed sewing commissions, sanded and painted window frames to pay our rent. When the Balls came for the weekend we moved onto the boat. They were happy with the arrangement and, when workshop problems entered the conversation, they proposed we build them a potential caretakers cottage that David could use as a studio, while in the meantime he could set himself up in the basement.

Following months meticulously crafting a desk and chair for the Winstones Craft Biennale competition, we drove to Auckland hopeful of winning the ten-thousand-dollar prize that would transform our lives. At the opening the judge proclaimed the desk an equal to the seductive glass bowl that he had chosen for its primal appeal. Totally bereft we visited Roger the Rogue, who cooked us a roast dinner in his bachelor pad. Following reminiscing about the Caribbean and Catherine, we realised that his invitation did not include an overnight so, confirming that *"We are staying just around the corner,"* we drove to a quiet back street and bedded down in Beatrice with David, Billy, and I bunking in the back while Sam stretched across the front seat. Awakening to the crisp light of a Remuera dawn, we rearranged our crumpled clothes and joined the throng of those who had slept in real beds. After buying a bandsaw, circular saw, and planer, we started home laden with heavy machinery and sleeping children. All was well until Beatrice's headlights faltered as we drove the winding back road. Fortunately, they ignited again, but half a mile from Smugglers Point we were plunged into total darkness. Clambering out, I ran in front, illuminating the rough road with a torch. We set up the machines in the cramped basement, then David started making a chess table from pōhutakawa and kauri while Billy carved a rhinoceros to accompany his camel and giraffe.

One weekend the Balls came up and we set to staining the weatherboard exterior, listening to a tape of Laurie Lee's *Cider with Rosie*, Don Ball striding about in gumboots directing the kids as they sloshed shit green stain at the walls. Literature and fine wine had become Winnie's tactic for managing his jolly jamborees. Maybe it was the appalling sight of Ball's belly bursting free from the buttons of a lawyer's shirt which had delivered its last writ that prompted Winnie's retreat into a bucolic haze where, oblivious to the campaign being waged, her mind wandered the lanes of pastoral England, lonely as a cloud. While Winnie had no need to take risks, her sharp quips indicated that she had chosen to abstain from the proceedings of her life, wearing subtle shades of tailored linen, the uniform of those middle class, middle aged women, who aspired for elegance and achieved atrophy.

Our only means of escape to the islands was a South Pacific party. After decorating Smugglers Point with foliage and woven mats, our friends arrived wearing grass skirts and lava lavas, for a feast, vigorous dancing, and fireworks. It was a brief intermission. While the tranquillity of David's makeshift workshop made up for its limitations, selling his furniture was a mission and when promised commissions came to nothing he decided to create a new piece. He began where his carvings left off, creating a sculptural chair with a triangular seat of pale matai, suspended on a frame of dark rosewood. When the Auckland War Memorial Museum purchased the *Pacific Seat* for their permanent collection it marked a turning point. However, despite David's growing reputation, we remained temporary residents and when immigration demanded that Brad guarantee that he would employ David on a minimum wage of eighteen thousand dollars a year, we wondered if we would ever be free of our nemesis.

As spring drifted into summer we prepared to repaint Hornpipe's interior, ripping up floorboards to find that spongy sawdust left over from her construction had seriously eroded the steel hull. David began chipping rust in the forward cabin and when the ring-ding of his hammer was interrupted with a volley of expletives I knew something was up. He yelled, *"Linda, come here a minute!"* and I was there in a flash, expecting a bloody thumb. Then he quietly said, *"Just put your finger there,"* removing his to expose an oozing hollow that defined its every intention of sinking our ship. I plugged my finger into the blue lens and David rowed ashore in search of something to bodge the hole. As I applied pressure my mind ranged through a script of possibilities, *"What if David never came back? If that overflowing puddle became a gushing geyser would I have the guts to rouse Obelix and run Hornpipe onto the mud flats to prevent her sinking?"* At last David returned with a plug of epoxy putty and a wooden wedge that clamped over the leak. While our days overflowed with preparations for that vital haul out, sleep conjured vivid projections of sunken wrecks. Then in late November, David received funding to attend a craft conference in Canberra which he could not resist. And while I kept watch on the primitive patch that held our home together, he stayed with the Cyclone family and interacted with likeminded people.

On David's return, we embarked on a harrowing haul out, contorting for endless hours of grinding, spraying our faces and bodies with stinging particles of steel, patching the hole and finding others. Bouncer hated those times. He had just finished stringing a perfect, symmetrical web with the promise of good hunting and feasts to follow when the lapping waves were silenced, his ears shattered by the sound of shrieking metal. Before long, the sticky strands of his glittering web were black with dust, visible for every Tom, Dick, and Harry of a fly to gloat over. Soon those naughty insects would be bouncing on its wondrously crafted centre, and there would be lean times for Bouncer as he waited for the dust to settle. Meanwhile we toiled through long days when, despite wearing breathing apparatus our heads reeled with the toxic epoxy. Finally, when antifouling the hull, David fell from the ladder and cracked his ribs. The job had to be finished so he suffered the shock and pain. It was long after dark when, on driving home, Beatrice sprung a puncture. The following morning she sustained another and it was then we remembered that, in our hurried departure, we had forgotten to close a sea cock. With the yard due to launch, our only option was to pump air into the bald tyre, and race onward, with a hope of reaching Hornpipe in time. Our yacht was already in the air when we scrambled on board to the crane operator's shout, *"She'll be right! We could have launched Hornpipe without you."*

Following a day of cleaning Hornpipe's filthy interior we moved out of Smugglers Point, driving away as the Balls rolled up, their Land Rover overflowing with fine food and expensive alcohol. After a frenzied shopping spree, we motored to Russell where we had hidden Sam and Billy's present. And at dead of night, while I rowed the Scarlet Pimpernel out through the waves, Father Christmas wrote a letter in shaky handwriting, drawing his reindeer sledge flying through the sky with the Optimist in tow. Then we sailed to Deep Water Cove for our annual walk to the lighthouse, before anchoring in Dicks Bay for my job at the Jack and Jill's campsite. David resumed painting the deck and engine room while Sam and Billy raced their Optimist with the boys who regularly camped on the nearby point, never imagining that in years to come Pug would exhibit alongside David in Milan. And between renting out the campsite's watercraft I wrote to my man, *"Way out by the boat I see three butterfly wings, as the Optimist sails drift quietly, or so it would seem. Everything looks tranquil, but no doubt the still air is full of chatter. In the midst, you are transforming Hornpipe, fixing those broken things we've lived with so long. It's good and honest to respect what we have instead of greedily using up the world's gifts, but it's slow, humbling work, and what others call patience is just another word for endurance, and skills that are almost redundant in our society. And in all this I guess I am just trying to say thank you for all that you do."*

On one of those carefree weekends of diving, swimming, and windsurfing, Billy rowed Jolly Boat to win a race at Urupukapuka Island's fun day. His determination never diminished and as he grew bigger, the boats became smaller. At university, he would train in single sculls, moving on when his initial enthusiasm had dissolved, eventually finding freediving. He created a career teaching the complex techniques in both English and Italian, running courses in Europe and the Bahamas where the locals welcomed him as their own, saying, *"William's a Bahamian now."* But legal acceptance takes time for those living an alternative lifestyle. Following two uncertain years our New Zealand passports arrived, stamped with resident visas, and the next morning we awoke to see a family waving from the shore. Al and Jill with their children Dan, Jo, and Ami had emigrated from England and when they explained how easy it had been, it cast a new perspective on our passage halfway around the world and the challenges of proving our worth. I remembered that Billy had been a baby when Al last visited us on Tormentil with Pete and Hank in tow, that on seeing the alcohol they hauled aboard I had worried about them sinking our boat – by mistake, or just for the hell of it.

Then Cyclone Bola hit our bay with fearsome gusts that swung Hornpipe from side to side. While Sam and Billy retreated into a game we rowed ashore to secure Smugglers Point's gable windows that were threatening to implode. Then I helped David complete a furniture commission before our long-awaited visit to England and cruise to New Caledonia and Vanuatu. Before leaving we sought out a British couple to enquire about the radar they had mounted on their yacht's mast. Betty had just made flapjacks and when she and Robert invited us for coffee it was the start of a friendship that would transform our lives. Shortly after, Catherine and Roger visited us for a weekend and, while she was elusive as ever, his ardour had not diminished. Years passed before a surprise phone call, *"Ahoy Hornpipers, Roger here! Not so good, cancer you know! Any news of Catherine? No, me neither, but I'll catch up with her!"* Years passed before a surprise phone call, *"Ahoy Hornpipers, Roger here! Not so good, cancer you know! Any news of*

Catherine? No, me neither, but I'll catch up with her!" And we thought that this was Roger the Rogue's final volley, until an answerphone message, that same unfaltering voice announcing across the ether. *"This is Roger: Romeo-Oscar-Golf-Uniform-Echo;* a ghost from a long forgotten past, entering our world as though it was yesterday once more.

In early May, we left our friend Christine in charge of Hornpipe and drove Beatrice to Auckland to deliver a table for Al and Jill, before flying to England with my parents paying. Determined not to miss a thing, Sam remained awake, while Billy sprawled across our recumbent forms. Two days later, after long waits in Hawaii, Los Angeles, and New York, we arrived in London smelling like kippers, having spent the final leg in the plane's smoking compartment. With our floral cottons and belongings in striped laundry bags, we looked like an island family and as we wandered into the British night I shivered with exhaustion. When a portly middle-aged man hailed us, I wondered, could this be my brother? After hugging my parents and telling our stories I curled into my familiar bed and all the adventures melted away. Then began a round of visits to castles, museums, and zoos with Sam and Billy lapping up the attention and cultural entertainments. But how could we repay my generous parents when parking a car cost more than a day's wage? Driving north to visit old places and friends was like moving unseen in a crowd. Reggie our yachting companion relished our company and on discussing the futility of teaching our boys to tidy their rooms his comment, *"Are you educating them to be cleaners or executives? Be pleased they are intelligent enough to avoid mundane jobs,"* made me think. Following heart-breaking goodbyes to my parents we journeyed south to the Isle of Wight, where we wandered the forlorn tourist sites with David's mother. On briefly meeting my yoga teacher in London, I felt that he alone understood why we had shed our past. And then we flew away, but not before Sam and Billy had sat in the pilot seat of Pan Am plane Maid of the Seas, that would explode over Lockerbie some seven months later. Then on to Hawaii to visit Polly and a familiar tropical lifestyle, never realising her fairytale romance was doomed, and after retracing our passage over the Pacific Ocean we landed in New Zealand ready for new adventures.

A WING AND A PRAYER

"*I dreamed a glimpse of sapphire blue*
in the wave's crest
a sea bird's wing
the star's trail
a wish come true."

Linda Trubridge

Winter was cold and damp on the boat. Night mists chilled our bodies and condensation ran down the walls as we prepared Hornpipe for the passage to New Caledonia and Vanuatu. While I sewed a lifeboat cover for Jolly Boat, David set up our new radar and then Claire returned, bringing me a copy of Jung's *Man and His Symbols*, inscribed, "*To Linda, I never dreamed I would deliver this to you in person. You instigate miracles.*"

On the eighth of July, we sailed for Whale Bay and on to Whangaroa Harbour where we waited for the fresh northerlies to abate. The following evening we hoisted Hornpipe's sails and switching on her radar, sailed out through the narrow heads into a choppy sea. As the gathering gloom of seasickness crept over me, I tried a new drug, devised by a trio of sailing doctors who had explored the connection between the symptoms of motion sickness and middle ear infections. As the Stugeron took effect my nausea relented; at last I was free to enjoy sailing. When the wind shifted to north east we wondered if a front was coming but despite our concern, Hornpipe's reefed mainsail set a rapid pace. Suddenly a powerful light beamed close on our port bow and where we should have been way out to sea our chart indicated that it could only be the North

Cape Lighthouse. With no clue as to how we had strayed so close to land we abruptly changed course.

The following day the wind eased and the children forgot about nausea as they tore open a huge package from the New Zealand Correspondence School, thoroughly appreciating the novel assignments. Rain had smoothed the sea to a consistent swell, but we were still playing cat and mouse with the front and as night fell the squalls died, leaving us intermittently motoring or sailing a port tack. Eventually the wind settled and by noon of the thirteenth of July we had reached half way. Despite making rapid progress our course discrepancies were a concern, especially when the day proved too overcast for a navigational fix. As night fell the only stars were those in the phosphorescent ocean and when persistent clouds obscured the following day's noon fix David turned to a book Reggie had given us, David Burch's *Emergency Navigation: how to find out where you are and get where you want to go without compass, sextant, or electronic instruments.* The forward by our mentor, Doctor David Lewis, boldly stated, *"This is the book you need when all else fails."* And it was proving true. As David grappled with our course deviations he became distant and uncommunicative but eventually he identified our problem; that welding the metal bar along Hornpipe's scuppers had compromised her compass magnetism. Although we had re-swung the compass to correct upright deviations we had not considered the heading would be dramatically altered when our yacht heeled. It was reassuring to know we could maintain our course by observing the waves, swell, sun, and stars, but anticipating negotiating a route through the shallow banks off New Caledonia's Isle of Pines made for sleepless nights.

The uncertainties had triggered my anxiety. At such times I inadvertently invested random acts with a deeper significance, and as I steered by the stars I searched for something to hang my hopes on. When a blazing light flashed across the sky it left a trail of wishes and a poem that played over in my mind. I found myself repeating the comforting words of worship I had learned as a child. I remember a friend showing me her illuminated Mary and Jesus statues, that I had said, *"I will make my own choices about what I believe."* While David decries his religious upbringing, I retain a sense of something beyond our being, and when fear overwhelms me, Om Shanti, the primal vibration of creation brings comfort. Although we had avoided imposing our beliefs on our children, I wondered whether they craved reassurance and hoped that on finding themselves on the brink of despair, they would find the strength to overcome their challenges, to find a peace beyond comprehension.

It was a thousand miles to Isle of Pines. Most of the trip was bad weather the Passage.

Sailing to the Isle of Pines ST

It was a relief when the morning of the fifteenth dawned clear and once David had calculated his sight of Venus we had the security of knowing where we were. Everyone felt better. Billy and Sam persevered with school work, while Hornpipe flew with her sails goose-winged, climbing mountainous waves, plunging into valleys of water; rising and falling, riding the ocean's roller coaster. As for David's harness! Raising the stanchions had somewhat dissolved my fear, the company of another woman balanced our energies and time had tamed the tiger. Some decades later I would learn that a new generation of Aotearoa's tangata whenua *waka* sailors had replaced the word harness for *whenua*, implying an umbilical cord connection to the earth. Would a meaningful terminology have defused our battle? Could David, or anyone, question the value in maintaining a bond to the mother vessel, to life itself?

With Hornpipe on an even keel I opened our food cupboard to discover that our wheels of Dutch cheese were going rancid. After hanging them in nets where a cooling breeze would dry them I lifted the bilge hatch to find that our onions and potatoes were rotting. We had no option but to drag the sacks of vegetables into the fresh air, to turn them loose to roll around the cockpit, creating an additional obstacle course. By midnight the high seas and strong wind had escalated into vicious squalls that prompted David to drop his trousers and hurl them overboard. Although I suspect that my man had hoped to dissolve our fears in laughter, his profanity was no less crazy than my private prayers.

David's bottom failed to impress Neptune, for during the night tumultuous seas and a howling wind forced us to reduce canvas to the staysail and storm jib. His dawn star fix had thrown no light on our proximity to the treacherous Torch Bank which lay between us and the Isle of Pines. I steered for most of the day, leaving David free to navigate, while Claire, who could not manage the helm in challenging conditions, cooked simple meals for hostile weather: beans on toast, spaghetti, stew, and mash. My man and I were already spent as we entered yet another wild night, standing endless hours tethered to the steering column, encased in yellow oilskin, eyes fixed on a star, taut as Hornpipe's canvas; a vigil that was only relieved by forays onto the deck. There we wrestled with ropes and rigging as, falsely secure within the spreaders' circle of light we barely noticed the unfathomable inky chasm beyond and below. And on releasing the sails, our bird of the night spread her wings to fly through the black sky. Sometime later, Claire abandoned her forward bunk and stumbled into the cockpit, announcing, "*Sometimes I'm airborne!*" And while her logbook entry summed it up as, *"THE ULTIMATE EXISTENTIAL EXPERIENCE!"* when Claire confessed to wearing her raincoat and boots in bed, I recognised anxiety in her bravado.

Days of vague navigation had heightened our physical and emotional exhaustion but Claire achieved a small miracle in the pitching galley, cooking apple fritters with a gentle sweet taste that bolstered our energy for whatever lay ahead. By dawn the clouds had dissolved, however the star fix we needed to estimate our precise position from the Torch Bank was vague. Approaching New Caledonia's treacherous reefs would be disastrous after dark. We must reach land that day. Choosing speed, we reset our mainsail to balance the poled genoa and headed downwind at a wild eight knots and at nine thirty the hazy line of the Isle of Pines emerged from the ocean. David stood at the bow, scanning the ragged waves that reared up to claw the broken horizon, seeking the Torch Bank, muttering, *"Where is it? Where is it?"* throwing arms wide in his all too familiar gesture of despair.

Our reckless flight filled me with terror. I gripped the helm and sensed the sails pulling us towards the Torch Bank's treacherous shallows. How much worse could that turbulent sea become before we foundered? Was this the moment; would we end that day drifting in Jolly Boat, victims of the treacherous waves? I hardly breathed as my toes recoiled, knees folded in dread of those coral jaws tearing at Hornpipe's hull. I had no choice but to power on, eyes raw from staring into that terrible unknown. My mouth was too dry to pray, yet I clung to the wheel, holding firm as I had through the days and nights of that seemingly endless passage. Meanwhile David hung onto the pulpit of our bucking boat, scanning the seascape. He was debating whether to drop the mainsail and make a more tentative approach, when a sound in the sky caught his attention. A speck of an aeroplane sparkled in the sunshine; a shining avatar of hope. Scrambling for the VHF he called up the pilot and asked where the Torch Bank was. And a precise French voice resounded through the ether, "*You 'ave passed the area of worst water.*" It was a voice from heaven. Whatever and wherever the Torch Bank was, fate had allowed us to pass over to the other side.

It was midday when we reset the mainsail to continue our cracking downwind pace north towards the haphazard graffiti of land. As we slid along the island's eastern profile the waves dispersed and by four o'clock we were anchored in Ugo Bay. The rigorous trip had challenged us all. David and I had steered and navigated through days and nights, had huddled in the cockpit grasping for brief moments of sleep. Sam and Billy had quietly occupied themselves while Claire sustained us all with hot meals. Hornpipe had heroically born us through the area of worst water. The greater torment had been that lack of knowing whether the situation would relent or become worse and we rated those hours surging towards the Isle of Pines as our most anxious. Since that day, whenever overwhelmed by physical or emotional challenges, I find myself wishing for a plane to metaphorically fly overhead to indicate when the crisis, *the area of worst water,* has passed.

The passage had dissolved into a wish come true. Five exhausted bodies plopped into the turquoise sea, to float suspended in light, and as we rocked in our bunks, held in Hornpipe's embrace, we dreamed the sleep of heroes. Waking, we registered the white sandspits of land coiffed with the Araucaria pines that had given the Isle of Pines their name. Then we sailed on a favourable wind and current that thrust us through the Havannah Passage and on to Nouméa. Claire explored Prony Reef with us before flying home and when rain and strong easterlies trapped us in the noisy capital we visited the aquarium and museum. Then we motor-sailed to Port Epic and on to Port Ouen, where while teaching Sam and Billy to windsurf we met Ian and Cathy who were cruising with their kids Rosemary and Buster on yacht Saltheart. On the eighth of August, we returned to the Isle of Pines, Kuto Bay. There we established a lazy routine with the children completing their school work before breakfast, leaving the day free to construct race tracks for hermit crabs and play beach boulle with coconuts. On finding a scrubby pen enclosing baby turtles they released the captives, clearing a path through the sand, whispering encouragements to urge them towards the ocean and although we wholeheartedly endorsed their action, concerns that the turtles represented a local's livelihood led to us moving on to avoid trouble.

Helping the big hawksbill to freedom

Titches sorrowful face.

Neptunes hand reached out to take Bealey from the grasps of man

Freeing the turtles ST

One afternoon we walked up Pic N'ga to look out over the translucent coral sea. David was scrambling beneath a scrubby bush to escape the savage sun when a long thorn stabbed his ear drum. Fearing permanent damage, he tried to keep out of the water but when our friends on Saltheart and Catriona M joined us, the temptation to dive became too great. On a hunter gatherer binge we scoured the islands for heart of palm and coconuts, the reefs for clams, to enjoy a beach barbecue until waves and a surge of yellow and black sea snakes engulfed the flames. One afternoon we borrowed Saltheart's tiny windsurfer to fly in the wind and dance with the waves. Three yachts sailed to Nokanhui atoll and after strategising a way through the shallow pass, keels scraped and nerves frayed, however we all made it through to anchor beside a sand bank for another crazy barbecue. Those were carefree times with Billy rowing over to visit Rosie on Saltheart, David and Ian night diving the luminescent coral for lobsters. Departing, we raced the zany Aussies to Îlot Brosse, before borrowing their bikes to visit the ruins of a prison that had been built to incarcerate captives of the French revolution. The following day we hitched to an unassuming clump of trees and followed directions through the jungle to where a tumble of rocks and creepers revealed a gloomy limestone cavern. Blindly groping our way, we blundered into glistening stalactite fingers, squandering thousands of years of petrified droplets. Then, lacking torches to venture further, we stumbled out into sparkling sunlight and clouds of fluttering butterflies.

August had slipped into September and when Saltheart departed we set out to explore the island, skimming on a rising tide into Gadgi's maze of waterways. The sheltered reefs were perfect for the children to sail their Optimist, for us to enjoy our own company while repainting Hornpipe's topsides. The weather was disappointingly cooler than the more northerly Pacific Islands and, despite wearing a wetsuit, I was chilly. However, this did not stop me windsurfing in the ideal conditions, and with the consistent wind and shallow water, after endless repetitions David achieved a water-start. Together we made a family board game based on the idea of cruising the Isle of Pines, with participants throwing a dice to designate tide and wind direction. At anchorages, the model yachts were awarded nature resource cards of shells, fruit, rocks, birds, and fish. Along the way they encountered penalty *sea snake cards* that Sam illustrated with zany cartoons, *"Magic motor use once – Idiot crew arrives"* etc. Creating the game added an extra dimension to our sailing venture, fond memories when played in land locked habitations on Christmases to come.

Despite posting the kids' assignments to Wellington, a lack of response from the Correspondence School made us fear they had been lost. However, despite investing so much creativity into their projects Sam and Billy didn't seem to care. On completing their school work, they headed for the beach, and one day they became so engrossed in building an obstacle course for hermit crabs that seven hours passed before they appeared for food. Friends through thick and thin, one day something set them arguing, and we banished them to the shore, where they stubbornly, separately began excavating a limestone overhang. At some point their tunnels met and, caught up in the momentum of the activity, they forgot their disagreement. A beach was neutral territory, with no pressures or possessions; a space where arguments and animosities were irrelevant, a playground that would seemingly be there forever.

On my birthday the children made breakfast and decorated the boat with flowers and foliage. Sam on his eleventh birthday revealed a maturing sensitivity as he opened his gifts, followed by homemade croissants and yoghurt. Never tiring of the sun and sea, we sailed Jolly Boat out for a picnic on a sandbank and an epic dive which became a heart pounding escapade for David when, on spearing an enormous grouper, a shark gave chase. After a harrowing escape that wrecked his spear, a stocky local appeared, rowing towards us, beaming a radiant smile. The Kanak was not much taller than our kids with a shock of fuzzy hair and skimpy leopard patterned shorts that made us think of Mowgli from the *Jungle Book*. Following an invitation for birthday cake Geoffrey established himself as Sam's friend, *"Mon copain."* Taking advantage of the moonlight, David and Geoffrey caught five big coconut crabs that we kept in the wash tub for later consumption. The following day we all sailed to Gadji in Jolly Boat and while the children played around Geoffrey's thatched hut David and I rode his decrepit bikes to retrieve our post. Our friend accompanied us when we made our way back to Nouméa, following the inaccurate chart through the reefs and spending a sleepless night setting anchors in the dark. Although Geoffrey was a bubbly guest, joking with the children, repeatedly playing Bob Marley's *No Woman, No Cry*, we were relieved at being alone again. After rectifying the compass' heeling error, we visited Martine and Benoit, who had been Sam and Billy's hero since his legendary twenty-seven metre dives in the Tuamotus; we found they had exchanged their adventurous life for parenthood, Chrysalis for a house in the suburbs.

On the first of October, we cleared immigration and sailed to Baie de Prony and Aiguille where we dived on an eerie pinnacle that projected from a great depth. Anchoring in the Bay of Carenage we ventured up a river that tumbled to the sea. David photographed us luxuriating in the waterfalls, capturing Billy asleep in a bubbling pool, curled in an angelic foetal position that now seems a premonition of his future. Billy could sleep anywhere, any time. On a school camp, he had fallen from a top bunk and when his teacher roused him, he had no comprehension that he was asleep on the ground. Sailing on to Rada de L'Est, we climbed a muddy track to the lighthouse, to gaze one last time over the Isle of

Pines, before motoring through the Havannah passage for an overnight sail towards the Loyalty Island of Lifou. After picking up the blip on our radar we drifted along the coast to Cap Lefevre and beat into the wide bay to anchor off the straggling habitation of Gaitcha. David and I slept until midday before venturing ashore to marvel at the carvings in the little village church and on stopping to talk to the locals they wrapped a fish in leaves and threw it on the embers of a fire. As darkness fell we munched the gritty flesh, pulling bones, leaves, and charcoal from our mouths as we combined eating with the islanders' natural dental care. Following an early night, David roused me at three thirty to set off around Cape Aime, reefing our mainsail in a brisk north easterly. A noon wind shift set us on a close reach with boisterous waves pounding against Hornpipe's hull, raining down into the cockpit. Then, despite a fickle wind and concerns about reaching land before dark, the day concluded with a fast reach into Port Vila.

After clearing customs and a reunion with Saltheart and Catriona M, we introduced them to the *Isle of Pines* game. However, a minor scratch on David's foot had flared into a reoccurrence of the staph infection that had plagued him in the Tuamotus and when the inflammation proved unresponsive to regular antibiotics, the hospital administered an injection and insisted we remain in Port Vila until it improved. Meanwhile we immersed ourselves in the museum where displays of ethnic craft and cultural videos taught us about Vanuatu's scattered islands which their British and French colonists had named the New Hebrides, before they claimed their independence. We discovered that the islanders, with their hundreds of regional languages, had evolved a pidgin communication called Bislama. Their long descriptive phrases rendered a bra as, *"Basket blong titi"* a piano became, *"Bigfala bokis-Yu kilim emi singalot."* While *"Kilim"* implied hitting, *"kilim he ded,"* indicated total annihilation.

When David's infection subsided we joined Saltheart at Hideaway Island, and when the anchor slid down the sandy ledge into deep water, David and I had to haul it together, tearing muscles and backs as we clawed up the combined weights of anchor and chain. Collapsing on the beach, we sipped icy cocktails, watching Sam and Billy play volleyball and dance with the Vanuatuans. And on their suggestion, we rowed Jolly Boat up through the milky pools of a nearby river that reminded me of a winding chasm that I had followed to the source of a river in Jamaica. When David's foot healed, we sailed north for Pélé, Nguna, and Emae Islands, briefly stopping at Moso Island off Efate's northwest coast, before ploughing into steep seas and a forty-knot wind that funnelled through a treacherous channel. The relatively recent volcanic islands had no protective reefs and few sheltered bays however, on finding a safe anchorage off the coast of Havannah we enjoyed days of windsurfing and diving. It seemed that the Vanuatuans preferred trading for usable items, so I exchanged five new shirts and shorts for a handmade model of an outrigger. And as David wove hats the children resumed a routine of schoolwork with a playful activity that evolved into a diving competition, where they swum to the ocean floor and spun upward with a handful of sand or stones as proof of their prowess. Surfacing with lungs bursting they climbed on board to switch on the depth sounder and discover what they had achieved. Being equally determined, neither claimed supremacy, nor did they forget the depths they reached, and William recalled, *"Our frenzied spurts took us to fourteen metres at ages eight and eleven, and our father could disentangle an anchor at twenty metres (all facts we proudly wore like badges in conversations with other boating kids)."* William would eventually go beyond everyone in this athletic discipline, composing a simple poem reminiscent of those childhood aspirations.

3oo feet under the sea

2 bare feet

1 breath

With no other contender for his world record in constant weight without fins, William decided to take his discipline to ninety metres, and in December 2009 he fulfilled his promise when, on a single breath, he dived with bare feet to a depth equalling three hundred feet.

When the weather scuttled our attempts at meeting Saltheart, we sailed to northern Efate, where we anchored off the village of Kakula and went for a dive. Becoming cold I swam home alone but, as I glided over the rippled sandscape, I became aware of two huge shapes crossing my path, a few metres below. Although almost sure the sharks were benign, my heart was pounding fit to burst as, willing myself to ignore their presence I continued swimming. Next day we sailed Jolly Boat to Tikilasoa village on Nguna Island where a meeting house shaped as a huge upturned canoe rested amongst the humble huts. As we wandered a path beneath flowering trees, we gathered a gaggle of children who chattered about their aspirations of becoming Olympic athletes. They showed us their school and challenged Sam and Billy to a game of football, with language no barrier to having fun. Then, having seen that the locals had few possessions, our kids gathered a bag of toys and carried them to the schoolteacher, who insisted on playing the board games to learn the rules.

Sailing on beside the hazy coast of Epi we hooked a mahi mahi, but on hauling it aboard, David's thin skin sustained yet another savage cut. Beset with a depressing foreboding of infection, we went ashore to explore a disused plantation, and it was there that a gaggle of girls begged us to take them out to the boat. When a scrawny woman demanded a dress I resisted and despite having given away most of my clothes, I regret that lack of generosity. After a hasty lunch we sailed downwind to Malekula, sighting misty views of Lopevi, hooking another mahi mahi, and ripping our worn mainsail from luff to leach as we gybed in a strong wind off Port Sandwich. The murky bay was surrounded with dense jungle and as we passed a couple on a yacht they shouted a, *"Don't go in the water,"* warning that the bay was notorious for shark attacks, that a baby had been taken from its mother's arms as she fished from a dugout. On learning the locals habitually slaughtered cattle at the water's edge, it seemed that news of the bloody banquets had reached the shark community. Ironically, when hanging the washing, my best sheet blew overboard and while it was not worth reclaiming it from the sinister depths, we dreaded fouling our anchor, the dilemma of whether we would retrieve or abandon that vital piece of equipment.

It was unusual for us to spend even a day out of the water but Sam and Billy found other ways to have fun, paddling outrigger canoes with the local children, while David and I rowed ashore to embark on an extensive mainsail repair. Chickens had roosted in the rafters of the dusty copra shed where we set up my sailmaker's sewing machine. After sweeping the floor we dragged out the heavy canvas and while he fed the material to me I operated the hand crank and guided the needle along the tear. Once we had washed off the chicken shit and cleated the sail to Hornpipe's mast, we felt proud of having completed a major repair in primitive conditions. When Saltheart and Catriona M unexpectedly arrived, we walked up to the plateau of Lamap village to watch a football match played against a magnificent backdrop and that evening we braved heavy rain to light a reluctant bonfire and soggy fireworks, for an incongruous Guy Fawkes night, followed with a final game of *Isle of Pines*.

Hugging farewells, we escaped the oppressive bay and sailed for Port Vila. Spreading her sails Hornpipe soared over the midnight sea. The jewelled heavens mirrored a glittering gown of phosphorescence and I lay on the cabin roof, wrapped in a blanket, keeping watch over my loved ones asleep on the ocean. I felt that momentary hesitation as Hornpipe gathered herself in the troughs, a quivering shudder as she surged over the swells. Hypnotised by her swaying mast, I momentarily slipped into a dream, shaking myself awake only to surrender again to the limpid night. Entering a timeless realm of visions, I held tight to a single star, a fragment of light that watched over us, showing the way. Hovering on the margins of consciousness, mesmerised by the whispered lullaby of creaking ropes and rippling canvas, it seemed that I sailed through an eternity of galaxies and stars; on and on over oceans of sky, through waves of fluid light that swept against cosmic shores. And when I could no longer resist, I called David to his watch. Succumbing to dreams I drifted into sleep, saving that sensation of sailing amongst the stars, a memory of what it is to be one with the infinite universe.

As the night progressed, David guided us around Eradaka (Retoka) Island to Devil Point and by dawn we were anchored in Port Vila where a letter informed us that our sail-maker friend, Claire Jones, was eager to crew on our return passage. Having heard of an abandoned plantation we ventured inland; the children climbed the palms gathering hordes of coconuts. But while scrambling through the foliage I had brushed against a toxic plant and following a feverish night, the locals sympathetically explained that there was no cure; that the burning rash would last seven to ten days. On returning to town the children blew their savings on a much-anticipated scuba dive. But being accustomed to swimming down to thirty or forty feet without tanks, they were bitterly disappointed with the shallow dive. After challenging the instructor, he agreed to David taking them out in the harbour, when having known the freedom of unassisted diving the tanks still felt cumbersomely unnatural, an experience that our kids never repeated.

Claire arrived ready for an adventure and we set sail into a heavy squall, followed by calms. After motoring past Erromango, dawn yielded a gentle

'We rise slowly and steadily upwards from the depths' ST

south westerly breeze. Hoisting our sails, we were drifting on a silken sea laced with algae when the tranquillity was interrupted by the buzz of a fish on the line. Once we had reeled in the bonito we randomly threw out the lure and had started preparing a late breakfast when the line spun again. Even from a distance we could see this was a huge fish. On hauling in the creature, we saw it jump and, recognising the unmistakable marlinspike, David could only think of the strained muscles and torn flesh that would be incurred in hauling it on board. Shaking his head, he said, *"There's no way we can handle a marlin."* But as I wound in the line the huge fish appeared docile and when it came alongside David grasped it by the bill. *"You can do it,"* I encouraged. *"You must be crazy!"* he retorted. But I persisted, *"Go on, give it a try."* What was I thinking, I who was so cautious? David started swinging its great body from side to side, with a slow pendulum momentum that culminated in a heroic lift, up and over the railing, onto the deck. There was no fight from the Marlin, and we motored on, debating what to do with all the fish. As a south-easterly sprung up we sailed again and when a billowing cloud appeared over the horizon, we presumed that it was the usual cloud that hovered over an island, before realising it was sulphurous smoke emanating from Tanna's volcano. On entering Port Resolution bBay, named after Captain Cook's ship, we encountered a local paddling a dugout with a little boy in the front. Charlie introduced himself and after forming a shy friendship we lowered the marlin into his canoe for him to share with his community. And that night we all feasted in the orange glow of the volcano that reflected off the clouds like the lights of a great city.

When we visited the tiny village of Malepouri and enquired about climbing the volcano we learned that a dugong inhabited the bay and, on consulting our book of marine creatures, we learned that, "*a dugong is a most friendly sea creature.*" So, Billy, Sam, and Claire set off in search of the amiable sea cow. Although they found gorgonians, cowries, and a dangerous fire coral that could render a nasty burn, there was no sign of the dugong. They were returning to Hornpipe when what they had thought was a coral head made its move. When an elephantine beast with a drunken smile enthusiastically rubs its barnacled body against yours, it is alarming and, although the dugong's amorous advances were most likely the desperation of a solitary soul, our intrepid three did not wait to find out. They clambered onto the nearest coral which the dugong playfully circled until a passing local paddled them home in his dug-out. After listening to their story David was eager to engage with the zany beast so we rowed over and slipped in, to swim along its leathery girth that seemed to merge with the cloudy water. While he enjoyed the dugong's boisterous ways, it loomed too large and licentious for me and when we saw the locals hurling vegetables and small children at its thrashing bulk we realised how the lonely creature had developed its wayward habits.

After deliberating on how to reach the volcano, we set off accompanied by a gaggle of Vanuatuans, including a crooked youth who husked coconuts with his teeth. As the light faded we walked on with hopes of a volcanic light show. A violent thunderstorm sent us running to a tin shack where we shared our sandwiches with the gang and when the rain became torrential we retraced our steps, sloshing through rising streams with Sam relentlessly singing, "'*Excuse me sir' said the thousand-legged worm,*" while Billy hugged his intrepid Mickey Mouse. At last, as Sam reached his

We learned that 'a dugong is a most friendly sea creature' ST

two hundred and forty sixth verse, we arrived at our submerged dinghy and as David rowed home we swum through the darkness, completing the day with a hastily prepared shepherd's pie.

It was already the fifth of December when we motored towards Sulphur Bay for our second summit attempt, but as we rounded the headland we encountered a huge swell that would render anchoring impossible. Maybe our previous endeavours had proved us tough, for at this point Charlie agreed to guide us to Yasur from Port Resolution. After anchoring and rowing ashore, we started along a meandering path through verdant gardens. The way bustled with villagers who resembled the earthy yams that filled the baskets they bore on bent backs. Deep in the undergrowth we saw rotting camouflage tents and the rusted remains of a tank and Charlie told us of an American serviceman *John From* who, having remained to distribute the surplus supplies at the end of the Pacific war, had acquired a cult status, with the locals worshiping him and awaiting his return. Charlie and his wife Mary were government teachers proud of their cavernous classroom but when I asked whether they had many books they reticently replied, *"not really."* Following this, Sam and Billy gathered a bag of books they had outgrown and on seeing them Mary's eyes pooled with tears. Only then did they reveal that the school had been denied all teaching resources until the locals ceased their adulation of *John From*.

Our determined party strode through the jungle, skirting the volcano's flanks, goaded on by Yasur's rumbling. Eventually, blinking and bewildered, we stumbled from the luscious shade into a scorched gulley. Beyond that last battalion of burnt trees the barren scree slope angled towards a summit. Clambering up that splattered scoria of crusted clots and jagged clumps we imagined them gushing as molten lava from the fiery cauldron. Plumes of sulphurous smoke blackened the sky and our heads resonated with a roar that emanated from beneath our feet. Climbing higher, our fingers clawed that black pyramid, blood surged through our brains, our belief in a passive planet eroding with each sliding step. The children's minds were afire with visions of monsters and mayhem. At last, in breathless awe, our little group approached the rim, as one would a shrine. We stood on the brink, as insubstantial as a row of cut-out paper dolls, gazing over the crumbling edge at falling ashes rushing headlong to the depths, shuddering as we experienced our mother earth at her most primitive. Yasur's burning breath seared our throats as, with senses kindled and eyes dilated, we heard her groan: witnessed the womb of creation, heaven, and hell – felt the pulse of that subterranean ocean within our souls.

It was past four when, with scorched feet, we turned from the dread landscape to begin the long journey home. David and Billy ran down the scree slope while Claire, Sam, Charlie, and I plodded on our weary way. But once amongst the trees, the dappled light soothed and sustained us. Wandering that shadowy path we stepped aside for an old woman laden with a basket. On seeing Sam, she paused to lightly touch his golden curls and glowing face. She gazed in wonder at his radiant eyes and entreated, *"Remember me one time,"* her whisper a memory that would last forever. It seemed that mythological visions haunted those tracts. An ancient patriarch, whose sinewy body and flowing beard invoked the bestial image of William Blake's *Nebuchadnezzar,* passed so close I smelt the earth he inhabited. Dusk had deepened to darkness when our way opened to Resolution Bay. Flopping into the water we swam home to Hornpipe and dinner with Charlie, and on leaving I gave him a bag of rice and a tin of dried milk so that he could make more of the rice pudding that he adored.

Next day, as we nursed our aching bodies, Ronnie the chief appeared with a gift of vegetables and something on his mind. The words tumbled forth as he spoke of his friend John, how before returning to America he had said, *"You don't need to do anything, I will return with everything your people need."* Through the years, John's followers had awaited their saviour. Ronnie explained his concerns for John, how he had sent letters to the American embassy to no avail. He wondered why his friend and messiah had abandoned the people of Tanna, when he had promised so much. What could we say? As Ronnie talked, we found ourselves empathising with this dignified intelligent man who talked of history as though it was just yesterday that Captain Cook and the missionaries arrived, to tell the Vanuatuans that the God Jesus had died on a cross to solve their problems. But what use was a dead chief? John from America had given them trucks, tents and really useful things that must surely have come from heaven. How often had we wished we could load Hornpipe with society's discarded items, and distribute them to the Vanuatuans who had nothing? How easy it would be to make that promise without seeing that their lives were rich in simpler measures, or considering the effect our philanthropy might have. At Ronnie's sad conclusion that the government had even confiscated John's American flag, I inadvertently let slip that we had one. He could not have been more ecstatic if I had revealed that we had the Holy Grail hidden on board. I had acquired the faded flag at a jumble sale with the thought that it might serve as a bedspread and, as I went below to find it, I battled with the sense I was dabbling in something I knew little about. While I was gone Ronnie diplomatically asked David to change his shirt and wash his hands to prepare for the ritual. When I returned Ronnie was standing, head bowed in supplication, palms open to receive the folded flag and as he left with the precious bundle in a paper bag David looked at me shaking his head.

On the dawn of our departure we were awoken by a tap on Hornpipe's hull and when I emerged from the cabin Ronnie presented me an exquisite woven basket. Then he paddled away in his dugout leaving us wondering about our irresponsible action. On farewelling those brief friendships, we took with us lasting memories of the most exotic location and fragile people we had been privileged to know; a culture where we had been perceived as rich beyond compare. And as we set sail we wondered why we were returning to a society that sometimes treated us as vagabonds. On leaving, Charlie had asked us to take with us two young Vanuatuans who needed a lift to the neighbouring island of Aneityum. Those gentle boys with their soft black curls, wild eyes, and ragged shorts had no possessions other than a delicate thread of flowers one wore about his neck. They were as trusting and free as the day they were born. We knew nothing about them and our inability to communicate ensured we would forever remain a mystery to each other. An erratic headwind made for a frustratingly slow sail and it was already dusk when we arrived at

Anall-un-se Bay. The boys slept on deck, curled in blankets, and then we rowed them ashore, where they disappeared into the undergrowth of that seemingly deserted island.

After sailing south to Anelghowhat Bay we reluctantly prepared Hornpipe for the passage home, taking time off to explore, dive, and practise yoga. In the steady wind of that last day I managed a windsurfing water start and by the time we had dismantled the bimini and hoisted Jolly Boat on deck it was dark. Feeling too tired to launch into a night of sailing we postponed our departure. Then, wishing we could stay forever, we waved goodbye to white sandy beaches and set sail into a fresh easterly that propelled Hornpipe on a fast, close reach, to rapidly leave Aneityum in our wake. The erratic splashy sea sent us below to read, play chess, and sleep, with brief intermissions to eat. That night Billy stood watch for an hour, alone with the new moon, recording a characteristically cute, *"Hello Moon, Hello Stars,"* in the log. As Hornpipe raced into a squally thirteenth of December, Sam took his turn, countering with a dry, *"Nothing to report."*

Hornpipe was steaming along and on plotting the noon sight, David discovered we had covered a hundred and ninety-five miles in our first twenty-seven hours. After catching a big wahoo, we dedicated the afternoon to gutting and filleting fish. By Thursday the fifteenth of December we were half way home. We celebrated with a chocolate party and when the wind strengthened to a southerly, pulled on duffle coats and put the clock forward. Claire, who had squandered two cups of water on washing her hair, clambered on deck to reduce sail where she was boisterously baptised by Neptune. Later that afternoon we became conscious of a sloshing sound beneath the saloon and on lifting the hatch, I discovered the bilge was awash. Our captain jumped to the pump and I fished for the flotsam that surged on the swell of that captive sea. While we were fortunate that the soggy toilet rolls had not clogged the pump, I had been unforgivably stupid to store paper in the bilge. Hornpipe swooped and dived through the mountainous sea and as we pumped I wondered where all the water was coming from. Then, as our yacht lunged through a wave, David saw water gush in through her bilge outlet pipe and was struck with an immediate realisation. When renovating the pump, he must have reconnected the hoses in reverse order. At sea, thousands of actions go unnoticed, but one flaw has the potential to sink a ship. A simple oversight had led to us pumping the salty Pacific into our boat. Hornpipe shook her head and resolutely battled on over the ocean and once David had turned the pump back to a sensible configuration our sense of humour saved the day.

Claire's log book comment, *"Lulls in wind, Sea Yuk!"* said it all. But the cold, clear night heralded a tranquil dawn and as Hornpipe reverted to the aimless drift we knew so well, we progressively shook out her reefs and hoisted ever larger sails. At dusk on the eighteenth of December, a pod of dolphins and a glimpse of North Cape welcomed us home. After motoring through the night, a south easterly forced us to tack, but once we had passed the Cavallis we had an exuberant reach to the Bay of Islands, rounding sail rock with Sam and Billy blowing a fanfare on the fog horn and Triton's trumpet.

MAKING WAVES

"I am one of you
a vulture I have been
The falcon is my face
You'll see that I am more
I am one of all
all that we see as sacred
they are all in me
all of man's divinities
deceased I am from the mortal world
yet I resurrect in the depths below"
Aeternus Litany of Ra

LT

Claire had proved herself a heroic, fun companion and, although our first passage with an experienced crew had been stormy, we had been more relaxed. She walked home to her little house that overlooked the bay while, with Christmas looming on our horizon, we hastily prepared for a picnic at Roberton Island. On the day, we collected the Jones and Parker families from Russell pier and sailed into a stiff breeze that blew out our foresail. As we ate lunch Gayle said, *"It wouldn't be Christmas without an overdone turkey,"* referring to Al's English legs, which were looking festively florid and, indeed, his face well basted with sun cream was done to perfection. Al was a contrast to the robust Kiwis, whose perpetually tanned, buff bodies were at home in a singlet, shorts, and gumboots, no matter the weather.

The following day we battled to Waipiro Bay through an easterly gale that blew out our mainsail. Following a meeting with the Balls we decided to build their caretaker's cottage; to exchange our efforts for ten years of using it as a workshop. Mr Ball drew up a legal agreement which we all signed and, after welcoming in 1989 at a Smugglers Point party, we made a start. Building a two-story dwelling with a high-pitched roof perched on a clifftop was a dizzy task, but apart from a plank falling from the roof rendering an excruciating blow to my elbow, we remained intact. When the timbers framed the sky, we invited everyone within a stone's throw to a roof shout. Imagine our surprise on finding that most of our neighbours had never met, while despite our not owning property in the bay we knew them all. Although we worked efficiently, building consumed all of January, February, and March with no earnings, but thanks to Betty Lowe's secret instalments to purchase David's chess table for her husband Robert's birthday, we made it through the lean times. In early April, we installed the machines and tuck box. As the light faded, Bouncer ventured into the spacious studio, singing to himself, *"This is it. I'm here to stay,"* as he started weaving a new web.

Following the success of correspondence school, we requested that the children continue. After moving into Smugglers Point we established the attic as a schoolroom and when the stormy summer culminated in cyclone Delilah we had a comfortable place to live and work. One blowy day with nothing vital to accomplish, I drew a clump of trees that sinuously undulated in the wind, giving myself up to that intense focus that only creativity, meditation, or sex can fulfil. Spontaneity, plus the space to make a mess, presented a range of creative possibilities and after pulping paper in my friend's food processor, I sculpted the fragments into faces that emerged as through a mist.

While our children had always been receptive to music Sam's taste had evolved from Michael Jackson to the edgy Roger Waters, and the Beatles appealed to Billy's sunshine personality. On seeing him improvise on a piano, his hands caressing the keys, I resolved that he should learn; and bought him a portable keyboard that he carried on and off the boat and up to my friend Beate's for lessons. Although the kids longed for a pet our nomadic lifestyle thwarted a relationship with a dog or cat, so we bought guinea pigs and, despite Mr Ball's fury at

LT

their intrusive presence in a corner of his garden, Nutmeg, Gingernut, Walnut, and Peanut thrived on cuddles. As the Nut family multiplied Sam and Billy learned vital lessons, including the need for separate hutches, to prevent the males fighting. They invested their love of collecting things into assembling a museum above the studio, exhibiting the shells, rocks, and stamps that had expanded their knowledge of the world. Although we teased him about his broken glass and rusty nail collections Sam the magpie was captivated by textures and stories and in time would collage his foraged metal objects into sculptural figures. On one occasion Sam would become so absorbed in transforming metal detritus into muscles and sinews, he inadvertently welded his house key onto the torso of a squatting gimp, chained to a leaden book on which its typewriter key fingers had punched pages of philosophical passages titled *From Flesh to Steel*.

David enjoyed his independent workspace but occasionally, with a large piece of wood to cut or plane, he returned to rent the Dicks Bay workshop, where predictably he had to clear the abandoned barn, sharpen blades, and sand the rusty machines to render them usable. After being awarded an Arts Council grant he developed his *Pacific Seat* into what became the *Sail Chair.* The seat of this chair emulated the bellying sail of a Polynesian sailing canoe, with a frame that evoked the tensile strength of mast and rig to suggest a female-male, yin-yang, water and air relationship. While constructing and assembling the fragile frame David often called it the *Never Again Chair,* however he would create many more design interpretations. And on finding a pōhutukawa log washed up on Elliot's Beach he carved it into a powerful figurative base supporting a wing of lighter wood to form a seat.

Meanwhile I was working to maintain the house, help David with his furniture, and the children with their school assignments. Despite winning top prizes in English, maths, and art, their isolation gave them the impression they were not very accomplished. Although Sam's standards dropped when I relaxed, I now realise my encouraging advice often implied more could be done; that I should have simply said, "*That's wonderful, let's stop there.*" Years later, Billy would acknowledge my efforts in the kindest way, "*My mother, who hand-sewed stuffed animal toys, quilts, and costumes for my brother and me, who consummately praised us for whatever we did while propelling us to something greater, represented a distillation of altruism that inspires me to this day. By coaxing and encouraging us – to write it a little clearer, to paint it a little more attentively, to play it a little more fluidly – she taught me that there was always more inside: more creativity, more potential, more depth. Thanks to my mother, I believe in myself and the infinitude of our capacity at whatever we set our minds to.*"

The kids returned to Russell School for sports days where, despite being reprimanded for swimming underwater, Billy won all the prizes, with Sam achieving second, third, and fourth place. Sam punctuated his weeks with Scouts and, although we abhorred its military attitudes, the regular excursions nourished his independence. The wicked ways of their *Bad Boys Band* went no further than pelting each other with fruit and cutting steps in the cliffs, and after school and work we often gathered the gang for surfing at Elliot's Beach. Their enthusiasm for Dungeons and Dragons had gathered momentum, garnering a lecture on the sins of that "*Evil game,*" on asking the charity shop ladies if they had any books. However, the interactive gaming was a healthier preoccupation than television, and their fantasies evolved into exploring the wilderness beyond the house, cutting labyrinths in the rushes, stalking each other through the pine plantation as they visualised the castles and landscape of another world.

Billy still struggled to keep up with the older boys and I became concerned when in a school assignment he wrote that Mickey Mouse was his only friend. So we celebrated his ninth birthday with a big party. Races, spotlight dancing, and a treasure hunt were followed by a taste test with the blindfolded kids attempting to guess various herbs and spices. We quickly realised that our family's eating habits had widened Sam and Billy's taste. Years later, when William

Dragons ST

mysteriously lost this sense, investigations failed to reveal the cause or how he could retrieve his ability to discern salt from sweet, bitter, and sour. He never complained, continuing his alkaline, high-carbohydrate, vegetarian diet; abstaining from sugar, alcohol, or caffeine, valuing the aroma and texture of foods that reward him with some sensory pleasure.

On windy nights David walked to the cliff edge and shone a torch on Hornpipe or drove down the road to direct Beatrice's headlights over the bay to where our yacht rode the waves, straining at her anchor. The Ball's weekend visits often coincided with storms that made moving back and forth a frantic affair. While David travelled to Wellington for a mid-winter *Quality by Design Exhibition*, Dan, Jo, and Amy came for a holiday, to roam the countryside returning with stories of warfare with rival gangs and how Amy had fallen from a cliff to be saved by Billy grabbing her rope of hair. After wading through the mangroves they proudly presented me with filthy parore fish that tasted of mud and then, during a game of hide and seek, the hapless Jo fell from the roof. He had climbed out of the bathroom window when, losing his footing, he slid like a possum down the tiles to mercifully land in one piece. Although I fed and cared for them, their crazy schemes made me shudder and on spending a daily hour untangling Amy's Rapunzel locks I comprehended my mother's insistence on my practical bob, and recalled the secret pride I had felt when she described my hair as *"black as a raven's wing."* I had always cut my boys' hair and apart from Billy growing a rat's tail braid to a record six inches, we were unconcerned about appearances, until an exhibition opening made me realise we had no appropriate clothes.

Our friendship with Robert and Betty developed and despite their nine grandchildren they welcomed Sam and Billy as their own. They were an incongruous couple: Robert, tall and detached with a savage intellect, had retired from his vital role as Dean of a London Hospital where Betty had looked after him and everyone else. Although our children were far from their grandparents, the Lowes' warmth and wisdom invested them with respect for an older generation, and where familial relationships are often fraught with expectations, Betty's habit of spontaneously inviting us for *"a little bit of dinner that needs using up,"* was invariably a banquet. She bustled about, sensing everyone's needs, taking a mischievous delight in seeing our happy faces while Robert discussed issues with Sam and Billy as though they were adults. Acutely aware of the passing years, Robert prowled the house like a caged beast, forever planning new ventures. And although Betty would have been content with a quiet life, she supported them all, until he came up with the idea of making the first Pacific Northeast passage.

One stormy weekend when the Balls were up, the Lowes insisted we stay. They already had a full house when, unable to curb their generosity, David and I slept in the living room, spotting shooting stars through the windows that stretched from floor to ceiling. The following morning we woke early to bake croissants for a breakfast party and in the evening played a game of *Murder in The Dark*, creeping through the house, clustering in a giggling gaggle to await the sudden encounter and wild scramble that culminated in a victim. The children soon joined the Lowes in games of Bridge, and William would go on to emulate Robert's analytical intellect, joining bouts of poker on Long Island until the locals barred him making the bets that were boosting his funds.

I kept a net in the bay and caught large rays with vast wings that I transformed into many a delicious sweet and sour stingray dish, and on the Balls' visits they began allowing us to stay in the house on the understanding I provide the meals. We remained on our best behaviour, compliant with the rituals that punctuated days, when the casual comment, *"at about this time we often..."* followed by the gracious invitation, *"would you care to join us?"* would lead to us adjourning to the patio for morning coffee, the gazebo for an evening drink. Unfortunately the Balls' benevolence masked an innate irritation. One windy day, when Billy forgot to fasten the heavy front door, it slammed with a resonant bang! But not so loud as Ball's violent retort, *"You've just killed a cat!"* Billy's colour drained as his mind grappled with the terrible truth. Rosie, the beloved Burmese, must have been crushed. A sweet life was lost because of his neglect! But it was not true. Although Ball had felt his feigned catastrophe would assert the gravity of Billy's lapse, it was a ruthless way to treat a gentle child who loved animals. Winnie was different. One could not place her in the same sentence as her husband. She lived a romantic charade, forever seeking some part of herself that was forever denied. Having been warned about Ball's habit of abandoning all attire but for a sunhat and gumboots, we usually made a noisy approach to Smugglers Point. The surprise came in another form, when one warm weekend we glimpsed an ethereal vision of Winnie, naked upon the stairs. With a little cough, she was gone, but in an unhurried way as though secretly glad we had witnessed her immaculate body.

I began teaching the kids yoga and most days they ran, while David and I walked around the bay. Exploring an overgrown track, we came upon a crop of marijuana and warned the kids to keep their distance, fearing they might encounter the illegal growers. Sam immersed himself in drawing and, on finding a young fruit rat cowering in a boot, he illustrated the cuddly creature as it washed its face, slept, and ate. Then on making a working trip to the boat I discovered chewed paper and a trail of droppings. There was a rat on board! Guessing I had carried it there in my bag of tools, I became fearful of the damage it could wreak. I set a trap and, after the stowaway had nibbled through a plaid shirt and a glow stick the kids had saved for a special occasion, we resorted to green

Ratty ST

poison. A toxic aroma led us to the prone body and no doubt the rodent still haunts Hornpipe, illuminated by the eerie glow of that last supper.

En route to Auckland for the second Winston's Craft Biennale, we picked up a happy Billy from a riding camp where he had written, *"I climb onto the saddle, squeeze with my legs. The horse is in the wind, and I am on the horse."* As for the competition: the judge had awarded the prize for clever craftsmanship and where previously David's extravagant desk would have won, his *Sail Chair* required an eye for design. Driving south to the Whakapapa ski resort, we took to the snow, clad like Wombles in yachting macks, woollies, and wellies, terrorising the skiers by sliding the slopes on a tractor inner tube. Billy was soon shivering and later, on glimpsing Sam's comment, *"Not being able to ski was the biggest disappointment of my year,"* I knew we had let him down. Our kids harboured few expectations, made no demands, and I wished David had won, that we could have splashed out on ski passes and rented gear. They made up for it when, on arriving home, they returned to their watery element, gaining expertise on their small windsurfing rig or surfing polystyrene boards with Billy's little arms and legs sticking out of an oversized wetsuit.

Sam windsurfing

WT

Sam manifested his commitment to Scouts with a Bob a Job fundraiser for a summer jamboree and a six mile hike to a deserted barn where he ate his evening meal and slept amongst the hay bales. Waking at dawn Sam returned, bright as morning sunshine, describing his rite of passage, *"I felt independence flow over me."* The secure environment nurtured a resourcefulness that our sons applied to their careers. Sam would train his mind to drift in a receptive state while retracing his consciousness from waking, back through a night of dreams; developing an awareness that inspired his *Sleep/Wake* performance. The opening scene of Sam's production developed from sleep science research into a script, intoned by an imposing, androgynous figure whose rendition of the Egyptian Litany of Ra heralded a menagerie of masked animals and lyrical dancers that told their story of sleep and dreams. Sam's collaborations with a composer generated a syncopated soundscape that brought the subconscious to life. As one's heartbeat gathered momentum, an underwater projection of William's breath held tremors of birth or death morphed to a mournful intonation of the aria from Monteverdi's *Orpheus* to compound the screened tragedy of a couple's romantic Skype meeting on opposite sides of the world. The mesmeric fusion of sound, movement, and narrative concluded in an image of my son's foetal body falling through space, with the audience reflecting on contemporary society's frailty in the wake of the apocalyptic 9/11.

As with Sam's previous productions, *Sleep/Wake* evolved in an alternative venue before featuring at Auckland's Town Hall as the main attraction of the 2009 Art Festival. Finally, in March 2015 *Sleep/Wake* toured to New York's La Mama theatre where it was the star of Sam's New Zealand Festival. Amidst the nightmare images, a macabre four-legged thing, composed of two dancers locked in a battle to separate themselves from opposite ends of a faded sleeping bag, evoked a Hieronymus Bosch painting. The bag had done good service; some forty years before, it had accompanied my adventure in Crete, I had slept in its warm embrace that first night beside David on the fell above Mount Pleasant, and Sam had carried it on his hike to the lonely barn. On snuggling into its feathered cocoon, did any of us dream it would end its days on the sacrificial altar of a spectacular performance?

As the sinister creature tore the sleeping bag asunder, feathers drifted through the audience and my mind returned to that day when I first met Aphrodite. My boyfriend and I had been wandering sun shocked along a street in Cania, when the local women gossiping on their doorsteps lured us into their circle. Aphrodite won us over and, although we shared no common language, I submitted to her clothing me in a lascivious dress and anointing my body and hair with olive oil. They plied us with food and drink and as we danced I fended off Aphrodite's amorous husband. When she insisted we sleep in her house it was too late to protest. I awoke with the evening's excesses demanding an imminent evacuation, to recall that the toilet lay through the bedroom of our sleeping hosts. With no time to waste, I chose the lesser evil and burst into the still sleeping street. But it was already too late and a sand pile offered the most immediate – the only – place. Guilty as a cat, I crept to the harbour to wash before negotiating a labyrinth of streets, trying to recall the house where I had left my boyfriend and clothes. We walked on over craggy mountains where the gods dwelt. An old rucksack wore my shoulders and new boots blistered my feet, so I went barefoot down the rocky Samara Gorge, and trod on, thirsty beside the surging sea. I told no one of my sin and the ancient civilisation that venerated the priestess and bull kept my secret. On returning to Athens we slept in a rooftop dormitory beneath the stars and visited the Acropolis where, insisting on a photograph, my boyfriend dropped his shorts and clambered onto an empty plinth. Convulsing with laughter I snapped his bronzed body and absurd white bottom that resembled the marble statues of those iconic ruins.

The Balls' three-month tour of Europe made it convenient for David's mother to visit. As the winter chill dispersed, she arrived to knit us patterned waistcoats and watch David as he worked on a commissioned cabinet to accompany his *Sail Chair.* My projects were less creative, a new mainsail cover and a weekend helping the Lowes cut paths on their daughter's farm. David remained with Gran, discovering a distance that extended further than the miles that usually separated them. On my return we spotted a pod of orcas playing like dolphins in the bay, and hurriedly rowed Jolly Boat out to Hornpipe. From the deck we watched their languid forms sliding beneath her bow, their black and white bodies weaving together as one. We gazed into their huge eyes, and wondered what those benevolent, much maligned creatures thought, whether they considered her hull another great mammal. Our human interactions were less harmonious. At eighty, Josslyn was active and obstinate; I always assisted newcomers in negotiating our skittish dinghy but she refused help, saying it made her feel old! Gran had always insisted that, when incapable, she would move into an old people's home. When in her nineties Josslyn was moved into the *"beastly home,"* she found herself surrounded by *"old people."* David, who had resisted the plan of uprooting his mother from her familiar surroundings, felt that the sterile place exacerbated her dementia and deeply regretted she had not been allowed to end her days in her own house.

Following Gran's departure, David and I gutted Hornpipe's living area in preparation for a haul-out that coincided with a kids sailing course. We hardly stopped during those fourteen hour days of grinding the rust that had been lurking behind the forward bunks, welding patches beneath the galley and shower. With Robert and Betty's help we launched on time.

On our return to Waipiro Bay, we replaced the chart table with an L shaped settee and invested in a new stainless-steel cooker and sink. But the pressures of spending while earning nothing made us dread Christmas. Apart from brief afternoon interactions, we had neglected the children while, accustomed to Hornpipe renovations, they had embarked on their own projects. Sam relished the novelty of sleeping in the tent and Billy wrote a forty five page story *The Quest of Callum* before carving a bowl and Sam a fish for Betty.

Although we had cleaned Smugglers Point, Hornpipe was a mess when the Balls arrived earlier than planned. Once again Robert and Betty invited us to stay, the children to invest their festive spirit into decorating a tree before our friends departed for Christmas with their six noisy grandchildren. Christmas Eve saw David and I finishing Hornpipe's interior and hastily wrapping the kids' Christmas bikes. They were up and away before dawn, hurtling down the stretch of tarseal at Te Uenga Bay, and after a day of sleeping and eating we moved aboard to the delights of a sparkling new saloon and galley with a window box of herbs over the sink. On the first day of the nineties Sam set off for his long-anticipated Scout Jamboree. Alone for the first time in his life, Billy occupied himself carving a marlin head, until the Lowes whisked him away on a sailing trip with their grandchildren. And after a few carefree days with the Parker family we sailed home on a balmy evening breeze, dragging the kids through the water in the way Big John had described as *"trolling for sharks."*

When New Zealand celebrated the 1990 sesquicentennial of the treaty between Māori and Pākehā, we sailed to Waitangi, where a fleet of waka had assembled from all over Aotearoa. Tribes of tattooed warriors hauled huge canoes to the ocean and paddled over the rolling waves as statuesque women intoned their karakia from the shore. The sombre wailing of the *kuia* filled my soul with love for this culture, these people, my country. And I realised that despite missing old friends, Aotearoa had opened our hearts and minds to a new way of being. Once a flotilla of waka, tall ships, and planes had welcomed Queen Elizabeth, we gathered for a reconstruction of the treaty being signed. Entering the spirit of the day, we watched Taiaroa Royal engulf the meeting house in a flickering fire of gestural storytelling before moving on to traditional dancing from the Cook Islands. Sam and Billy had wandered away and we found them at the feet of contemporary bard Sam Hunt, and though artist Tony

Fomison died that day at Waitangi, he also influenced Sam's creativity, despite them never meeting.

Work had begun but the holiday was never over when our home was both classroom and playground with the freedom of sailing to a beach and diving to claim a fish for supper. Sam took first turn with the spear gun, shooting two, followed by Billy who was eager to share the satisfaction of providing supper. On other afternoons we drove to Elliot's Beach where David and I lay beneath the huge pōhutakawa of Pahi Pa, lulled by the sound of happy children and gentle waves. Soon after the school term began we hauled up the anchor to sail north for a Correspondence School summer camp at Coopers Beach. It was then we saw Mr Ball burning the beach huts Sam and Billy had built from the flotsam and jetsam on the seashore, and it being too late to stop him, we said nothing to the kids who had taken great pride in constructing their dens. Following a nauseous sail, we spent a night in Whangaroa Harbour before tacking out into the tide and lumpy sea settling onto a broad reach for the Mangonui inlet. While the children encountered computers for a first time, we squandered those quiet days painting Hornpipe's deck and taking the students on a sailing excursion. Moving on we spent a night beside the white beaches of the Karikari Peninsula, fleeing the exposed bay to head up the coast against a blustery wind, and when a squall tore the old mainsail, we motored into the sheltered harbour of Houhora. After exploring the treasured shells, butterflies, and antiques of the local museum, we caught a ride to Ninety Mile Beach, where we frolicked in the surf. And fortuitously a couple drove us home in time to summit Mount Camel and see the sun set on a spectacular view along the coast to Spirits Bay.

Our return was that rare occasion when sailing seemed the most natural thing in the world. After scrambling to the top of Stephenson Island we slid down the grass and continued to the Cavalli Islands where we scrubbed Hornpipe's hull and overnighted before cruising home to Waipiro Bay. Following an invigorating two-week holiday, we felt totally refreshed, but the kids were devastated on coming across the burnt remnants of their dens. They could not comprehend why an adult would do such a thing saying, *"They meant the same to us as Smugglers Point does to the Balls."* Sam and Billy had helped maintain Ball's trees and paths and the dens had been far from the areas he frequented or owned. They appreciated the consequences of actions and when friends caused havoc or disrupted

Scouts, they pronounced them immature and stupid. Having encountered many who were happy with nothing, they harboured no envy for those with more and Sam would remark, *"When I was young it was always the child who wasn't playing the game that kicked all the pieces over."* And while this explained Ball's behaviour, it did not excuse his lack of compassion.

David began making a bench settee and table for a *Make it in Radiata Award*, that was intended to promote innovative ways of using New Zealand's plantation pine, which was rather soft and bland for fine furniture. Despite balking at my irreverent suggestion that he paint his furniture, David's use of contrasting dark and light woods had paved the way for colour. In staining the radiata he invested its bland grain with character. He wove strips of purple, blue, and green into a latticed back and complemented the colours with a seat of natural Oregon pine. The effect was repeated in an accompanying coffee table, with a hard wood surround that protected the pine. Through years of managing David's workshops Bouncer had appraised his furniture with a critical eye. He was thrilled to see *The Maker* stain the boring wood with the fresh colours of sky and sea – the rich purple of night. *"This is me. I needed a change!"* cried Bouncer, as he recklessly dipped his toe into a sapphire puddle.

Before driving south to exhibit David's furniture at Auckland's Fisher Gallery we had a studio preview, and to our surprise Christine bought the pōhutakawa and matai stool, though where she would put it in her house truck home was a mystery. After the opening event we explored the Coromandel Peninsula, with Sam proudly guiding us through the mining tunnels of the Karangahake Gorge he had visited on his jamboree. But on our return to Auckland, we learned that, despite enthusiastic responses, nothing had sold and it seemed that David's furniture had entered the volatile realm of luxury goods, where market fluctuations were as unpredictable as wind shifts on the ocean. With no foreseeable funds to pay our way we drove home under a gloomy cloud. The children appeared unfazed and on leaving Billy at a riding camp, the responsibility of caring for his horse and the freedom of cantering across open country elevated him above our ups and downs.

Our fortunes changed overnight when David won the five-thousand-dollar award for his radiata bench, and on learning that his *Sail Chair* had sold we were ecstatic. When the Lowes told us of their plan of sailing to Tonga and offered us their house for the winter, we were overjoyed. Then

Robert and Betty revealed a scheme for teaching me to drive, that in the three weeks before their departure they would loan me their car and son Simon to prepare me for the test. I have omitted to explain Simon's schizophrenia and wicked sense of humour! On one of those daily drives he and I were kicking rubbish sacks into a pit at the Russell tip when Simon sagely gestured towards the screaming gulls circling overhead with the comment, *"Looks like a scene from an Alfred Hitchcock film."* A voice in my head questioned what I was doing with a schizophrenic at a remote dump. However, despite Simon's distracting way of conversing with his mind, he lacked all potential for violence and his calming presence eased my fear of driving; I passed the test, thanks to Betty, Robert, and Simon for the most empowering gift I ever received.

After racing to Kaitaia for the birth of their latest grandson, the Lowes loaded Windrace with a trampoline for a Tongan village and sailed away, leaving us to enjoy their comfortable house. A few days later Billy turned nine, an age when he could join Sam at Scouts. And with the endorsements of my citizenship and driving licence I once again braved Bay of Islands College. Following an early morning summons, I donned smart clothes and flagged down the school bus in which the Ngaiotonga and Rāwhiti students suffered three hours of every day, juddering along the twisting road to Kawakawa. My classes were often unruly with many of the predominantly Māori roll coming from families that had never known employment. A patient optimism got me through and, even as I journeyed home, a perceptive youth commented, *"Hey Miss, you even smile in your sleep."*

Once David had untangled an old bike that had lain hidden in Hornpipe's engine room, he began riding to Smugglers Point, returning for lunch with Sam and Billy who accompanied him for the afternoon. While never lacking our contribution they enjoyed their independence and always had something on the go, with Billy making bows and arrows, Sam illustrating and inventing stories. Unfortunately Billy was frustrated by lessons that catered for a limited attention and his insistence on developing projects far beyond the school's requirements caused migraines. While there was little we could do to dilute his intensity or determination to keep up with Sam, I resolved that my children should never suffer the torturous waste of time that I witnessed daily; but how was I to compare the local college with others? Maybe they were all the same?

Driving awarded me the versatility of travelling to country schools where, following a creative workshop about trees, a class leader thanked me, saying, *"Although we had expected someone bigger, we had a wonderful day!"* While teaching a week of art at the Bay of Islands College I was reminded of my London experiences. Although I had learned to stand strong, creativity offered more opportunities for disruptions, stimulated emotions suppressed in other subjects. I was comforted in knowing that, at the end of the day, I could shake off my responsibilities, but enduring those adolescent frustrations was taking a toll; I was becoming intolerant of my own children and my stomach was wracked with pains which were diagnosed as a stress related peptic ulcer.

Through the winter, flu did its rounds and, despite feeling as ill as those teachers who called in sick, we needed my earnings. I became renowned for being dependable, teaching all subjects, including horticulture, *"Learning how to grow good dope, Miss,"* and while being a mother helped me connect, my students refused to believe I had children of my own, *"You're too small, Miss."* Lacking a handbag, I used my Vanuatu basket and, when a student commented *"Hey Miss, that's a strange kete,"* I told her about the dugong, the volcano, the flag, and bag. On finishing she said, *"Who would believe that a kete could tell so many stories?"* When teaching in Jamaica I had been known as *"The lady with the basket,"* for carrying my belongings in a cane basket, and today David uses a similar one to carry his laptop and lunch to work. On hearing the Māori story of the *Three Baskets of Knowledge,* I recognised a universal wisdom that relates to the yogic principles of body, mind, and spirit, that must be balanced if we are to live in harmony. It goes that, when Earth's creation was complete, Tāne was sent up to the heavens to receive the knowledge that humanity needed for living on this earth; he was given the information in three baskets. *Kete Aronui* contained the knowledge of the natural world. *Kete Tuauri* revealed the workings of the mind, and *Kete Tuatea* encompassed a spiritual wisdom. David had been seeking a theme for his Milan installation and as I told him the story he visualised the symbolic vessels and immediately began creating his interpretation as a series of lights with a contemporary message, and on showing his *Three Baskets of Knowledge* at Milan's furniture fair, he received a huge response from the international audience.

Our lives were full of simple rewards and despite their solitary schooling our boys had many social opportunities. Following a Scout leadership course, Sam's fascination with group dynamics prompted him to organise and attend more events and at the end of an advanced learning camp he gave a magnificent speech. Although our kids were tiring of friends who wasted time at Scouts, the activity had introduced them to wider issues. One weekend they rode to Elliott's Beach, gathering rubbish that had been tossed from cars, and long before they reached their destination the bags were full, their minds made up on conservation issues. We joined Martyn Evans, Chris Booth, Pat, and Gil Hanley for the poignant dedication of Chris' Rainbow Warrior Memorial Sculpture, situated on the clifftops that overlook the Cavalli Islands. And as we reflected upon an event that had touched all our lives we recalled those first impressions of a land that had become home.

Despite the struggles, teaching had boosted our finances, so when an acre plot in Parekura Bay came on the market for eighteen thousand dollars, we optimistically paid a deposit. There was a sea view and access to a bay where neighbours Wayne and Beth anchored Tern. Christine lived nearby, Robert and Betty's house was a five-minute walk away and despite having spent all our money we speculated about building on *our land*. Soon after, we loaded a year's worth of David's creative furniture into our friend's van and drove the snowy Desert Road to exhibit at the Crafts Council in Wellington. David's show integrated art, craft, and design as One. He had applied the practical skills of a sailor, combined with the construction processes he had observed on Samoan houses, the canoes and stick charts of Melanesia. Dispensing with the western tradition of cutting to create fragile joints, he had crafted jute lashings to form strong, flexible connections that could withstand use, in the way a sea-going craft weathers the wind and waves. David's furniture referenced sails, rigging, waves, and canoes: concepts that had evolved from his life as a navigator and a voyager who had crossed oceans. A Polynesian influence was evident in the kava bowl form of a table, a *tiki* shaped stool; in wall sculptures that suggested Micronesian navigational aids, the crescent of a sextant or the sun's arc across the heavens. Ten years later David would develop those themes into a sculpture that acknowledged Hawke's Bay as the first place to witness the year 2000. Only a navigator could have conceived the *Millennium Arch* sculpture that stands on Napier's waterfront. The single arc of steel with its gigantic stainless steel disc that David had angled to reflect the rising sun on that dawn of a new epoch.

While in Wellington, the boys and I visited their Correspondence School and caught a bus up to the imposing Art Gallery that overlooked the city in a building that would become Massey University, where Sam would teach spatial design some fifteen years later. Once the television arts programme had filmed David, we drove home, satisfied with the extensive coverage and glowing reviews. However, the catastrophic stock market crash of 1989 had struck and only one jewellery box sold. Commissions were not forthcoming and David said, *"What's the point."* But he could not give up. He diversified, making *Itsy Bitsy*, a whimsical wall sculpture composed of plywood squiggles that emulate an abstract figure in a saucy bikini, along with many others, including a butterfly, and a fish swimming through fronds of weed.

Though we could not afford extravagant mistakes, when Beatrice's frequent break downs led to us buying Emma, our finances sank as her faults rapidly surfaced. David was increasingly pessimistic about making a living in the Bay and I was under pressure to accept a permanent job at the local college; an implausible proposition when I thought of our children having to attend the unruly classes. At the Crafts Council's suggestion David phoned Jacob Scott of the Hawke's Bay Polytechnic and when offered an artist's residency with a studio, stipend, and house, it took but a moment for us to decide to try our luck in the bay area that, in my imagination, was shaped like a bird.

A bay shaped like a bird LT

On Robert and Betty's return I cooked a celebratory dinner and when they left on a South Island holiday Simon remained, to smoke, play bridge, and wander the beach. I continued teaching on request, while helping with the haul-out. During ten years of ownership we had stripped and painted Hornpipe's entire exterior and interior, but rust never slept and if the tiniest molecule lay hidden in a secret crevice it would flex its muscles to eventually burst free. Worn weary of grinding and painting we staggered into the light, eyes red with dust, bodies cramped from contorting at impossible angles. When David put his back out he became hysterical with frustration and we wondered if it would ever end and was any of it worthwhile?

With Christmas imminent, the children became intoxicated with excitement, decorating a pōhutakawa tree and making presents for the Parkers who camped on our land. We saw the old year out beside a blazing fire beneath a full moon and then the Balls celebrated their combined birthday with all the pomp and circumstance of fireworks and a flute recital starring Uwe Grod. We sensed a desperation in Winnie's eloquent remark, *"The worst thing about growing old is knowing that you will never fall in love again,"* barely disguising her torment. After building a defensive wall around her spirit Winnie had discovered she was locked inside with the beast. She was not blind to the aspirations I had for our children, but when she suggested finding our boys places at a prestigious boarding school, Winnie was offering cake to beggars. Our children's learning experiences had been so different from David's privileged school that harked back to a culture dating from Tudor times. My education had lacked all refinement, so when Billy professed a desire to go to a real school wearing a little suit and tie, I empathised with his desire to be a part of something and longed to fulfil his wish, but David insisted that tradition was a straitjacket that impaired freedom.

Before the holidays ended we had sailed to the Black Rocks to gather mussels, when amongst the boulders, Sam's glance alighted on a silver threepence that must have fallen from someone's pocket some hundred years before. The boys jumped off the cliffs, but having lost my nerve for heights I cowered in the shallows. On returning to Indico Bay we scooped scallops from the sandy sea floor before drifting home to Waipiro Bay trailing the kids from ropes at Hornpipe's stern. While we never equated those simple pleasures with the price we had paid in maintaining our yacht, we regretted curtailing those activities just as Billy and Sam were becoming more involved with sailing, diving, and windsurfing. As the school term began they worked alongside David in my studio; Sam immersing himself in diverse high school subjects; Latin, technical drawing, music, and chemistry. The Balls embraced the novelty of hoisting a semaphore of flags to signal phone messages from school, with the sight of a red and yellow ensign fluttering over Smugglers Point setting me in a spin. Within minutes I would be clad in my decent dress, rowing ashore to catch the school bus, and after the Balls' departure, Robert updated our communications with his VHF radio. Once again, we sailed north for the Correspondence School camp and clear waters of Matai Bay. Spontaneously taking advantage of a favourable wind, we returned to the Cavalli islands, using the radar to enter the bay with a pod of dolphins darting here and there, greeting us with their squeaks and squeals.

When David's last commission was cancelled we thanked our lucky stars that he had accepted the residency and eagerly anticipated our opportunity to develop creative ideas, for Sam and Billy to experience a school community. One glorious day we windsurfed for hours, returning exhausted and elated to a barrage of *Dungeons and Dragons*. But that summer's blustery winds caused David increasing concern. Sound rigging was the equivalent of decent tyres on a car, and it was vital we replace ours before sailing south. There was no alternative but to borrow from the kids' savings, and when you have no money, you become an expert in all things, so David rigged the mast with my help before climbing on the workshop roof to seal the tiles and put up flashing and battens that would safeguard the building in our absence. I was called in to teach until our day of leaving, taking that step into the unknown as lightly as our previous lifestyle change, except that this time we had no choice.

On hoisting Hornpipe's sails, Sam and Billy blew the conch and as that mournful sound echoed around Waipiro Bay, our friends came out on their decks. Damian watched until Hornpipe was out of sight and his mother said that he was heartbroken, scanning the anchorage every day for our return. He would remain a loyal friend, visiting us in Hawke's Bay, arriving barefoot in his bedraggled tracksuit and pudding bowl hairstyle, carrying a bag of books. Damian capitalised on the individual tuition of a rural education, becoming Dux of Bay of Islands College and eventually a Professor of Mathematics. But before this he would join our boys at

Auckland University, performing in Sam's productions of *The Tempest* and *Henry V*, playing Ivan in William's adaptation of Dostoyevsky's *Crime and Punishment*. And William would say that Damian was "*A subconscious influence in my first tentative months of freediving, appeared in my sleep to tell me, 'stand in your dream.'*"

Robert and Betty had supported us through those challenging years but soon after our departure they moved to be nearer their daughter and grandchildren. Robert would campaign for Mayor of the Far North District Council, but when I asked whether the office required that he be a New Zealand citizen he fell silent. Amidst the hype of rallying support, he had overlooked that detail and, despite having the integrity and ability to transform the district, he was not eligible. Betty and Robert's wisdom and generosity had a lasting influence on our lives and it was they who phoned with the terrible news that Billy's friend Ben had met with a fatal accident. He and a friend had been driving a speedboat in the dark when they hit a moored boat, suffered concussion, and drowned; a tragic rite of passage that could have happened to either of our boys. We could not imagine the overwhelming grief of his parents and Billy could not immediately grasp the finality of that loss.

During our time in the Bay of Islands we had transcended from nomads to landowners. As our patrons saw us outshine their expectations a perceived power shift had occurred, with some becoming envious while others radiated an abundant generosity. Perhaps it was the secluded bay that undermined its residents' equilibrium, for in subsequent years many suffered personal hardships. Isolation may be paradise or hell depending on whether you live in plenty or poverty, and it was tragic to hear that a woman living a squalid life no more than a stone's throw from Smugglers Point had run amok with an axe. Sometime later the couple who introduced us to New Zealand separated and he suffered a fatal heart attack. Trees grew and spread their leafy shade, babies became adults, and eventually the rough road was sealed. Christine lives on in her house bus, designing opulent buildings, weathering into a wise woman while, beyond her jungly garden with its multiple yachts in various stages of construction and decay, luxurious houses blossom on sections that had been empty when we bought our land.

Going About

"As the waves rise and fall, I watch them from without and within.
Thoughts froth in the foam of their passing.
And I gaze through this glassy surface and beyond, to when this wave
reaches the horizon of the mighty ocean that touches us all, You and I."
Linda Trubridge

When we moved the tuck box back on board, Bouncer peeped out and, barely recognising Hornpipe's fresh white cupboards, thought he must have mistakenly booked into a fancy hotel. While our spider was curious about the journey south and wondered whether he would be seeing icebergs, we were just as excited. Over five years in the Bay of Islands we had explored all its islands; the overhanging cliffs and twisted pōhutakawa trees had become as familiar as a garden and maybe that was an indication it was time to move on. So, after filling our water tanks and a night at Otehei Bay, we made an early start, passing between Piercy Island and Cape Brett, briefly following the coast before heading out to sea. The hazy day drifted by, the Poor Knights' pinnacles slowly emerged from the mist, and Billy began writing an illustrated account of our voyage. *The Trip of The Trubridges* was not short of superlatives! *"Captain David never seasick, Linda cooks the best meals ever, Bosun Billy none as fit as him rushing around and always sighting land before anyone else. Of course, there's sailor Sam the fearless, always reading, sleeping, or eating."* And after anchoring off Maromaro Bay we rowed into Rikoriko Cave where, as Billy wrote, *"We had a great time with some very friendly fish."*

Easter dawned late on that last day of March, but long before the autumnal sun appeared the kids had cracked their Easter eggs. Then we motored beneath the spectacular rocks and arches of the Poor Knights, stopping for an ocean swim before heading over an oily sea of swirling currents that was abundant with leatherback turtles, sharks, and dolphins. Our path south was conveniently scattered with islands where we could briefly explore a new place and refresh ourselves with a sleep before sailing on. The first of these was the Mokohinau Islands where Billy cooked a Thai dinner for a school project. We dressed in a rag bag of oriental clothes and ate on deck, gazing at a view reminiscent of a Chinese watercolour. During our game of mahjong a full moon rose to shine on Hornpipe, lyrically rolling within the crescent of rocks. Then, as Billy wrote, *"We went to sleep under the stars and mosquitos."*

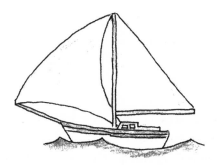

Hornpipe WT

When the kids woke they thought we had eaten their chocolate eggs, but of course we had hidden them for an April Fool's joke. After rowing around the larger of the islands, we dived their coral arches and returned to the boat with a tame wrasse following me like a stray dog. Then we hastily climbed the cliff for a view of where we had been, and forward towards our next anchorage at Port Fitzroy, Great Barrier Island. There we set off up the track, past the kauri dam to Mount Hirakimata's two-thousand-foot summit, where we ate the Kendal Mint Cake that Robert and Betty had given us as a reminder of England. Returning with an easy swinging pace, we washed in a stream and headed home to bed. The following morning our exertions and a passing front caught up with us, but after a day recovering we sailed for Great Mercury Island where we went ashore to walk over the rolling green hills. Billy wrote, *"Linda and David are picking mushrooms while Sam and I follow them without letting them know... Then we go back to the boat where we have mushroom pizza and mushroom soup.*" Ever a forager for free food, I fell just short of making a mushroom cake, while as always my family enthusiastically ate whatever I concocted.

That evening we hauled Jolly Boat on deck in preparation for an early start and were away before dawn, with Billy describing the nomadic transition he accepted as normal, *"Wake up and find we are sailing from Mercury Island to Mayor Island."* Following an easy sail past Aldermen and Slipper Islands we motored the last stretch, and as the day diminished, David and I hurried up a winding path through dense pohutukawa trees, hoping to catch a last glimpse of the view. The children had remained on the shore, fascinated by the glistening black obsidian boulders, that Māori flaked into axes and blades which, having been found throughout Aotearoa, are evidence of their people's extensive travel and trade. Billy's foraging experiences prompted his exaggerated account of the rock's lethal capability, *"I cut two fingers to pieces but succeed in getting two dagger like obsidian pieces."* After a beer at Mayor Island's unpretentious beach bar, we reluctantly set off to motor through a night of rolling swells, passing White Island in a windless daze. Billy was up before dawn, logging his impressions at a later date, *"We go to bed and at about nine o'clock David starts the motor and we set off for East Cape. I have a watch at three thirty to five o'clock on a seventy degrees course. Sam steers for half an hour and then I steer for another half hour listening to music of all sorts. This goes on for a long time, then we round Cape Runaway and the East Cape. Do my diary then go to sleep while we are heeling over at about a thirty degrees angle. Linda and David hardly get any sleep because they have to constantly change the sails."*

When Cape Runaway appeared out of the mist we goose winged to follow the rocky coast to Lottin Point, gazing longingly up at lush pastures backed with forested mountains. After deliberating whether to overnight at Hicks Bay, the only sheltered anchorage on the bleak coast, we decided to take advantage of the serene weather and slack tide to round East Cape. Dropping our flopping sails, we noisily motored several hundred metres from the shore's steep dry hills that were pocked with slips, resulting from the eradication of native forests for sheep farming. All was peaceful on that still, sunny afternoon with David sat on the cabin top steering with his feet, the children reading on the deck with the occasional glance at the land slipping past. I had set to tidying away the lunch when the engine fell silent. Darting to the cockpit to help hoist the sails I stopped in confusion. There was no breeze, the broken coastline was too close for swimming, and as David disappeared into the engine room I asked the obvious question, *"Why did you stop?"* And when he briskly replied, *"I didn't,"* I realised that Obelix had taken things into his own hands.

The boulder strewn shore loomed closer, the swirling tide rippled with menacing currents, and on sparing a glance overboard the seabed appeared as close as a cobbled road. With no means of propulsion we were doomed, yet I chose to stand at the helm pondering our sweet and sour relationship with Obelix, pleading with the inert mechanical beast. And when David emerged from below I steered clear, knowing that when the shit hit the fan it was best not to ask, that a concerned, *"How's it going?"* could ignite a fuse. When David shook his head, I feared the worst. Then he pressed the start button and without hesitation the engine burst to life. As he thrust Obelix into gear I gave a shuddering sigh, welcoming the thundering roar that rattled our bones. And when the gap between our precious home and the savage shore had widened, David explained how he had diagnosed Obelix's ailment as a cracked fuel line, that after cutting away the shattered copper he had reconnected the pipe using a flare tool. He had miraculously bought the specialised tool just a month before, thinking that it could be a vital piece of equipment in a dire situation. And if not for his foresight, Hornpipe would have surely foundered on the rocks of the lonely East Coast.

The East Cape is renowned for its hazardous rips and treacherous tidal waves so it was a relief to sneak between the island and headland on a benign sea. But on turning the corner, a fierce wind struck from the south and when a sudden squall ripped the genoa, we reefed the mainsail. There would be no rest for us as we clawed our weary way south, tacking through the fickle winds, making constant sail changes. The previous sleepless night and long day had been exhausting, so for safety's sake we stayed clear of the coast. I took first watch, standing strong through the passing hours. When anxiety overwhelmed me, I escaped into a mental indulgence, visualising every detail of a luxurious bath, dressing for a special night out. And while my imagination lingered on perfumes and potions, my mind held true to Hornpipe's compass, alert to the wind and waves, focused on sailing our course. The thread of thought sustained me and by the time David woke, my fears had dissolved. By dawn of Sunday the seventh of April, we were off Moutara Bluff and as we beat into Poverty Bay we caught a couple of skipjack tuna. When the wind and waves eased, David and Billy swam before motoring, sailing, motoring, and eventually making a safe landfall. Billy completed his story, *"Finally we arrive at Gisborne and are hurried away to the yacht club where we are bought drinks. Go home supper...bed...snore. Snore."*

The weather was unsettled so we delayed our departure, and as the rain became heavier, the squalls more violent, we became increasingly grateful we were safe in Gisborne's inner harbour. A huge surge rolled into the bay and when a yacht limped in we heard that the delivery skipper had spent the week endlessly tacking against ferocious winds, barely avoiding being swept onto the shore. When the weather subsided, we waved a farewell to our new friends and motored out through a mountainous swell that was rolling onto the cliffs of Young Nick's Head. As a gentle easterly sprung up, we hoisted our sails to swish past Table Cape in the diminishing twilight. On clearing Bull Rock, we gybed in a fresh northerly that blew us past Portland Island into Hawke's Bay. A seascape confounds definition and there was barely a ripple in the vast open bay that had been a raging cauldron the previous week. Despite a desire to equate a location with certain characteristics, an ocean constantly reinvents itself; the weather creates a sense of place. While I had come to accept that I needed some control over my circumstances, David claimed that uncertainty was one of sailing's great attractions, yet in practice he was often frustrated by the unpredictable.

Fifteen miles out from Napier, Hornpipe's most southerly passage concluded in a tranquil calm. And as dawn illuminated the coast, unfamiliar sights emerged from the shadows to become forever associated with that arrival. Along Marine Parade a line of Norfolk Pines marched in a regimented battalion, and as the sun's rays spread over the Kaweka Range, a huge cross emerged from the mist to remind me of an incomprehensible dream; although I presumed this icon to be a gigantic monument, it was nothing more than a group of trees.

That passage had provided an intermission for letting go of old ways and opening to new experiences. It would be Sam and Billy's transition from childhood to adolescence, from water gypsies to school students who would wear uniforms and adhere to conventions. And while they would run with the pack and claim an identity through their academic prowess, the ocean would beckon and seduce them with an irresistible siren song.

Tying up at the marina in Ahuriri's inner harbour, we dozed until Jacob Scott arrived to drive us to a welcoming meal at the Otatara studios. Then, abandoning Hornpipe, we moved ashore to immerse ourselves in separate activities. The children attended intermediate and high school, with Sam involved in art and drama, while Billy pursued chess and guitar, wondering why other children improved until he realised they were practising, a self-discovery that was worth any amount of nagging. William would write an article, *The Bane of Natural Ability*, that explains the uncompromising attitude of one who controls the most vital instinct. *"With so many elements that must come together in the training of a depth freediver – breath hold, technique, mental calm, flexibility, patience – it is highly unlikely that any one person will be born with natural abilities in all of them. Alone, one of these abilities will only get you so far, and so the remainder must be cultivated. And this means that the most important quality for any freediver will always be their dedication and application."*

This was a new beginning and though our accommodation lacked the luxury of opulence or the purity of frugality, that was not my concern. Turning my back on the squalor, I immersed myself in creative explorations, however it often seemed that I would suffocate in the stagnant smell of others' feet and pets. Filthy windows obscured the light of those dwellings and sleeping within a walled enclosure was stifling after an open boat. We did not miss our ocean life. This was a chance to feast on a cultural stimulus our family had never known. After school the children walked up to the Otatara studios, reconnecting as they played amongst the old buildings, interacting with the other artists. Julia Van Helden shared David's affinity with nature, expressing this in ceramic sculptures that investigated the exposed edges of the earth. Liz Maw was claiming a quirky identity. Ricks Terstappen created a menagerie of metallic creatures with lopsided smiles, collaborating with Jeff Thomson in bending and welding iron into seriously zany sculptures, covering Jeff's decrepit station wagon with corrugated iron, driving it around the Bay until Te Papa claimed it for their national collection.

The fertile Heretaunga Plains had been partitioned into orchards. Apples lay rotting on the ground, while further inland the hills undulated to the Kaweka and Ruahine ranges. There we spent our weekends, and a four-day hike in the early spring that took us above the snowline. Our hobbled outdoor gear was marginally safe and, in a misplaced attempt at encouraging the children's participation, I had allowed them to choose the food; our rucksacks of potatoes and heavy saucepans dragging at our backs as we endured a blistering climb from grassy pastures to one thousand seven hundred metres, a greater height than any mountain in Britain. We met hunters and hardened trampers; a father and son, out for a week with a gun, a dog, a bag of oats, and a *"She'll be right"* that would get them through anything.

WT

Those rugged mountains awoke David's fascination with the patterns in the environment. Cutting slithers of wood, he stained and spiralled them like autumn leaves on the walls of his studio. Splitting raw wood into textural slabs, he portrayed Aotearoa's geological origins, her tectonic plates, lava flows, and braided rivers. While David's artistic explorations had their own value they also influenced his design, and on exhibiting at Napier's Museum, he complemented his crafted furniture with a backdrop of expressive wall sculptures.

Meanwhile I had taken up an appointment teaching art and drama to the senior students of Colenso High School. Learning on the job, I drove them to events, striving to conceal my lack of experience behind a wheel. Accompanying a class trip to Wellington was a revelation, especially the amount of leftover spaghetti and salad from a meal that I had calculated based on my family's appetites. As I chomped through yet another untouched salad, a concerned student commented, *"You don't need to eat that horrid stuff Mrs Trubridge."* Once again I was mortified at the valuable time wasted on confrontations and questioned a culture that showed little respect for learning. Sam and Billy had found themselves far ahead of their classmates and they understood why when they saw how much time was wasted. When visiting England, our friends had asked us about

New Zealand's soaring rate of suicide and child abuse; why a people and land rich in natural resources harboured such sadness. Maybe the statistics reflect Aotearoa's isolation but I suspect they relate to a culture that endorses a caricature of a man as if he was no more than a hard drinking thug. I feared for our boys, for although we had taught them to be sensitive and caring, they had entered a world beyond our control.

On arriving at the polytechnic, David and I attended life drawing classes with thirteen-year-old Sam joining us to further his artistic talent. I remember following him into class and realising he was walking on the spot. Despite his uninhibited upbringing, the sight of an unclothed model surrounded by a circle of artists was all too much. While Sam somehow made that giant step through the curtained door into his artistic future, I began reclaiming my creative voice. My thoughts returned to those art college days of painting and sculpting; evenings of art history, film studies, and life drawing. Stripped of conventions, castigated for being *precious* about my creations, I had been devastated when, on the fourth day of an observational drawing, my tutor insisted I rub it all out and start again. But it was a revelation to draw a body and discover a spiritual presence. Just as scientists and doctors develop a familiarity with enzymes and flesh, nakedness no longer embarrassed us. Unaware that our models kept their profession secret, we never knew that, for a generation of working class Britons that had never seen their matrimonial partner undressed, nudity assumed a pornographic dimension. We wondered why our male model arrived in a business suit, laughed at his briefcase that contained sandwiches and a hand sewn g-string. And while we students could barely contain ourselves when the irate husband of our model stormed through our studio's easels and canvases to deck the principal a crushing blow, we felt for his shamed wife, a gentle woman with a quiet dignity.

On choosing to specialise in sculpture, the time between concept and completion became greater. My head was full of creative ideas but the processes of carving, casting, or welding consumed so much time. A year of investigating organic subjects culminated in an aluminium *Sculpture for the Deaf* that distorted the surrounds in its reflective surface. During my final year, I pursued a dream of creating sculptures for audience participation; a room filled with expanding and contracting inflatables. Obtaining a drum of liquid latex from a balloon factory, I experimented with dipping the innocent dolls of my childhood, inadvertently dunking my hair in the tub whereupon it congealed to a rubbery clot. While my appearance had outstripped fashion, anxieties about my final show kept me awake at night and sleep brought visions of empty exhibition halls and monsters that pursued me across a barren land.

Following years of making stuff and seeing results, a friend introduced me to the ancient yoga practices. It was a revelation to spend hours seemingly achieving nothing. The practices stilled my turbulence, saved my exhibition and life. And while yoga asana reveals few of the hidden treasures that lie within, the craft of writing amounts to reflections that appear to yield nothing but words on a page. Opportunities to live as an artist are rare; so, despite achieving a first-class honours degree, I chose a teaching profession. However, my creative education and final exhibition had lain a foundation for future explorations, prompted a reviewer to write, *"Linda King's sculpture has a cohesive appeal, with the basic theme of life forms shown in globular clusters made of plaster aluminium and resin. Some are erotic, others grotesque, but they all have a sensual, tactile appeal."*

Women readily sacrificed their bodies and souls to their family and though my husband and children had filled my focus, quenched my creativity, I was ready to make a new start. My studio was soon populated with gestural figures and faces that combined sculpture with painting, art with drama. After fabricating the masks and costumes for a theatrical production I concluded the year with an exhibition that sprung from the pageantry of my imagination. *Breaking Free* made few sales, but it posed many questions, *"Why is the pathway to paradise so painful? Everyday news describes cruelties beyond our imagination and we turn away saying, 'This is of no concern to me,' forgetting that this was done to someone's child or loved one."* My intensity was tempered with a lighter touch, *"In all my works it is carnival time. In living, death is ever present; many feelings abound: sorrow and joy, moon and sun, god and devil, clown and muse. I have been a daughter, wife, mother, and teacher. Have built a home on land and sea, nourished and protected my family while living at the mercy of the elements. For many, survival is a luxury. We who aspire for more than physical sustenance should consider the survival of our spirit."*

That time in the wide awake, brittle bright atmosphere of Hawke's Bay had been intended as an intermission. We hardly noticed that we had evolved into a new way of being, but as the year progressed we questioned our next move. Although we had friends, a studio, and land in the Bay of Islands, David's struggle to earn a living there had ground us down.

The children's education prospects were limited and returning after that era of growth seemed pointless, and on proposing a trip to the Pacific Islands the kids said, "*We like it here, can't we stay?*" And we realised that a teenager's paramount need is for friends and independence. We visualised a creative life in tranquil surroundings with an active cultural scene. But where? Nowhere was perfect, so when I saw an advert for a part time art teacher at a private girls' school in Havelock North, I applied and had an interview. In the same post as the job offer from Iona College, a letter arrived from our friend Jos whose family had spent summer amongst the Hebridean Islands. She described visiting the Island of Iona and walking the coast of South Uist, where David and I had honeymooned; that in the bay where we had sighted a mysterious sailing yacht, they had seen and hailed a boat. They couldn't believe their luck when they were invited on board, and how astounded they were when they saw that it was named Hornpipe. Overwhelmed by the coincidence I accepted the job at Iona.

Hawke's Bay is an affluent community where David felt sure he could make a living, but while we knew that we could not afford both a house and yacht, Sam and Billy had not imagined giving up Hornpipe. Having finally won the battle of the rust, we should have enjoyed the fruits of our labour, but just like the nightmare drip, drip, drip of water that had cursed our Northumberland home, it seemed that no sooner had we resolved a problem than we lost faith. Before finishing at Bay of Islands College I had borrowed their video camera to film ourselves, the land and workshop, neglecting to take any footage of Hornpipe; maybe because we had not conceived life without her. Home was my security but Hornpipe was much more. She had been a trusted companion, an abiding presence through years of travel, and it was incomprehensible to think that we had sailed our last ocean passage encircled in her hull; that the subtle sounds of chuckling waves and flapping sails, her wheel in our grasp, that tremble of her rigging as she ran before the wind, would all fade into memories. For David who was so entirely at one with the sea, it was a huge price to pay. While it is in his nature to keep moving on, being slow to adapt I felt the loss of a way of life that had been perfectly in tune with nature; that I was giving up on an old friend, a part of myself.

Forcing a decision, we chose a locality near my school to find that houses in our price range were disappointingly bland, except for one that Alan Duff, an aspiring author, was renting while finishing his novel *Once Were*

Warriors. We commiserated about the lot of artists and when the owner/ architect John Scott toyed with a partial swap with our Northland plot, I staked my hopes on it and enrolled Sam at Havelock North High School. When negotiations fell through, the dilemma of where we would live remained. Then, immediately after Christmas, we sailed for the Bay of Islands, intending to resolve matters in Waipiro Bay before delivering Hornpipe to an Auckland marina. Work colleagues Geoff and Pete accompanied us as, following a well-worn pattern, we motored out of Napier in a flat calm only to discover that the engine's manifold pump was leaking. There was nothing for it but to wait for wind and after a bout of scrubbing the keel we spent a pleasant evening going nowhere. At two in the morning a light north easterly sprung up and at first light we slid between Mahia Peninsula and the purple shadow of Portland Island. Off Table Cape the wind turned northerly and as we tacked towards Gisborne we debated going ashore for a new pump seal, but with specialist shops closed it seemed best to continue. The wind died at dusk and once again we were sitting with our sails listlessly hanging, watching black squalls build over the land only to die as they drifted across the sea.

Eventually we risked motoring at half revs through flat calms that persisted all the way up that coast. We were compensated with spectacular views of Mount Hikurangi, a swim, and two tuna that provided sushi for lunch. Shortly before closing on East Cape a light north westerly lifted our spirits and set us to tacking, past Hicks Bay and Cape Runaway. During the night, the wind died, leaving us motoring through a lumpy sea until dawn brought a gentle breeze. As the wind increased, Mercury Island appeared and just south of Cuvier Island a savage squall broke our backstay block and whipped the sea to frothing waves. When the storm abated, we ran under our storm jib and triple reefed mainsail to anchor outside the crowded bay of Great Mercury Island. And when the forecast warned of a fast-approaching westerly we joined the armada of noisy revellers, and oblivious to their New Year celebrations, collapsed into sleep.

It was 1992 when we emerged to find Sam illustrating our crazy passage and, as we sailed on past Great Barrier Island, we were rewarded with a gentle wind that carried us through a perfect night. Dawn saw us passing the ragged silhouette of the Poor Knights before running with a buoyant breeze, downwind, for Cape Brett. Then we all crowded Hornpipe's cockpit as she surged past the portals of Piercy Rock, riding high on the

Chaos in the galley ST

voluminous waves that climbed the cliffs; flocks of gulls ascending on the updraughts, filling the sky with a welcome.

On rounding the entrance the waves subsided, and after motoring into Waipiro Bay, Geoff's partner joined us for a crowded night. Our crew drove away leaving David and I desperate for time alone, relieved when the children went ashore to build huts in the bush, leaving us to discuss the studio repayment with the Balls. On contacting a broker, we were advised to advertise Hornpipe at a hundred and twenty-five thousand dollars but when another valued her at a hundred and sixty David was sceptical. While we had stripped our yacht of engine dependant gadgets, and had attached a solar panel to replace the wind generator, few shared our values, and a potential buyer turned Hornpipe down because she lacked a freezer. As David set to painting the deck and engine room I reluctantly constructed a new cockpit cover. On finishing we made a brief escape, diving for scallops, and gathering mussels for a feast of *kaimoana* with Windrace, Iron Butterfly, and Blackbird, before heading for Deep Water Cove where the boys camped ashore, spearing fish, and fending for themselves. Finally, we turned up the Rolling Stones and danced on deck to the primal beat, *"This could be the last time,"* as Hornpipe drifted into the sunset.

Following more farewells, Claire arrived and as the brilliant day faded to a starry night we set sail for our last passage on Hornpipe. In the early morning, Billy and Sam stood watch as a gentle north westerly blew us to Kawau Island where we anchored amidst a crowd of boats. Next day we sailed past Rangitoto in a misty drizzle, weaving through the hundreds of yachts that were participating in the Waitemata Regatta. Then, dropping Hornpipe's sails to motor under the Auckland Harbour Bridge we headed out to Westhaven Marina to greet a flood of brokers and buyers and after many favourable comments Hornpipe was listed at one hundred and thirty-five thousand dollars. Claire left on the bus and we were relieved when Jill Parker collected the kids to stay with Dan, Jo, and Amy. They had suffered enough disruptions and we did not want them to witness our uncertainty. Sam and Billy could not conceive of giving up the only home they had known and the finality of turning our back on hard-won freedoms filled us with doubt.

Selling Hornpipe was more than parting with a property. Insurance had always been prohibitively expensive, and we had lived with the knowledge that if we lost our home, our only posesion we would be lucky to be alive. Hornpipe represented a way of being, a magical carpet that could transport us anywhere. I moved to Hornpipe's rhythm, knew every inch of her hull, deck, and sails. Had come to love her. David was turning his back on those profound understandings that united him with nature. He had never felt so fulfilled as when collaborating with the stars, sun, waves, and wind on our ocean passages. Our children's lives had been shaped by living afloat; the vast solitary seas had formed Sam's perception of the world and inspired him to become a creative magician. William had no memories before Hornpipe. He had slept in her belly, rocked to her rhythm. The ocean had awakened his soul, formed a resolve to accept whatever came from his relationship with the depths. Hornpipe had taught us how to live in tune with the elements, shown us a spiritual freedom, which we longed to express in an enticing new life. But if we had known what lay ahead we would not have had the heart to part with her.

Leaving David to negotiate, I caught a bus and set off to join the Iona teachers in planning the school year. Previous trips had taken us through the central plateau but this was the first time I had travelled by road to Hawke's Bay. At last the coach crested the mountains before descending into the Mōhaka Valley. The Heretaunga Plains spread before me with the mirrored ocean scything a curving crescent across the view; and as a shaft of light illuminated the Havelock hills my heightened senses transformed the scene into a promised land. After walking a last mile to the car at Otatara, I drove to Pete and Ani's Hastings house; their sleep-out that would provide a temporary home. Then I joined the staff, discussing the curriculum and learning computer skills. But Iona's rituals seemed as foreign as life on Mars and as the dilemma of leaving Hornpipe played in my head I found myself craving the familiar taste of salt on my skin, a horizon beyond the tartan carpets and rose bushes.

Usually when I sought a cool word of wisdom I would spontaneously open the I Ching so, when Ani suggested that I throw the runes, I knew that the time was right. Carrying them into my room beside the chicken coop I climbed into the white cavern of mosquito netting and slid my hand into the bag of stones. Without hesitation, my fingers found Othila and as I drew the tablet into the light its simple lines leapt like a fish out of water, seeming to represent the sea, or a face like my own. A book explained that the rune represented a current need to separate from past beliefs, behaviour, and property. Reaching for another the stones slipped through my fingers, until one came to rest. I marvelled at the rune *Perth*, and the discourse on my circumstances, *"You may feel overwhelmed with exhaustion from meeting obstruction upon obstruction yet you always have a choice: you can see all this negativity as bad luck or a challenge specific to the initiation. Each setback and humiliation becomes a test of character. Patience and perseverance are called for. Keep on keeping on."* Transfixed, my fingers curled around the stone *Dagaz*, to reveal an inscription like two wide eyes, similar to my own, that reminded me of the traditional fairytale ending, *"And they all lived happily ever after."* The rune implied a conclusive transformation, *"In each life, there comes at least one moment which if recognised transforms the course of that life forever...the moment may call for you to leap empty handed into the void. The darkness is behind you, daylight has come, seize the opportunity before it passes."* And as I reflected on the runes' uncanny relevance and wisdom I felt a sense of deep peace; that no matter what the future held our family had made the right choice.

Throwing the runes had connected me to my intuitive self; helped me understand the helter-skelter of events. So when the workshop was complete I set off for Auckland, to collect the children and our belongings in readiness for the school term that would commence on Monday. As I drove and drove I sang to fill the silence and arrived at midnight to find that David had spent days preparing Hornpipe for sale, his nights reading our logbooks and journals, reflecting on our sailing life. Spending time alone had intensified his doubts about selling Hornpipe and his scepticism had been confirmed by a first offer of ninety-two thousand dollars. With just one day to pack there was no real opportunity to talk but in our final moments David and I concluded that to grow we must sell Hornpipe. On Sunday afternoon Sam, Billy, and I loaded the car with our belongings and drove away feeling empty and uncertain. Emma was labouring with a mysterious mechanical ailment. She struggled up the hills, but at last we saw Hawke's Bay in the distance as, coasting into the Mōhaka Valley, we arrived in Hastings and moved into the sleep-out to face the toughest year of our lives.

FULL CIRCLE

"Dive deep, O mind,
into the ocean of Divine Beauty,
you will discover a new gem
instant after instant. "
Sri Ramakrishna

Immediately on seeing the photograph advertising an acre and a half plot with established trees and a brook I recognised it as our land. Although I could have lived anywhere, I knew that David would be imprisoned by the houses we could afford, that this chance would not come again. So, the day he arrived we viewed the section and despite concerns that it was shut away and far from the ocean, we took the plunge. When our unconditional offer was accepted, we asked ourselves, *"Did we really want this commitment?"* With barely a month to settlement day we wondered how we would find the finances in time and although it was too late to question or concede we could not help but deliberate. We had expended all our energy on renovating Hornpipe, building the workshop in Northland, and developing David's reputation, but it had all come to nothing. Was New Zealand the country for us? Hawke's Bay the area? That pastoral section the place?

The Land, as we called it, was situated down a long drive, off a quiet street on the edge of Havelock North. It was close enough for Sam and Billy to bike to school and for me to walk to Iona. Plateaus steeply sloped to where the Herehere stream bubbled beneath walnut, poplar, and willow trees. A wind pump, reminiscent of a structure on the fell above our house in Northumberland, towered over the garden. It had dispensed stream water to the stock troughs in the days before *Old Eric* grazed his sheep and carved the tiny model of an axe that we found in his tumbledown shed. On the last day of settlement, we fortuitously banked the money from our plot in Northland which sold for twice its value the year before and this, along with a loan from my parents, saved the day. The land purchase had stripped our finances and though few realised our need, Billy's school generously paid for him to attend his class camp.

Life afloat had allowed us to maintain a comfortable distance from society, but on arriving in Hawke's Bay we found ourselves renting a suburban bungalow, surrounded by people we had no connection with. After assembling second hand mattresses, a trestle, and plank table, with paint drums for stools, we had a home we called the Ghetto. At weekends we swam at Ocean Beach and cleared thistles on *The Land*. While our boys excelled at art, maths, English and geography, which they understood from an experiential level, they were fishes out of water and must have often questioned the choice that had been made. At first Billy said that the children in his class were *"Boringly normal,"* and he retained a friendship with a Japanese boy from his previous school. Six weeks passed before I realised that Sam was merely treading water, that his school had neglected to inform us that their high achievers class was full, the numbers too great to place him as promised. While Sam had avoided bothering us, the only solution was to move him up a year; where he faced catching up on more than a year's work, making friends with those who considered him an outsider.

Building a papier mache *Dungeons and Dragons* landscape was our kids' last fun project before Sam became overwhelmed with schoolwork, and when David's expectations of continuing to rent the Otatara studio were dashed, he searched for another space. When his efforts proved futile he moved into the Ghetto's cramped garage, buying time on friends' machines while waiting to collect his from Northland. Hoping that free publicity might generate work, we allowed the Village Press to write a feature, along with a window display of David's furniture. When his lashed *Kava* table won three hundred dollars at the Hawke's Bay Craft Exhibition, he expected that the endorsement, combined with an exhibition at a winery, would generate commissions and sales. But all to no avail. The inability to provide for his family attacked the core of David's being and as stress compounded into incapacitating back and groin pains, he dreaded cancer. It was a huge relief when a chiropractor traced his problem to trapped nerves from the broken leg and twisted pelvis he had incurred in his twenties. While treatment released the physical constrictions, the disempowerment from circumstances beyond David's control would take longer to shift.

Our lost freedoms had not been replaced by any form of fulfilment, and we could barely hold onto a dream for the future. The stamina and patience that had won respect in my previous teaching jobs were superfluous at Iona and, while I gave my all to surpassing their expectations, the part time job barely covered our rent. As a teenager, I had longed to break free of my family, to attend a boarding school, and now the inconceivable had become a reality, I felt like a fraud. On enquiring whether more teaching was available, I was met with *"So what's your jolly husband doing?"* And it seemed that those who had spent their days in Hawke's Bay's abundant sunshine could not understand why we had chosen to live as Water Gypsies; did not care that David had established a reputation in Britain. Our family had become an island. Although travel had stimulated our creativity, we were now high and dry, grieving for the ocean. I wrote *"I wished so much, but all my stars have plummeted to earth, too heavy to soar across the heavens."*

When Hastings' freezing works was demolished to make way for a shopping centre, David Ricks and Jeff went along to salvage the beams that would provide a superior timber to fast grown wood. After class I joined them, never stopping until darkness fell, limping home to lick our wounds. In a last-ditch investment, David recycled jarrah wine vats into seats and table tops, learning to weld and fabricate the steel frames for his range of outdoor furniture, which he planned to exhibit in the Auckland Gardenz show. When the car collapsed the day before David was due to depart, he heard of a sixties Holden that a farmer was using to round up his stock. Though Martha had holes in her floor and lacked a radiator cover, she appeared sturdy so he paid the farmer six hundred dollars and loaded her to the gunwales with tables and chairs. Martha made it to Auckland, where David stayed on Hornpipe and met potential buyers Pete and Bev, who offered him a miserable eighty thousand dollars for our yacht.

On receiving a letter from my mother, saying that she was going into hospital for a routine hysterectomy, I knew she was disguising her fear. I had no energy to support her and an overseas phone call was an unaffordable luxury. When my father called, his shuddering "*Lindy...it's Daddy,*" reminded me of that terrible Christmas when we had grappled with Mum's breakdown. The operation revealed extensive cancer in my mother's womb, bowel, and liver, that once again my parents needed my help. I tried to reach across the vast ocean to comfort them, but my reassurance was hollow; I lacked money to fly home and my boys could not manage without me.

During the May holidays we set off to collect our belongings from Northland, stopping on the way to listen to Billy's story *Whale in the Bath*, that featured on the *Ears* radio programme. Swapping Martha for Jill's horse truck, we drove north to the Bay of Islands. Our friends gave us a fun intermission while, despite reuniting with Damian and Morgan, Sam diligently maintained his studies. Following an excursion on Windrace, we loaded David's machines and drove to Auckland where our purchasers Bev and Pete requested a sea trial, "*To consider Hornpipe's performance.*" After that last sail and night afloat, we continued south in the old truck with David and I sat up front, Sam and Billy shut in the back, perched above the cabin. For eight hours we ground uphill at a walking pace with a queue of drivers backed behind. At last, with Hawke's Bay in sight we hurtled down the last long slope, and when I screamed at David to "*brake, brake*", he yelled "*I am, I am,*" above the screaming engine. As a stench of overheated brakes filled the cab seconds stretched into last moments. The jaws of death opened to swallow us; and then the slightest rise in the road gave David the briefest opportunity. He slammed the gears into third, the truck faltered, and with a shuddering lurch, slowed its headlong pace just before the road swung into a bend. David pulled over and we let the kids out the back and fell on each other sobbing with relief. As the drama unfolded Sam and Billy, who were helplessly dozing in the back, had felt the escalating pace, heard our shouts; and as always had no control over their fate. We arrived home in time for Sam's ninjitsu class, and he clambered from the horse truck, no doubt glad to see the back of his family.

After unloading the machines into the shed and filling the redundant Emma with junk, David was about to drive the empty horse truck to Auckland when a policeman delivered an urgent message to contact

Robert. Our inability to pay the phone bill had led to us being cut off, and fearing bad news I waited at home and on David's return I could not bear to hear. When he said, *"It's your dad,"* my grief erupted in a wail of despair. The last time we spoke, Dad had been distraught with concern for my mother. She had heard his cry, the sound of his fall; had found his inert body on the ground. My father's heart had stopped, stress had taken his life. I recalled my parents visiting us in Northumberland shortly after Sam's birth, Dad telling me that alcohol was ruining his health. Following my suggestion, he had turned from booze to meticulously record his life's story in a beautiful script and although Mum had lacked the strength to read about their past she had understood how therapeutic that writing had been for my dad. I wished he could have experienced the landscape of New Zealand and sailing on Hornpipe. But now, all that remained was his last letter in the post.

When Mum insisted I give her time to adapt to the changes, it seemed best David keep to his plan of meeting with our purchasers, who were criticising Hornpipe's mechanics and driving a hard bargain. In David's absence, I reflected on my father. Tim had said that he was the saddest man he had ever seen and as I recalled Dad's dark eyes overflowing as from a deep well of grief, I wondered how he had suffered my teenage years, never mentioning his lack of opportunities. Through all his years spent fixing turbines, no one had ever commended him for doing a good job. My heart ached for his lost life, and I recalled that little shrug he gave, as though trying to cast off his troubles. The way he sat, slumped in his rocking chair, his Siamese cat on his shoulder; a suburban pirate surfing the TV channels.

Our buyers paid eighty-four thousand dollars for Hornpipe and although this was far less than her worth, the heartbreak was over, or so we thought. Shortly after we received a letter from a yacht broker, claiming to have introduced us, and demanding a third of Hornpipe's sale price. I recalled my brief encounter with the broker, his attempts at converting me to his sect of fundamental Christianity, and that on divulging my commitment to yoga, he called me a devil worshiper. It seemed that the broker's god endorsed those who stole from the vulnerable. After receiving threats and a lawyer's writ we re-established contact with Pete to question his first encounter with our boat. On stating that the couple who had alerted him to Hornpipe had left on an ocean crossing we set to tracking the yacht with a radio message. As soon as the yachties reached civilisation they sent a letter confirming the truth but in the meantime, the bullying broker had made those months seem like years.

Meanwhile another legal battle was underway. Although our contract to build the Balls' cottage in Northland had stated they would compensate us if we were forced to leave, they disputed any such decree. We were not asking for charity when, after less than two years' use of the workspace, we requested some form of reparation. Winnie may have valued our friendship sufficiently to honour the debt, but she had no say and we could only assume that the lawyer was proud of outwitting us. David and I had signed his agreement as naively as when we surrendered Mount Pleasant to our Northumberland friends; chosen to accept circumstances that contributed to our departure and eventual arrival in New Zealand. But Ball's exploitation of our efforts and trust was immoral and unjustified.

Since coming ashore we had sunk into persistent misfortunes. My father had died; my mother was terminally ill. Sam was struggling to keep up with students a year older and although Billy never mentioned the bullying at school our kids were heartbroken when a dog broke into their guinea pig pen and ate them all. An exhibition table was smashed on delivery, the car constantly broke down, and every trip was fraught with difficulty. After losing thousands on Hornpipe's sale and giving up the workshop we were embroiled in disputes with a broker and lawyer. David was virtually unemployed, we were struggling to live off my frugal wage, and everything seemed to be slipping away. While I longed to give our sons the home and opportunities they deserved, only later would I realise the vital lessons those hardships taught them. David would use the metaphor of Aotearoa's volatile geology of volcanic eruptions and earthquakes to define that time as entering the element of fire. Was there worse to come, would our metal refine into steel, or be destroyed in the furnace?

Billy became notorious following an article entitled *A Casualty of the Education System* that featured him wistfully gazing into the distance, along with the claim that schools failed their brighter students, concluding, *"Often those with outstanding potential are not fully realised."* Consequently, his teacher seized every opportunity to catch him out while his classmates labelled him, *"gifted child,"* genuflecting and chanting, *"We are not worthy,"* when he entered the room. Regardless of the *Tall Poppy* mindset of cutting the exceptional down to size, Billy came top of his class and was crowned Hawke's Bay's junior chess champion. But the stress exacerbated migraines which Sam diagnosed as Billy's brain threatening to explode from overuse. His intense focus excluded all else and one day I returned to find him reading, oblivious to the water from a burst tank flowing around his feet. Billy was acutely aware on a deeper level, and on seeing a farmer set his dog to tear a rabbit to pieces he abstained from eating meat. Most Kiwis considered vegetarians weird and when I saw him eating sausages at a barbecue I realised that hunger had forced him to abandon his principles.

Attending his ninjitsu group gave Sam a sense of a community and although he was so overwhelmed with his academic work to progress far the teachings nurtured his emotional equilibrium. Sam and Billy often looked after our neighbour's boys and the reward of playing with their Border Collie sustained them through tough times, with Shelley saying one day she found Billy curled up with Tessa in her kennel. He had covered his wall with an intricately drawn map of his imaginary world inscribed with mountains, forests, and oceans, so when he and Sam joined us at life drawing classes, it was no surprise that they instantly grasped proportions. In spare moments Billy sat for me while I sculpted his elfin face in a ceramic portrait that mercifully survived the firing. When David taught a *Ways with Wood* class, Billy accompanied him, throwing himself into every activity, signing up for individual chess tuition, and joining the tables of old ladies at the Bridge club. Although the youngest in his year, he excelled in cross country and swimming, where he moved with an unconventional but efficient technique. On accompanying his Mathletics group to a tournament, I watched their earnest young heads grapple with the complexities and glow with exultation on winning an eighty dollar prize. Their determination would lead to the highest awards, with Geraldine and William's art folios ranking in the nineties, Melissa destined to become a brilliant chiropractor who would maintain our twisted spines in years to come.

As autumn turned to winter it became bitterly cold in the ghetto. Billy thought there was an earthquake every Saturday until he discovered that the washing machine was shaking the flimsy, uninsulated house. Maybe our frugal circumstances undermined our health, for that winter we came down with the worst flu ever. Sam suffered stress related bouts of chest infections, but as always he soldiered on, accepting whatever life dealt.

He vented his frustrations on his bicycle which devised cunning ways of outwitting its rider. Sam and his bike were irrevocably locked in combat. Either the snaking chain writhed around the cogs or the wheel spun off to continue its solitary passage along the road. With no time for rebellion, Sam took to plodding his weary way on foot. He diligently spent hours at his desk, writing stories and filling his folio with stylised paintings, capturing my likeness in crystalline forms and sepia tones.

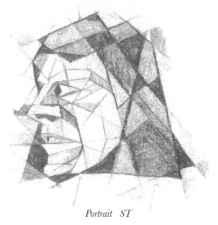

Portrait ST

The tide turned when David was awarded third prize and a grant to exhibit and accompany his *Canoe Chair* to *Anticipation 92* in Chicago. On his way through Hawaii he looked for Polly, to hear that she and her three little boys had returned to England after separating from her alcoholic husband. On his return, David finalised our house plan with advice from a local architect and Martyn Evans, who regularly visited the Bay. However, owning a home remained a dream until at last we found a bank willing to risk a loan. In late September, Jeff and Ricks came to help dismantle the old windmill. But as we gazed up at the kinetic wheel rotating in the wind, we asked ourselves, why? And on measuring our plans, we saw that the structure fitted into a corner of the living room. And so it remains, towering over that inner sanctum where sheep once sheltered beneath a grove of trees. In keeping with Māori tradition, the local *kaumātua*, Waru Kupa, blessed the land before we made that first cut. When a procession of storms passed through, the stream burst its banks and became a raging torrent. Even when the rain stopped, water continued seeping through the clay, rendering the site a muddy mess, the track inaccessible, and it was exasperating to be told, "*It's not normally like this.*"

David project managed the builders who, being unfamiliar with block construction, made many mistakes. Wet days gave him a respite to work on commissioned dining tables and chairs for organic farmers Vicki and John Bostock, and my teaching colleague Graham and partner Graeme. David's back constantly ached and he endured sleepless nights worrying over finances, not least our unreliable car. Almost every trip involved a jump start or tow home, but despite the setbacks, by November the house foundations were complete. Sam's school year ended with the boost of learning that he had not only won the geography prize but passed all his exams with high marks. And when Iona's final assembly concluded with a song of the sea, tears flowed as my memory returned to happier times.

> *"When the coast is left and we journey on to the rim of the sky and the sea, be the sailor's friend, be the dolphin Christ lead us on to eternity / When the clouds are low and the wind is strong, when tomorrow's storm draws near, be the spirit bird hovering overhead who will take away our fear."*

Where previous festive seasons had seen us working to meet a deadline, that year was no different. As the walls went up we started visualising our rooms and when the builders finished, our family took over, labouring from dawn to dusk cleaning the terracotta Marseilles tiles that had been recycled from Hastings Boys High School. The solidarity of work united our boys. Billy scrubbed with gusto while Sam stoically loaded them in Martha. We had hoped to get the roof on by Christmas, and almost finished to plan, the special day passing in a haze, with time off and a swim the biggest treat; then, at Mum's request that I come when she needed me most, I flew away over the oceans leaving David building the house, the children in charge of cooking.

I arrived in Britain for the winter of my mother's life. Mum bravely hid her dwindling energy, but chemotherapy had stolen her apple cheeks and her eyes appeared translucent as though her soul had washed away. She found most pleasure in buying us gifts and cooking me cakes I had no stomach for. Her generation had been the first to possess more than life's bare-essentials, and my parents' supreme achievement had been taking us on summer holidays to Weston-super-Mare. I remember donkeys plodding beside a murky sea hauling shabby Cinderella coaches packed with sandy children. And although the tumbril's interiors were rough and unpainted, they fulfilled promises that would some sixty years later be mocked by Banksy's satirical *Dismaland*. One beach day when Mum, ignoring my protests, undressed me with a, *"Why would anyone want to look at you,"* I threw sand in her face and ran off along the promenade, pursued by my father, who smacked me in front of a critical audience. Funny that as an adult I would shed those reserves, or was that childhood rebellion my only resistance to those who sought to control me? But despite my parents giving me the very best of their lives, my presence was of little comfort in my mother's time of need. And although I knew it was forever, when we hugged our goodbyes I could not bridge the distance between us. Briefly visiting friends in Devon, I absorbed enough of the lush countryside and their warm company to strengthen my return and that first sight of the sapphire sea and emerald land of Aotearoa revealed where my heart lay. The children had adorned the ghetto with flowers from our garden and when David took me to see their progress on the house, I lay on the warm grass and knew that I was home at last.

Shortly after my return David gathered New Zealand's leading sculptors for a Pine Symposium in the woodland slopes of the Eastern Institute of Technology. After discordantly singing our revised version of *Redemption Song* at the welcoming *pōwhiri*, the action began. Bronwyn Cornish formed a giant earth mother, covering her with a log blanket and setting the structure alight to fire through the night. David constructed a sky pathway from slices of wood suspended between Douglas fir trees, and Billy carved a garden altar. On coming upon John Bevan Ford completing a totemic *tiki* I helped the men heave it up to stand amongst the trees. Only then did I realise that my female presence had breached Māori protocol; but when I apologised, John gently acknowledged my action, *"You were here, you are here, you should be here. All is well."* A cultural lapse could not taint the mana of a beloved artist, whose images of *korowai*, birds, sea, and sky continues to inspire my creativity.

After considering subdividing our land for extra funds we decided it made more sense to build David a studio in the orchard beside the house. The school year began with Billy joining Sam at Havelock High while I took charge of Iona's art department, teaching fulltime along with building and caring for my family. After David had completed our home's ceilings and interior walls, a plasterer rendered the thick blocks that insulated temperature and sound. Then, along with finishing cupboards, shelves, and doors, David began constructing his workshop while the boys and I painted the plaster and waxed the tiles that flow from the living centre into our personal spaces. During our house sits I had never dared dream of owning a home, but there was no time to celebrate when, amidst the upheaval of moving, Iona called me in to help with a weekend sports event. On Saturday, March the thirteenth 1993, eleven years after setting sail from Gibraltar, we slept our first night in the house we had built on the other side of the world. Shortly after, my friend Sue presented a stress workshop for the teaching staff, and when she took me aside to explain that my Dad's death, Mum's terminal illness, financial problems, a new location, and job with increased responsibilities ticked every box, I assured her I was through the worst.

Our family had exchanged a boat for a house, the sea for a stream, childhood for adolescence. Adverse circumstances had drawn us closer and, even though we lived out of cardboard boxes with David's circular saw dominating the living-room, our home was full of sunshine and birdsong. Whenever a child visited they stopped, spellbound, pointing at the colours and flickering light. Our house relates to Hornpipe. The windmill's frame snuggling into a corner of the kitchen is reminiscent of her mast stretching up through the galley to the heavens above; the whirling wheel of clanking steel reminiscent of the percussive rigging. Our kids instinctively chose rooms that replicated Hornpipe's bunks, with Billy on the port side, Sam to starboard, while our bedroom, situated like the back cabin at the opposite end of the house, appears to rise upon a swelling wave of grass, with the tinkling brook and wind in the trees to soothe our dreams.

Late that year Great Aunt Julia visited and set about teaching Sam to drive; *"So, after school every day we would go off along the roads through orchards and past farms. This may have been easy, had Julia not also decided to use it as opportunity to help me with my French studies at the same time. Conversations and instructions took place completely 'en Francais' as I tried to navigate the Rubik's Cube of gears, and control this machine that was twenty times larger than my bicycle. I still gabble in French when I am stressed, remember her 'mon copain' and knowing wink."* David's mother followed and, when the Parker family arrived for Christmas, Al burst into tears on the doorstep. Jill had left him, to eventually get together with Pete, who would swap sheep farming and stone walling in Northumberland for the decadence of sunshine, a job sticking labels on wine bottles, spending their spare time trapping predators on conservation land.

Sometime after New Year my mother died and I journeyed home for the funeral where she was remembered for performing as a clown in an orange wig to amuse the kids at the village fete; her last stand in battling cancer, a poignant image of how in reaching out to a new generation she had transformed heartache into happiness. Those lonely nights were haunted by the ghosts of my childhood and on curling into the familiar bed, I clutched a small shell; holding tight to memories of home and the beach where David had

LT

found it on the day of my departure. Each morning I awoke with its shape imprinted in my flesh. When all was sorted, I caught the bus into Leicester and sold my mother's golden jewellery to cover the cost of my flight. I kept her silver seahorses and bracelet of palm trees I had played with as a child, that held happy memories of the mother I had loved. After packing a few practical items my parents had treasured – Mum's coloured mixing bowls, walnut napkin rings my father had made, and a pottery rabbit he won at the fair on their first date – I stepped over the threshold of that house stripped of their presence. This had been their first home. On returning from Bermuda they had briefly lived in Plymouth; moving on to stay with my grandparents in Bath, while my father bought his way out of the Navy. When Dad was offered an engineering job with the English Electric Company, they travelled to Leicester by train, caught a bus to Cosby, and walked through the village to that house. Setting cardboard suitcases on the bare boards, they hung bright Caribbean prints on the grim walls and made a start. All those years lay hidden in the archaeological strata of layered wallpaper, in empty rooms that held secrets of my evolution from child to adult – until that day. Closing the door, I left with the hum of the heating system my father had perfected ringing in my ears. And his engine room, still running, years after his death, would forever resound a note of warmth in my heart.

On my previous visit, Mum and I had planted bulbs around a wooden seat that she dedicated to my father. And as I walked the lane for that last time I saw their golden buds bravely emerging through the snow and knew that crocuses would forever remind me of the comfortable place she had created for children to play, lovers to meet. I had planned taking Mum on a last trip to her childhood village near Cheddar Gorge; had hoped we could walk up onto the Mendips where my father had asked her to marry him. She had wanted to scatter his ashes from those ancient rocks, but the journey was too far for her failing energy. Following her death, it seemed appropriate to honour her wish, to climb to that high point and throw my parents' ashes to the winds, and in doing so, unite their spirits. But my brother saw no purpose in making a pilgrimage to a place he saw as irrelevant to our parents' lives, insisting they remain in the garden they had toiled over. My brother and I were so different; even death could not bring us together. I recall him introducing me to his friends, saying *"This is me mad little sister!"* his banter reminding me of my mother's breakdown. Yet, some twenty years later, when his son visited the house at 1 Elm Tree Road, its owner revealed a last secret. That on demolishing Dad's shed he had discovered a hidden trapdoor to a store of whisky! As my nephew walked amongst the apple trees where his father had scattered the ashes, he reflected that *"Unlike childhood, it was a finite space (I remember it going on forever, and the orchard as a forest)."* And when he wrote of picking and planting an apple, so that as an old man he could make his grandfather's chutney, I realised how appropriate it was that my parents had come to rest beneath those trees that had provided us with their sweet fruit and a place to play.

Once the Cosby house had sold, we bought a reliable vehicle and on that first drive it seemed that we flew, the safer car diluting my hyper-vigilance on journeys. Martha was exchanged for Rick's piano and Billy took lessons, but when the honky tonk proved itself a pig to play, we swapped it for a crate of wine. Billy's love of music would lead him to compose and enter chamber music competitions, however it would be the guitar that survived his transient lifestyle. Financially secure for the first time since leaving England, we found that life was easy when freed of the frugality that had led us to scythe, and even borrow a friend's cow, to tame our grass. Violet had seemed a logical solution until we discovered that behind her brown eyes and buttery hide raged a ferocious beast. We had no fences so we tethered our bovine lawn mower to a fisherman's anchor until, on learning she could drag her anchor, Violet made chase with it bouncing along behind. In a flash, I had bolted up the walnut tree, where I waited on her munching the grass below. A machine proved docile, less gregarious. In time, our rough paddock became an undulating lawn and after building a studio for my art and yoga we constructed two bridges over the stream.

Where many homes are devoid of character, ours had a heart and soul; however, we never imagined it would also provide us a living. Our concrete block supplier had agreed to subsidise his price in exchange for demonstrating their product and, when customers visited, their first question was *"Who designed this house?"* David was soon discussing plans with clients sitting around our kitchen table, utilising his naval architecture training along with the decades of furniture making that had taught him to visualise in three dimensions. His navigation skills helped him position houses to benefit from passive solar heating and ambient sunlight, while experiences of having built in block, timber, and stone supported David's designs of more than thirty Mediterranean style houses that complement the landscape of Hawke's Bay.

Before Sam left for university, the Lowes lent us their yacht and we sailed north to Whangaroa Harbour, reliving our past life. Sam and Billy had grown into able crew, Stugeron ensured I need never be seasick, and satellite navigation meant any idiot could press a button to find out where they were and which way to go. Where dawn and dusk had seen us changing sails to match the erratic wind fluctuations, one tweak of the roller furling sail was all it took on Windrace. After Sam's departure, Billy felt a restless need to join him. He reclaimed William as his name and became involved in teenage pranks, swimming naked by midnight in the Iona pool, consuming junk food and excessive alcohol. But despite the rebellion, he never ceased his academic and athletic pursuits, competing in chess, debating, rowing, tennis, cricket, cycling, destined to become a scientist, writer, translator, actor, director, party animal, and Sam's best mate. A spontaneous action would predict William's outcome, *"At New Year's Eve going into 2001 I was at a rock concert in Napier (NZ) when on a whim just before midnight I walked outside the venue and down to the beach, stripped to my boxers and jumped in the sea. As the distant crowd chanted out the countdown I took a breath and ducked underwater for the final seconds, re-emerging in a new year. I didn't become a freediver that year, or the next, but in hindsight it seems like that night was a window to the future."*

Throughout those years I somehow continued my creative endeavours, shaping life sized fragmented figures, paintings, and prints. But the whirlwind of teaching and nurturing my family was exhausting. I bled, burned, and thought I would die in that fiery pyre of menopause, and then as a phoenix I was reborn from the ashes of my womanhood. Meanwhile David's furniture had become ever more original in its concept and construction. When his kit-set Hornpipe Bench, named for its balanced form and happy colourful pieces, won the second pine competition, the prize was a trip to Japan, a country we had always been curious about. We flew there over the jewelled waters of the Isle of Pines where we had sailed a lifetime ago and on seeing David's *Canoe Chair* taking pride of place in the foyer of the New Zealand embassy, we recalled how depressed we had been when it failed to sell at its first showing. On returning he began creating tables that integrated art, craft, and design in their figurative supports; complementing their bases with tops inscribed with carved motifs. Each table was accompanied by a woodcut print that recorded the process of construction, its layers of textural carvings. At each step, I helped saturate the table top with ink before hand-rubbing each print in a series of *Offerings* that express David's homage to nature.

On a solitary mountain walk, David reflected about what to create next and realised that it was time he revisit his naval architecture training. As he experimented with methods of nautical construction, steaming and bending individual pieces of ash wood, his concept condensed into a monocoque structure resembling a Polynesian canoe. Meanwhile, Bouncer had settled into the garden workshop, finding it convenient to slip outside to sample an apple while adding the odd squiggle to what he considered collaborative works of art. But where had all the gadgets come from and what purpose did they serve? Bouncer was constantly surprised by the unexpected processes, like the steam box fed from a boiling kettle. He remembered when the tuck box of tools had been enough and wondered what would happen next.

In the autumn of 1999, twenty years after David's visit to the *Earl's Court Boat Show* that propelled us into sailing, we travelled to London to exhibit his *Body Raft Lounger* at the Earl's Court *100% Design Show*, and when a visitor to our stand asked if the raft floated, I replied, "*It will float the dreams of whoever sleeps on it!*" Embracing the millennium with a bonfire party, we invited friends to burn objects that symbolised their obsolete past. David initiated the destruction, heralding a creative spark by sacrificing his obsolete design templates. And as the cleansing flames consumed those discarded plans, photographs, clothes, and toys, we embraced a new era. In response to an Italian manufacturer's request that David adapt his *Body Raft Lounger* for mass production, he designed a rocking version and in 2001 he transited to Milan through LAX airport, wielding a shrouded package resembling a giant banana. On first sight of *Body Raft* at Salone Satellite, renowned Italian designer Cappellini purchased the unique design. David's uncompromising passion for innovation and change had made the impossible happen and his subsequent regular presence at Milan's Furniture Fair would maintain that international profile, however organising, setting up, and welcoming visitors to the aptly named *stand* demands a colossal commitment. I have helped my man carry furniture through the city streets, paint and assemble his show and, when things went wrong, restrained him from bashing the *"useless piece of shit"* to bits. David's design has been elevated to worldwide acclaim, however a casual onlooker's response to his *Body Raft*, *"This is empty yet so full,"* remains the greatest recognition.

Meanwhile our summer holiday escapes had become increasingly extreme and on those land voyages across the mountains of the South Island we carried rucksacks laden with food for ten or twelve days in the wild. High in the ranges of the Nelson Lakes we set off up a mighty scree slope that swept to where Mount Franklin culminated in sky. As we climbed higher and higher I was so intent on keeping pace I never noticed the increasingly acute incline. Drawing breath beneath the battlements of an ice cliff, I turned my gaze down the gully to where, beneath my feet, a swathe of tumbling scree and boulders swooped to the valley floor. Numb with terror, I swayed on the narrow ledge. It would be too treacherous to return the way we had come and David was all for ascending the sheer ice that led towards the mountain's crest. He began cutting steps and I followed, jabbing my stick for stability, my knees shaking uncontrollably. Knowing that a fall would precipitate a relentless acceleration to inevitable death, I whispered, *"I can't go up there."* Hesitantly I returned to the ledge, to crouch, methodically nibbling a sandwich, restoring warmth to my shivering body, avoiding gazing up the ice face or down into the void. There was not so much as a blade of grass on Franklin's Mordor of a mountain, and my trusty stick was all I had to remind me of the living world. I waited, and at last David retraced his steps and sat beside me. He conceding that going up or down was not possible, that he would check a side route and after exploring he returned with a plan, our only option. Following a harrowing scramble up the slab walls of *thunder gully* we found ourselves amongst huge boulders perched above gigantic rock falls. With no assurance of success, we began threading a way down, weaving our way around cliffs and brittle scree runs. At last the gradient became less extreme and, overcome with the jubilation of being alive, I threw my trusty stick in the air. Falling to the ground it shattered on a rock. Having served to reassure me on the icy slopes, it lay broken, nature having dealt with it as brutally as she could have done for me.

Undaunted, we returned the following year for twelve days in Mount Aspiring Park, discovering that the momentum of walking harmonised body, mind, and spirit into a meditation. We clung to each other as we forded deep rivers, bathed in a stream that had melted from a glacier, and drank from peaty puddles. One night we slept on a high plateau, looking out at the icy face of Mount Awful, before descending into a lush valley where the midges pattered as rain upon our tent. During the summer of 2002 we walked from the Kaweka Ranges of Hawke's Bay to Lake Taupo, celebrating Christmas in a solitary hut and sharing tiny presents before tramping on with balloons flying from our packs. That passage saw us crawl along tracks choked with storm debris and, as always, I kept on until my legs and the path would go no further. The following year David injured his knee, so we took to the hills on mountain bikes where his adrenaline addiction set him hurtling with *wheels on fire* down Takaka Hill. And while our bodies were still indestructible, we slept on the beach beneath our windsurfer sails, watching stars and wandering the shore at dawn.

Through those many years I taught a life drawing class, with the family accompanying me, covering lengths of wallpaper with pastels and paint. Ambient music transformed those sessions into deep meditations and I recall a girl, immaculately clad in white lace, elegantly dipping quills in ink, while others smudged and rubbed charcoal on screeds of paper. In summer, we drew in the leafy privacy of our garden, chasing dappled shadows over the model's form. Evenings were filled with yoga classes that also spilled outside, concluding with pot luck dinners that transcended into winter sessions when Thai soup bubbled and bread machines baked in readiness; on completing our rigorous routine, we spread a cloth to feast in the place where we had practiced. Yoga and creativity combined to express an inner dimension. A pregnant model invoked a Madonna, her body glowing with magical light as she shared that memorable evening before her baby's birth. If a model failed to turn up I took their place; alternating between tutor, muse, and artist rewarded me with an intimate understanding of the creative process. There is no shame in nakedness, as David and I discovered when sharing communal bathhouses in Japan when, on abandoning their clothes and identity, the bathers revealed the dignity and beauty of humanity.

The yoga class LT

With David and I sharing a car, it remained convenient to teach a walkable distance from home. Apart from stints darting over the road to teach at the rival girls' school, Iona's motto *Love, Joy, and Peace* permeated my life. Over the years my students created murals, theatre sets, and costume masks and body decorations for *A Midsummer Night's Dream*. During an arts festival, I led the pupils and staff in forming terracotta figures, to represent themselves in a sculptural *"Self portrait of a school."* While I taught a classic foundation of observational drawing that led to painting, sculpture, printmaking, and design, I noticed that teachers who chose easier options failed to develop their students' potential. As the curriculum changed, creative expertise turned to bland appropriation. I had been a novelty amongst the serious students on Exeter University's education course and my tutor Ted Wragg, who would influence teaching strategies on a world stage, had encouraged my individuality, called me *'Butterfly'* for my exuberance. But two decades of teaching had drained that enthusiasm and it was time to turn to yoga and self-expression.

The stopping and starting that compromised my art practice made me recall a retired friend who, having realised a dreamed of time to write, found that the years had stolen his passion. As an art student I had followed my intuition in creating organic forms and, despite barely understanding myself, my thesis *The Circle* investigated the ouroboros and archetypal female. My interest in symbolism opened the way to studying yogic philosophy and creative explorations of spiritual and sensual themes culminating in a series of sculptural shrines. On winning a commission for Waipukurau's town centre my patrons requested I keep the sculpture under wraps until a ceremonial unveiling. So it was that Ricks Terstappen, William Jameson, and I presented my stylised CorTen and stainless steel hawk, *Kanohi O Te Kāhu,* as a reference to a local Māori proverb that tells of *"The Eye of The Hawk"* that sees all and is a *kaitiaki or* guardian over the land and its people. Where an affirmation of intent might have dissolved my objective before it had fully formed there was a power in keeping the secret that took flight in the sculptural image of the hawk as it transcended to the spiritual realm. When in 2004 I won the opportunity to produce my *Wall of Wings* for the centre of Havelock North it endorsed a similar theme. The sculptural wings, comprised of six panels pierced with stylised patterns, were inspired by *korowai*, Māori cloaks and its position in the heart of my village gives me a sense that my spirit has found its home.

A wall of wings LT

While I awakened to an inner landscape, David's overseas exhibitions allowed him to gather inspiration from the world's wild localities. Together we presented workshops in France, Tasmania, and New Zealand, combining yoga and creativity to stimulate transformative design experiences. When David was awarded an artist residency in Antarctica it was a dream come true. However the opportunity to explore Earth's most remote continent came just as his business gathered momentum. David's search for a manager proved futile and as his workload escalated he tempted fate by saying, *"Things couldn't get any worse."* When he broke his leg falling from the steps of his workshop, the injustice of the accident, the thwarted Antarctica trip, magnified his despair. This was the same leg that had been broken in the car accident, but just as before, the catastrophe heralded a transition and when he recovered David was able to take control.

A year later David was given another chance to go to Antarctica. He set off agog with anticipation, but just after he had flown out his brother phoned to say their mother had died. Although Gran had remained determined to the end, age had transformed her, and David had already experienced a sense of loss. His mother's death added poignancy to the icy wasteland from where he wrote her epitaph. *"Dear Mum, thank you for all that you did for me. Thank you for being a mother. You gave us the most precious gift of a happy childhood bonded by love. That became the foundation for so much that is important in my life. During the same year that you were born, 1910, Scott arrived in Antarctica for his ill-fated polar attempt. His story haunted my childhood. Its sense of adventure, discovery, and exploration - of living near the edge – became part of my life. Now 94 years later at the end of your long life I am writing this at Scott Base in Antarctica from where Scott set out. So please forgive me for not being there with you one last time. Once again, my thirst for adventure has kept me away. I know that my traveling so far from you saddened you. But I know also that you cherished that poem in The Prophet, by Kahlil Gibran, about parents letting go of their children, like arrows from the archer's bow."* David's mother had introduced her sons to the wonder of nature, left them memories of a happy childhood and an endless supply of knitted socks. And while Josslyn had completed her passage through life her nemesis would outlive her by ten years. On hearing of Julia's passing Sam wrote, *"Julia has always been an inspiration and support for Billy and me. When I read that she has gone, I stopped...to spend some time with my memories of her. I turned the TV off, my girlfriend went to bed, and now I sit with Julia for a while."* Farewell Julia, and tally ho.

THE OCEAN WITHIN

"We shall go to sea my brother

Where three years hence an anchor lay

Past coral gardens on soft blue sand

In fathoms nine, Where sharks patrol and stingrays play

Breathe deep, my mother's other son, Let us raise this arrow, this hook, this

ship's tether, from its rest, Lift this anchor from the sea's deep bed

Hang it from a cloud of divers' breath, Let it bob upon the

swell awhile, Before its weight pulls it back to sleep

Let it fall from the light and waves, Let it plummet into the deep

Home again beneath the sea once more

Home again on the ocean's breast."

Sam Trubridge

David responded to his Antarctic experiences with an exhibition of photographs and art works that included the huge steel triptych *On Thin Ice.* This he submitted to the Nobel Peace Centre of Oslo, avoiding excessive transportation by commissioning a local manufacturer to cut and construct the piece. When his triptych won the prize for best sculpture David chose to stay away. Although his creative practice was founded upon a concern for the environment some business trips are unavoidable, however his conscience could not rest easy with squandering natural resources to fly halfway around the world, so he never attended the ceremony or the exhibition that toured to Brussels, Monaco, and Chicago.

After working alone and unacknowledged, David began employing a secretary and friends to assist him in the garden workshop. As his business expanded, David felt that others could learn from his experience and wishing to ensure they avoid the hardships we endured, he and fellow artist William Jameson established Cicada Studios' Design Incubator. The programme offered emerging designers machinery, mentoring, and opportunities to supplement their earnings making furniture. When some appropriated David's designs he said that it was better to have trust abused than live with suspicion – but when overseas companies copy his products they receive a lawyer's letter. The advent of computer technology as a tool and communicative device had transformed David's design and made an international business possible but when his marketers suggested he expand we questioned their motives; after struggling to earn a living with your hands you do not gamble or incur debt. David chose to diversify his range of products and when the speculators' bubble burst we survived.

David's Coral light overcame the tyranny of distance and, in a world of sterile designs, its connection to nature gives it a universal appeal. Although he has become a designer rock star, David has earned his success - and the opportunity to step away from laborious procedures. Many designers expect to shortcut such processes, and when a young worker commented, *"I can't see the point of mucking around making stuff, I just want to be a designer like you,"* David could not help but reflect that after forty years of making furniture, sculpture, buildings, boxes, and jewellery he had gained a knowledge that could never be found sitting at a computer. Having been the forester, cabinetmaker, sander, mechanic, accountant, photographer, designer, computer programmer, salesperson, and businessman, David has experienced every part of the process. Lacking the luxury of excessive time, he has learned to work efficiently, and while each piece remains an exquisite example of fine craftsmanship, along the way David has gained humility and respect.

On casting my eye around David's exhibition that accompanied his book *So Far – A Maker's Journey*, I saw *The Lovers* wood carving that he finished on the day we met, a carved sculpture of myself doing my windsurfing *Head Dip*. But only a fraction of hundreds of his hand-crafted works could be shown, for most claim too precious a place in people's hearts and homes to be spared. Just as when David disappears over the horizon on his windsurfer or outpaces all others in climbing a mountain, his endeavours are driven by a love of nature. In this era of disposable products, his designs emanate an innate connection to the environment. He is recognised as a leading light in sustainable design and yet we have always lived by these principles. The business supports numerous charities, we look after our workers and every Friday they share a banquet equal to that first meal David and I enjoyed together. David has no separate office, preferring to work alongside his team, sharing knowledge, leading by example. And where some achieve from climbing on others, his wish is to take everyone to the top. While my man has stepped into the light, age has clothed me in a cloak of invisibility, but that supportive role rewards me with a secret accomplishment and I am content to be the ahi ka, to keep the home fires burning. Harmony is a subtle affair and I am honoured to contribute to what is defined as *manaakitanga aroha*, the Māori practice of caring love.

Yoga has opened my heart and taught me *samtosa*, contentment; a harmony of body, mind, and spirit that eternally seeks the light. Truth is the compass on a never-ending passage on an unpredictable ocean; freediving a pinnacle of that self-realisation. I am forever grateful for yoga's powerful breathing, dynamic positions and flowing sequences that calm my emotions and keep me agile, despite the scoliosis and spondylolisthesis that accompanied me from birth; And when I die, bury me in that primitive foetal position that brings comfort and eases this spine that is twisted like the ivy vine I referred to, so long ago. On glancing down at a woven mat I use for yoga, I see a splash of cream paint and smile as I remember a day spent painting Hornpipe's deck in the Perlas Islands. During my London years, I strode through Finsbury Park wearing a Mexican poncho, throwing it on the ground to use for yoga. My most beautiful mat was crafted of pandanus from the island kingdom of Tonga, where a man is a mountain, woman the earth. If, like Tongans, we wrapped ourselves in the golden circumference of our mats, it would remind us to manifest yoga in our every action. During years of preserving that ritual on sandy beaches or

LT

425

our yacht's rolling deck, I overcame the distraction of children, insects, onlookers; and now I ask myself, "what is there to stop me practicing yoga on my mat and in my way of being."

A true yoga teacher is a conduit/passage through which the light of an ancient knowledge shines. Yoga has the potential to fill a vacuum of abuse and addiction that accompanies spiritual damage and if those healing practices were taught in public institutions our people would be happier, safer, fulfilled. A belief that the community is an extension of our family, that we are responsible for its damaged and vulnerable, led me to volunteer at my local prison. So began my most rewarding teaching experience, but it broke my heart that most of the inmates were Māori, to see those warriors stripped of their freedom and identity; how our indigenous culture suffers from social imbalances. Those journeys *inside* are brief tastes of another reality. As my students engage in breathing and stretching, their grunting and groaning subsides. They make uninhibited comments, *"Miss, you're hypnotising us."* And following a meditation, a young man says, *"That was the most difficult part, it reminded me of how I miss my kids."* Over the years, I have met battered old men with hollow chests and vacant expressions, skinny youths whose restless bodies and minds dart here and there. I learned that many who cannot read hide their inadequacies behind faces and bodies etched with the insignia of gang cultures that have become their only family. Their ferocious tattoos do not disguise the lost child of their true self. Where they could have crushed me, I trusted my intent, and on complimenting a formidable mob leader on his warrior pose he responded, *"You look pretty mighty yourself."* And when he claimed that yoga had turned his life around, I knew that others would follow, that I was in the right place.

And what of Hornpipe? Gerry recently met her owners to discover they had converted the kids' forward cabin into a workroom, installed a washing machine and dryer in our back cabin; that despite different values they love her and have weathered many storms together. We had exchanged the buoyant ocean for a stream and pond, but there are reminders of Hornpipe in the reflected water that fills our home with patterned light, lawns that undulate as an ocean swell and spreading trees where birds fly like fishes around a coral head. Blossom drifts as fragrant foam and an indigo swamp hen, a pūkeko, strides across the lawn, followed by punctuations of fluff, stumbling on stilt legs. They scurry away when a hawk hovers overhead but I cannot resist these gregarious creatures that squawk and take food from my hand. On one occasion I saw a determined friend pacing uphill with some small thing in its beak. Delicately placing the object on a tile, it tapped the glass to attract my attention to that fragile wisp of a snail shell, a gift of appreciation for years of crusts.

After buying land at Mahanga on the Mahia Peninsula, we built a beach house, a place of air and light; a melding of past and present where I choose to remember Hornpipe sailing past on her last, most southerly passage. Over time we cleared the prolific brambles and planted hundreds of trees, sponsoring schemes that preserve the native forests. The area has proved a prime windsurfing location and one memorable day I made a dramatic start, hanging on for a two kilometre reach. Hours passed as I tacked against the strong wind and as my energy failed, I invoked the dolphin that inhabited Mahia's bay, *"Help me Moko,"* I silently pleaded. A gentle nudge to my board jolted a primal fear. It was the dolphin. Weariness became joy, my arms held the wind and as I increased speed Moko leaped around me. We skimmed the waves together until, laughing, I lost control and hit the water, taking a briny gulp, welcoming this unity with the dolphin. Then I lay on the board, my arm around Moko's dolphin body, sensing his being, absorbing that moment. I saw David stop, look my way, register concern; and I waved in jubilation, to indicate that Moko was with me, that I was with the dolphin. When Moko became restless, I hauled the sail from the water and, bracing my body, attentive to the wind, I hung on, speeding over the waves, singing and shouting, the dolphin leaping and circling my board. David saw us against the sun, a plume of a water in front, sometimes behind and, after wondering a while he realised. When a speedboat ran parallel, Moko left me for the new playmate, while somehow, sick with exhaustion, I made it ashore, jabbering my story, resolving to protect the ocean and her creatures.

The final day I windsurfed the sea was a vibrant turquoise tossed with white. On making it through the waves, my stamina faded. David had disappeared over the swell, but as I came ashore through the pounding surf he was there to save me. After, as I massaged my hero's solid back we talked of his impending show in Milan, and how he would follow his successful *Three Baskets of Knowledge*. David was seeking inspiration for his latest work in a creative evolution that corresponds to the *chakra* elements of earth, water, fire, air, and ether. Our earthy foundations in

Northumberland had flowed into a water phase that taught us to accept life's offerings. Aotearoa's trial by fire had cleansed and prepared us for that era of air, ether, and light, the essence of the gods that is everywhere and nowhere. On suggesting that David consider the ethereal story of Icarus for his installation he responded with a vast constructed sun orbited by three wing forms, a contemporary interpretation of the Greek myth, a message to a society squandering its resources. True to our philosophy of reducing our environmental impact, we travelled with the pieces of the installation packed flat in our suitcases, and on arrival spent exhausting days assembling the complex airy structures. The enthusiastic crowd witnessing our exhibition never imagined the blood, sweat, and tears of its creation, or that it would be purchased for the permanent collection at Paris' Pompidou Centre.

Chakra sculpture LT

When David rediscovered a model boat with individual planks and wooden pins that he had made as a teenager, it prompted a return to making boats, boards, and windsurfers. The most mysterious of these, the Melanesian *thofothofo* outrigger canoe, makes one question the purpose of the spiked antenna that protrudes from its bow and stern and when David featured a skeletal *thofothofo* as centrepiece of his 2015 Milan installation *At Eye Level*, its form drew attention to the plight of the island communities threatened by rising sea levels. When our family sailed the Atlantic and Pacific those oceans appeared pristine and inviolable, yet three decades later all has changed. It is tragic that the descendants of the great Pacific seafarers, those least responsible for global warming, should suffer the consequences of climate change and it is vital we lend our voices and actions to a world in crisis, to combat the irresponsible consumerism and pollution destroying the life blood of our mother Earth.

I wonder whether we were truly brave when we set sail into the unknown. An audience craves excitement, and on being asked about our voyages, the first question is of the storms we must have endured. Yet it was the sleepless nights and unpredictable circumstances that held the greatest potential for disaster. My years afloat have made me anxious about balanced objects. The precarious position of a kettle on the edge of the cooker makes me uneasy and I am reminded of David urging me to photograph him on the brink of a two-thousand feet cliff in Yosemite's National Park; of when, sextant in hand, he stood on Hornpipe's heaving deck, trusting to the mercy of the fickle waves. How I silently watched, knowing that to speak would increase his defiance. We were locked in a primal battle. The woman cowering in dread of losing her man; her reckless hunter making ready to shoot the sun. And on considering the potential for disaster I feel that fortune has blessed us with far more than our survival.

The adventures are never over. Early on that morning of March eleven, 2011, a helicopter flew overhead, warning us of a tsunami, but at lunchtime the radio informed us that any threat from Japan's catastrophic earthquake had passed. The sky was bright and a lack of wind rendered the conditions perfect for paddleboarding. It was only when David and I were off Happy Jacks Cove that I saw colossal waves pounding the shore. On catching up with David we sat there, rising and falling on the mountainous swell. Home looked so near. Longing to be there I tried to ignore my shaky knees and the shoulder I had damaged falling down a cliff. If I could not paddle hard enough I would be lost. But there was no other option. David calculated the rollers and after a gigantic set we paddled with all our might. Mercifully a wave swept us through the cove's narrow entrance, breaking with a raging roar upon the rocks at either side. Safe within we stopped to look back, and it was then that the tide turned, dragging me towards the clawing waves. David, with his feet planted on the ground grabbed me, and as the bay emptied we clung together while the water rushed past; horrified when it met the breakers in a tumult of spume. Escaping, we dragged our boards over the mud and when a man who had watched from a hilltop came near he commented, *"And I thought you were much younger!"*

When I think back on our years afloat, it appears we were suspended in a time warp. David and I spent evenings playing games, reading, and listening to music we had heard many times. Our children appreciated small things, valued friends with a loyalty they would bring to their adult relationships. With no access to films or television, all too few books, resources or toys, our family made the most of what we had, enjoying a self-sufficiency and synchronicity with nature few will ever know. In this culture of mind-dominating technologies, the body and spirit are often neglected. We humans are overstimulated yet deprived of real experiences. Absorbing life's simple pleasures takes time. Nurturing a child is similar to crossing an ocean, and it is only when the experience has passed that we are finally prepared for that which is gone. Our boys' evolution from children to adults coincided with a journey that laid down a lifetime of impressions. Fragrant memories of an era that was as fleeting as sunlight piercing a wave, traces of magic that are revealed in today's accomplishments.

A legacy of that extreme lifestyle is that Sam and William see the best in others and, although this renders them vulnerable in relationships, their generosity of spirit endures and nourishes those around them. Although they have accomplished extraordinary things they find the greatest satisfaction in giving; express their gratitude to the oceans by protecting its habitat and creatures, with William writing, *"I've always believed that creativity, innovation and perhaps even positive energy in general have a kind of syphoning quality to them: the more you draw from these pure mountain waters, then the more will spring up to replace it, while on the other hand hoarding leads to stagnation of the source. It's thanks to those who share a similar view that I am where I am today, and as long as I am able to help others myself then I will still have access to the clean source that is nourishing my own growth."* And in 2010 he mounted a campaign that would both fund his thirteenth World Record and support New Zealand's endangered Hector's dolphin.

William invited the public to purchase individual metres of the fluorescent dive rope that would guide his Hectometre dive to an unassisted one hundred metres. Failure would incur a huge debt and, following two aborted attempts things were not looking good. William had also tweaked a neck muscle, so before sleeping he took anti-inflammatories and my advice of propping his head with towels. The thirteenth of December dawned chilly, with clouds obscuring the sun. William shivered as he entered the water and on plunging beneath the surface, some air was forced into his stomach. He returned with a groan of dismay. Then grasping a glimmer of hope William swam ashore, climbed in his truck and set the heater to maximum. After roasting himself for twenty minutes he returned to complete his preparation in the water. He has few memories of that dive apart from entering the freefall, pulling a tag from the plate and telling himself to *relax and flow* as he commenced his long swim towards the light.

William wrote, *"I remember coming to the surface, reminding myself to concentrate on doing the protocol correctly to ensure a valid dive. And I remember erupting into celebration with my team the moment the judges displayed their white cards."* It was an auspicious achievement. Shortly before William's birth, legendary freediver Jacques Mayol achieved a hundred metre *No Limits* world record, descending on a sled before being pulled to the surface by a lift bag. Not only had Jacques broken new ground, he had faced fears that the body could never withstand the pressure below fifty metres. The zen master's explorations of yoga and meditation, his affinity with the ocean and her creatures, had gifted a freediving legacy for others, particularly his student Umberto Pelizzari, who inspired William. And some thirty-four years later our son would dive for the dolphins; plunging to a hundred metres and swimming to the surface using only the propulsion of his bare hands and feet.

Meanwhile Sam had chosen an equally unique means of entrancing an audience. His way of beguiling his students into magical experiences led to them fondly calling him *"The Space Poet"* and *"Pied Piper of Performance Design."* Turning his passion towards the environment Sam researched twentieth century farmer, H. Guthrie-Smith, whose *Tutira – The Story of a New Zealand Sheep Station* documents the development of his land. In November 2011 Sam presented his *Ecology in Fifths* to parody the devastation colonisation has wrought on the New Zealand landscape. The production commenced with a symbolic death of a last tree on a stage composed of a central square of turfed lawn, whereupon four dancers manicured and fenced the grass, transforming it into an arena of ritualised conflict. Their destructive force intensified into a mesmerising act of rolling away the turf to reveal barren soil. The dance culminated in a primeval figure emerging from the earth, and at this point the stage was abruptly shrouded, blinding the Wellington audience to all but the violent cacophony being waged within that hidden space. When the black curtains opened they revealed a charred, desecrated landscape that heralded Christchurch's devastating earthquake and Japan's tsunami; events that remind us of our volatile planet, that we are victims of our own demise.

From his flat, *The Crow's Nest*, with its expansive view over Wellington harbour, Sam is elevated beyond limitations. Although a child when we cast off from Britain, his interactions with people and places provide seeds of influence for written and directed works which are a commentary on social and environmental concerns. In 2012 Sam affirmed the impact of his seagoing childhood in a speech at Queensland University of Technology in Brisbane, *"Hornpipe was built in Brisbane, so in a sense it is fitting that I begin this research trajectory here, thirty years later. The life lived on a fluid, ever-moving surface, within the play of volatile elements, defines a philosophical outlook and practice common to much of my research. Playing in this environment as a child necessarily led to an ongoing interest in transforming limited resources (spaces, toys, playmates) into diverse imaginary landscapes,"* he continued, *"It is possible to compare performance design with nautical navigation,"* concluding, *"This is in some sense a part of the aboriginal notion of the 'dreaming', where landscape, mythology, and the individual become indistinct from one another."*

In 2015 Sam created a collaborative interaction between visiting artists and the athletes competing at William's Vertical Blue event. *Deep Anatomy* presented a full circle of Sam's philosophy that concluded with his own creative performance portrayed in the poem that begins this chapter. Sam experiences a rich fulfilment in staging *The Performance Arcade* in shipping containers on Wellington's waterfront; creating a yearly performance event

Nomad ST

where anything might occur. Sam's circus came to town when, of recent years, his studies for a PhD investigating nomadism led to new ways of experiencing the land. In Sam's *Night Walk* he traverses various terrains within an inflated sphere fabricated from plastic rubbish sacks. In the heat of the Australian desert the walker generates a captive weather system, and as his passage erodes the flimsy black bubble of plastic, pinpricks of light appear; as do the stars in the night sky or phosphorescence on the indigo ocean. Sam's explorations illustrate how movement and change may be a catalyst for growth, that security and permanence degenerate into stagnation. Sam is a nomad and who knows where he will go next.

You ask: and what became of Bouncer? When once upon a time the tuck box had transported the spider from place to place like a magic carpet, it had come to rest in a very different site. He recalled the tiny workshop in Tortola, where he had strung his web from one side to the other; the magnificent furniture he had created in Mo'orea and those months at sea, when he had longed to sling his hammock from a palm tree. Bouncer had hung on for the ride, gone with the flow, or the tuck box so to speak! He had accepted the nomadic instinct that lurked in his spider spirit, and along the way he had realised that the tuck box got him out of one scrape, only to drop him in another. Recently Bouncer had grown creaky and spindly, seldom going beyond his web, but on hearing rumours that the tuck box had made another move, he decided to shake a leg. Stepping out, he found himself in a room that extended further than Hornpipe, almost as high as her mast. And when Bouncer enquired about the humming sound, he learned of a machine that could achieve more in a single minute than *The Maker* had in a week of toil with a chisel and spoke shave. He saw workers assembling all sorts of stuff that was carried away by trucks or in the arms of happy customers. Lights were everywhere, sparkling like galaxies of stars, and after Bouncer's years before the mast he knew all about stars. He felt at home amongst the beautiful forms and fantasies that had somehow evolved out of the tuck box and as he wandered the glorious space, Bouncer was soon surrounded by a small crowd who, enthralled by his foreign accent, pressed him with questions. As the throng fell silent he told of his life, the magical tuck box, and *The Maker* who, with Bouncer's help, had thought all these wonderful things into being. Bouncer began his story in Dyke Head where his forebears had dwelt, rarely venturing beyond the ancient walls. He recalled that day when playing hide and seek he had climbed into the tuck box and eaten the crumbs of chocolate that lingered in the corners. How he had fallen asleep with a tummy ache; had woken in a foreign land to discover he was on a real adventure. Bouncer knew he must tell his tale before he forgot the interesting bits. And so, we leave him, sitting in that circle of webs, surrounded by little spiders with fidgety legs who keep saying, *"What happened next Bouncer?"* And the wise ones that hush them as they try to remember every word, knowing their turn will come all too soon.

Throughout my life I have questioned the social convention of religious expression. Creativity and yoga have illuminated my path on that search for the inner light. We are instinctively spiritual beings, who have from the earliest time expressed ourselves through art, ritual, and mythology. Cave art records humanities earliest attempts to comprehend and define their relationship to the world. While the artist taps into universal truths, the yogi encounters the divine. Travelling opens the heart, and when David and I set sail we embarked on a spiritual experience of being truly alive. Those nomadic years had unfolded with a momentum of their own, but I sometimes wonder how one who craves stability, and the space to dance and create, made a home on that fluid element. While those passages awakened our deeper potential, I know that I could never have endured the ultimate price of freedom, that in the light of today's stateless, homeless refugees our struggles were trivial. While we believe that no one should be excluded freedom, imprisoned within a country, we forget we own that increasingly rare privilege of considering ourselves citizens of the world. That recurring nightmare of finding myself in a dreary passage of creaking boards that undulated between wooden walls with locked doors has passed. Whatever lurked behind those apertures, beyond the curve of the corridor, had been too awful to contemplate. Fear of the unknown is often greater than the consequences and as I awake to sunlight patterning my walls, surrounded by beauty beyond comprehension, I wonder if I deserve the happiness I have found. When my son tests the limits of human endurance on a daily basis, it seems rash to claim a *happy ever after*, yet this is all I ever wished for.

I have never met anyone who lives as fully as William, whose every dive demonstrates his absolute determination to return to the world. Maybe that closer proximity of death awakens a realisation of why he is alive; an appreciation of every moment. The sanctity of life sometimes eclipses the reason for living, constrains our breath and being. As William wrote, *"The proper function of man is to live, not to exist. I shall not waste my days in trying to prolong them. I shall live them, because I think that if you die doing something you love that will be the best way to go."* When in April of 2012, the crew of the American *60 Minutes* programme travelled to the Bahamas to film William's world record attempt with fins, Sam called the depths from the dive platform while his brother performed. And despite a marginal lapse of surface protocol that cost William the opportunity to hold all three depth records, the grace with which my son accepted defeat set him above his failure.

In 2015 William, Sam, and David travelled to the Himalayas to hike the foothills of Kangchenjunga while, grounded by back issues, I remained at home. In his absence hurricane Joaquin devastated William's island and when he returned, wasted and sick, his home looked like a war zone. Nature's fury wracked a symbolic conclusion to the destructive marriage that had threatened his life, tainted his happiness and career. I cannot imagine how William endured the violence and emotional abuse. Should I have taught my sons to be less generous and open? I remember that affectionate little boy who had been all heart and wonder whether his compassionate nature made him more vulnerable. In 2016 our family descended on Long Island to support William's Vertical Blue event, witness his transformation and see him achieve two world records in freediving's free immersion discipline. Then, after battling to maintain that athletic peak, William made a second televised attempt at taking his no fins world record to one hundred and two metres. During the weeks, days, and minutes before William's dive he targeted niggling thoughts with the mantra, *"Now is all."* And as we watched from the studio in Auckland I knew that all of New Zealand was behind my son, willing him success.

When a gypsy read my palm, she concluded with a gesture towards a meadow of wild flowers. *"That is you,"* she said, *"Unseen, beautiful, they just are!"* I am content with that analogy, thistles, brambles and all. In this telling, I could have presented myself as a heroine but that would have been dishonest, the reason for writing lost. I abhor categories. We are first and foremost humans beings but amid the maelstrom of the "Me Too" movement I am concerned at the risk of demonising males. This is a power issue. I have suffered at the hands of women, known and shared my life with sensitive, respectful men, and while I don't doubt or condone thousands of years of male dominance and abuse, the pendulum must not reverse its swing. I long for that harmony between male and female that thrives when society values and respects everyone's unique qualities, regardless of gender, race, and age. And though I no longer attempt to keep up with David, I cannot deny the challenges of maintaining a voice when surrounded by brilliant men. The bond between parent and child is eternal and those years afloat still stalk my relationship with my boys, for in demanding situations they unconsciously assert their authority over the mother who knew them at their most vulnerable. Does this explain why women have often been historically and culturally subjugated? And if as an old woman I lapse into behaving like a rebellious child or a Tongan grandmother then it may be because I never wanted power, just the freedom and fun of being myself.

David recently returned from Milan to nonchalantly present me a little packet of designer pegs, shaped as blackbirds to perch on the washing line. As I mustered enthusiasm for this delightful domestic gift, David searched a deeper pocket and with an *"Oh I almost forgot!"* he drew out a small bag. Inside I found a circle of polished steel lightly holding a glowing ruby in its open embrace. The tinkling gem, dancing within the ring's circumference, affirmed the everlasting freedom and love we have found. It reminds me of a weekend that never ended, of our secret marriage, so many years ago. And though our bodies have become worn and familiar as a child's favourite toy, I see the person I fell in love with as clearly as if it was yesterday that David carried me to the van with my ankle broken from that first leap into the unknown.

When asked how we met, David said, *"It was inevitable that we would come together,"* adding, *"Every person grows and realises more of themselves through others, particularly their partners and children."* The symbiosis of our spiritual connection has blossomed into a summer's day. Conversations lapse into those silences that are more important than words, and while I restrain myself from spontaneously voicing my emotions, David persists in never offering an opinion until he is certain. Standing beneath his eye level, I beat on David's chest, jump up and down and wave my arms to claim his attention, while he scans the horizon, seemingly oblivious to my presence. Decades passed before we realised that a tricky situation could be resolved through humour and a hug. And just as dolphins maintain their social harmony by constantly brushing each other as they move through the water, that touch may heal a hurt or defuse anger, in no lesser way than the hand of god reaching across the void.

I have been blessed with many lives, a spiritual awakening that led me on this passage, to discover the fulfillment of love, family, and creativity. I reach out to the heavens and earth - dance and sing my gratitude to Papatuanuku and Ranginui, our earth mother and sky father. And there are times when I have wished I could slip into my past to see the silhouettes of my joyful children; to comfort the mother who tried so hard to overcome her inadequacies. I would throw my arms around her saying, *"Don't worry, it will be all right – in the here and now and the happy ever after, as we weave through the waters of our lives, reaffirming our connection with each dolphin touch; in an adventure that is ever changing, never ending until our return to the ocean from whence we came."* And in a similar way, I hope these passages will give those who struggle the strength to laugh, love, and carry on. Change is inevitable but the spirit will endure.

LT

REFERENCES
AND BIBLIOGRAPHY

"Noa Noa, Gauguin's Tahiti" Original manuscript, Nicholas Wadley, Phaidon

The Bhagavad Gita – translated by Juan Mascaro - Penguin Classics

Exeter College of Art Diploma Show: Reviewed by Jon Culverhouse, Exeter Post, 1971

"Call Me Jack" The autobiography of A. M. King - unpublished

"So Far" David Trubridge - Potter and Burton

Sam Trubridge address Compass Points: Locations, Landscapes and Coordinates of Identities - ADSA conference at Queensland University of Technology Brisbane, Australia. July 2012

On Sea/At Sea Richard Gough & Sam Trubridge - Routledge Taylor & Francis Group

"Cheating death in the deep" Claire Harvey, Canvass magazine: February 2, 2008

"Oxygen" William Trubridge – Harper Collins

ACKNOWLEDGEMENTS

"One is in oneself the whole of mankind, and one's fate
is the fate of the whole of mankind."

D H Lawrence

Passages tells of my family's travels on our yacht, Hornpipe, woven together with reflections on how those years afloat influenced our lives. I am grateful for David's journal account that, along with Hornpipe's logbook, prompted my memories. Sam and William persuaded me to write and their voices accompany ours in describing those adventures that transformed us all. They lived the life we chose, forgave our mistakes, and say that they never wished for anything more.

My parents grew out of an age that derided qualities that are valued today; they were ahead of their time and I learned much from my mother's perseverance, my father's acceptance. A quote from his memoir, *"I trust this may be of benefit to my children and future generations of my family,"* reminds me they deserved the joys we experienced and the fulfilment we found.

Thanks to everyone I mention in these passages and met along the way, for they all contributed to our growth. Gratitude to Amelia and Sachiko for the love and happiness they bring to Sam, and to William's life. To my Auntie Sylvia, the matriarch of my family and my brother who was there for my parents when I was far away. To Susan Dugdale, whose wise words got me started; Marilyn Taylor, for her honest critique; and Wendy Glasgow, whose enthusiasm reminded me of why I was writing this story. This book was written and illustrated with technical help from Josh Lynch, Bobby Cheng, and Ben Pearce, with the design assistance of Reuben Maybury. My gratitude to Barbara Sumner and her daughters, the Sumner sisters Bonnie, Rachel, and Ruth, who helped birth this book. Personal thanks to my supportive friends Rondi, Jan, Naomi, and Rachel, who led me to David. My respect to those teachers, Jim Newnes, who guided my first steps into a creative career and adventurous life; for Alan Babington who revealed the silent power of yoga. And all gratitude to those three doctors, Robin Tattersall, Richard Morrison, and Robert Lowe, who I believe saved our lives; Betty who welcomed us into her home and heart.

This story is for all explorers. The passages we weave through our lives find their truth in those we touch along the way.

LT

Afterword

To find out more about my life and art, sign up to my newsletters through:

www.lindatrubridge.com

I will send you occasional newsletter with updates on my life and work.

Did you enjoy this book?

If you enjoyed Passages, I'd really appreciate if you could leave a review on Amazon.com. Thank you!